FOR GOD AND IRELAND

For Roger and Betty McCabe

FOR GOD
AND
IRELAND

The Fight for Moral Superiority
in Ireland, 1922–1932

M.P. McCABE

IRISH ACADEMIC PRESS
DUBLIN • PORTLAND, OR

First published in 2013 by Irish Academic Press

8 Chapel Lane
Sallins
Co. Kildare, Ireland

920 NE 58th Avenue, Suite 300
Portland, Oregon,
97213-3786 USA

www.iap.ie

Irish Academic Press

British Library Cataloguing in Publication Data

McCabe, Michael P., 1977-
For God and Ireland:
the fight for moral superiority in Ireland, 1922-1932.
1. Ireland--Social conditions--1922-1973.
2. Catholic Church--Ireland--History--20th century.
3. Fianna Fail--History--20th century.
4. Religion and politics--Ireland--History--20th century.
5. Ireland--Politics and government--1922-1949.
I. Title
941.5'0822-dc23

ISBN: 978 0 7165 3162 3 (cloth)
ISBN: 978 0 7165 3194 4 (ebook)

Library of Congress Cataloging-in-Publication Data
An entry can be found on request

Printed by CPI Group (UK) Ltd, Croydon CR0 4YY

Contents

Acknowledgements

This book started out as a doctoral thesis at the University of Oxford. Like many other historians of modern Ireland, I owe so much to Roy Foster. He was an exemplary supervisor, and his continuing support, advice and encouragement have made this work possible. Special thanks also to Richard English and Marc Mulholland, who were excellent examiners and who made writing this an easier and more fulfilling experience. I am also greatly indebted to Tim Wilson, who has been a tremendous friend, supporter and critic.

I am grateful to many scholars for their advice and support, especially Senia Paseta, Chris Davies, Huston Gilmore, Matt Kelly, Robert Lynch, Ultán Gillen, Lauren Arrington and Frances Flanagan. Many useful suggestions were raised over a glass of wine or a pint of Guinness that have made this a much better piece of work. On top of that, it has been a pleasure to call them colleagues and friends for several years. My thanks to Shane Murphy, Tom Devine, Oonagh Walsh and the late George Watson for starting me down this path, Brian Griffin for making Chapter 2 a better piece, and Diarmaid MacCulloch and the staff at the *Journal of Ecclesiastical History* for helping tighten up Chapter 3. Thanks, also, to Michael Wheatley, Mary-Lou Legg and Patrick Maume for sharing their encyclopaedic knowledge of the Irish press, and Owen Dudley Edwards for his many ideas over a delicious dinner.

None of this would have been possible without the patient assistance of many people at several different archives and libraries. Special thanks to David Sheehy and Noelle Dowling at the Dublin Archdioceses. Vera Orschel, formerly at the Irish College, Rome and Marcel Chappin, S.J., at the Vatican Secret Archives, both of whom have helped more than they realise. The staff at the archives at UCD, especially Séamus Helferty, Kieran McConville at the Tomás Ó Fiaich Library in Armagh, Joe Summerville at the Killaloe Dioceses, Tom Kilgarriff at the Galway

Dioceses, Fr Brendan Kilcoyne at the Tuam Archdioceses, Fr Nicholas Irwin at the Cashel Archdioceses, Brian McGee and the staff at the Cork City and County Archives, the staffs at the National Archives and the National Library of Ireland, the British Library Newspaper Archives in Colindale, the Public Record Office of Northern Ireland and the Bodleian Library.

I owe much to Lisa Hyde for being a most patient and supportive editor and the staff at Irish Academic Press for correcting my many errors and turning my mess of a manuscript into a beautifully finished product. Thanks also to Dave and Marianne Meyer for their help with Church doctrine and generally for being there for me when I needed them. A huge debt of gratitude is owed to Betty McCabe for being a fantastic mom, and Christopher and Sarah Sharp for their hospitality, generosity and support. An immeasurable debt is due to my beloved wife, Melanie, who has been so helpful, supportive and amazing throughout this whole process. Finally, I want to thank those who did not make it to see me finish, especially Eric Meyer, my grandma, Anna Reed, and my dad, Roger McCabe. Their unfailing support and friendship were largely responsible for getting me to the point that I could even start this project.

M.P. McCabe
July 2012

Abbreviations

AARIR	American Association for the Recognition of the Irish Republic
A.E.S.	Archives of the Congregazione degli Affari Ecclesiastici Straordinari
AOH	Ancient Order of Hibernians
CAA	Cashel Archdiocesan Archives
CB	*Catholic Bulletin*
CCCA	Cork City and County Archives
CDA	Cork Diocesan Archives
CE	*Cork Examiner*
CRO	Cumbria Record Office
DAA	Dublin Archdiocesan Archives
DJ	*Derry Journal*
DP	*Derry People*
DWNTH	*Derry Weekly News and Tyrone Herald*
FIF	Friends of Irish Freedom
FJ	*Freeman's Journal*
FS	*Free State*
GAA	Gaelic Athletic Association
GDA	Galway Diocesan Archives
GHQ	General Headquarters
IC	*Irish Catholic*
ICDA	*Irish Catholic Directory and Almanac*
ICH	*Irish Catholic Herald*
ICR	Irish College Rome Archives
IER	*Irish Ecclesiastical Record*
II	*Irish Independent*
INBMN	*Irish News and Belfast Morning News*
IPP	Irish Parliamentary Party
IRA	Irish Republican Army

IRB   Irish Republican Brotherhood
ISDL   Irish Self-Determination League
IT   *Irish Times*
KDA   Killaloe Diocesan Archives
NAI   National Archives of Ireland
NLI   National Library of Ireland
NUIM   National University of Ireland, Maynooth Archives
PP   *Plain People*
PRONI   Public Record Office of Northern Ireland
RA   The Royal Archives
RH   *Roscommon Herald*
RIC   Royal Irish Constabulary
RUC   Royal Ulster Constabulary
SF   *Sinn Féin*
TAA   Tuam Archdiocesan Archives
TCDA   Trinity College Dublin Archives
TD   Teachta Dála
UCDA   University College Dublin Archives
UVF   Ulster Volunteer Force
WP   *Wicklow People*

Introduction

Despite efforts to more fully objectivise the events of the past, some spheres of study remain oddly resistant. The study of Irish history is now more inclusive of the multiple variations of Irish society that do not fit within the constricting nationalist-Catholic classification. Unfortunately, impartiality has not yet been universally achieved. Because of a tendency to grant the Catholic Church, and especially its leaders, a large measure of amnesty regarding political activity, the history of Catholicism and the Catholic Church in Ireland is still often written in a manner that is inadequate to understanding the Church's role in politics and society.

The history of the Catholic Church in Ireland during the late nineteenth and early twentieth centuries has not suffered from a lack of scholarly attention. Broad studies covering the Church and its relation to Ireland abound. Prior to the 1980s, Emmet Larkin, Patrick Corish, J.H. Whyte and David W. Miller each added their own contributions to this genre.[1] Since then Dermot Keogh and, most recently, Patrick Murray have added their own works.[2] Barry Coldrey, focusing on the Christian Brothers, and Kevin Collins have each written on clerical contributions to the Gaelic Revival and Irish-Ireland movement.[3] Nor has there been a shortage of works on individuals affiliated with the Church. Gerard Moran and Denis Carroll have each contributed studies of radical priests, and Carroll has written a biography of Sinn Féin's Fr. Michael O'Flanagan.[4] Catherine Candy has written an interesting book on clerical authors of the early twentieth century, providing one of the most recent studies of the fictional works of, among others, Canon Patrick Sheehan.[5] Some biographies have also been produced on individual bishops, including an Australian cottage industry centred around Archbishop Daniel Mannix,[6] though given their importance within the framework of Irish life and politics, fewer prelates than might be expected have been studied, though with the recent biographies of Cardinal Logue and Archbishop Byrne, this deficiency has been slightly rectified.[7]

Since Ireland is an overwhelmingly Catholic country, even those scholars who have not written specifically about the Church often feel compelled to incorporate it into their study of Ireland and treat the two as if they were inseparable. For scholars like Tom Garvin and Richard English, Catholicism infused itself into the mindset of the nationalist people to such an extent that to understand the conflict of the early twentieth century requires an understanding of the Catholic upbringing and beliefs of those involved. Many authors who write about those involved in the 1916 Rising cannot but discuss their devotion to the faith, and this is a pattern that can be transferred to those who became involved in the struggle for Irish independence afterward.

Many fine historians have successfully incorporated elements of the Church and Irish spirituality into their studies without losing their perspective, but the historian who can do so while focusing primarily on the Church is a rare one indeed. The marriage of Catholicism and Irish politics has not been an altogether healthy one within the context of historical study. Those historians who have written about the mixture of the two have often demonstrated a sympathetic mentality towards the Church that only devout political partisans would show for a political party or organisation. A reading of Larkin's interpretation of the bishops' involvement in the ending of Parnell's career shows that fault lies completely outside the sphere of the Church. A careful reader would be hard-pressed to demonstrate within the considerable collection of Monsignor Corish's work a coldly objective examination of Church policy in relation to the Irish state. Coldrey's often-cited book on the Christian Brothers' contribution to Irish nationalism, while beneficial in its ground-breaking subject matter, offers little more than praise for the order's schools and exaggerates the Brothers' influence in the Irish-Ireland movement.[8] Kevin Collins performed a similar role by attempting to reduce the importance of the Anglo-Irish tradition within the Gaelic Revival and giving the lion's share of credit to Catholic priests. Oliver Rafferty defends the Church's activities in the face of the 'Fenian Threat' that attempted, according to Rafferty's analysis, not only to deny the clergy direct involvement in Irish political affairs but also contributed to the breakdown of the identification of nationalism with Catholicism,[9] a contention discredited by the works of Vincent Comerford and Owen McGee.[10] Biographies of priests and bishops by clerics, such as Joseph Brusher's work on Peter Yorke,[11] and B.A. Santamaria's and Michael Gilchrist's books on Mannix are little more than hagiographies, despite the highly controversial and sometimes questionable political involvement of their subjects. Historical works on lay Catholics can often take on the same flaw when the subject's religion comes to the foreground. The writings of Fr. Brian P. Murphy, with a mixture of devotion to the faithful and attacks against those who dare question the Church or its members, demonstrate the extreme to which Catholic apologies can reach. Too few have emulated Lord Acton, who, as Regius Professor of History at Cambridge, maintained his devotion to Catholicism while submitting popes, cardinals and bishops to the same critical analysis as secular leaders. He is known for his aphorism: 'Power corrupts, and absolute power corrupts absolutely.' What is not so well known is that he wrote this to Bishop Mandell Creighton, chiding him for being insufficiently condemnatory of former popes.

Authors who have restricted themselves to abiding by the decisions of the hierarchy suffer from the same myopia as the men and women who adhere to a particular political doctrine, and so often cannot write dispassionately about the opposition. Contemporary works like those by Dorothy Macardle and Frank Gallagher on the republican side, or Piaras Béaslaí and Ernest Blythe on the Free State side suffer from similar deficiencies. Political and social histories, though, are no longer primarily the property of partisans. Less so can that be said about ecclesiastical history. Of course, there has been an array of anti-clerical literature that is hyper-critical of the Church's involvement in Irish affairs. These pieces, though, provide little of interest for this study beyond an interesting look into various mentalities that conflicted with the mainstream. Irish anti-clericalism is a fascinating subject, but is not a matter for this book. Commentaries that criticise the bishops and clergy with scant or biased evidence do not provide an adequate counter-point to those works sympathetic to the faith and its leaders. What is needed is a broader historiography of works genuinely objective and critical of the Catholic Church and its involvement in Ireland beyond the scope of religion. To date, this branch of Irish history is sorely lacking.

There are notable exceptions to this rule, including Mary Harris's critical examination of the Church's role in the formation of Northern Ireland, and Tom Inglis's look at the role of the Church in Irish society in the twentieth century. Work by Jérôme aan de Wiel has carefully analysed the evolution of ecclesiastical attitudes towards Sinn Féin during the turbulent years of the First World War.[12] However, aan de Wiel's insistence on limiting his study to the timeframe of the Great War omits analysis of ecclesiastical opinions during the war against the Crown, when bishops' positions altered greatly. Tom Garvin's collected works were groundbreaking in their investigations of the Church's role in politics with a keen critical eye. Historians and political scientists alike owe him a debt of gratitude for blazing this trail. Dermot Keogh also deserves mention. His pioneering book, *The Vatican, the Bishops and Irish Politics, 1919–39*, has been instrumental in proving that the Irish hierarchy was not a group that was prone to homogeneous political thought. However, twenty-six years after its publication, the subsequent release of documents and source materials that would have affected his interpretation had they been available have rendered a re-examination of the pivotal Civil War years both necessary and, thankfully, possible.

Such re-examination was attempted earlier this millennium with Patrick Murray's *Oracles of God: The Roman Catholic Church and Irish Politics, 1922–37*. The book is well-researched but, like many other works focusing on the Irish Catholic Church, his text suffers from a lack of critical analysis. His acceptance of the bishops' self-justifications for their actions demonstrates a deficiency common to Irish history. Like Corish and Larkin, Murray displays the weakness of granting Church leaders largely uncritical coverage, allowing the offices to protect men who occupied them. He claims that to focus narrowly on the Church as a power structure and political agency is a distortion, as the political assertiveness of the ecclesiastics and clergy cannot be explained simply as an impulse to exert power for its own sake. Church leaders had in mind the greater goal of ensuring and protecting the well-being of their flocks whenever they engaged in a move for power.[13] Such a statement could be applied to many responsible and civic-minded political leaders, yet this does not immunise them from criticism. Furthermore, whatever the bishops' overarching motivations, episcopal actions during this period demonstrated inconsistencies with previous statements, personal thoughts and sometimes even Christian teachings, and whether or not they were attempting to protect their flock, these inconsistencies require a greater degree of analysis than Murray is prepared to undertake.

For example, Murray states that for the bishops the moral issues presented by the Civil War were clearer than those which had confronted them during the war for independence. They were no longer obliged to condemn violent deeds of both sides impartially or to give the impression of moral ambivalence.[14] He does not challenge this hierarchical philosophy, although (as republicans rather convincingly stated on multiple occasions) the guideline issued by the Vatican was for religious leaders to maintain a strictly neutral stance while dedicating themselves to working for peace. It seems almost too simple to point out that publicly uncritical acceptance of the Free State government's policies towards its enemies, especially when compared to the reactions of bishops to the activities of the northern government, is not defensible by using the well-being of Catholics as an excuse. As will be examined in Chapter 4, episcopal silence in the face of executions of prisoners, almost all of whom were Catholics, without trial, and the continued internment of thousands of untried men and women for months after the end of the military conflict was not morally justifiable, but rather politically expedient.

As religious figures, then, Ireland's Catholic bishops present a strong front to the historian and theologian. Had any of them engaged in a theological line not approved by the Holy See, the pope would surely have involved himself and reinstated Church doctrine as necessary. Therefore, the bishops' theological actions can be questioned and commented upon, but as they conformed to the rulings of the Vatican, they have to be accepted as Church law. However, the same rules do not apply to the political activities of the hierarchy. As will be discussed in Chapter 3, the Vatican was extremely reticent about involving itself in Irish politics and therefore generally remained silent on the bishops' political activities. Without the papal blessing for their temporal deeds, the bishops left themselves exposed to criticism and even rejection of their judgments. This course of action was never tremendously popular within Ireland, and it has been a line of critical analysis that has been sorely lacking from studies of the Church and its role in politics.

The bishops were men who had benefited from excellent religious training and little in the way of political education, a fact the Fenians had reiterated time and again. They were men who were as prone to biases, strong emotions and mistakes as any other. They held grudges and, despite their protestations, did not always act in the interests of their faith. They came from the same backgrounds and classes as the leaders of the Free State government. They often had the same intentions as the secular leaders, and – it needs to be mentioned – they shared many of the same financial interests as secular leaders. Therefore, their political activities deserve the same degree of analysis and criticism as those of anyone else. This is especially true as their involvement served to impose their political and moral preferences on many people who did not want or welcome them, which became characteristic of the Irish state for much of the remainder of the twentieth century. Their religious offices may protect them in spiritual matters, but the same rules do not apply to temporal issues.

*   *   *

David Miller and J.H. Whyte both focused their works on the interaction of the Catholic Church and mainstream, popular nationalism.[15] Miller's book is an interesting examination of the Church relationship with the mainstream organisations of Irish nationalism during the first decades of the twentieth century. This focus, though, ignores the equally important Fenian militant separatist tradition that contributed as much to post-Rising Sinn Féin as the quasi-constitutionalism laid out by Arthur Griffith.[16] The Fenian-separatist tradition was another movement with which the Church had to contend, and the relationship between the Church and Fenianism was much more contentious.

The Fenian tradition was important to the relationship between nationalism and the Church for several reasons. The IRB had been condemned by Pope Pius IX at the behest of the Irish hierarchy in 1870. As a secret, oath-bound society, it violated Church laws. Equally importantly, its goal of Irish independence through violent means defied the bishops' strong, unified support for political change through constitutional methods. The popularity of the post-1916 Irish Volunteers, the infiltration of both the Volunteers and Sinn Féin by the IRB and the unification of the Volunteers and Sinn Féin under the leadership of Éamon de Valera in 1918 brought all strains of separatism together in a way that made it difficult for the bishops to issue any condemnation. This was made worse by Dublin Castle's decision to lump quasi-constitutionalists and militants together and to treat them as a single group.[17] The bishops had begun to give their public support to the nationalists, but this required temporary acceptance of Fenianism.

With the Anglo-Irish Treaty of 1921, the possibility of a return to non-violent politics was the opportunity for which the bishops had been looking, especially once the anti-Treaty movement showed itself to be dominated by its militant wing. Republicans maintained their connection to Fenian separatism that Free State supporters cast aside for peaceful means, though the majority of participants on both sides sought the same end. In this respect, hierarchical opposition to the republican movement fell in line with their traditional rejection of militant separatism. The fact that the majority of the IRA sided with the Treaty opponents only served to aggravate the bishops further.

Prior to 1916, Fenianism contained elements of what could be described as anti-clericalism. The chief propagator of this was Charles Kickham, perhaps best known for having authored *Knocknagow*.[18] As one of the chief editors of the *Irish People*, Kickham wrote many articles and responses to correspondence conveying a simple, straightforward notion that clergymen of all religions were to be respected for their spiritual functions. This respect given by the people had allowed priests to enter into the political arena and take political power. The Fenians did not deny priests the right to hold political opinions, but their clerical offices should not add weight to those opinions. Because of their clerical education, priests were likely to be worse politicians than other men. They were ensconced in theology from a young age, isolated from the people until they left the seminary, and chose to take an active part in politics with no political training.[19] Kickham defended the position of the Fenians by arguing that differing with a priest was not a subversion of the faith and a corruption of morals, as Cardinal Cullen had charged. Kickham retorted to Cullen's charges: "'If faith and morals have been subverted in [a bishop's] diocese, let him charge it to his own imprudence, or attribute it to his own neglect.'"[20] Both Kickham and O'Leary urged priests to remove themselves from politics for the good of their flocks, themselves and the Church in Ireland.

This was hardly anti-clericalism as it was practiced on the continent, but it demonstrated enough of a challenge to the political power of the hierarchy and clergy to be seen as a threat. Elements of this desire to purge politics of the activities of the clergy can be found in the republicanism of the Civil War as well as, sometimes, ironically, from the pens of priests themselves. However, 1916 had changed the nature of Irish separatism. In terms of political personnel, beliefs, practices and assumptions, there was a great deal of continuity during the pre- and post-Rising years, but the deeply religious and sacrificial nature of the Rising changed the terms of the debate, and expectations were dramatically altered.[21] Post-Rising separatism became a movement that melded together patriotism and spiritualism as never before experienced in Ireland. This book sets out to examine, carefully, this relationship between the Church and separatists from the Civil War to Fianna Fáil's ascension to power. Unlike most studies, which tend to give the Church preferential status, this work has endeavoured to treat the opposing sides as equals, and has granted republican rhetoric the same degree of validity as ecclesiastical pronouncements.

Acceptance of the Treaty caused a shift away from the amalgamation of nationalist philosophies and approaches, as Treaty supporters adopted a pragmatic, purely secular tactic to the founding of the new state and aspirations for greater independence. With foundering popular support, military victory growing increasingly elusive and a largely hostile church, republicans redoubled their usage of spiritualism as defence of their movement and their continued battle, while maintaining the Fenian tradition of expressing disapproval of allowing religious authorities to give their political statements added weight because of the social leadership brought about by their religious positions. The reasoning behind this and a closer examination of republican spiritual rhetoric, as well as reactions to it and the seeming paradox of using faith and morals to describe a movement yet criticising religious leaders for involving themselves in such a movement, are the subjects of Chapter 1.

Chapter 2 explores the bishops' opposition to anti-Treaty republicans and contends that the severity of episcopal language, both as individuals and a unified body, indicates that the bishops perceived republican attempts to promote their cause as the continuation of the holy cause of the 1916 martyrs as an acute threat to their power base. The other motive to be found in the strong ecclesiastical support of the Free State government was the bishops' desire to gain as much influence as possible over the apparently weak fledgling government and to maintain a firm grip on the social issues which had largely been their domain for decades, namely education and health care. Rather than submit, though, republicans chose to plead their case to the Vatican in the hopes of embarrassing the Irish bishops and lifting the ban of excommunication placed against them.

The potential for the Holy See's involvement in Irish affairs was a matter that caused consternation amongst the bishops, the Free State government and even some within the republican movement. The bishops feared the pope issuing a statement which might contradict their decisions, or, worst of all, the appointment of a Vatican representative, who would infringe upon their control of the Irish Church. The Free State government also displayed strong objections to the Church's interference in Irish matters when the republicans appeared so close to defeat. It was only the republicans who welcomed the Apostolic delegate, and then only after it became obvious that he could be used to the movement's advantage. These concerns and the Vatican activity that heightened the bishops' fear to near-panic are the subjects of Chapter 3. The papal-initiated visit of Monsignor Salvatore Luzio to the Irish Free State and the mixed reception he received while there is examined in detail. Due to the recent opening to the public of the Vatican papers of Pius XI's papacy, I have been the first Irish historian to study Luzio's mission using his own report, shedding light on many of the questions Keogh asked in 1986.

Chapter 4 focuses on punishment of republicans by the Free State and the difficulties the bishops faced in silently accepting arguably immoral actions by the state to allow it to strengthen as the ministers deemed necessary. Though some bishops worked quietly to alter government policy in the face of questionable executions and internment, their silence benefited the government, which used its perceived weakness to act without fear of hierarchical condemnation. More importantly, those bishops were in the minority, raising questions about the motives and desires of their fellow members of the bench. For republicans, hierarchical silence was further proof of the bishops' political partisanship. This was also made evident by their changed attitude towards the republicans' revival of the weapon of hunger strike, which had been accepted and even praised by members of the hierarchy during the hunger strike of Terence MacSwiney. Post-Treaty republicans who engaged in the same activity, even Terence's sisters, Mary, Eithne and Annie, were not treated to the same sympathetic attitude, but rather condemnation which had spiritual grounds that were shaky at best.

Though their political involvement had relatively little long-term impact on inter-denominational relations in the twenty-six counties that became the Free State, the same cannot be said in the northeast, where the bishops unintentionally served as perpetuators of the continuing sectarianisation of Northern Irish politics. Their social presence frightened northern Protestants, who actively sought to distance themselves from Catholic Ireland. Partition and the problems posed by a Protestant-dominated Northern Ireland are the themes of Chapter 5. Whereas the bishops had been the staunchest opponents of partition prior to the Treaty, after its ratification their collective attitude changed drastically. Republicans could have used this to their advantage in their conflict with the bishops for moral and principle high ground, but like so many others in the Free State, republicans seemed content to jettison the north amidst waves of rhetoric and bluster that masked general apathy or even relief to be rid of an area dominated by Protestant unionists.

The conclusion examines the Church's relationship with those who left Sinn Féin and formed Fianna Fáil, thereby moving republicanism into the realm of legitimate parliamentarianism. With mainstream republicans swearing off violence in favour of taking their seats in the Dáil, the bishops had to once again readjust their attitude towards the men and women they had just a few years prior excommunicated. Conversely, those excommunicants had to accept Church leaders not as their enemies, but as men who could (and to some degree would) help them dislodge Cumann na nGaedheal's monopoly on power in the Free State.

*   *   *

This book is, primarily, an attempt to observe and study trends across both sides of the ideological divide that separated republicans and the bishops. Given that the hierarchy was comprised of a small number of men, only some of whom chose to involve themselves in political affairs, most bishops who were politically active receive a voice in this work. Several, either due to age and illness or personal motivations, avoided the Civil War and politics as much as possible. All the bishops were very private men. They left no memoirs and very few of the Civil War era bishops have been the subject of a biography.[22] Their private letters seem to present one of the few tools available for getting at the heart of their fears, concerns and hopes. Because of this, I have aspired to incorporate their letters as much as possible. Unfortunately, two of the most politically active members of the hierarchy left virtually no political papers. Archbishop Harty ordered his personal secretary to destroy his political papers, which he dutifully did, and Bishop Cohalan made a point of not keeping anything involving Civil War era politics any longer than necessary.

On the opposite side, those who supported the republican cause through their words constituted a larger group, but were still small in number. Because of this, I have found it possible to discuss many of them in great detail. Unlike the bishops, many republicans were very open about their lives. There are many memoirs, published and unpublished, diaries and biographies available on the leading men and women of the anti-Treaty movement. Others discussed in this book, especially those who acted solely as letter writers, have left much less of a personal imprint on public memory. Information gleaned from their correspondence has been utilised in this book, but several of them remain little more than a name, and that only when they chose to identify themselves. Of special interest have been the papers of the priests and members of religious orders who defied the wishes of the bishops and supported the republicans. The Hagan collection in the Irish College in Rome contains dozens of letters from priests, nuns and seminarians informing the rector of their displeasure and disbelief at the positions of their spiritual leaders. The pseudonymous political writings of Fr. Patrick Browne of Maynooth have been instrumental to this book. I only wish that he had kept his personal papers, so that more about this fascinating man could be uncovered.

This book also seeks to examine some of the theological concerns raised by both sides during this turbulent period but only insofar as they were important to the debate. It is neither a work of theology nor a history of theology. It is also not a study of the Catholic Church. Because of this, the basic organisation and workings of the Church are not discussed and are simply understood. There are several sources available to better understand this topic. Whyte's text begins with a very short examination of the Catholic Church's structure, and Tom Inglis studies the matter in a highly critical, one might say anti-clerical way.[23]

NOTES ON TERMINOLOGY

Because this book focuses on the Catholic Church, and generally more specifically the Catholic Church in Ireland, the word 'Church' is used to mean that institution specifically. This is done simply to reduce repetition and does not imply a preference for any particular faith. Whenever other denominations are referenced, their full names are used. When the Catholic bishops are referred to as a group, 'hierarchy' is generally used, as this is one of the recognised terms for a nation's bishops. The Anglo-Irish Treaty of December 1921 is generally referred to as the 'Treaty'. Those who opposed it are discussed with multiple words: 'republicans', 'militants', 'separatists' and 'Irregulars', this last one only in the context of quotations. The terms are not entirely interchangeable and I have tried to distinguish them as necessary. The terms 'north' and 'northern' are meant to indicate the six county area of Northern Ireland, whereas 'Ulster' is generally definable as the traditional nine-county province. However, when used within the context of unionism, 'Ulster' refers to Northern Ireland. Finally, I have endeavoured to adhere to the spelling of words as I have found them in various sources. I have included all accent marks in words and names derived from Irish. I have refrained from italicising words in Irish to maintain a more consistent style. In quotations, I have maintained spelling and emphasis as they appeared.

NOTES

1. See *inter alia* Emmet Larkin, *The Roman Catholic Church and the Creation of the Modern Irish State, 1878–1886* (Dublin, 1975); Emmet Larkin, *The Roman Catholic Church in Ireland and the Fall of Parnell, 1888–1891* (Liverpool, 1976); Patrick Corish, *The Irish Catholic Experience: A Historical Survey* (Dublin, 1986); Patrick Corish, *Maynooth College, 1795–1995* (Dublin, 1995); J.H. Whyte, *Church and State in Modern Ireland, 1923–1970* (Dublin, 1971); David W. Miller, *Church, State and Nation in Ireland, 1898–1921* (Dublin, 1973).

2. Dermot Keogh, *The Vatican, the Bishops and Irish Politics, 1919–39* (Cambridge, 1986); Dermot Keogh, *Ireland and the Vatican: The Politics and Diplomacy of Church-State Relations, 1922–1960* (Cork, 1995); Patrick Murray, *Oracles of God: The Roman Catholic Church and Irish Politics, 1922–37* (Dublin, 2000).

3. Barry M. Coldrey, *Faith and Fatherland: The Christian Brothers and the Development of Irish Nationalism, 1838–1921* (Dublin, 1988); Kevin Collins, *Catholic Churchmen and the Celtic Revival in Ireland, 1848–1916* (Dublin, 2002).

4. Gerard Moran (ed.), *Radical Irish Priests, 1660–1970* (Dublin, 1998); Denis Carroll, *Unusual Suspects: Twelve Radical Clergymen* (Blackrock, 1998); Denis Carroll, *They have fooled you again. Michael O'Flanagan (1876–1942). Priest, Republican, Social Critic* (Blackrock, 1993).

5. Catherine Candy, *Priestly Fictions: Popular Irish Novelists of the Early 20th Century* (Dublin, 1995). See also Lawrence W. McBride, 'A Literary Life of a Socially and Politically Engaged Priest: Canon Patrick Augustine Sheehan (1852–1913)' in Gerard Moran (ed.), *Radical Irish Priests*, pp.131–48.

6. B.A. Santamaria, *Daniel Mannix: The Quality of Leadership* (Carlton, 1983); Colm Kiernan, *Daniel Mannix and Ireland* (Dublin, 1984); Michael Gilchrist, *Wit and Wisdom: Daniel Mannix* (North Melbourne, 2004).

7. See John Privilege, *Michael Logue and the Catholic Church in Ireland, 1879–1925* (Manchester, 2009), and Thomas J. Morrissey, *Edward J. Byrne, 1872–1941: The Forgotten Archbishop of Dublin* (Blackrock, 2010).

8. Dáire Keogh's forthcoming history of the Christian Brothers should correct some of these inadequacies.

9. Oliver Rafferty, *The Church, the State and the Fenian Threat, 1861–75* (London, 1999), p.21.

10. R.V. Comerford, *The Fenians in Context: Irish Politics and Society, 1848–82* (Dublin, 1985); Owen McGee, *The IRB: The Irish Republican Brotherhood from the Land League to Sinn Féin* (Dublin, 2005).

11. Joseph Brusher, *Consecrated Thunderbolt: Father Yorke of San Francisco* (Hawthorne, NJ, 1973).

12. Jérôme aan de Wiel, *The Catholic Church in Ireland, 1914-1918: War and Politics* (Dublin, 2003).

13. Patrick Murray, *Oracles of God*, p.419.

14. Ibid., p.409.

15. See David W. Miller, *Church, State and Nation in Ireland, 1898–1921* (Dublin, 1973), and J.H. Whyte, *Church and State in Modern Ireland, 1923–1970* (Dublin, 1971).

16. For an exemplary study on the course of Fenianism during the late nineteenth and early twentieth centuries, see M.J. Kelly, *The Fenian Ideal and Irish Nationalism, 1882–1916* (Woodbridge, 2006).

17. David Miller, *Church, State and Nation in Ireland*, pp.431–2.

18. To date, the best biography remains R.V. Comerford, *Charles J. Kickham: A Study in Irish Nationalism and Literature* (Portmarnock, 1979).

19. John O'Leary, *Recollections of Fenians and Fenianism, Volume II* (London, 1896), p.15.

20. Ibid., pp.48–9.

21. Richard English, *Ernie O'Malley: IRA Intellectual* (Oxford, 1998), p.9.

22. The exceptions being Logue and Byrne (see above) and J.J. Murphy, *The People's Primate: A Memoir of Joseph Cardinal MacRory* (Dublin, 1945). This last work, though, is amazingly concise; 72 pages, and completely uncritical.
23. See J.H. Whyte, *Church and State in Modern Ireland*, pp.1–3; Tom Inglis, *Moral Monopoly: The Rise and Fall of the Catholic Church in Modern Ireland* (Dublin, 1987).

1

The Gospel of Irish Nationalism

> They have conceived of nationality as a material thing, whereas it is a spiritual thing ... They have not recognised in their people the image and likeness of God. Hence, the nation to them is not all holy, a thing inviolate and inviolable, a thing that a man dare not sell or dishonour on pain of eternal perdition.[1]

Patrick Pearse uttered these words against the leaders of the Home Rule movement. He would never have imagined that seven years later similar ones would be used against men who had fought beside him in the GPO in 1916; men who had embraced the same desperate cause, many for the same abstract reasons. Historiography of the Civil War has examined in great detail many of the reasons for the split in Sinn Féin and the IRA; how the division occurred along class and geographical lines,[2] and the loyalties and rivalries that contributed to the divisions.[3] The importance of these factors cannot be questioned, but in a conflict which centred on issues of principle and morality, certain aspects of the convictions of those who defied the popular government and their religious leaders must be examined more closely than they have been by historians. While analysis and debate on the respective interpretations and connections to the principles of democracy have been thorough, the same cannot be said about the role moral convictions and principles played from the signing of the Treaty onward.

Rigorous academic study has enriched our understanding of the conflict over the Treaty and the ensuing war through analysis of the nuances of the political principles of the era. However, Paul Bew's contention that the historiographical debate has existed 'without any precise reference to the real interplay between Catholic popular piety and the political practice of radical nationalist movements' is as apt a statement for the post-Treaty era as it is for his chosen topic of the Land War.[4] One branch of this deficiency has been the lack of adequate examination of republican convictions as a motive for their activities in the aftermath of the Anglo-Irish Treaty of 1921. It was, after all, these convictions that inspired Treaty opponents to challenge the Catholic bishops on issues they accepted as involving morals and principles and which served as the sources of inspiration for the propaganda and rhetoric that established the republican cause as the superior one. Chapter 2 examines the conflict between these groups after the bishops became vocal on the subject. This chapter focuses on the republicans and the rationale behind their post-Treaty principles.

RELIGION AND NATIONALIST RHETORIC

Republicans' strong convictions were rooted in a foundation of an organic marriage of Catholicism and nationalism that dated from the nineteenth century. Roy Foster uses A.M. Sullivan's *The Story of Ireland* to show that national aspiration was the subject of religious portrayal as early as the 1860s. Though he was an advocate of moderate home rule, Sullivan's work included references to crucifixion, burial and a glorious rising.[5] In his extensive study on Irish nationalism, Richard English shows that by the 1880s Catholic teaching and thinking were so pervasive in Irish society that the crude application of power through direct clerical involvement in politics was not necessary, though often still utilised. By this period, Catholicism and nationalism had become so intertwined, English argues, that the aspiration to nationhood had, in a sense, become a religion.[6] Vincent Comerford describes the development of a nationalist Catholic identity as the 'largest political fact of Irish life in the mid-nineteenth century'.[7] Coinciding with this was the emergence of a Catholic nationalist middle-class, as shown by Patrick Maume and Senia Paseta, which was resentful of the repression and lack of opportunities they faced due to the privileged status of the Ascendancy and the lack of viable university education acceptable to members of the Catholic Church.[8] England's official Protestantism only served to increase the links between nationalism and Catholicism, as the 'Gaelic' Irish, both in reality and fiction, came to be identified with their Catholic faith to differentiate them from the Protestant 'outsiders' and 'aggressors'.[9]

Mary-Lou Legg's outstanding work on the Irish provincial press of the second half of the nineteenth century has shown that the press played a pivotal role in the spread of Gaelicisation.[10] The same must also be said of the press's role in the merging of Catholicism and nationalism. Publication of episcopal and clerical statements and sermons was common and served to disseminate the clergy's increasingly involved views on temporal issues. With the creation of specifically Catholic publications, a wide variety of issues became topics of discussion through the lens of Catholicism. Even though the Church generally remained aloof from secular issues and the bishops often disagreed, definite lines of consensus became obvious and the 'Catholic' perspective more defined.

Emergence of a Catholic press began in Edinburgh in 1832 with the founding of the *Edinburgh Catholic Magazine*, which appeared intermittently until it began regular circulation in 1837. The first stable Catholic journal was the *Dublin Review* founded in London in 1836, followed four years later by Frederick Lucas's *The Tablet*.[11] Except for the brief re-location of *The Tablet* to Dublin during the final years of Lucas's life, Catholic publications did not spread to Ireland immediately. Aside from a few short-running local papers, the *Irish Catholic* marks the first successful venture, dating from 1888 and continuing to the present. Also of note were Charles Diamond's *Irish Catholic Herald*[12] (1921–34) and the *Catholic Bulletin* (1913–39). While not as widely read as the *Catholic*, each title was well known and propagated strong views on politics and religion.

Priests also contributed to the growing market of Catholic newspapers. *The Tablet* had been purchased by Fr. Herbert Vaughan in 1868 and remained under the control of the Archdiocese of Westminster until it was sold to Catholic laity in 1935. The Dominican Order began publication of *Irish Rosary* in 1897 and the Jesuits followed suit with *Studies* in 1912. *The Catholic Bulletin*, while published by M.H. Gill & Son under the editorship of laymen J.J. O'Kelly and later P.T. Keohane, had a strong clerical element in its writing. Bishop Cohalan of Cork contributed until 1918, Fr. John Hagan, then vice-rector of the Irish College in Rome, wrote the 'Notes from Rome' section under the pseudonym 'Scottus' and Fr. Timothy Corcoran, S.J. imposed his own unique perspective on the journal from 1922.

A new phenomenon that emerged in the second half of the nineteenth century also served to move Catholicism from the realm of the purely religious – the priest as author. The popular works of fiction of Canons Guinan and Sheehan exposed a large audience to an incontrovertible merging of Catholicism and nationalism that, in Sheehan's case, even sanctified the heroic Fenians he had admired as a child.[13] In 1905, Monsignor Michael O'Riordan wrote his five hundred-page rebuttal to Horace Plunket's *Ireland in the New Century*. In his tome, O'Riordan promoted the Catholic perspective on most of the era's hot topics, including government, agriculture, education and the role of the Church in society.[14] In the wake of this groundbreaking clerical entry into secular issues, priestly literary output grew even stronger, including pamphlets on a gamut of issues that had only the most tenuous link to faith and a collection of essays by eleven priests that discussed such issues as the Irish language, history and rural life.[15] By the 1920s, the *Irish Messenger* was publishing an entire series of pamphlets written by priests focusing on social action.

In this environment, it was only natural for the language of Catholicism to permeate even the most extreme varieties of nationalist rhetoric. Though the original members of the IRB had attempted to build their organisation into a purely secular and non-sectarian one, the attractiveness of using the language of Catholicism proved too great, and given the religious beliefs of the majority of members, was simply organic. Crucially, the tenets of Fenianism, propagated by Charles Kickham, John O'Leary and James Stephens, which called for the leadership of the benighted masses towards the ultimate goal of independence, synchronised very well with the example set by the Catholic Church of contempt of electoral politics and majority rule.[16] Moreover, the Fenian attachment to the abstract 'Irish Republic', which continued uninterrupted into the twentieth century, demanded, to use Matthew Kelly's phrase, 'a leap of faith' that appealed to the Catholic mindset.[17] The similarities of psychological demands shared by Catholicism and Fenianism made the bringing together of the two easy for any who wanted it, even if the bishops had condemned the Fenian movement, and John O'Leary, one of Fenianism's chief ideologues, possessed a strong anti-clericalism inspired by his experiences in France. By the time Pearse entered the political arena, '[t]he seepage of religious terms into political language' had been, according to Michael Laffan, 'widespread and instinctive'.[18] Irish nationalists, by and large, viewed their nationality as tightly interwoven with the cultural language of Catholicism.[19] Pearse's rhetoric resonated well because he was speaking to a highly receptive audience.

By the beginning of the twentieth century, religiosity had permeated nationalist rhetoric to such a degree that C.S. Parnell, formerly denounced by the Irish bishops for his immoral behaviour, had become the subject of Christological metaphors granting him the status of a sacrificed saviour figure.[20] However, the more extreme elements of sacrifice remained strongest amongst the coterie of advanced nationalists who were ultimately responsible for the Rising. Ben Novick's exceptional work on the advanced nationalists' propaganda of the First World War shows that some separatists, the most extreme of them being Terence MacSwiney, were responsible for 'demands which expressed an extraordinary degree of masochism that went beyond even Pearse's promotion of sacrifice'.[21] MacSwiney's pre-Rising rhetoric was especially filled with Catholic themes and the idea of martyrological sacrifice. In the wake of the Rising, however, Pearse stood out as the quintessential hero/martyr, granting his writings and orations a place at the top of the canon. MacSwiney had to wait four more years before he could make his own ultimate sacrifice for Ireland.

It was in large part due to the First World War that the public became receptive to this language of sacrifice, a trend that occurred across Europe as the language of sacrifice and sanctification of dead soldiers became common.[22] Coupled with this was the intensification of wartime discourse that involved its brutalisation and increased aggression.[23] The letters of Maud Gonne demonstrated the shifting mentality that resulted from these changes. In a letter to Yeats written during the first year of the War, she described a wild reel she had been hearing in her mind that was drawing together the thousands of Irish soldiers who had died on the front. She believed that many of these had died with a definite idea of sacrifice to an ideal:

> they were held by the stronger & deeper Rhythms of the chants, leading in wonderful patterns to a deeper peace, the peace of the Crucified, which is above the currents of nationalities & storms, but for all that they will not be separated from Ireland for as an entity she has followed the path of Sacrifice & has tasted of the Grail & the strength they will bring her is greater.[24]

Over-exposure to death also carried the price of growing callousness of the general populace. Gonne, again, expressed this in a letter she wrote after the sinking of the *Lusitania.* 'I suppose the constant familiarity with Death will end by making everyone reckless or indifferent.'[25] While Gonne's esoteric interests were not shared by the majority of advanced nationalists, let alone the Irish populace at large, her correspondence are just some of the more colourful examples of the fact that the language of loss and sacrifice had permeated Irish society, allowing the traditional appeal of sacrifice and martyrdom that ran through both Irish nationalism and post-Famine Catholicism to become part of contemporary, everyday life.

In the midst of this shift in the public discourse came the Easter Rising, during which the usage of religious and sacrificial rhetoric in advanced nationalism climaxed.[26] Pearse's words, the symbolism of voluntarily sacrificing one's life for Ireland, even the opportune timing linking it to Christ's self-sacrifice, all made the coming together of sacrifice-oriented Catholicism and separatism in the public conversation a certainty, especially after the executions of the leaders turned the masses against the Crown. The Rising popularised martyr-worship to an extent never before or since experienced in Ireland. The Rising and its aftermath made sacrificial-political language popularly acceptable, so that a religious/cultic ethic imbued with concepts of blood sacrifice, martyrdom and the sacredness of the national movement permeated the ranks of Sinn Féin from 1916. The extent of this can be found in the fact that the executions of the Rising leaders spawned 'a veritable micro-industry' of propaganda pieces and commemorative kitsch that perfectly, if rather tastelessly, married popular spirituality and militant separatism in items such as tricolour rosary beads and a colour print titled 'His Easter Offering' which featured a dead Volunteer lying at the feet of Kathleen ni Houlihan in a style strongly reminiscent of the countless works depicting the body of Jesus resting in front of his mother.[27] Mass-produced portraits of the executed Rising leaders served as a focal point for the public's newfound enthusiasm for sacrifice.

The Rising also served to imbue separatists with a newfound sense of urgency. The idea of the republic became as sacred as Ireland itself and could not be eradicated for any reason, even the democratically displayed desires of the living Irish. Using the old Fenian argument, the people were to be guided along the correct path, but the motivation was now holy rather than political. These spiritually focused separatists did not constitute the entire movement, but they were largely responsible for its public persona and ideology, and for this reason alone, they are worth examining. In this regard, Patrick Murray's work on the Catholic Church and Irish politics is deficient in the limited attention he pays to post-Treaty lay separatists. One of the distinguishing factors of the rhetorical fight of the era was that lay Catholic republicans gave their arguments the same moral and spiritual leverage as those of their religious leaders. To dedicate a mere twenty pages to this aspect, as he does,[28] does not do the matter justice and certainly does not allow for a thorough enough examination of what is one of the primary subjects of this book.

The examination of the relationship between religion and nationalism hits a snag with the signing of the Anglo-Irish Treaty of 1921 and the division in the nationalist camp that resulted in the opposing sides of the Civil War. Jeffrey Prager attributes the war to the inability of Ireland's polarised ideologies, Irish-Enlightenment and Gaelic-Romantic, to work together. The problem with this interpretation is that the opposing sides were not made up of people who adhered to differing polarised ideologies. To accept this dichotomy implicitly grants Treaty opponents a greater degree of 'Irishness' when in fact the rhetoric of both sides was imbued with cultural revivalism.[29] Tim Wilson's recent comparative work on Ulster and Upper Silesia indicates that it was the need to define 'hard' boundaries in Upper Silesia due to lack of obvious differences between the opposing sides that brought about the atrocious acts of violence which marred the region in the aftermath of the First World War.[30] The same model could be applied to the Irish Civil War. One of the few differences that republicans could highlight was their self-ascribed moral superiority and continued adherence to the goals laid out by the leaders of the Rising, which had become sacred. They were the true inheritors of the legacy of Pearse. Free State supporters, by contrast, had embraced the pragmatic tactics, and, Kissane argues, the values and status hierarchies of the Parliamentary Party.[31] They were seen as sell-outs, careerists and morally weak.

While there had still been a possibility for co-operation between the opposing sides, republicans focused their ideological aggressions against the British, who, for them, represented Protestantism and the evils of secularism and modernity. After the start of hostilities, though, the matter of justification changed as the new opponents were nationalist, Catholic Irish. Republicans defended their position as one of continuing the fight against the English which had yet to be won while denouncing the very existence of the Free State. With the general election of 1922 and the shelling of the Four Courts, the republicans found themselves to be a minority engaged in a fight against superior military forces – which had the backing of the majority of Irish. At that point, they delved 'into republican theology for answers and explanations as to why a revolutionary world no longer conformed to the needs of their predestined republic.'[32]

POST-TREATY REPUBLICAN RELIGIOSITY

Amongst those who have studied the leadership cadre of the post-Treaty republican movement, there has been a traditional view of doubting the authenticity of their convictions, an idea which was widely distributed in the contemporary, predominantly Free State supporting print media. V.S. Pritchett, an English journalist who reported from Ireland during the Civil War,[33] was one of those responsible for this line of thought. He informed his largely international audience that the talk of principle was superficial and that personal bitterness and jealousies amongst the political elite were the real motivating factors for the conflict.[34] David Fitzpatrick formerly adhered to this stance and argued that the ethical defence of republicanism was not a viable cause for the Civil War as 'almost all leading republicans had long since compromised their demand, whether in pursuit of nationalist solidarity or of a negotiated settlement.' For him, the struggle was caused more by personal and factional divisions within the leadership than ideology.[35] Once the need for public solidarity had waned, rivalries and philosophical differences came to the fore and caused the fracturing of the movement. This was obvious as early as the Dáil vote on the Treaty. Garvin agrees with Fitzpatrick's assertion, citing the rivalry between Collins and Mulcahy on one side and Stack and Brugha on the other.[36]

It cannot be denied that most of the anti-Treaty leaders had compromised their positions, including Éamon de Valera, the man who served (and to a degree still serves) as the scapegoat for the cause of the Civil War among Treaty supporters. The reasons for de Valera's rejection of the Treaty remain a contentious issue. Some of the most vocal critics of his motives were members of the Cabinet who had supported the Treaty and who had expected that they could count on de Valera's support, as his concept of External Association had freed him from the straitjacket of extreme republicanism. They were taken aback at what they viewed as his betrayal of them. They could only make sense of his adoption of uncompromising republicanism as a political power play.[37] Blythe believed that de Valera rejected the Treaty because he could not find a way to deny Collins credit for it, and Laffan finds it credible to assert that he was not averse to compromise but rejected this particular version because it was not his.[38] Owen Dudley Edwards offers an interesting counterview that de Valera, having had very little contact with his Cabinet ministers, was shocked that the Cabinet voted against his wishes regarding the Treaty.[39]

Even with the benefit of hindsight and copious amounts of source materials, modern historians cannot authoritatively offer an answer. Rather than acting on his own initiative, Kissane argues that de Valera acted as the representative of his followers and that his reasons for opposing the Treaty were consistent with the objectives of the Sinn Féin movement.[40] Archbishop Harty was of the same opinion even as he and the other bishops prepared the April pastoral. He informed an interviewer 'that it would be impossible for De Valera [*sic*] to accept it [the Treaty].' He had a mandate from the people to accept nothing but a republic and it would be impossible for him to take any other line.[41] It is difficult to believe, though, that the man who had provided such strong leadership and whose record demonstrates that his interpretation of the principles of democracy favoured the 'general will', especially during this period, would submit himself to the will of his constituents to such a degree. Much more plausible is the argument that de Valera acted in the manner he did to keep Treaty opponents united and to prevent hardliners from taking complete control of the movement. His attempts at maintaining Sinn Féin unity, first through his desperate attempts to get widespread acceptance of Document No. 2, then through the failed pact with Collins, shows that he was primarily concerned with keeping the movement as intact as possible and feared that inadequate leadership would cause the anti-Treaty side to splinter into the multiple factions of which it was composed.[42] Diarmaid Ferriter's recent work on de Valera demonstrates that his actions during the Treaty debate and Civil War indicate a man who was unrealistic and stubborn, especially in his belief in his own ability to unite the opposing sides.[43] Perhaps Hopkinson best sums up the challenge of understanding de Valera's motives during the Civil War. He had a 'tendency to cloak political compromise and ambiguity in the language of principle ... It was difficult to ascribe ordinary politicians' considerations to the much revered and abused Chief'.[44]

Though de Valera described himself as guided by reason and therefore unfit to lead doctrinaire republicans,[45] his actions during the Civil War seem far from logical and reasoned for a man who obviously had ambitions to be a leader. There is something to be said for taking his language of principle as more than a mere cloak. De Valera's rejection was expected by many and was widely accepted as an honest but mistaken decision.[46] Fr. Pádraig Ó Cleírig of St Columban's College, Galway, questioned: 'Is it that De Valera [*sic*] is going to sacrifice himself, just to hand down to posterity the national ideal, or is it that he is going to try by every means to swing the country and the Dail with him.'[47] Fr. Michael O'Flanagan argued that had de Valera only been interested in power and personal gain, he could have accepted the Treaty, become head of the Free State government and avoided the imprisonments, defamations and general inconveniences of being a fugitive on the run.[48] Both John O'Carroll and Owen Dudley Edwards maintain that de Valera earnestly believed in the principles on which he had made his stand, and Edwards believes de Valera saw those who defected from his line as worse than traitors; they were accursed defectors who had abandoned their sacred calling.[49] Many republicans adopted this mentality against their opponents, who were regularly described in republican rhetoric as fallen.[50]

Scholarship has recently begun to re-examine the Civil War as a conflict caused by republican leaders' attempts to regain the principles they had largely abandoned in an attempt to end the conflict with the Crown through compromise, primarily in the form of de Valera's Document No. 2. One historian who has promoted this claim is David Fitzpatrick, who had modified his stance by the time he wrote *Harry Boland's Irish Revolution*. In it, he theorises that '[t]hough the debate over the Treaty was construed by most leaders of both factions as a contest between principle and pragmatism, its underlying thrust was a disagreement as to which form of compromise was most expedient.'[51] While the members of the republican leadership had compromised themselves and were willing to go further, it violated their principles, and so they were somewhat relieved when the Treaty supporters rejected their offers. 'The eruption of Civil War brought much-needed moral relief to opponents of the Treaty ... whose republican principles had been compromised through the search for a settlement. It enabled them to reclaim membership of a virtuous minority pitting its purity of principle, as in 1916, against the superior force of the Republic's internal and external enemies.'[52]

Contemporary documentation certainly shows that principle was a deciding factor. Monsignor Hagan, rector of the Irish College, Rome, made one direct attempt to resolve the crisis, in August 1922, at the behest of Seán T. O'Kelly. In his letter to Mulcahy, Hagan implored the Free State government to show itself to be open to peace negotiations because the war against the English had shown how difficult it is to exterminate an enemy who is prepared to give all in the name of an ideal.[53] Though negotiations proved exceedingly slow, Hagan finally wrote to Rory O'Connor and Liam Mellows in early September stating that their desire to meet with the prisoners' commanders in Kilmainham was perfectly acceptable from a moral standpoint. 'In doing this you will be giving away no principle',[54] indicating that this was an issue for them. Aside from this incident, the desperate actions of the republican leadership indicate that for many it was a desire to regain principle rather than rivalries that guided them. Despite Garvin's contention that Cathal Brugha's alignment during the war was largely attributable to jealousy of Collins's powerful position and his own gradual marginalisation,[55] Brugha's charge into Free State bullets was not the action of a man who had an axe to grind with his opponents. In light of his death, it is difficult to counter Owen Dudley Edwards's description of Brugha as 'the implacable zealot for the Easter Republic unalloyed by pragmatism'.[56]

There is a lot to be gained by expanding the study of post-Treaty republicanism beyond the sphere of the top echelon of power. Even if the motives of the leadership were questionable, there was more to the struggle than elite psychology;[57] post-Treaty republicanism derived much of its ideology from rank-and-file members. A large portion of the rhetoric examined in this book was written by such supporters of the republican cause. Seminarians, prisoners, anonymous pamphleteers, semi-literate Irish Americans, nuns and doting mothers genuinely believed in the words they were writing, and these were the people who gave religious republicanism its true strength. This had been one of the lessons of 1916: it was only after the people gave their full support to the cause of the executed rebels that Sinn Féin began its momentous spread. Anti-Treaty republicanism retained the backing of rank and file supporters who treated the dead as martyrs and the republic as a sacred gift from God, and this support base was much more important than the questionable principles of the leadership. Furthermore, despite what the leaders may have said and thought in private, they were telling these followers exactly what they wanted to hear by filling their propaganda with religious motifs.

Treaty supporters, many of whom had been believers in and contributors to the religious-political language of the war for independence, no longer spoke of the national struggle along such lines. In 1913, Ernest Blythe had written about the national soul being yielded to the conqueror if the succession of martyrs failed.[58] Once the Treaty was signed, he, like other Free State supporters, abandoned the religious rhetoric of the nationalist movement except for the occasional reference to the Treaty and new state as a gift from God. Given the Catholic bishops' almost instantaneous endorsement of the Treaty, leaving religious rhetoric to religious leaders was a natural choice, and one that allowed for a more secular message which could appeal to the Free State's Protestant residents and possibly even alleviate the fears of Northern unionists.

While Free State supporters turned to a pragmatic nationalism that promoted a gradual move towards full independence within the Empire, republicans re-embraced the spirituality that had become one of the hallmarks of the nationalist movement. This is something that deserves greater analysis, as spiritual nationalism was just one avenue republicans could have pursued, and not the easiest one at that, it should be noted. Once they chose spirituality, they ran the risk of incurring the wrath of the Church, which in retrospect seemed inevitable, though the religious nature of the post-1916 fight had attracted the positive attention of many of Ireland's priests and even the eventual, albeit often begrudging acceptance of many of the bishops.[59] Clerical endorsement of the Treaty made republican spiritual defence a risky venture. Insistence on genuine self-determination and a stronger fight against the injustice of partition would have proven safer and more theoretically sound lines of argument for their militant opposition to the Treaty, but this would have failed to adequately inspire those who remained loyal to republicanism.

As Richard English perceptively points out, '[w]ithout understanding the religious conviction shared by these Catholic Revolutionaries, the nature of their commitment will elude us; in particular, the sacrificial element within Republican thinking was pervasive, and was accentuated by the painful Civil War.'[60] Despite the overall inadequacy of Prager's interpretation of the Civil War, his analysis of the mentality of the men and women he describes as the Gaelic-Romantic type is apt for this book, though its usage must be more refined and sparing than he allows. He contends that these men and women saw the republic as imminently real and possible. More importantly, though, this meant that to them the national ideal was open to only a single interpretation and demanded absolute realisation. 'Doctrines were either correct or incorrect, and compromise for the sake of expediency could not be tolerated.'[61] They were, in his words, 'men of faith. They were infused with the Catholic conviction of the union of spirit and flesh.'[62] Prager's critic, Garvin, agrees, claiming that the republicans saw the republic as a moral and transcendental entity analogous even to the Church and whose citizens were duty bound to defend it with their lives. Although Garvin believes that republican leaders were guided by ulterior motives, he seems convinced that the same cannot be said about the rank and file, describing them as 'a moral community created by a single and irreversible plebiscite and sanctified by the blood of martyrs; Irish republicanism was not a political theory but a secular religion.'[63]

It is difficult to countermand this line of reasoning in light of the grim situation faced by many republicans, who would have found life much easier had they accepted the new state. Personal ties, loyalties and other non-ideological motives undoubtedly contributed to the divisions at the initial split, but once the republican cause was a lost one, it is difficult to see these factors retaining their importance. The rank and file who had nothing to gain in terms of power and authority and everything to gain by accepting the Free State were acting conscientiously. Over ten thousand internees would not have been locked away for months without trial, parents would not need to have written to government ministers and bishops complaining of the treatment of their children, and priests would not have faced suspension or transfer for their political beliefs. Furthermore, the dearth of republicans volunteering to sign a promise to accept the authority of the government and swear off violence against it, knowing that it would result in their freedom and return to a peaceful life, only serves to affirm the importance of principle to them.

A letter from Charlie Daly, a young republican prisoner, to his parish priest serves as an excellent example: 'I would never have thrown away the prospects which were mine twelve months ago and gone through all this painful business with the knowledge of possibly meeting such a fate as mine without having been actuated by the purest of motives.' Regarding his activities during the Civil War, were it not for his 'strong convictions as to its morality and righteousness I would never have taken part in it, or persisted in it afterwards, not against the common enemy but against our own comrades and dearest friends we have been compelled to turn our arms.'[64] Daly was one of four prisoners executed as a reprisal for the shooting of Captain Bernard Cannon in March 1923.

A large part of this need to re-embrace republican religiosity was due to the lack of tangible elements in the anti-Treaty ideology. On the surface, de Valera's Document No. 2 was similar enough to the Treaty that Cardinal Logue, who was never lacking for disparaging words regarding de Valera, criticised the difference between the two as 'a thin, intangible, unsubstantial vapour' and lamented that this minute difference had been responsible for the Civil War.[65] Those with keener political minds were even less kind to the republican alternative to the Treaty.[66] Even some of those who opposed the Treaty remained unconvinced that de Valera's option was a legitimate substitute. Kathleen Clarke, widow of 1916 Rising hero Tom Clarke, staunch opponent of the Treaty, and a woman who had few kind words for some of her fellow republicans,[67] informed de Valera after reading his document that there was 'scarcely the toss of sixpence' between it and the Treaty and that she would not support him in trying to get it passed in the Dáil.[68] Post-Treaty republicanism carried on the tradition of pre-Treaty Sinn Féin by being an organisation that was most easily defined by what it opposed rather than what it believed in. Still having no clear definitive plan for their independent state, republicans could offer little in the way of how their utopian option presented a brighter future. Even the hallowed 'Republic' was no longer part of de Valera's goals, which consisted simply of allowing the Irish people to freely choose their preferred form of independent government.[69] The Treaty gave enough freedom to please most of the people, and with Collins compellingly promoting his stepping stone programme, the majority of Irish were convinced that it was just a matter of time before complete independence was within reach. The republican plan, then, offered little appeal to pragmatic, war-weary nationalists. Talk of achieving similar ends through more bloodshed required moving the debate to a more abstract plane.

Many within the republican camp maintained the traditional separatist obsession with complete separation from Great Britain. For them, much like the Fenians of the nineteenth century, the many aspects of the budding nation would be sorted out once Imperial authority had vanished from the island. It was this simplistic and naïve mentality that kept spiritual republicanism alive. The escalation of the conflict against the Free State supporters coupled with the termination of widespread public support for the republic and the increasingly obvious inevitability of a military loss served to reinvigorate and intensify this re-spiritualisation of the movement. With little or no recourse to popular pressure or military strength, republicans returned to promoting their cause along lines of principle and morality, as the men and women of 1916 had done. Abstract concepts of superiority did not depend on physical realities and remained unassailable regardless of the situation. The result was a movement in which 'contradictions and inconsistencies' abounded.[70] For republicans, though, no contradictions or inconsistencies existed. In their minds, their actions were guided by the highest of principles.

Perhaps the best example is the post-Treaty view on democracy and popular consensus. The Declaration of Independence, passed by the Dáil in 1919, emphasised that the 'overwhelming majority' of the electorate seized the first occasion available, the General Election of 1918, to declare its firm allegiance to the republic that had been declared in 1916 by the army in the name of the Irish people. The official republican memorandum presented to Clemenceau and the members of the Paris Peace Conference also utilised the will of the majority as valid reason for granting self-determination.[71] In March 1921, de Valera said that the elections of 1918 had given the republic an unassailable foundation which had not existed beforehand. Those who questioned the moral validity of the republic now were in effect challenging the foundations of democracy and the constitutional rights of people.[72]

Less than two years later, Eithne MacSwiney questioned Archbishop Byrne's right to demand obedience to the will of the majority, as he and other Irish bishops had thrown scorn on the will of the people when they demanded a republic in 1920 and 1921, a common republican argument against the bishops' calls for the acceptance of the will of the majority. Referring to what she believed to have been their attitudes during the conflict against the Crown, MacSwiney informed Byrne that '[i]f you could ignore the "voice of the majority" when it willed the Holy Right of Freedom, surely I may ignore it when it wills the perjury and dishonour of my Race.'[73] It must also be remembered, MacSwiney noted, that the majority were responsible for condemning Christ to death, while a majority of bishops in several countries were responsible for the abandoning of Catholicism for Protestantism. These were arguments that were utilised in a large quantity of small propaganda posters that questioned the rights of the majority, including an anti-Semitic piece that rhetorically asked if the majority of Jews had been right in killing Christ.[74] Fr. Patrick Browne, who had served as an electoral agent for Sinn Féin in 1918, now questioned the fundamental principle of liberal democracy:

> To come to the question of the 'Will of the People', which is now almost the sole source of strength for the Free State Party. Do you, educated men, really accept the new interpretation of this sacred principle? You must know that majority rule is an imperfect institution. You, disciples of Him who was unjustly crucified by the people, must know that there are limitations to the 'will of the people'. If numbers are to make right, there is an end to all morality.[75]

De Valera's statement from less than two years prior defending the voice of the majority and lashing out against those who opposed the republic seems to have lost all its authority once the majority used their voice to express a desire that conflicted with the goals of the republicans.

Democracy had been a useful tool while it was available, but the will of the people had never been the ultimate concern for die-hard republicans. There were greater principles at stake than the will of the people. Republicans had equated freedom to a divine gift; 'the Holy Right of Freedom' to use Eithne MacSwiney's phrase. Naturally, the men and women who fought for freedom were raised to the same plane as the heroes of 1916. 'Next to God is freedom' *The Connachtman* informed its readers 'and next in greatness to the roll of martyrs to God is the roll of martyrs to freedom.'[76] A resolution passed by the Roger Casement Sinn Féin Club (London) illustrates how ingrained this belief had become in the republican mentality. 'THAT we recognize that Erskine Childers by the sacrifice of his life for the Faith of Irish Freedom, has added his name to the long list of Martyrs in the cause of National Freedom.'[77]

With an estimated seventy-five per cent of the Free State population favouring the Free State, republicans had to defend their position, which had formerly been held up by the electoral victories of 1918 and 1920, by a means that circumvented the democratic values they had previously embraced. Once again, the Fenian tactic of guiding the benighted masses towards what was best for them was adopted, but with a strongly spiritual bent. While the IRA admitted that its resistance to the Free State was unpopular as early as July 1922, 'democratic principles of legitimacy were unimportant compared with a competing set of principles that were essentially of religious origin.'[78] To this end, they returned to the sacredness of the Irish nation that had been preached by Pearse.

Popular opposition to the continued fight for complete independence did not deter republicans, but merely forced them to alter their ideological motivation. Whereas these men and women had found public sympathy throughout the twenty-six counties during the war for independence, they now faced opposition and so resorted to intimidation and retracted into their 'self-justifying reveries of the ideal republic, maintained their futile campaign of destruction, and waited in vain for the people to awaken from their slumber.'[79] Instead of listening to the will of the people, the republicans validated themselves by proclaiming that the people had been held hostage by the British, led astray by the media and the Catholic Church or were morally weak. This formed the basis for the reaction that was inspired by Garvin's 'general will', but that general will was also steeped in moralistic motifs. Republicans were therefore able to re-embrace the spirit of 1916 in an attempt to achieve the same goal of leading the people towards the correct end for the good of Ireland.

SPIRITUAL RHETORIC

One of the republicans who displayed a penchant for employing spiritualist rhetoric was Éamon de Valera,[80] though according to his private words such rhetoric was nothing more than a tool for him. He admitted to Mary MacSwiney that her stand for fundamentalist republicanism placed her 'on the plane of Faith and Unreason.'[81] When, in a meeting between Eoin MacNeill and de Valera, MacNeill criticised de Valera's stance as lining himself up with doctrinaire extremists with whom he did not agree any more than MacNeill, de Valera responded 'these people have one thing. They have faith.'[82] Within this context, it is not clear whether he viewed this as an asset or as a hindrance.

He certainly used that faith to his advantage when it suited him. De Valera, who was a life-long devout Catholic, appealed to the expectations of other devout Catholics by emphasising ritual in his politico-religious ceremonies and by preaching along orthodox and fundamentalist lines.[83] In a letter to Archbishop Mannix, who had been converted to the cause of republicanism largely through the efforts of de Valera, he wrote that human nature would have to be recast before Irishmen and women, who believed in the national right and the national destiny as in a religion, would consent to acquiesce in the selling of the national birthright for what they regarded as an ignoble mess of pottage. Paraphrasing the former bishop of Limerick, de Valera wrote: 'As Dr. O'Dwyer said, as long as grass grows or water runs, men and women will be found ready to dare and give up their lives in the cause of Irish freedom, and will deem the sacrifice virtue and not sin.'[84]

Many republicans displayed the resolute faith in republicanism that seemed to evade de Valera and held to their moral superiority and the spirituality of the fight against the Free State. A letter writer to Hanna Sheehy-Skeffington proudly announced that he and fellow members of the Roger Casement Sinn Féin Club of London were working to keep the 'Republican Gospel' before the people.[85] A Treaty opponent writing under the pseudonym 'Miles Republicanus' credited the men who stood by the republic as believing in their cause as a just and holy one. They were defending what they believed to be right nationally as ardently and as steadfastly as they would defend their religious faith, unlike Free State supporters, he implied, who were willing to fight as mercenaries for gold careless of the justice of their cause or the morals and motives of their leaders.[86]

During the five weeks republicans occupied Cork city, the *Cork Examiner* was turned into an anti-Treaty daily that pushed the spiritual superiority of their side. An article titled 'Magna est Veritas' argued that the republic was not merely the symbol that the Free State supporters claimed it was. It was a living reality and the expression in concrete form of the aspirations of centuries' worth of Irish. More importantly, symbols, the writer contended, are outward marks of living reality. Making a transparent link between Irish republicanism and Christianity, the article continued:

> Men have died in every age for symbols such as ours. What is the Cross but a symbol of the greatest of all realities? What is the flag of the nation but a symbol of its glory and independence, and have not the best and bravest in every age died in defence of that symbol? We do not suffer and die for the symbol itself. We suffer and die for the reality which it expresses.[87]

The Free State had its own symbols, the writer added, 'And the Oath of Allegiance is but a symbol too, but one and all are symbols of surrender, the surrender of the underlying reality – of the principle which distinguishes the souls of fire from the souls of clay.'[88]

Propagandist Aodh de Blácam described the entire struggle as a spiritual one. The fight against Britain was one of spirit against force, and the collapse that led to acceptance of the Treaty was spiritual, not material.[89] In a published article, he expanded on this idea, claiming that the real tragedy took place with the acceptance of the Treaty. 'The awful sin of December, when they [Collins and Mulcahy] broke faith with President de Valera, and perjured themselves, handed them over to influences too bad and too strong to be got free of. So broken faith and perjury led on to the sin of Cain.' Interestingly, he theorised that had unity been maintained through an act of bad faith, the disaster that would have befallen would have been much worse than the present war.[90]

Many connections between Free State supporters and those who had fallen from grace were made. 'Like Lucifer, they have fallen: like Lucifer, would they shut close the gates of Heavenly freedom and force us all through the devouring fires of Civil War into England's bottomless pit.'[91] An account of the 'overheard' dialogue of two soldiers, in which each soldier took a doctrinaire line, had the Treaty opponent informing the other: 'In what you now accept, the magnificence of the bribe has blinded you and wrapt you up in the bribe is that same slavery. Satan had brought you to the mountain top, tempted you and you have fallen.'[92] An article titled 'Right against Might' described the Free State supporters as having given in to the temptation of the Treaty. They had once been amongst the great men and women of Ireland, the article noted, but they were comparable to Judas amongst the Apostles: 'But even among the chosen Twelve fell one from grace; and among those whom we honoured were those whose faith was weak, whose souls were not attuned to the greatness of Pearse and Clarke and Connolly.'[93] In early April 1922, the short-lived and enigmatic *Plain People* published an article that, ironically, asked the readers to look past the verbiage of the Free State and see the situation in Ireland for what it was. Supporters of the Treaty were tempting republicans with peace, prosperity and all manner of material things in return for acceptance of the English king, surrendering of the national birthright and willingly embracing common citizenship with their racial foes. In case the readers had not made a close enough link to loss of principle, the paper compared the situation to Satan's temptation of Christ in the desert. Christ asked what a man gets if he gains the whole world but loses his soul. 'What doth it profit a country if it gain material prosperity and lose ITS soul, its nationhood, its birthright, its title to legitimacy!'[94]

Republican women, whose dedication to the cause has been extensively examined by Margaret Ward,[95] strongly advocated the religious interpretation of the movement. A group of unnamed republican women worked with Count Plunkett to produce a statement that praised their sons and relatives for recognising that material gain was unworthy of being fought for and that if they did not throw off the foreign yoke that Ireland would be bound to a Godless nation.[96] The MacSwiney sisters, Mary, Eithne and Annie, wrote many letters about the morality of republicanism and aspects such as hunger striking and the pronouncements of the hierarchy, many of which are discussed throughout this book. Insisting that her support of republicanism was perfectly justifiable, Mary wrote to Archbishop Byrne: 'The morality of the acts of war committed by the Republican forces depends on the justice of their fight for freedom. If our fight is wrong to-day then every fight ever carried on for freedom in Ireland was wrong.'[97] In her letter to the hierarchy pleading with them to remain aloof from the Treaty debate, MacSwiney made several references to the holiness of the cause of republicanism and not just temporal but also spiritual freedom. She emphasised the fundamental moral concerns of accepting British dominance, as it would lead to corruption and bribery, as well as the betrayal of the cardinal principle of the republican movement.[98] During a speech in Tobercurry, County Sligo, she praised the martyrs of 1916, claiming that 'what Pearse and Connolly succeeded in doing saved the soul of the Irish nation.' Referring to those who had voluntarily given their lives, especially her brother, she said that the rest of the world came to realise that 'there must be something holy and sacred in the cause for which they were dying.'[99]

One of their favourite topics was the oath required by the Treaty. In the same letter in which Eithne scolded Archbishop Byrne for unquestioningly accepting the will of the majority,[100] she informed him that the republicans would continue their fight regardless of the pronouncements of the bishops:

> and if we have to break bridges in the fight, we shall do so, believing that broken bridges are far less evil than broken oaths, and that while material damage can be easily repaired at any time, the spiritual evil that comes from turning to ridicule the sacredness of an oath and making a mockery of all Principles of Justice and Honour can only be fought and conquered here and now.[101]

Oaths and vows were common elements in post-Treaty republican rhetoric. In February 1922, *The Connachtman* published 'Our Vow', in which the litany of Irish heroes and martyrs was listed. The second half of the piece focused on the dedication of the contemporary fighters:

> We have not faltered in the fight,
> Our martyrs not in vain
> Have died when darksome was the night,
> And poured their blood like rain;
> To Pearse and Plunkett's land we're true –
> True to the dead who died
> To raise the flag of Roisin Dhu
> One glorious Eastertide.
>
> We have not faltered in the fray,
> To God and Granuaile

> We pledge our fealty to-day
> With hearts that shall not quail;
> Come weal, come woe, we'll ever be
> To holy Ireland true
> Until the flag of liberty
> Waves over Roisin Dhu.[102]

A piece that appeared on multiple occasions, 'Padraig Pearse's Oath', moved from a prayerful recitation of religious figures to a chronological listing of notable Irish events and people. The merging of the two sets of imagery culminated with a final statement: 'We swear the oath our forefathers swore, / That we will burst the bondage of our Nation, / Or fall side by side. Amen.'[103]

Constance Markiewicz, a convert to Catholicism during her imprisonment after the 1916 Rising, used religiosity to attack the Free State and its supporters. She accused the Free State of using the same cant and hypocrisy employed by the British throughout the world to convince people that they were the true patriots and acting according to the precepts of the dead patriots. By linking themselves to the dead heroes and honouring them, '[t]hey betrayed the dead even as they betrayed the living, the Republic, and Ireland ... It is an insult to our holy dead that mass should be said and military honours given them by these men'. Proof of their hypocrisy was to be found in their treatment of republicans who had refuted the Treaty. Free State forces raided the homes of heroes who lived, many of whom were then imprisoned, as well as the families of those they were honouring.[104]

Notably absent from the spiritual debate was a large contingency of anti-Treaty clergymen. Interestingly, while Patrick Murray's book has shown that they existed in sizeable numbers, their contributions to the rhetorical debate tended to focus on other aspects of the conflict. Fr. Michael O'Flanagan, for example, rarely made mention of the spirituality of the republican cause, preferring to focus on democratic principles. As 'Western Priest', he castigated the actions of the plenipotentiaries and even compared the occupation of the Four Courts to those in the GPO during the 1916 Rising.[105] O'Flanagan, then vice-president of Sinn Féin, was sent to the United States in March 1922 to represent opponents of the Treaty and counter Free State attempts at gathering support. He gave many speeches attacking the Free State and championing the republic during his extended trip, but one that was very interesting was a speech he gave in Pittsburgh. In comparing the notions of 'Free State' to 'republic' he compared the U.S. to Canada. When the U.S. proclaimed independence, its population was three times that of Canada; now it was fourteen times as large. O'Flanagan attributed this to America's status as a republic, a simplistic statement that would confound respectable American historians. By accepting Free State status, Ireland was limiting its growth potential and dooming itself to a fate worse than that of Canada, as Ireland was so close to Great Britain, the Governor General would have the ability to use his powers over the government.[106]

It is interesting that republican clergymen did not concentrate on the spiritual aspects of the movement more than they did. Rather, most of those who defied their superiors and spoke on political matters utilised the arguments of the original Fenians that priests and bishops had every right to speak on political matters as individuals because they were citizens, but they did not have the right to speak as religious figures and they certainly could not use their religious offices to promote their personal feelings. This was one of the central tenets of O'Flanagan's defence of his political activity during his numerous suspensions and reprimands. He was especially vociferous in the run up to the by elections of March 1925. He was 'pained and grieved and ashamed' to see that 'the evil of turning the churches into political meeting houses' had been resumed. The Irish people, he said, were not required to sit through such things. 'It was, moreover, not merely their right, but their duty to leave the church as a protest against such a desecration.'[107] At a speech he gave in Castlerea, Co. Roscommon, he told his audience that he had been told personally by Pope Pius to say nothing of politics. He interpreted this as abstaining from politics from the altar. He did not feel obliged to refrain from politics in general though:

> Why, he asked, should they leave nationality all to the laity? Why could not the clergy have some of it, too. A priest was a citizen, and it was not right that he should be muzzled in that way. There should be certain things in which he had to submit to the directions of his Bishop, but it should be different when it came to a matter of exercising his civil functions.[108]

Personal separation of politics and religion was a concept Patrick

Browne incorporated into his writing on multiple occasions. 'Morality breathes in every sphere of men's activity. And the Irish priest may and should enter every department of Ireland's life, as of right and not upon sufferance or by popular courtesy. But he must deport himself very differently in the political and national sphere, and in the purely religious departments of Ireland's life.'[109] In a published oration commending the victims of the Castleisland ambush, Father Allman, an admitted opponent of the Free State, paid tribute to the sacrifices of the men who had died for Ireland, referring to them as martyrs. He used some of the spiritual words that had permeated all of republicanism, referring to the 'faith' and 'sacrifice' of those who had died for the nation. Overall, though, his oration was surprisingly secular. He discussed Imperial strategy, civil strife and the government.[110] Despite what seems to be an almost automatic interjection of religious terminology, Allman displayed a desire to keep religion out of the national issue.

There were exceptions, however, including Patrick Browne. A priest and Professor of Mathematics and Natural Philosophy at Maynooth, Browne was a widely respected academic during his life; Oliver St. John Gogarty described him as 'possessor of one of the greatest brains and the best memory of any Irishman.'[111] Besides publishing academic works, Browne also wrote poetry under the Gaelicised version of his name, Pádraig de Brún, and republican essays under the pseudonyms 'A Priest', 'Colm Cille' and more commonly 'Columban na Banban.' He was a man who completely embraced Pearse's spiritual nationalism, and his many pseudonyms shielded him from episcopal condemnation and probably inspired him to reclaim some of the spirituality of the republican movement.[112]

In 'False Pastors' he described the republic as 'a Christian and a holy thing. It is a shrine wherein rise the sacred incense of Ireland's devotion and Ireland's holy aspiration.'[113] In an essay which is more sermon than political treatise, he urged his readers to do their duty and support the republic. 'Believe me, there is more at stake than the Independence of our Country. This is a battle between right and wrong, between Heaven and Hell. God is calling us to save a degenerate world and show the nations the strength of moral beauty.'[114] While the men and women of the last several years had answered the call, 'Collins and Griffith preach the heresy of expediency, compromise and dishonour; and they strive to draw you from your allegiance to God's holy cause.'[115] Furthermore,

Ireland's cause, being a holy one, could not be destroyed by its enemy. 'In our fight with England Heaven will be with us as it has been since 1916, and the Mother of God and the Saints of Erin will obtain us victory.'[116] He finished his essay by appealing to supporters of the Treaty. While rejection would almost certainly mean renewed war with England, at least Ireland would be reunited in that fight – a line of argument he had adopted from the Four Courts' leaders.

In a section of 'Ghosts – Other Ghosts or the Priests and the Republic', an essay inspired both in title and subject matter by Pearse's writings, he even appealed to clerics who endorsed the Treaty by portraying the entire conflict in religious terms. 'At the root of your position is the fact that you have never understood the meaning of the 1916 Rising, and have never accepted the gospel of Pearse and [Terence] MacSwiney. Become converts even at this late hour. Ireland cannot become great without you. The best of our manhood and womenhood [sic] have taken that gospel to their hearts, and they are determined to see that it becomes the faith of the Nation.'[117] He continued this theme when, promoting the religiosity of republicanism, he went on the offensive, especially against the bishops:[118] 'I expect some of our infallibles sneer when I mention Irish prophesies – well, I will not argue with you. You are a heretic crowd. You have no faith. You had no faith in 1920 and 1921. You have no faith in the triumph of right and bravery.'[119]

Other priests who engaged in spiritual and moral defence of republicanism often did so from the safety of another nation. The Scottish edition of *Poblacht na h-Eireann* published a recap of an address by Father Torley, who featured in the paper regularly. He informed his Glaswegian audience that the Irish people did not want the 'Free' State, and to sidestep the democratic manifest given to the Free State, he added that the Irish nation consisted of people of the past, present and future, 'and if we renounce our Fenian baptism, then like a rust-worm [sic] link we will be replaced by one of pure steel.'[120] While the sacredness of the republic was unquestionable, he said, honour, truth and love of country were also sacred, and if they were not, then neither was religion. Turning against all opponents of the republicans, Torley believed that '[t]hese men who renounce their allegiance to the Republic are worse than Judas. Judas saw his crime and hanged himself; but these people think themselves patriots.'[121]

Archbishop Mannix of Melbourne was the best known foreign

prelate who utilised spiritual rhetoric in defence of the republican cause. His fiery statements had resulted in the British refusing him entry into Ireland in 1920 and even as late as 1925, Richard Dawson Bates, Minister for Home Affairs for Northern Ireland, issued an order prohibiting him from entering the six county area as he was deemed a threat to the preservation of peace and order.[122] Like so many others within the republican camp, Mannix viewed the conflict as a moral rather than a political one. Colm Kiernan attributes his conversion to full-fledged republicanism, fittingly enough, to the display of self-sacrifice and piety that surrounded the hunger strike induced death of Terence MacSwiney. MacSwiney's death inflamed Mannix's sense of moral outrage and terminated his belief that compromise with the Crown was possible.[123] From that point on, he was a republican in the mould of MacSwiney's own sisters, one who saw the Treaty not only as a mistake but as immoral.

Time and distance did not moderate Mannix's stance on the issues pertaining to Ireland.[124] During his 1925 trip to Ireland, he informed a Dublin crowd that there were only two types of people who favoured the Treaty: Imperialists and those who had jobs for themselves or relatives,[125] using the popular republican expedient of labelling opponents as materialists and sell-outs, thus morally and spiritually inferior. Mannix's high religious position and permanent Australian residency protected him from detention or prosecution. His arrest by British forces and forced residency in England in 1920 caused outrage throughout the Catholic community in Ireland and caused the Irish hierarchy to release a sharp statement against the treatment of their fellow prelate. With only the pope as his religious superior, Mannix was also free from the potential religious repercussions of publicly advocating his political position.[126]

His 1925 trip, though, did not generate the same enthusiasm within the Irish hierarchy or lay Irish Catholics as had his previous trip. While in Rome, he had been urged by de Valera to end the pilgrimage of Australians in the Holy See, thus allowing him to visit Ireland as a private individual. De Valera had been warned that the hierarchy would ignore Mannix if he arrived in Ireland in an official capacity and he did not want to give them any excuse to ignore the archbishop. According to Kiernan, Mannix's sense of moral outrage at what he saw as the temporising of conscience that allowed Free State supporters to abandon the drive for independence ensured that he would not agree to this.[127] In fact, Mannix was completely snubbed by both the Irish bishops and the Free State government. There was no public recognition of his existence by either institution. He was not invited to visit Maynooth, and Byrne did not invite him to stay at the Archbishop's Palace in Drumcondra. When Mannix went to stay with his sister in his home-town of Charleville, Co. Cork, he found a large gathering of people to greet him, but the Catholic church locked up and dark. As had been the case with Monsignor Luzio two years prior, Mannix left Ireland embit-tered and resolved to never visit the island again. He went so far as to end all written communication with friends and relatives.[128]

Why republican priests were more reticent to focus on republican religiosity than their lay comrades probably rests with their attempts to distance themselves from the Church and its politics. As will be shown, the bishops became fervent public supporters of the Free State government, and so did the majority of clergymen, who often spoke of the benefits of embracing the government and condemned republi-cans from the altar. For republican priests, to criticise their clerical opponents for these actions while infusing their rhetoric with large amounts of spirituality could come across as highly hypocritical. It was also probably a self-defence move. Separating their religious and political ideas so completely would, many hoped, protect them from the wrath of their bishops, the scorn of their fellow clergymen and the criticism of religiously-minded opponents. As Archbishop Mannix's 1925 trip demonstrates, the Irish Catholic Church was unbending in its rejection of clerical supporters of republicanism, especially when placed within the context of official Church representation. Finally, those republican priests who chose to air their opinions were no doubt aware that careful examination of their cause under the microscope of Catholic doctrine would reveal many aspects that conflicted with such notions as justifiable war and legitimate authority. Even the most provincial of republican priests had had enough theological education that they knew if the debate moved into the realm of Catholicity, their side would most likely lose. Fear of Vatican involvement in the Irish situation had been an important factor for some, especially Monsignor John Hagan, rector of the Irish College in Rome, and they presumed that any papal intercession would work against them and ultimately force Catholic republicans to choose between their political convictions and their religion.[129]

There was widespread fear that republicans would eventually find themselves faced with the question of choosing either their political stance or religion, and that many would follow the example of French republicans and leave the faith, possibly even become vehemently anti-clerical. Bishops definitely feared the worst with regard to republicanism's effect on its adherents, especially since the Fenian variety could trace its origins in part directly to mid-nineteenth-century France. However, they had little to fear from the twentieth-century interpretation of Fenian republicanism and even less to fear of republicans leaving the Church. With exceptions such as Liam Mellows, Liam Lynch and Liam O'Flaherty, modern republicans abhorred the anti-clerical nature of French republicans and were, according to all who have studied them, very socially conservative. Richard English describes them as matching their opponents in the severity of their social conservatism.[130] De Valera informed the Vatican's delegate that he was of the opinion that republicans were even more conservative than their Free State opponents.[131] During de Valera's premiership, Fianna Fáil would prove this to be largely true.

REACTIONS TO SPIRITUAL REPUBLICANISM

Many within the Free State and the Free State supporting press chose to highlight republican religiosity as a sign of their detachment from popular opinion, their hypocrisy or to indicate that republicans' inability to put the lives of Irish before their hallowed ideals made them dangerous to society and the stability of the nation. The *Free State*, a weekly propaganda piece written, edited and published by government ministers and their cohort, was relentless in mocking the spirituality of republicans. In a scathingly satiric piece called 'How it is Done: Instructions to Would-be Hiberniors', a term that mockingly placed them, in the time-honoured cliché, in the ranks of those who tried to be more 'Irish' than the Irish,[132] Michael Tierney, future Cumann na nGaedheal TD, Senator and president of University College, Dublin, renamed republicanism 'Hiberniorism' and stated that it was a mixture of political party, army and religion. Tierney's humorous mockery of republicanism came before the start of the Civil War. Once the conflict had begun in earnest, the paper's tone became more sombre. Seamus O hAodha wrote a piece in mid-August that again underscored the religious nature of republicanism, but his article was very serious and tinged with sadness. Centuries of fighting for Ireland had exalted nationalism to an artificially high place in the minds of people. Nationalism and religion seemed to be embedded in the subconsciousness of the Irish people. The philosophy proper to religion, with disregard for death, principles at stake, a wariness of the slippery slopes of material prosperity, had been transferred to nationalism 'until a current political issue like acceptance or rejection of the Treaty comes to be discussed in an atmosphere of spurious asceticism.'[133] The problem with this, as O hAodha saw it, was that religion and nationalism had radically different subject matters, and the practices and principles of one could not be applied to the other without grievous harm. He offered republican rejection of the Treaty along moral lines as the strongest example. The Treaty did not contain a moral issue of right versus wrong, but rather whether acceptance or rejection best served the interests of the nation. While the republicans maintained their politico-religious exaltation, he gloomily contended, it would be impossible to discuss important matters with any of them. Argument with them was useless. All Free State supporters could do was await a military decision. Only then would a new situation be created where reason could resume its proper place.[134]

Piaras Béaslaí, writing for the soldiers of the National Army, produced a story about the ghost of a Black and Tan who visited one of the Free State's barracks on Christmas night and had a conversation with a soldier. Béaslaí has the ghost defending the Black and Tans' actions. They had been told the country was full of murderers and scoundrels. They saw their comrades getting killed and the whole population against them. They were, frankly, waging war against the Irish people, but the republicans were now doing the same thing, claiming to do it out of love for Ireland. Again mocking republican religiosity, the soldier replied that the ghost could not understand the 'lofty-souled idealism, the divine enthusiasm' which inspired them.[135] Béaslaí also chose to combat the increasingly spiritual nature of republican rhetoric by making light of their concept of martyrdom. In a limerick written for *An tÓglách*, he mocked republican religiosity by juxtaposing it with drunkenness and criminality:

There was a young man of Kinsale
Mopped up gallons of whiskey and ale
Then he went out for loot
But, being drunk, couldn't shoot,
And now he's a martyr in jail.[136]

Liam de Róiste, whose pragmatic, pro-Treaty republicanism caused supporters of both sides to question his allegiance, was a harsh critic of republican religiosity and adherence to principles. 'From all the disputations, I find that not one of those who proclaim they stand for the ideal and principle contained in the term "Irish Republic" seem to have analysed what it means. It seems clear enough as a ideal [sic] of thought, but worked out in the realm of concrete fact and of prosaic things no one can say what it means.'[137] He regularly rebuked republicans for failing to explain their political goals. What, he wanted to know, was the republic for which they were fighting? He was most disapproving of their moralistic high-handedness:

> There are some intellectuals who argue that the arrangements with the English are a form of 'spiritual surrender'. But, what some at least of the 'intellectual' snobs seem incapable of understanding is that there is no high, pure idealism, no noble principles, no spiritual incentives in the minds of many of those whom they – the intellectuals – fancy are 'fighting for Ireland'.[138]

Again a few months later, he lambasted republican notions of the infallibility of the cause of Irish independence. Infallibility, he said, is based on eternal truths, and relations between states are not eternal truths: 'Right and wrong are eternal … but to find an absolute right and wrong as between *all* relations of states and nations is, I judge, an impossibility.'[139] Using a powerful historical image that was popular with both sides, he compared modern republicans' self-proclaimed moral superiority and the infallibility of their political platform to that of Oliver Cromwell and the Puritans of the English Civil War.

Rather than treat republican religiosity as a joke or a shame, the *Irish Catholic Herald* took great offence at their description of their cause as holy. 'Their cause is a "holy" one indeed! And their methods of supporting it are "sacred", whatever form they take! Was such perversion of all moral sanctions ever witnessed among a civilized people?'[140] Their use of words like faith, sacredness and liberty was nothing but blasphemy, the paper argued. By passing death sentences on members of the Free State legislature, they were showing themselves to be more savage than Red Indians.[141] Republicans were more dangerous than rabid dogs, which are recognisable on sight. 'These people go about as ordinary citizens, with the doctrines of hell in their hearts and in their pockets deadly weapons ready for use.' That there were apologists for people like this was a portent, the *Herald* noted. Once again the spirit which pervaded the reformers of the sixteenth century had made itself manifest. The followers of Calvin, Luther and Knox who killed Catholics and burned churches were animated by such mad passions.[142] The next month, the *Herald* altered its source for comparable evil. Republicans were now guilty of paganised patriotism: 'The Car of Juggernaut was not a more terrible instrument of human depravity and tyranny than is the "creed" of the latest form of Irish "patriotism".'[143]

The paper was so concerned about republicans' assumption of moral and political rectitude that it chastised the people of the Free State for their widespread neutrality toward the struggle: '[T]here is a mildew of moral and physical indifference covering the land which makes men and women impotent or unwilling to distinguish between good and evil, between duty and neglect of it ... While this spirit of cowardly compromise prevails the destruction of Ireland will go on.'[144] The *Herald* assured its readers that the republicans were not adhering to any noble ideals, but rather their revolt was largely due to ineradicable national vices, such as jealousy, envy and spite. Republicans who were professing to seek the will of God were merely pursuing their own evil wills: 'It is the true spirit of religious revolt, of black heresy.'[145]

Just to highlight how despicable the republicans truly were, the paper contended:

> There is to-day in Ireland more moral, patriotic, social and individual perversion to the square yard, more jealousy and envy, more misdirected and decadent activity of body and energy of mind, than is to be found anywhere else in Europe, except, perhaps, in some of the Balkan areas, where sects and paganism and Mohammedanism have struggled for centuries and spread moral blindness.[146]

Returning to public duty, the populace was reprimanded again for not taking the side of right in this struggle against what was so clearly evil and heretical. There were no neutrals when Luther and his allies attacked the Church, or when there was a war in Heaven. By not opposing the republicans, people were helping lead Ireland down the slope of destruction.

ECCLESIASTICAL INVOLVEMENT

The *Herald* marked the extreme anti-republican position of institution-supporting Irish Catholicism. However, the Catholic Church as a whole was eventually drawn into the fray and very pronouncedly spoke against the republicans. By the autumn of 1922, the Catholic bishops became politically active and willingly used their religious offices and associated powers against those republicans who were either engaged in or supportive of the armed revolt against the Free State. Rather than rely on spiteful and hyperbolic rhetoric, as had been their wont against Crown forces during the height of the war for independence, the hierarchy utilised their weighty public authority, widespread communication resources and the punishments available to them through their ecclesiastical positions to wage their battle against republican religiosity that lasted beyond the end of the Civil War. As will be demonstrated in the next chapter, the purposes of their activities in this sphere were twofold. Firstly, they hoped to link themselves closely to the emerging power structure to maintain close control over social areas which had been their domain for decades, more specifically education and healthcare. Secondly, the spiritual authority republican leaders sought for themselves and their cause demonstrated a direct threat to the dominance of the bishops, and these statements were intended to reclaim complete spiritual authority.

That Irish bishops were inserting themselves into national politics was nothing new. A strong clerical strain of political involvement was in no small part attributable to the lack of a lay Catholic leadership cadre as a result of the religious persecutions of the seventeenth and eighteenth centuries. With no landed, Catholic gentry to lead the rural communities, the task fell upon the bishops and clergy.[147] Bishops had been involved in a multitude of national questions since Daniel O'Connell had enticed them with the campaign for Catholic Emancipation. Members of the hierarchy had spoken against the Fenians, favoured the Land League, fought Parnell and his supporters after the O'Shea affair, and had been integral to the Irish Parliamentary Party ever since. Some had even embraced Sinn Féin, and episcopal statements of condemnation of British tactics during the war for independence were released on numerous occasions.

Patrick Murray agrees with Emmet Larkin that republicans never went so far as to claim that the Church had no claim to power and influence in Ireland.[148] This is, of course, true, because to make such a claim would have been politically suicidal. This does not mean, though, that many republicans did not hold that very opinion and worked to deny the bishops power and influence within the political sphere. More importantly for this book, rather than deny episcopal rights to power and influence, republican rhetoriticians attempted to circumvent the bishops by claiming a spiritual authority for their movement that transcended episcopal authority. This spiritual authority came down from generations of Irish patriots who willingly gave their lives for their country, culminating in the holy martyrs of 1916. The Catholicity of the Rising and the spread of the cult of martyrdom which had attracted so many clergy to the Sinn Féin movement was now being used against Church leaders and the clerics who had sided with the Treaty supporters. Once this religiosity conflicted with the Church, the bishops refused to tolerate it. The result was an acrimonious battle of words and symbolic actions between republicans and the bishops that lasted until well after the war had ended. Relationships between the groups often remained strained even after de Valera and Fianna Fáil came to power in 1932.

While this chapter has examined republican religiosity predominantly along ideological lines, this has served only as a way of introducing the essence of this aspect of the debate from the anti-Treaty perspective. Due to clerical involvement in the political debate, there was a very pronounced strain of questioning of the bishops and clerics who challenged republican principles. Republicanism acquired a very strong element of what can be categorised as spiritually-inspired anti-ecclesiasticalism, which is discussed at length in the next chapter. It was not, it needs to be noted, anti-clericalism as such because criticisms against priests were based on their acceptance and acquiescence of particular hierarchical edicts. Clerical support for republicanism was sought and encouraged. Several memoirs of republicans indicate that they drew strength from knowing that their cause had at least some sympathetic priests within its ranks. There was an element of anti-clericalism within the republican movement,[149] but that is not the primary subject of this work.

With ever-fading hope of bringing republicans in line, the bishops issued a series of statements, both personally and as a unified hierarchy, urging, pleading and finally attempting to pressurise republicans into abandoning their armed resistance against the Treaty. Having re-established the spirituality of their cause as justification for the continuation of the conflict, republicans fought back, some by criticising the bishops' involvement in politics, others by choosing to engage in a debate of spirituality and morals. Republicans had re-embraced Pearse's spiritual separatism and were not prepared to abandon it, even at the behest of the bishops. As will be demonstrated in the remaining chapters of this book, the Civil War would offer many opportunities for both sides to fire fresh volleys in the conflict, and republicans especially would be presented several opportunities to attempt to claim the moral high ground over the religious leaders of the majority.

NOTES

1. Pádraic H. Pearse, 'Ghosts' *Collected Works of Pádraic H. Pearse: Political Writings and Speeches* (Dublin, 1919), pp.224–5.
2. See especially Peter Hart, 'The Geography of Revolution in Ireland, 1917–1923', *Past and Present*, 155 (May 1997), pp.142–76.
3. There are several studies that examine this in depth. See David Fitzpatrick, *Politics and Irish Life, 1913–1921: Provincial Experience of War and Revolution* (Cork, 1998); Michael Farry, *The Aftermath of Revolution: Sligo, 1921–1923* (Dublin, 2000).
4. Paul Bew, 'A Vision to the Dispossessed? Popular Piety and Revolutionary Politics in the Irish Land War, 1879–82' in Judith Devlin and Ronan Fanning (eds), *Religion and Rebellion* (Dublin, 1997), p.137.
5. R.F. Foster, *The Irish Story: Telling Tales and Making it up in Ireland* (London, 2001), p.8.
6. Richard English, *Irish Freedom: The History of Nationalism in Ireland* (London, 2006), pp.215, 219.
7. R.V. Comerford, *The Fenians in Context: Irish Politics and Society, 1848–82* (Dublin, 1985), p.31.
8. Patrick Maume, *The Long Gestation: Irish Nationalist Life, 1891–1918* (Dublin, 1999), p.5; Senia Paseta, *Before the Revolution: Nationalism, Social Change and Ireland's Catholic Elite, 1879–1922* (Cork, 1999), pp.103–4.
9. For literary examples, see Lawrence McBride, 'Imagining the Nation in Irish Historical Figures, c. 1870–c. 1925' in Stewart Brown and David W. Miller (eds) *Piety and Power in Ireland: Essays in honour of Emmet Larkin* (Belfast, 2000), p. 92. See also James Murphy, *Catholic Fiction and Social Reality in Ireland, 1873–1922* (London, 1997).
10. Marie-Louise Legg, *Newspapers and Nationalism: The Irish Provincial Press, 1850–1892* (Dublin, 1999), pp.93–108.
11. For more on Irish Catholic influence in the British press, see Owen Dudley Edwards and Patricia J. Storey, 'The Irish Press in Victorian Britain' in Roger Swift and Sheridan Gilley (eds), *The Irish in the Victorian City* (Dublin, 1985), pp.158–78.
12. Diamond's New Catholic Press Company and Scottish Catholic Printing Company owned

nearly forty weekly newspapers at the time of his death in 1934. Owen Dudley Edwards and Patricia J. Storey, 'The Irish Press in Victorian Britain' in Roger Swift and Sheridan Gilley (eds), *The Irish in the Victorian City*, p.175.

13. Catherine Candy, *Priestly Fictions: Popular Irish Novelists of the Early 20th Century* (Dublin, 1995), p.70.
14. See Michael O'Riordan, *Catholicity and Progress in Ireland* (London, 1905).
15. Irish Priests, *The Will and the Way* (Dublin, 1915).
16. Tom Garvin, *1922*, p.46.
17. M.J. Kelly, *The Fenian Ideal and Irish Nationalism, 1882–1916* (Woodbridge, 2006), p.135.
18. Michael Laffan, 'The Sacred Memory: Religion, Revisionists and the Easter Rising' in Devlin and Fanning (eds), *Religion and Rebellion*, p.176.
19. Richard English, *Irish Freedom*, p.241.
20. M.J. Kelly, *The Fenian Ideal and Irish Nationalism*, pp.254.
21. Ben Novick, *Conceiving Revolution: Irish Nationalist Propaganda during the First World War* (Dublin, 2001), p.223.
22. Modris Eksteins, *Rites of Spring: The Great War and the Birth of the Modern Age* (New York, 1989), p.236; Paul Fussell, *The Great War and Modern Memory* (Oxford, 1975), p.119.
23. Ben Novick, *Conceiving Revolution*, p.222.
24. Gonne to Yeats, 7 Nov 1915, No. 313, in Anna MacBride White and A. Norman Jeffares (eds), *The Gonne–Yeats Letters, 1893–1938: Always Your Friend* (London, 1992), p.363.
25. Gonne to Yeats, Sunday [May 1915] No. 308, ibid., p.357.
26. Michael Laffan, 'The Sacred Memory', in Devlin and Fanning (eds), *Religion and Rebellion*, p.176.
27. Ben Novick, *Conceiving Revolution*, p.203.
28. Patrick Murray, *Oracles of God: The Roman Catholic Church and Irish Politics, 1922–37* (Dublin, 2000), pp.222–42.
29. Tom Garvin, *1922*, pp.149–50.
30. See T.K. Wilson, *Frontiers of Violence: Conflict and Identity in Ulster and Upper Silesia, 1918–1922* (Oxford: OUP, 2010).
31. Bill Kissane, *The Politics of the Irish Civil War*, p.28.
32. John M. Regan, *The Irish Counter-Revolution, 1921–1936: Treatyite Politics and Settlement in Independent Ireland* (Dublin, 1999), p.47.
33. See Jeremy Treglown, *V.S. Pritchett: A Working Life* (London, 2004).
34. Bill Kissane, *The Politics of the Irish Civil War*, p.99.
35. David Fitzpatrick, *The Two Irelands, 1912–1939* (Oxford, 1998), p.124.
36. Tom Garvin, *1922*, pp.97–8.
37. Maryann Valiulis, '"The Man They Could Never Forgive" The View of the Opposition: Éamon de Valera and the Civil War' in J.P. O'Carroll and John Murphy (eds), *De Valera and His Times* (Cork, 1986), pp.94–5.
38. Michael Laffan, *The Resurrection of Ireland: The Sinn Féin Party, 1916–1923* (Cambridge, 1999), p.353.
39. Owen Dudley Edwards, *Éamon de Valera*, p.10.
40. Bill Kissane, *The Politics of the Irish Civil War*, p.6.
41. CAA, Harty papers, interview with Harty, 4 April 1921.
42. For more on de Valera's attempts at maintaining unity prior to the start of hostilities, see John Regan, *The Irish Counter-Revolution*, pp.5–67.
43. Diarmaid Ferriter, *Judging Dev: A Reassessment of the Life and Legacy of Éamon de Valera* (Dublin, 2007), p.70.
44. Michael Hopkinson, *Green Against Green: The Irish Civil War* (Dublin, 1988), p.71.
45. UCDA, de Valera papers, P150/657, de Valera to Mary MacSwiney, 11 November 1922.
46. Tom Garvin, *1922*, p.49.
47. ICR, Hagan papers, O'Cleirig to Hagan, 10 December 1921.
48. *Roscommon Herald*, 1 July 1922. Needless to say, de Valera's opponents did not find this argument convincing. See Michael Tierney, *Eoin MacNeill*, pp.307–11.

49. J.P. O'Carroll, 'Éamon de Valera, Charisma and Political Development' in O'Carroll and Murphy (eds), *De Valera and His Times*, pp.21–2; Owen Dudley Edwards, *Éamon de Valera*, p.69.
50. See below, pp.33-4.
51. David Fitzpatrick, *Harry Boland's Irish Revolution* (Cork, 2003), p.261.
52. Ibid., p.306.
53. ICR, Hagan papers, Hagan to Mulcahy [copy of letter sent on 30 August 1922].
54. ICR, Hagan papers, Hagan to O'Connor and Mellows, 7 September 1922.
55. Tom Garvin, 1922, p.98.
56. Owen Dudley Edwards, *Éamon de Valera*, p.76.
57. Bill Kissane, *The Politics of the Irish Civil War*, p.100.
58. Quoted in Michael Laffan, *The Resurrection of Ireland*, p.216.
59. Bishop O'Dwyer of Limerick was exceptional, having endorsed Sinn Féin from shortly after the Rising. On the other side, Cardinal Logue stood out as the most vocal opponent of Sinn Féin's aspirations up until the Treaty.
60. Richard English, *Ernie O'Malley: IRA Intellectual* (Oxford, 1998), p.93.
61. Jeffrey Prager, *Building Democracy in Ireland: Political Order and Cultural Integration in a Newly Independent Nation* (Cambridge, 1986), p.55.
62. Ibid.
63. Tom Garvin, *1922*, pp.151–2.
64. Quoted in Dermot Keogh, 'Éamon de Valera and the Civil War in Ireland, 1922–1923' in Gabriel Doherty and Dermot Keogh (eds), *De Valera's Ireland* (Cork, 2003), p.69.
65. *INBMN*, 12 February 1923. John Regan and Tom Garvin contend that de Valera's manoeuvrings, especially the concept of External Association, were politically astute moves to try to keep the divergent strains of nationalism unified, and Owen Dudley Edwards describes External Association as a pathfinding proposal for Commonwealth relations. Ferriter describes Document No. 2 as far-sighted about the future of the Empire. Diarmaid Ferriter, *Judging Dev*, p.124.
66. For example, see Michael Tierney, *Eoin MacNeill: Scholar and Man of Action, 1867–1945*, edited by F.X. Martin (Oxford, 1980) pp.304–8, 311. Tierney served in the Dáil, 1925–32; Seanad, 1938–44; Council of State, 1940–4. Martin reports that Tierney, MacNeill's son-in-law, was slated to be the next Minister for Education, but Fianna Fáil's election victory ended the prospect.
67. See Kathleen Clarke, *My Fight for Ireland's Freedom*, edited by Helen Litton (Dublin, 1997) for her descriptions of Cathal Brugha, Mary MacSwiney and Constance Markiewicz, among others.
68. Ibid., p.190.
69. UCDA, de Valera papers, P150/1654, de Valera to Bishop Amigo, n.d. Hopkinson states that most members of Sinn Féin, even Mary MacSwiney, admitted that the electoral victories of 1917 and 1918 were won because of a desire for independence rather than because of popular desire for a republic. Michael Hopkinson, *Green Against Green*, p.5. Piaras Béaslaí attributed the electoral victories not to conversion to republicanism, but rather a popular anti-IPP vote, as well as a gesture against the English government's actions in Ireland. Piaras Béaslaí, *Michael Collins and the Making of a New Ireland* (London, 1926), Vol. 1, pp.250–1.
70. Diarmaid Ferriter, *Judging Dev*, p.69.
71. *Documents on Irish Foreign Policy: Volume I, 1919–1922*, Ronan Fanning, et al. (eds), (Dublin, 1998), Document No. 13, p.24.
72. DAA, Byrne papers, 'President de Valera States the National Position' (from interview on 30 March 1921).
73. UCDA, Mary MacSwiney papers, P48a/195, Eithne MacSwiney to Byrne, 28 February 1923.
74. See the republican propaganda file of the Ernie O'Malley papers, UCDA, P17a/246.
75. AAA, Patrick O'Donnell papers, 'Ghosts—Other Ghosts or The Priests and the Republic'.
76. *The Connachtman*, 29 April 1922.
77. ICR, Hagan papers, O'Brien to Hagan, 29 November 1922.
78. Tom Garvin, 1922, p.141.
79. David Fitzpatrick, *The Two Irelands*, p.132.

80. Owen Dudley Edwards's biography of de Valera is especially informative on his use of Catholic ritual and transferring spirituality, especially martyr worship, into the political sphere. See Owen Dudley Edwards, *Éamon de Valera*.
81. UCDA, de Valera papers, P150/657, de Valera to Mary MacSwiney, 11 November 1922.
82. Quoted in Michael Tierney, *Eoin MacNeill*, p.309.
83. Owen Dudley Edwards, *Éamon de Valera*, p.12.
84. UCDA, de Valera papers, P150/2909, de Valera to Mannix, 6 November 1922.
85. NLI, Sheehy-Skeffington papers, MS 41,178/52, Tomas O'Suilleobain to Hanna Sheehy-Skeffington, n.d.
86. UCDA, de Valera papers, P150/1653, 'Miles Republicanus', 'Episcopal and Clerical Injustice: Grave Responsibility of Churchmen', 8 August 1922.
87. *CE*, 5 July 1922.
88. Ibid.
89. UCDA, FitzGerald papers, P80/736, de Blácam to Hanna Sheehy-Skeffington, 27 July 1922.
90. *CE*, 31 July 1922.
91. Ibid., 15 July 1922.
92. *The Connachtman*, 29 April 1922.
93. *CE*, 20 July 1922.
94. *PP*, 9 April 1922. (Emphasis in original.)
95. See Margaret Ward, *Unimaginable Revolutionaries: Women and Irish Nationalism* (London, 1983) as well as her biographies of Hanna Sheehy-Skeffington and Maud Gonne.
96. UCDA, de Valera papers, P150/1653, 'Statement prepared by Count Plunkett on behalf of Republican women'.
97. UCDA, FitzGerald papers, P80/745, Mary MacSwiney to Byrne, 5 November 1922.
98. UCDA, Mary MacSwiney papers, P48a/192, Mary MacSwiney to Cardinal Logue and the Irish Archbishops and Bishops, 11 December 1921.
99. *The Connachtman*, 4 March 1922.
100. See above, pp.41–2.
101. DAA, Byrne papers, 'An Obedient and Loving Daughter of the Catholic Church' [Eithne MacSwiney] to Byrne, 28 February 1923.
102. *The Connachtman*, 11 February 1922.
103. *CE*, 10 July 1922.
104. *SF*, 16 May 1925.
105. *RH*, 25 March 1922, 1 April 1922.
106. Ibid., 1 July 1922.
107. AAA, O'Donnell papers, 'Republicanism in Ireland. Rev. M. O'Flanagan's Support', newspaper clipping [source unknown].
108. DJ, 25 February 1925.
109. AAA, O'Donnell papers, 'Ghosts—Other Ghosts or The Priests and the Republic'.
110. CE, 29 July 1922.
111. Oliver St John Gogarty, *As I Was Going Down Sackville Street* (New York, 1937), p.146.
112. The shielding failed when Browne was arrested during a CID raid of the Sinn Féin Suffolk St. headquarters on 12 February 1923. The arrest and Browne's alleged behaviour towards the Free State forces caused embarrassment and consternation amongst the hierarchy and President MacCaffrey of Maynooth. Despite prolonged discussions by the Standing Committee, no specific action was taken against Browne, but the sudden termination of his political activities indicate that severe, unrecorded warnings were most likely issued.
113. DAA, Curran papers, 'False Pastors.' p.6.
114. AAA, O'Donnell Papers, Box 5, 'An Irish Priest's Appeal'.
115. Ibid.
116. Ibid.
117. AAA, O'Donnell papers, 'Ghosts—Other Ghosts or The Priests and the Republic'.
118. Browne's writings against the bishops are discussed at length in the next chapter.
119. AAA, O'Donnell papers, 'Ghosts—Other Ghosts or The Priests and the Republic'.
120. *Poblacht na h-Eireann*, 9 September 1922.

121. Ibid.
122. PRONI, Home Affairs of Northern Ireland, HA/32/1/463, Ordered under the Civil Author-ities (Special Powers) Act (Northern Ireland), 1922, 29 September 1925.
123. Colm Kiernan, *Daniel Mannix and Ireland* (Morwell, Victoria, 1984), pp.154, 158.
124. See Colm Kiernan, *Daniel Mannix and Ireland*. Michael Gilchrist contends that after Mannix's return to Australia in 1921 his speech became increasingly moderate and, in fact, he rarely spoke about Ireland from the signing of the Treaty until 1925. See Chapter 5 of Michael Gilchrist, *Daniel Mannix: Wit and Wisdom* (Melbourne, 2004), pp.105–133. While it appears that Mannix rarely spoke during the four years between his Irish trips, his 1925 trip indicates that his views had, if anything, grown more radically republican.
125. NLI, Sheehy-Skeffington papers, MS 41,185/2, Telegram sent by Hanna Sheehy-Skeffington, recipient unknown, 23 October 1925.
126. After the ratification of the Treaty, however, Mannix's anti-Treaty stance alienated him from many within Melbourne and damaged his political and popular influence. Colm Kiernan, *Daniel Mannix and Ireland*, pp.174–5.
127. Colm Kiernan, *Daniel Mannix and Ireland*, p.188.
128. For more, see Chapter 10 in Colm Kiernan, *Daniel Mannix and Ireland*. For Luzio, see Chapter 3 of this volume.
129. See Chapter 3 of this volume.
130. Richard English, *Irish Freedom*, p.311.
131. Vatican City, A.E.S., Inghilterra, Posizione 167, fascicolo 14, de Valera to Luzio, 22 June 1923.
132. The original phrase being: '*Hibernicis ipsis Hibernior*'.
133. Ibid., 19 August 1922.
134. Ibid.
135. *An tÓglách*, 6 January 1923, 'The Black-and-Tan'.
136. *An tÓglách*, 6 January 1923, 'An Irregular Martyr'.
137. CCCA, de Róiste papers, U271/A/41, de Róiste diaries, 22 December 1921.
138. CCCA, de Róiste papers, U271/A/44, de Róiste diaries, 7 May 1922.
139. CCCA, de Róiste papers, U271/A/45, de Róiste diaries, 5 July 1922. (Emphasis in original.)
140. ICH, 9 December 1922.
141. Ibid.
142. Ibid.
143. Ibid., 6 January 1923.
144. Ibid., 27 January 1923.
145. Ibid.
146. Ibid.
147. David W. Miller, *Church, State and Nation in Ireland, 1898–1921* (Dublin, 1973), p.1.
148. Patrick Murray, *Oracles of God*, p.13, quoting Emmet Larkin, 'Church, State and Nation in Modern Ireland', *American Historical Review*, 80 (1975), p.1276.
149. See, for example, the works of Liam O'Flaherty and Peadar O'Donnell.

2

Moral Duopoly:
Episcopal Pronouncements and
Republican Reactions

> I could not restrain a suspicion that, though the Bishops
> claimed to speak merely in the interest of morality, this was
> not their only, nor even their strongest, motive. It was
> convenient for them to say so, as their pronouncement was
> thereby raised above hostile criticism. And some of them –
> their leaders – as I suspected, knew this well and calculated
> on it; putting it forward as a very efficacious shield to cover
> the real, or at least, more prevalent, motive, which was
> political.[1]

Fr. Walter McDonald, Professor of Theology at Maynooth, was in
no way an unthinking follower of his superiors. In 1909, he
defended Fr. O'Hickey against Monsignor Mannix, then president of
Maynooth, who pushed for his dismissal after the fight over making
the Irish language compulsory for matriculation. At the end of his life,
as the clergy were lining up behind Sinn Féin, he informed Monsignor
MacCaffrey that he refused to attend a college dinner that included
guests advocating the recognition of the Irish republic, as attendance
would be construed as implying support for their cause.[2] His treatise on
peace and war flew in the face of accepted nationalist arguments by
positing that Ireland had not been historically unified and had willingly
submitted to the rule of the English numerous times.[3] His posthumously
published memoirs were highly critical of the bishops and many of his
fellow clergymen, and thus were not received well by many within the
Church. Fr. Timothy Corcoran wrote a scathing review of the book
and chastised Denis Gwynn for being responsible for its publication,

as well as tarnishing McDonald's reputation amongst his colleagues.[4] So it is unsurprising that he provided one of the clearest voices of scepticism regarding the bishops' involvement in secular activities. He did not live to see the passing of the Treaty and the subsequent endorsement of the Free State by the bishops, but he had been suspicious of the motives of their political involvement since Parnell's divorce scandal. While he accepted that he was not the man to deny the episcopacy the right to interfere in politics, 'neither can I shut my eyes to the fact that their religious interests are too often used as a cloak, and that Bishops have acted merely as politicians while claiming to act in the interest of religion.'[5]

McDonald's memoirs were first published in 1926, but republicans had been issuing statements similar to his since early 1922, when it became obvious that the hierarchy would not refrain from speaking on the Treaty issue. Prior to this, though, the republicans had been enthusiastic about the clerical support their cause received, and even after the Treaty split, they took advantage of any clerical endorsement they could muster. In light of this relationship of convenience, it is difficult to harmonise republican rhetorical stances on the national issue and religion. As has been shown, their interpretation of the national question contained strong spiritual and moral elements. That they spoke in such terms and yet argued that the matter was not one in which the bishops had the right to interfere seems contradictory. Urging the bishops to remain neutral and preferably silent on the national question seems to have been a defensive ploy intended to increase the moral standing of the republican movement by removing the threat of denunciation by the recognised moral authorities. While republicans eventually shared McDonald's objection to the manner in which the bishops involved themselves in politics, it seems that they lacked the professor's principled argument and chose instead opposition along the pragmatic grounds that the bishops were no longer sympathetic to their cause.

ECCLESIASTICAL NATIONALISM BEFORE THE TREATY

When examining the attitudes of the bishops pertaining to the Treaty and ensuing Civil War, a comparison should be drawn with their individual stances before the end of hostilities against the British.[6] A pamphlet entitled *Irish Bishops on English Rule*, published in 1919,

attempted to explain the nature of episcopal positions and their importance to Ireland through the words of the bishops themselves. The
author showed loyalty to their lordships by claiming that they only
publicly commented on secular matters when faith and morals were
affected, a statement that was undoubtedly met with some raised
eyebrows. Traditionally, the author noted, they spoke in favour of
moderation and maintenance of the status quo. In the recent fight
against the British, their rhetoric had acquired a severity that could
shock foreigners but it demonstrated the appalling state of affairs in
Ireland.[7]

Bishop Fogarty of Killaloe, who was a fervently nationalist bishop
and was one of the trustees of the Dáil Loan, was quoted at length from
his pastoral of 1919:

> Ireland which has not had one years [*sic*] peace since greed and
> plunder brought a foreign power amongst us 700 years ago, is
> being tortured and harassed by that alien rule to a point of exas-
> peration which has become almost unbearable. In their insane
> attempts to extinguish the unquenchable fire of patriotism they
> have given us martial law for government, and turned our country
> into a prison.[8]

Bishop Hoare of Ardagh and Clonmacnois, in a quotation which could
have come from the most passionate republican, stated:

> We are a martyred race. We have been cruelly treated, persecuted,
> oppressed, robbed and insulted. For seven hundred years we have
> proclaimed and protested, and it is only in our own day that our
> cry has reached the nations to find them sympathetic. Our rulers
> dare not now deny us independence. All nations except England
> acknowledge the justice of our claim.[9]

In an address written for a Sinn Féin meeting in 1918, Bishop Hallinan
of Limerick contended that by condoning Carson's rebellion while
suppressing the Irish Volunteers the British government had killed
British constitutionalism in Ireland. For Ireland to continue to send
representatives to Westminster after this disparity would be to engage
in a 'silly farce'. He expressed his support for Sinn Féin's methods,
though he warned against rebellion and secret societies at the same
time, threatening to pull his support from the organisation if they

trusted in either method.[10] Archbishop Harty proclaimed that '[t]o-day our determination to be free is as fresh as ever, and we shall never cease until our country enjoys its rightful liberty.'[11] His 1920 Lenten pastoral contained elements which were overtly separatist: 'We are living under a Government which has proved itself an abject failure.' It had trampled on the will of the people and upheld the ascendancy of a pampered minority. It had excelled in acts of coercion and oppression: 'The remedy for the Irish upheaval is obvious, since freedom is the best solvent of political disorder.'[12]

In an interview conducted in April 1921, Harty spoke candidly about his politics. The interviewer reported: 'His Grace told me perfectly frankly that he was a Republican and thought that form of Government was the one which would be best suited to administer Ireland.'[13] While claiming to be a republican, he was somewhat surprisingly in favour of Dominion Home Rule for the entire island along the New Zealand model as a second best, and believed that eighty per cent of the Irish would be willing to work with that compromise. Showing a political aptitude which escaped several of his colleagues, he, like Byrne, was aware that de Valera would not and could not accept Home Rule as he had a mandate from the people to accept nothing less than complete independence. The interviewer asked if the bishops would declare themselves in favour of Dominion Home Rule if it was offered. 'He told me – No: that it would be quite impossible for them to make any such declaration in advance but that he hoped that, in the event of Dominion Home Rule being given without reservation they might be able to advise their people to give it a fair working and trial.'[14] Harty clearly understood the delicacy of the political situation, a fact which allowed him to act as one of the few moderating voices within the hierarchy during the Civil War.

Positive hierarchical attitudes towards members of Sinn Féin were not limited to their political activities. In 1919, Bishop Foley of Kildare and Leighlin, who had remained an Irish Party supporter until the party's final collapse, went so far as to admit that 'I can say without the slightest hesitation that as a body they [Sinn Féin members] are most exemplary in attending to their religious duties and living good, Christian lives.' This was clearly an important issue for him in the wake of the 1916 Rising. 'From conversations which I frequently had with them here,' he reported, 'I am satisfied that they are quite willing to accept the teaching of the Church, even when it may not be quite in harmony with some of their views for instance the lawfulness of the Easter Rising for the success of which there was no hope whatever.'[15] Foley was not alone among the bishops in this regard. It seems that the strong spirituality of Sinn Féin members won over many bishops, including those involved in attending to Terence MacSwiney's body in October 1920.

Archbishops Gilmartin and O'Donnell displayed the moderate, moral-force nationalism for which they were known and respected. As a rule, Gilmartin refrained from political activity, preferring to demonstrate his nationalism through strong support of the Gaelic League and the GAA. However, in 1919 he asserted that Ireland was knocking at the gates of liberty: 'as a nation, old in centuries, young in her manhood, strong in the justice of her claims and calm in the divine hope that truth must prevail in the end.'[16] A year later, he informed his flock that if they thought they were misgoverned, they had not only the right but also the duty to seek for a change of government. In doing so, however, they must adhere to the Ten Commandments.[17] According to O'Donnell, who had been the Irish Party's strongest episcopal supporter before falling out with Redmond during the Irish Race Convention in 1918, the misrule in Ireland had led to crime and vengeance that would disgrace even a savage government. In his opinion, '[t]he pity is that any of our people should give the oppressor a chance.' Echoing Gilmartin's sentiments, he stressed that immoral acts on both sides were wrong. A murder by nationalists was as much a crime against the majesty of God as one by Crown forces.[18] Neither man was prepared to accept the moral relativism which was a staple defence of militant nationalists, but their criticisms were generally expressed as moral instructions, with little threat of punishment of any sort.

The same cannot be said of Bishop Cohalan of Cork. A nationalist who had been one of the first members of the hierarchy to offer tentative support to Sinn Féin, he was heavily criticised in 1920 when he threatened excommunication on anyone in his diocese who engaged in violent behaviour. Nationalists took this as an attack on their legitimacy, but Dermot Keogh theorises that Cohalan's motives were in no way political. As he points out, the ban extended to people on both sides of the fight. Keogh contends that Cohalan, having witnessed the deaths of several clergymen and the burning of a portion of Cork city, did what he deemed necessary.[19] Judging from Cohalan's response to a complaint from the American Association for the Recognition of the Irish Republic, de Valera's replacement for the Friends of Irish Freedom,[20] this contention is almost certainly correct: 'I wish, as much as you do, the independence of Ireland. It is scandalous on your part to align yourself with those who ambush, who are useless politically and who expose human life without any protection to the dangers of reprisals and injury. The ruins of Cork are the result of your policy.'[21] In spite of this, Cohalan's ban was, whether inadvertently or not, biased against nationalists. A ban of excommunication by a Catholic bishop would obviously have no effect on Protestant members of the Crown forces, meaning that most Black and Tans and Auxiliaries could continue to act with impunity. He seemed to realise this when, in 1921, he informed the people of Cork: '[i]n emergencies like the present it is a serious difficulty to a Bishop in the discharge of his duty that when he condemns crime he seems to give heart to the oppressor who has no scruple about crime'.[22]

David Miller, specifically discussing Cohalan's ban, judges the excommunication to have been ineffective and only hurtful to the Church's interests.[23] Their indignant outrage aside, most nationalists showed little concern about the ban. Many of the priests in the Cork diocese ignored their bishop's directive. Fr. Dominic O'Connor, the republican Capuchin known for his involvement in the Rising and the Four Courts, was convinced that acts normally considered sinful, when performed under the aegis of the authority of the republican government, were not, and therefore did not fall under the ban of excommunication. Additionally, because these acts were committed to promote the rights of the Irish against an army of occupation, they were, in fact, meritorious. Just to be safe though, he recommended that IRA members refrain from telling priests when they had committed any of these acts.[24]

Even Cardinal Logue, who was known to enjoy socialising with British royalty, condemned British tactics. In a published letter, Logue gave a scathing account of British control of Ireland:

> It is true we are subjected to a sharp trial, to drastic repression, such repression as has been seldom paralleled in modern times, even by autocratic Russia or overbearing Germany, without any serious effort on the part of our rulers to apply the remedies which

would have infallibly obviated that present confusion and secured order and tranquillity.[25]

In November 1920, he stated that he was oppressed with sadness and despair after the murder of government officials by Collins's squad during what quickly became known as Bloody Sunday. However, while the murders of Sunday were terrible, the 'indiscriminate massacre of innocent and inoffensive victims which was perpetrated by the forces of the Crown in Croke Park was, if a balance were struck, worse.'[26] Assassination of individuals is a detestable crime and an outrage to God's law, he noted, 'but it is a greater shock to humanity and a graver outrage against the divine ordinance by which human life is protected, to turn lethal weapons against a defenceless, unarmed, closely-packed multitude, reckless of the numbers of innocent people who may fall victims. No amount of special pleading or misrepresentation can rob such an act of its horrors.'[27]

Logue's sharp bias against the Crown was not an automatic blessing upon Sinn Féin's political policies. Throughout these tumultuous years he maintained that aspirations towards an independent republic were 'ill-considered and Utopian'. He felt that these aspirations 'cannot fail, if persevered in, to entail present suffering, disorganisation, and danger, and is sure to end in future disaster, defeat, and collapse.'[28] He was insistent that Dominion status was the best possible course for Ireland. In 1920, Richard Pope-Hennessy, son of the former Conservative politician and colonial governor Sir John Pope-Hennessy, wrote to Logue praising him for dispelling the notion that the bishops supported Sinn Féin and opposed any solution which kept Ireland in the Empire,[29] though, in fact, he was actually praising Logue for his independent statements and not those of the hierarchy.

Individual statements by bishops carried a great deal of authority, but it was in their hierarchical pronouncements that the bishops possessed their strongest weapon of protest against the state of affairs in Ireland. The turbulent circumstances of 1920 resulted in two such pronouncements in which the bishops harshly criticised the British government for its handling of the Irish situation. On 27 January, the bishops met at Maynooth and issued a joint statement calling for allowance of an undivided Ireland to choose its own form of government. Their lordships declared that this was the only way that relations between Ireland and England could turn friendly. The Irish people were

entitled to this right, however they had been denied it by an oppressive
government, and the people 'subjected to an iron rule of oppression as
cruel and unjust as it is ill advised and out of date ... We would represent to the advocates of military rule in Ireland that government by
force, which was never right, is to-day wholly obsolete, and cannot
hope to prevail for long against the democratic spirit now animating the
world.'[30]

The January statement contained all the elements of a strongly
worded appeal to the British government urging it to rethink its
strategy in dealing with Ireland. By the time of their October meeting,
the bishops had hardened their attitudes. The resulting statement was
an acerbic criticism of British policy that made demands rather than
appeals. The bishops accused the British government of conniving at
and encouraging, if not actually organising, acts of terrorism and
savagery throughout the island, and allowing sectarian riots in Ulster to
result in the persecution of northern Catholics. They did not blame the
men who engaged in these acts, but rather their superiors, who never
showed any signs of issuing reproof or deterrent punishments, or
calling public investigations. To remedy this, the bishops demanded in
the name of civilisation and national justice that a full inquiry into
the atrocities be investigated by a tribunal which would inspire the
confidence of all.[31]

The bishops were prepared to criticise the Crown, but rejected calls
to speak in any way that would damage the nationalist movement. In
1919, the Bishop of Nottingham publicly urged the Irish hierarchy, as
a body, to denounce crime. Logue replied that the bishops spoke against
crime wherever it happened, but he displayed a reticence about the
issuing of a joint statement. 'But some people seem to think that the
clergy and the hierarchy should be continually harping on this string.
Even if they did, crime would be beyond their control, while the state
of things which gives an opportunity and some kind of pretext for
crime continues.'[32] The next month, the *Irish Catholic* lambasted some
English papers for their calls for the bishops to openly and publicly
denounce crime.

> They have performed their duty, and they can do no more; and if
> the warnings and admonitions addressed by them to their flocks
> sometimes go unheeded, so far as a small body of rash, ignorant,
> and misguided men are concerned, the fault is surely to be laid at

the door of our rulers themselves, who by reason of their misgovernment and the betrayal of the trust which they hold for Ireland, have directly conduced to the bringing about of the present deplorable state of affairs.[33]

Responding to the *Irish Times*'s call for an episcopal statement, the *Catholic* responded: 'Why should the Catholic Bishops, more than the prelates of any other Church, be called upon to denounce the commission of crime? ... Why, also, are political murders – if the adjective is really the proper one to employ – to be thus singled out for denunciation?'[34] It appears that Professor McDonald's scepticism was well-founded, as the bishops conveniently overlooked activities during the war against the Crown that they condemned just a few years later. Republicans, though, did not object to the hierarchy's pronouncements before the Treaty, especially when they found episcopal involvement, or lack thereof, helpful.

INITIAL EPISCOPAL REACTIONS TO THE TREATY

Treaty advocates, aware that many of their former comrades would oppose them, requested open support of the hierarchy immediately after the signing. The ambiguousness of a 'Free State', when compared to a fully-independent republic, left their cause politically and philosophically weakened. To bolster what would inevitably be a delicate and vulnerable government,[35] they turned to the strength and stability they could gain from episcopal support. As Liam de Róiste observed, the bishops wielded great power: 'part of the success of recent years has been due to their support, as of failures in the past have been due to their opposition.'[36] Some, though, were nervous about the effects of episcopal support on the tone of the debate. As Michael Collins and Archbishop Harty both noted, a hierarchical denunciation of de Valera and his followers was not necessarily the wisest of options, especially as the radicalisation of republicanism had made attainment of the republic a national and spiritual imperative amongst the growing ranks of the militants.[37] Mulcahy approached Patrick Browne about using his influence with the bishops to keep them from making a statement, as he feared the effects it would have on the IRB.[38]

Opponents of the Treaty, sensing episcopal sympathy going against them, appealed to the bishops to refrain from involving themselves.

During the Dáil debates, de Valera asked the bishops to refrain from making a public statement on the Treaty.[39] Mary MacSwiney urged the hierarchy to allow for Ireland's case to be pleaded before the international audience without prejudice by refraining from taking a side in the matter.[40] Monsignor Michael Curran warned Gilmartin against an episcopal announcement. The matter was purely political and clerical interference would 'benefit anti-clericals', he wrote. More importantly, when the final stage of what he termed the 'Irish Renaissance' came it would be important for the Church to be able to say it had not hindered progress.[41]

This was a marked changed from the calls for episcopal and clerical involvement that had been frequent in the recent past. Republicans had not been averse to using the bishops and clergy to their own political advantage when it suited them.[42] The year 1918 saw Sinn Féin approach the hierarchy in an effort to jointly confront the issue of conscription.[43] In 1919, Logue had expressed concern to Archbishop Walsh about Sinn Féin's attempts to use the priests for the same purposes as they were using the Lord Mayor.[44] Republicans had pushed hard for the hierarchy to formally recognise the authority of the Dáil prior to the 1921 truce, with de Valera making a trip to Maynooth to plead the national case on 21 June. Episcopal involvement, therefore, was not opposed on principle.

Despite Byrne's assurance to de Valera that the hierarchy would refrain from speaking as a body before the Dáil voted, individual bishops had been offering their personal opinions through sermons and published letters since shortly after the Treaty had been signed. In the *Irish Independent* of 8 December, Bishops Gaughran, Hackett, Hallinan and McKenna pledged their support for the Treaty, with the names of Logue and Gilmartin appearing beside these in that day's issue of the *Freeman's Journal*. Bishop Fogarty made his opinion known the next day in the *Irish Independent*, declaring the peace as God's gift. The Treaty, he said, was well worth the price paid for it.[45] On 10 December, the *Independent* listed thirteen bishops who favoured acceptance. Cohalan described the settlement as excellent, and Bishop O'Doherty stated that he could not understand de Valera's statement of opposition.[46] Bishops who rarely spoke of politics, including Naughton, Finegan and Brownrigg each praised the Treaty as marking a new beginning for Ireland and a chance to live in peace. Miller contends that these statements were made unaware of the deep division the Treaty would precipitate in the national leadership,[47] but given the requests made by de Valera, MacSwiney, Mulcahy and others, this is highly contestable.

The bishops did refrain from issuing a joint statement that indicated their preference while the debate continued in the Dáil. Breaking with the customary tri-annual hierarchical meetings in April, June and October, Logue called the bishops together on 13 December to give the Treaty their full consideration and, in his mind, prevent the plunging of the country into 'a more intensified course of burning and bloodshed'.[48] The statement expressed the hierarchy's highest appreciation for patriotism, ability and honesty of purpose in which Irish representatives have conducted struggle for national freedom. The bishops recognised that the burden of responsibility for deciding Ireland's destiny rested with the Dáil, and they were certain that the TDs had the best interests of the country and the wishes of the people at the forefront of their minds.[49] Logue, who was greatly impressed with the terms the plenipotentiaries had been able to win from the British, was disappointed with the statement, as he felt the bishops should have shown their support for the Treaty.[50]

As debate over the Treaty intensified, so too did the bishops' support of it. Towards the end of December, Fogarty proclaimed that rejection of the Treaty would be 'an act of national madness'.[51] In a letter published on 2 January 1922, Bishop Hallinan, whom Cohalan believed would find it very hard to accept a settlement that did not result in complete independence as late as June 1921,[52] wrote that while the Treaty was not perfect in his opinion, it still granted to Ireland a substantial share for which the republicans had suffered and fought. Utilising an argument popularised by Collins, he declared that those aspects of complete independence still wanting would come through the use of Ireland's newfound freedom. It was the duty of the representatives of the people, he wrote, to vote in accordance with the wishes of the majority, and those wishes were for peace and ratification.[53]

In their New Year's addresses, both Logue and Harty called for ratification of the Treaty. Logue declared that to reject it over mere verbal quibbles – a restrained yet cutting comment aimed at de Valera's Document Number 2 – would be a terrible calamity for Ireland, and that to do so would go against the wishes of the Irish not just in Ireland but all over the world. Harty contended that the new year would not be a peaceful one unless the Treaty was ratified. He also appealed to the representatives to pay attention to the wishes of the majority, who were clearly in favour of its passage.[54] Privately, Harty still gave his tacit support to republican aspirations. If there was any possibility that a republic would be recognised, he wrote, he had no doubts that the country would support this. However, there was none in his opinion, and he did not find enough difference between the Treaty and de Valera's External Association to risk the renewal of war.[55]

Few bishops withheld their support of the Treaty by the year's end. The most notable examples of silence came from several northern bishops, though interestingly their stances on partition were varied, meaning that it did not automatically play the influential role to be expected.[56] Bishops O'Donnell and Mulhern, both of whom had become resigned to accepting some temporary form of partition, chose to refrain from speaking publicly, as did the fiercely anti-partitionist McHugh. However, MacRory, who went so far as to refuse to personally deal with any member of the Northern government, spoke in favour of the Treaty. A few regularly vocal bishops in the Free State, including O'Dea, Hoare and Morrisroe, declined to comment. Byrne also maintained his characteristic silence. While he privately compared his views on the Treaty to those of MacRory, he made up his mind to deliberately refrain from speaking his mind on political affairs as long as possible, hoping that he could do more good by keeping quiet and acting as a mediator and conciliator.[57]

Edward Mulhern provides a fascinating example of how conflicted bishops could be. Mulhern was a strong nationalist who maintained friendships with moderate republicans even during the height of the episcopal condemnation of their movement. In December, he informed the *Irish Independent* by telegraph that he did not wish to interfere in the discussion at the present stage.[58] Privately, though, he favoured acceptance of the Treaty, which was, in his opinion, made great simply by sending British troops out of Ireland. He feared the possibility of a renewal of violence and what would happen if the British delivered on their promise of immediate and terrible war. Most importantly for him, the Church had to side with the people or find its 'influence of little weight at the end of this struggle' whatever the outcome. 'I believe that if we keep within our own special domain our people will love us more and listen to us even if we should now and then find fault with their doings.'[59] The fear of reduction of the Church's influence on the Catholics of Ireland, while rarely discussed, obviously played a large part in the activities of the bishops. Convinced that the majority of people were in favour of the Treaty, they clearly would have been reticent to oppose it even if they did so on moral grounds.

Like so many other nationalists, the bishops viewed the founding of the Free State as the best possible way to advance Ireland's aspirations for independence while avoiding further warfare, which seems to have been their predominant motivating factor. There was a strongly pragmatic streak running through the bishops' thoughts. Fogarty believed that the Treaty was acceptable because '[i]t was not possible to get one grain more out of the English.'[60] MacRory was convinced that 'there is no dishonour in bowing before the facts and accepting the better when the best is unattainable.'[61] Mulhern was concerned at the level of attachment republicans, especially women, held to ideals. He was of the opinion that the Church must, with Divine right, waive the exercise of these in their fullness to best secure what is for the good of the country.[62] This episcopal concern over ideological motivation evolved into antipathy towards the republican movement as its ideology promoted a stronger spiritually guided opposition to the Treaty.

JOINT PASTORALS

The growing tensions within the nationalist movement, culminating in the seizing of the Four Courts by republican forces, changed the nature of the bishops' arguments regarding the Treaty. Whereas previously they had urged for its adoption as a way of securing peace and advancing the final stages of independence, militant republicans' defiance of the Provisional Government caused the hierarchy to regard rejection of the Treaty as succumbing to paramilitary pressure and a guarantee of further war. In a sermon just two weeks before the bishops' April meeting, Bishop Fogarty, echoing his predecessors' admonitions of the Fenians during the late nineteenth century, described those who supported the republican military action as 'anti-Irish and unCatholic' and those who actively fought as bandits in uniform. He accepted that political differences existed, but urged his listeners and readers to settle those differences constitutionally.[63]

The bishops' statements against the IRA split commenced with a sermon read by O'Doherty on 1 April. Just days after the forming of the republican executive council, the Bishop of Clonfert informed the people of his diocese that in all civilised states the army was the servant, not the master of the people. It was bound to obey the will of the majority. With this in mind, he said that the only legitimate army in Ireland was the one which acknowledged the authority of the Dáil, and that '[t]hose who have repudiated that authority and set up an executive of their own may call themselves what they please, but they are not a national army.'[64] He informed the young men of his diocese that the republican IRA had no authority to claim obedience, and that any oaths it demanded of its members were non-binding: 'Death inflicted under their orders is nothing but murder. I wish to put these principles plainly before the young men of this diocese lest, actually by a false patriotism, they should be led into courses which may easily involve most grievous sin.'[65]

O'Doherty's sermon was highly praised by other members of the hierarchy. Logue stated that it was just what the people wanted. He asked O'Doherty to chair the sub-committee that would produce the April pastoral. Gilmartin and Robert Browne of Cloyne also believed that the people were eager for an episcopal pronouncement,[66] a notion that was supported by those within the press. The *Wicklow People* had repeatedly urged the bishops to involve themselves in the crisis for the good of Ireland. Its strongest cry came on 8 April when it asked that the hierarchy as a whole act as an intermediary between the rival camps. This was a pattern that re-emerged in the *Derry Weekly News* and *Donegal Vindicator* in September.

Following their April meeting, the bishops released a statement they hoped would help reunite the opposing sides and allow for a peaceful transfer to self-government. In this statement, the bishops recognised the question of the Treaty as a legitimate subject for national discussion, and that all Irishmen, including themselves, were entitled to their own opinions. They would not, though, obtrude their opinions on anybody, 'founded though they are upon a disinterested and anxious love of Ireland's welfare.'[67] For the first time, they announced, as a unified body, their approval of the Treaty and desire to see it passed, stating 'we think that the best and wisest course for Ireland is to accept the Treaty and make the most of the freedom it undoubtedly brings us for the first time in 700 years.'[68] The means by which the Treaty debate was to take place, they continued, could not involve violence or the suppression of majority opinion by an armed minority. Those who continued to hold the majority hostage were engaged in an immoral usurpation of the people's rights. Furthermore, any bloodshed that resulted from this armed confrontation would rest on the shoulders of the minority occupying the Four Courts. Any war they brought upon the country made them parricides, not patriots. The actions they engaged in would be criminal and sinful, not the legitimate acts of a justifiable war.

If the political passion the republicans felt for an Irish republic was wisely conceived, the bishops noted, 'their day will come in God's good Providence.'[69] The way to that republic could only come via constitutional means. Anything else would further entrench Unionist opposition in the North, suppress the civil rights of the Irish public and disgust the world. Therefore, those who believed they were acting as champions of liberty by continuing the fight for a republic were hurting their own countrymen and foolishly ruining Ireland's hopes for a peaceful and free future. Finally, the bishops decreed that they expected the priests to support the rights of the people and 'to wean our young men ... from evil tenets and evil ways.'[70]

The April pastoral was a demonstration of the bishops' attempting to remain within their spiritual realm while offering their opinions on the state of current affairs. It was, in essence, an invitation to republicans to cease their violent resistance and rejoin the political discussion before the situation got completely out of hand. Both Logue, still nursing the wound of not getting his way in December, and Harty had previously expressed this desire. Logue had wanted the bishops to make a bold pronouncement that avoided siding with a political party before the Dáil had voted on the Treaty. He reiterated this desire in April.[71] Harty was of the opinion that an episcopal statement on the necessity of freedom of election, speech and press would be beneficial: 'On the other hand if the Bishops were to take sides in the political issue I am of the opinion that their meeting would do more harm than good.'[72]

The pastoral was generally welcomed by the press and Treaty supporters. The *Cork Examiner* urged the young boys mixed up in 'this net-work of scandalous and incalculable criminality' to return to their homes.[73] The *Wicklow People* described the pastoral as the most important pronouncement the hierarchy had made. The editors were sure that the weighty statement would bring about a better state of affairs and end the troubles which had rent and distracted the country.[74] Liam de Róiste had no quarrel with the republicans' desired end, merely their methods for achieving that end, a mentality he shared with Bishop O'Dea.[75] De Róiste argued that despite their noble sounding arguments, those who claimed to uphold the republic through force of arms were, in actuality suppressing public opinion while engaging in dictatorial powers and terror. Their actions went against his notion of Catholic conscience. The bishops' statement was, he believed, clear and strong, condemning only what was wrong while choosing to provoke argument on other issues.[76]

Episcopal rhetoric against republicans turned increasingly aggressive after the issuing of the April pastoral. This was due, in large part, to the increased usage of spirituality in the movement once the fight against the Free State became desperate.[77] The republicans' viewing of their cause and themselves as morally above reproach was an extremely threatening position for the bishops. As the leaders of the Catholic Church, they were Ireland's moral arbiters. Republicans' claims to moral superiority meant that not only did they no longer feel compelled to abide by the decisions of the bishops, but they placed themselves at an equal and competitive position regarding moral issues. This threatened one of the primary power bases of the bishops.

From the onset of the Treaty debate, the threat of republican moralising was deemed a potential irritation. Bishop Hoare wrote to Hagan that he would not take lessons on theology and morals from de Valera any sooner than he suspected Hagan would take lessons from Mussolini.[78] As republican usage of morality arguments increased over the course of the summer, so too did the bishops' concern with the situation, with Cardinal Logue threatening excommunication of anyone who continued the immoral and illegal fight against Free State troops in July.[79] As autumn drew close, the bishops began their offensive in earnest, with the Bishop of Waterford firing the first volley in a new round of arguments.

In late August, Bishop Hackett, issued a very emotional sermon on the Irish situation that left him, according to press coverage, unable to speak for a few moments. Though he had previously remained silent about the political issues, the time had come, he said, to either speak or resign his position. He told his listeners that he was not adamantly in favour of the Provisional Government and if the republic could be fought for without sin, he would stay silent. However, that path had not been adopted, and republican leaders claimed that they had been enabled to brush aside moral law. Demonstrating the hierarchy's urgent desire to maintain its monopoly over morality, he told his audience: 'I am your teacher. I am the authentic custodian here of the moral law for you.'[80] He said that he spoke not as an individual, but as the possessor of the position he held, giving him the same power over his diocese that the pope had for the world. Those who set themselves against the teachings of the bishops were not fit to receive absolution: 'There was liberty for discussion before the bishops spoke, but all room for doubt is hereby removed.'[81]

Other bishops quickly followed suit and issued statements that demonstrated similar sentiments to those expressed by Hackett. Bishop O'Sullivan of Kerry, one of the more conservative episcopal critics of the republican movement, released a statement to be read aloud in all the churches in his diocese on 27 August which reaffirmed the authority of the bishops as laid out in the April pastoral. He referred to the hierarchy as the 'divinely appointed teachers in matters of morality, whose moral teaching you cannot disregard without imperilling your immortal souls.'[82] The pastoral, in his estimation, dealt with the fundamental truths of morality, and all Catholics were bound to acquiesce to its teachings. Furthermore, no individual priest or layman could detract from its doctrinal authority or lessen its binding force on the consciences of Irish Catholics.[83] The bishops, he continued, were the appointed rulers of the Church. They were each the sole authentic teachers of faith and morals in their own dioceses. Individual priests, on the contrary, had no right to teach on matters of faith and morals, except insofar as their bishops permitted. Those who acted in defiance of the moral teachings of their bishops could not salve their consciences with the un-authoritative teachings of these priests. Nor could the defiant individuals argue that the bishops had no authority to speak on political and secular matters, O'Sullivan contended. Theologians had taught that only bishops are competent judges as to on what they have the right and authority to pronounce.[84] Therefore, if the bishops said they had the right to speak on something, no one had the authority to question them, quite a self-serving Möbius strip of an argument. He concluded by appealing to the republican soldiers to quit the path they were on. Their sense of loyalty and rights as soldiers was false, and their

actions were morally indefensible and ruinous to the country they
professed to love.

On 24 September 1922, Bishop Cohalan read out a pastoral at Mass
that questioned and criticised the republicans' belief in themselves as
the morally superior defenders of the true Ireland. While they wished
to be regarded as good, loyal Catholics, he said, the fact of the matter
was they chose to continue a course of life which the bishops had
declared unlawful. Through false moral teaching, they had come to
justify their criminal actions, but the bishops were the leaders of the
Catholic Church in Ireland and it was their responsibility to determine
such things. These men and women had accepted the Catholic Church
as their faith. In doing so they had agreed to accept the moral teachings
of the Church and its pastors. If they were genuinely good Catholics,
they had to abandon their subjective speculations and judgments in
opposition to Church teaching.[85] As the activities of militant republicans
were clearly unlawful and in violation of the Church's teachings, priests
who refused absolution to republicans were in the right. For while the
Church regretted the loss of anyone from its fold, it would not hesitate
to punish and cast out sinners who failed to adhere to its teachings.

The bishops solidified the support for the Provisional Government
they had declared in April as well as their objections to militant republicanism when they met again at Maynooth and issued the October
pastoral. There has been widespread belief that the pastoral was inspired by a request by the Provisional Government for a statement to
coincide with the newly enacted Public Safety Bill and offer of amnesty
to all republican forces willing to surrender arms. While the Executive
Council did believe that such a pronouncement would be desirable,[86]
the statements made by bishops since the start of hostilities indicate
that they needed no prompting from the government. Furthermore,
while they were undoubtedly concerned about helping to support the
state, they were also gravely concerned about maintaining their own
authority in the face of the republicans' competitive stance on morality.

In a pronouncement to be read throughout the Catholic churches
of Ireland, the bishops expressed their anguish at the current state of
affairs. They declared that the Provisional Government was the
government set up by the nation. In what must be seen as an example
of the bishops' use of overstatement, they posited that those who
refused to acknowledge it had resorted to attacking their own country,

causing more damage in three months than the British had caused in three decades.[87] As the opponents of the Provisional Government had no legitimate authority, their 'war' was nothing more than a system of murder of National Forces.

Echoing Cohalan's pastoral, the bishops declared that even worse than the physical ruin was the demoralisation, especially of the young, 'whose minds are being poisoned by false principles'. Among these false principles was the republican belief that they could defy the bishops, 'whose pastoral office they would silence by calumny and intimidation' and still consider themselves good Catholics. 'It is almost inconceivable how decent Irish boys could degenerate so tragically, and reconcile such a mass of criminality with their duties to God and to Ireland.' Rebellion against the legitimate Government, set up by the nation and acting within its rights, was never justifiable, and as the Dáil of the Provisional Government had been 'elected by the vast majority of public opinion', it was clearly the legitimate government. Any person who continued fighting against the legitimate government or supported the continuation of the fight was 'guilty of the gravest sins' and so could not receive the sacraments of confession or Holy Communion. Priests who approved of the post-Treaty resistance were to be suspended and no longer allowed to carry out the responsibilities of their sacred office.

The bishops declared that they had decided to interfere in the political matter not because of a desire to help or hinder either side in the political debate, but because they could not stand idly by and watch the young men of Ireland participate in such un-Catholic activities. It was their duty to God and the people of Ireland that drove them to make the pronouncement, a statement most republicans found difficult to believe. As for the republican argument that they were bound to their oath, the bishops returned to O'Doherty's contention that no oath could bind men to carry out warfare against their country in circumstances forbidden by God's law. To even claim that such an oath was possible would be an offence to God and to the very nature of oaths.

The reaction to the pastoral in the Irish press was immediate and mostly supportive. The *Freeman's Journal* declared: 'Let us hope, then, that the words of these Fathers of the People may convince the minds and touch the hearts of those to whom they are addressed.'[88] The *Cork Examiner* issued an empathetic editorial stating that no Catholic could question the authority of the bishops to pronounce on such matters:

'No vestige of excuse of any kind is left to the youths who have been misled by the insidious teachings of amateur theologians, for the Church condemns the campaign that is being conducted by an armed minority in Ireland and declares it to be without moral sanction.'[89] The editor questioned the notion of patriotism that discarded the law of God which would intensify poverty and social chaos. The pastoral, he hoped, would cause reflection amongst those who had believed themselves fighting for Ireland by opposing the Free State and would result in them seeing the error of their ways.

Not all press coverage was completely complimentary to the bishops. The *Irish Times* asserted the pastoral was 'a truly significant index to the state of Southern Ireland'. The alarm of the hierarchy was entirely justifiable and their pronouncement should 'have a swiftly sobering effect throughout the whole country'.[90] However, it went on to state sardonically that it must be remembered that many good Irishmen had seen this taint of lawlessness long before the present situation, when British law was openly defied and no nationalist seriously protested; a remark, no doubt, aimed at the bishops' public endorsements of Sinn Féin from the General Election of 1918 onward. The paper concluded, appropriating Catholic terminology, that such lawlessness was not to be exorcised in a day. The *Derry Weekly News* was one of the few non-republican, nationalist papers that expressed outright criticism of the document. 'The Pastoral will make no change', the paper stated. 'Those who act upon their own initiative in matters of life and death are above Pastorals and regard them not. The guilty ones are not always on one side we fear.' The editors believed that fault did not lie solely with the pastoral's audience, but with the writers as well. 'We had hope from the Bishops [*sic*] pronouncement but it is argumentative and will quite certainly prove ineffective.'[91]

According to Emmet Larkin, the October pastoral was issued not because de Valera or his followers posed any real threat to the bishops' power or influence, but because like Parnell thirty years prior, de Valera no longer retained the confidence of the majority of the party and was therefore no longer the legitimate leader.[92] This statement is erroneous for two reasons. First, the pastoral was not about legitimacy of leadership. The hierarchy had expressed their approval of the Treaty in April and by the publication of the October pastoral, their stance was well known to be firmly in the Free State camp. Logue, Mulhern and Fogarty, among others, had all publicly expressed their displeasure and/or disbelief with de Valera's actions, so there was very little need to focus further on the matter. Even if there had been, they stated within the text of the pastoral that the issue of legitimacy had already been addressed. Second, given the severity of individual ecclesiastical statements culminating in the extreme warnings and threats contained within the pastoral, Larkin's argument that republicans were not deemed a genuine threat does not stand up. The fact that the bishops pronounced the demoralisation through false principles as more damaging than the physical ruin of Ireland, which was apparently greater than all damage caused by the British since the time of Parnell, proves how seriously they treated the attempts by republicans to justify their cause through morality. While it is true that the bishops were prone to hyperbole, their co-religionists were generally immune from such intense castigation. The sudden turnaround in this policy shows that they did deem the republicans an actual threat to their power and influence. With addresses like Cohalan's and O'Sullivan's setting the stage, this pastoral was the strongest message the bishops could send that they and they alone were Ireland's spiritual leaders. As Cohalan complained in December 1922, if an individual priest approved of the republican violence, his word was taken as gospel; 'but if the united Episcopate, the authoritative teachers of the Church, condemned both actions as grievously unlawful, it was considered a sufficient answer: "The Bishops were always wrong in politics".'[93] They were the Church's representatives on the island and they were the interpreters of divine law. Republican attempts to usurp this position had turned thousands of their flocks down the path of sin. With this document, the bishops declared that the republicans who preached the spirituality of their cause were not only wrong, but were leading Ireland towards ruin. This document was, above all else, an affirmation of their spiritual and religious authority in the face of what they deemed a mounting threat.

REPUBLICAN REACTIONS

Many in the republican movement did not deem the pastorals as spiritual documents. The Republican Election Committee of Tirconnaill expressed its concern for the consequences to Catholicism as a result of the April pastoral and the use of the altar for what could only be

construed as an attack on principles.[94] The *Plain People* denounced the
pastoral as proof that the bishops had cast their lot with the Free State.
Not only had they declared themselves 'Slave Staters' and decried all
those who stood by the Irish republic, but they had used their positions
'to frighten you into accepting England's flesh-pots of Egypt at the price
of your national souls.'[95] The majority of the article rehashed arguments that were common for the period. The author claimed that the
bishops had been opposed to Irish nationalism during the historic
periods of rebellion, all the way up to 1916. What made this rendition
unique was the contention that the hierarchy would not have dared to
issue a statement like the April pastoral for the past three years due to
national unity 'and, as politicians, the Bishops are, above everything
else, disciples of Expediency.' It was only due to the dissention caused
by England's seducing of Griffith and Collins that finally allowed the
bishops to throw their lot in with England.[96]

Most galling of all, the author believed, was that had the bishops
recognised the supreme authority of the Irish people to determine their
own form of government anytime before the truce, Britain would have
been compelled to recognise the Irish republic. Instead, they waited
until after the ratifying of the Treaty, once the majority of those who
had previously been loyal to the republic accepted the supremacy of Great
Britain, to make a statement. Readers were encouraged to maintain the
firmness of their convictions, despite the statement of the bishops,
'because the Hierarchy have clearly laid it down that this issue is one on
which "every Irishman is entitled to his own opinion".'[97]

The usage of moral concerns against the bishops' activities became
predominant as the year progressed. In a pamphlet from August 1922
titled 'Episcopal and Clerical Injustice: Grave Responsibility of Churchmen', the bishops and clergy were chastised for using their pulpits to
denounce the 'faithful in deed and word to the Republic which has been
baptised and sanctified in the blood of men of whom any country
would be proud.'[98] Rather than engaging in political denunciations,
which threatened to drive courageous, honest and faithful men from
the Church, the author suggested to the bishops that they call for a
national crusade of prayer to lead the people through the terrible
national crisis. At present, the bishops were engaged in 'upholding a
policy of cowardly yielding to threats; tampering with the sanctity of
oaths, and generally putting fleshpots before principle.' While these

views were shared by many within the republican camp, the hierarchy was not won over by this line of argument.

In an essay published in the *Cork Examiner* on 12 July which is more sermon than political treatise, one of 'Ireland's young "rebel" Priests' writing under the pseudonym Colm Cille, who was in all probability Patrick Browne,[99] urged his readers to do their duty and support the republic. He proclaimed that the Irish people had the right to expect guidance from their spiritual leaders but the Irish bishops had failed the people, just as they had in 1916 and 1920. If the bishops had supported the Irish nation in its fight against England, perhaps the terrible bloodshed that resulted from the Civil War would not have happened. As galling as this was, Colm Cille urged his readers to refrain from losing self-control: 'It would be foolish and disastrous were you to neglect your duties to God and your immortal souls, because of the actions of your Bishops and Priests.'[100] Unlike some on the republican side, Colm Cille did not accuse the bishops of loving the Empire. Indeed, he proclaimed that they loved Ireland, 'but they love her unwisely. They mean well; but they are guilty of weakness and timidity.'[101]

Browne's writings displayed a paradoxical set of viewpoints regarding clerical involvement in the national question. On the one hand, he opposed the Church's involvement altogether. He argued that to declare on the political question, as the bishops had done, assumed a level of authority not held by the entire Church, and if the Free State government had no lawful standing, the bishops had espoused and blessed a traitorous and murderous campaign. He also added that even though the bishops had decreed that the Free State government was the lawful government of Ireland, the Church had made no such pronouncements. The meeting that resulted in the joint pastoral had not been called by the pope. Therefore, the bishops had overreached their authority. Even if the pope had called the bishops together and they had spoken with the authority of the Church supporting them, their threats of censure against priests were completely powerless and unfounded. Even the pope could not censure individuals for actions which could be considered holy, and as Irish republicanism had not been condemned by the Vatican, the activities of republicans could very well be holy.[102] Browne failed to mention that the pope could very easily condemn republicanism and all its adherents, just as Pius IX had done with Fenianism, at which point his argument would be invalidated.

On the other hand, one of Browne's primary concerns was winning the approval of fellow clerics for republicanism. Browne appealed to the priests of Ireland to resist the bishops' attempts to exaggerate the rights and powers of the Church. Ironically, his argument bordered dangerously close to the tenets of Protestantism. 'Since the definition of Infallibility ... we tend to magnify the divine, and forget the human in the Church and the Pope, and to curtail the liberty of men's judgment.'[103] The bishops were not infallible, and it was the duty of the Irish priests to protect the people and teach them the truth when the bishops delivered false doctrine, of which their attack on Irish republicanism was clearly an example. As discussed in Chapter 1, Browne, like many other republican priests, seemed intent on separating religious and national responsibilities: 'As Irishmen or simple priests you can express your opinions; but as Churchmen neither you or [sic] the Bishops have any power or authority whatever to declare with certainty for one side or the other.'[104]

Being a priest himself, Browne opposed the anti-clericals within the republican movement and the strict Fenian notion of no priests in politics:

> There is an idea prevalent among many priests and lay people, that the Irish clergy have no duty to perform as Irishmen. This is a dangerous error. It would be bad for the Church and the country if Irish priests were to neglect the duties of Irish citizenship and patriotism. Although you have chosen the Lord for your inheritance, you are still Irishmen.[105]

However, he had no qualms borrowing from the Fenian traditions he criticised when he reverberated an old message of Kickham's with: 'We need never have any anxiety about the teaching of our Bishops on purely religious matters. But the position is not the same as regards National and purely religious questions. You know what your own experience and the history of the last century tells you of the Irish Bishops and Irish politics.'[106] Whereas Browne urged priests to play their patriotic role, he made it evident that their patriotic role must conform with his concept of patriotism. Any acts opposing that concept ruled a cleric, in this case bishops, unfit for political activity.

Browne dedicated a large percentage of his republican verbiage to criticising, chastising and denigrating the activities of the Irish bishops. His pamphlets were widely distributed and sometimes even ended up in the post of their lordships. Logue commented on receiving a copy of one, though he added that like other propaganda pieces he threw it in the rubbish without reading it.[107] Had he deigned to read it, the Cardinal would have found that Browne invoked the ghost of Columcille, who was 'cursing the Bishops of Erin, for that they threatened to falsify his prophecy, frustrate the plans of the Almighty, and mar the untold destiny God has in mind for the children of the Gael.'[108] Browne accused the bishops of opposing the independence movements of Ireland for over a century, culminating in their denouncements against the heroes of 1916 and the patriots of 1920 and 1921. When Griffith and Collins violated their sacred oaths and betrayed Ireland, the bishops gave their approval of these acts of high treason. With 'unspeakable profanity' they bestowed their benediction on the traitorous and murderous campaign that was waged against the soldiers of the Irish nation at England's bidding.[109] For these acts, the men who were bishops during the war for independence would be ranked with Diarmuid MacMurrough for treachery, shame and dishonour.

By involving themselves as they did in Ireland's political debate, Browne accused the bishops of arrogating for themselves powers beyond those of the pope, i.e. to pronounce on the question of the moral right of the Provisional Government. That right belonged solely to the Irish people, and it was still violently disputed whether the government had received any such authority to rule from the people. Until the political question was settled, the ethical side of the Irish situation could not be properly addressed, so the judgment of the bishops was premature. Seeming to contradict the above assertions, Browne wrote that while it must be remembered that the Church is infallible on essentials of faith and morals, it is not infallible on political issues. More importantly, the bishops were not the Church. They were not infallible in anything. Their duty was to deliver the teachings of the Church, not to make pronouncements in the name of the Church. 'It is the duty of the ministers of Christ to labour to secure and preserve peace; but they have no right to require unto that end the acceptance of their views.'[110] The bishops should have known that it was not within their power to deprive men and women of the sacraments because of their political affiliations. Furthermore, it was unheard of throughout the history of the Church to refuse absolution to men fighting in a war.

These strongly anti-ecclesiastical feelings were the result of the bishops' statements against the republican movement, especially the October pastoral, which Browne found especially offensive. In 'Reply to the Pastoral issued by the Irish Hierarchy in October 1922' written even before the pastoral was read aloud in churches, he declared the pastoral as the culmination of the bishops' ignominy. They had blessed the traitorous usurpation that called itself the Free State government and in doing so were 'worse than the Chief-Priests who were the sworn enemies of Christ'.[111] The pastoral, Browne argued, was based on the false notion that the Provisional Government and the Free State Parliament had been popularly elected by the people of Ireland. The election of 1922 had been held to elect members to the Third Dáil. The Dáil had been dissolved and the Free State Parliament had taken power in a coup d'etat. The pastoral was, therefore, 'a political prostitution of [the bishops'] sacred office, an abuse of their spiritual power and an open alliance with England's tools in a murderous attack on the defenders of the honour, the integrity and the independence of this nation.'[112]

The bishops' indifference, even contempt for the mandate the Irish people put forward in the elections of 1918 and 1920 made their sudden championing of the will of the people suspicious, Browne wrote. Their blindness towards the torture and murder inflicted upon republicans by the Free State forces was despicable, and their attempts to deny the true patriots of Ireland the sacraments was Cromwellian in its cruelty: 'Yea, they are worse than Oliver Cromwell, for it is their solemn bounden duty to feed and succour us, but they try to steal in our dire need the Divine Bread that God sent down to us through them from Heaven.'[113] In doing so, he wrote, the bishops had been false to both Ireland and God. In spite of all this, Browne was convinced that republicans would survive the pastoral and would do so without submitting to the Church on political matters.

Prior to the October pastoral, moderate republicans displayed, like the *Derry Weekly News*, a sense of disappointment in the statements of the hierarchy and a missed opportunity for potential resolution. J.J. O'Kelly, editor of the *Catholic Bulletin*, congratulated Bishop O'Dea for his prudent letters, which he regarded as the first attempts by the hierarchy to lead the nation's thoughts back towards peace. He feared that the statements of other bishops, specifically naming Logue, were regarded as lacking impartiality and so could not lead towards peace or aid in the interests of religion.[114] Hagan feared that the recent tone of episcopal pronouncements would do much harm in the years ahead. He too complimented O'Dea's writings, adding Mulhern as another voice of moderation.[115] A month before, Michael Curran wrote to Hagan from Dublin: 'The Bishops are as bad as anybody else, and will follow Killaloe and others of our friends into any wild series of denunciation of republicans that forms its staple of their daily conversation.'[116] Art O'Muireadaig, a seminarian in Canada with an arrest record from his IRA days, had hoped that the bishops would have attempted to stop the war, but as far as he was aware they had done the opposite, having encouraged Free State supporters and denying the consolation of religion to dying republicans.[117]

After the pastoral was issued, Hagan wrote to Curran that the bishops had written it due to their foolish conviction that the Civil War was within weeks of ending. He was saddened that when the bishops had an opportunity to preach peace, they had chosen instead to further divide the nation.[118] In a letter to Archbishop Mannix, de Valera described the pastoral as unfortunate: 'Never was charity of judgment so necessary, and apparently so disastrously absent. Ireland and the Church will, I fear, suffer in consequence.' In de Valera's estimation, those who believed in the national right and destiny of Ireland as in a religion would never acquiesce to the Free State, regardless of the statements of the bishops.[119]

Republican letters addressed to the bishops rarely displayed such a restrained tone, seeming to be largely used to vent frustrations and sometimes displaying rather harsh and/or unfounded allegations. In a letter to Archbishop Byrne, Art O'Connor, Dáil member and former Secretary for Agriculture, complained of the withholding of absolution from republican prisoners at Mountjoy jail, of which he was one. He informed the archbishop that in common with hundreds of thousands of Irish citizens, the republicans did not accept the authority of the Provisional Government, 'and we respectfully submit that if a priest holds an opposite view in this matter he is not entitled to force his view as an article of the Church's teaching and withhold absolution from those who refuse to subscribe to it.' He requested that Byrne grant the republican prisoners the ministration of unprejudiced priests in the interests of the Catholic faith in Ireland.[120]

O'Connor was not the only prisoner upset with the treatment he received at the hands of the Catholic chaplain at Mountjoy. In a pamphlet entitled 'The Refusal of Absolution in Mountjoy: Questions that should be answered', the author asked if the refusal of the sacrament of penance to republican prisoners, evidently on the orders of the bishop, had succeeded in making republicans believe that it is a sin to serve the republic. Definitely not, he concluded, for republicans still questioned the legality of the Free State government and their war against the republican cause. If these matters were at all doubtful, he argued, then the penitents were entitled to the benefit of the doubt, and if it was not given to them, then there was 'grounds for fear that the power and influence of Churchmen in Ireland is being once more used in the interest of Ireland's enemies.'[121]

Frank Gallagher, de Valera's press officer, described the language and misstatements of the October pastoral as 'hot and steaming from the party presses'.[122] Such evident bias forced Gallagher to conclude that the bishops had decided to use the sacraments as a political weapon. Proof of this bias was seen in the lies regarding the start of the Civil War. Whereas the pastoral stated that the republicans had initially attacked Free State forces, Gallagher was of the opinion that their lordships knew that the Free State had instigated the war when, acting under order of the British government, the Free State attacked the republican general headquarters, located in the Four Courts.[123] He noted that the sudden criminalisation of members of the IRA, while staggering, was just another series in hierarchical pronouncements against Irish patriots dating back to 1916. He claimed that when fighting against the Black and Tans, the Volunteers had been branded as murderers and criminals by the bishops. Little, therefore, had changed. The bishops were still siding with the enemies of Ireland. What made the pastoral worse than previous decrees of the bishops was the severity of the punishment for failing to succumb to their political biases: 'Moral infamy has apparently become an adhesive stamp to be affixed to the unsuspecting souls of one political group by the clerical supporters of another.'[124] It would have been better had the bishops simply confessed to their biases, rather than attempting to pronounce in favour of the Free State in the name of Christ: 'As if the doctrine of Winston Churchill is Christ's doctrine or that He whose attributes include Truth, Honour, Justice and Liberty could teach that a State founded on deception, dishonour and the surrender of ideals must be accepted under pain of separation from Himself.'[125]

Eithne MacSwiney wrote a letter to Byrne on 28 February 1923 which was more of a diatribe against the hierarchy than a defence of republicanism. She began by stating that republicans were not fighting against lawful authority, but rather continued unjust oppression. The bishops' sanctioning and blessing upon the Free State and its actions against the republicans were criminal. Their continued attacks against republicans would recoil on the hierarchy itself, as would 'the preposterous claim made for the Infallibility of their Pastoral' which was 'sheer heresy'. Their refusal of the sacraments to those who would not swear to God an oath of fidelity they meant not to keep 'is only comprehensible in the light that [the bishops] are all acting as Political Partisans and not as priests of the God of Truth.'[126] No republican questioned the bishops as the interpreters and teachers of the Law of God. However, the bishops had recently sought to impose the law of England on Ireland, insisting that it was the Law of God. That, republicans would defy.

Cathleen O'Moore lamented Ireland's lack of a Cardinal Mercier,[127] who told the invaders he recognised only their brute force and refused to tell the people to obey them. She maintained that the Irish respected their priests and bishops and were prepared to accept their teachings as regards religion, but not politics. They were not infallible and were liable to err – 'very liable in your political ideas' and, she continued, the laity claimed the right to use its judgment and conscience.[128] Philip Kettle made a similar statement in his letter of complaint about Bishop Morrisroe's recent actions. Laymen will take religious teaching from bishops, he wrote, but to have the business of civil life stuffed down their necks by the hierarchy leaves them with no earthly margin of liberty.[129] 'An Old Irregular' informed Byrne that threats of excommunication and sacramental deprivation would only make young republicans more solid in their political faith, while the Catholic clergy would, like the prosecutors and priest hunters of the Penal Law era, fail. '[Y]ou will go down unwept unhonoured and unsung.'[130]

Mary MacSwiney, then a prisoner in Mountjoy jail, defended the bishops' rights to support the Free State government, but only as private citizens. By officially condemning the fight for the republic, the bishops were driving many good Catholics from the Church. Their support of perjurers and materialists over those who stood for truth, honour and the sanctity of oaths was equally injurious to the nation.[131] In his response, Byrne passed on the opportunity to comment on MacSwiney's political beliefs and aspirations. However, he informed her that he loved his country and its people as much as many who more openly professed patriotism. His defence of the pastoral was very brief, stating that the bishops acted as 'divinely authorised interpreters of the Divine Law' to point out actions they deemed wrong.[132] They approached the matter with a full sense of their responsibility, and the necessity of such a pronouncement caused him great pain.

The idea that the hierarchy's actions were damaging to the Church was argued by many. In a letter prepared by Count Plunkett, 'Republican women' declared that if the course set out by the bishops was seen through it would be a grave scandal and could, quite possibly, drive people from the Church.[133] John O'Daly of Co. Meath wrote to the bishops to tell them that their short-sighted, intemperate actions had estranged many from the Church, perhaps even driven them out forever. 'What will you answer the gentle Saviour when He asks you for an account of your stewardship?'[134] In an anonymously written document titled 'The Case for the Republicans in Ireland', the Civil War was presented as more than just a struggle for Ireland's political future, as acceptance of the Free State put the very existence of Irish Catholicism at risk. Prior to the Treaty, the republic had been recognised as the legitimate authority in Ireland by a large number of priests and by several bishops: 'Besides explicitly teaching the justice of the Republican Cause, these ecclesiastics gave it such support as to amount to formal co-operation in acts of war, and so confirmed the people in their judgment that the Republic was their lawful government and that their war with England was a just one.'[135] However, the document continued, they faltered when England offered certain advantages in exchange for abandoning the rights of the nation. Rather than accept that the Irish people had spoken in favour, they tried to induce the whole nation to accept the bargain.

The Free State government imposed a constitution on Ireland which was alien and pagan in nature and proceeded to set up a government 'largely composed of Protestants and Freemasons and others who are equally hostile to our religion and our race.'[136] The situation was especially dangerous, the text noted, because republicans who remained good Catholics saw that the bishops were supporting this pagan government through their holy offices. They had no choice but to infer that the bishops were acting as mere politicians. Furthermore, the enemies of Catholicism were encouraged to mock the Free State because it had clearly become the priest-ridden land they had warned against for so long. They were using this opportunity to attempt to weaken the faith of Irish Catholics and spread anti-clericalism, which Ireland had avoided up until then. The only choice the republicans had was to appeal to the Vatican and urge the pope to get involved and rein in the hierarchy. Despite the concern the author felt for Irish Catholicism, it is noteworthy that the damage to the faith and the faithful inflicted by the partitioning of the island and the creation of a genuinely Protestant northern government is never mentioned.

Elements of republican supporters were strongly in favour of taking the offensive against the bishops. During the summer, Sinn Féin propagandist Aodh de Blácam wrote to Hanna Sheehy-Skeffington that while the Treaty opponents could not expect the pope to side with them, perhaps the strength of their case would warrant a pious appeal from his Holiness to the Irish hierarchy. This would drag all the bishops' intrigues into the light and expose them to massive publicity, which, de Blácam claimed, they dreaded more than anything else. He blamed the bishops for the failures of the national movement, claiming that they had always smashed it at the critical moment for simoniacal reasons: 'It was they who broke our late movement, and so next time we must work to make the people consciously hostile to clerical power in politics. Then the Church will either reform itself, or else stand in with us from fear.'[137] He viewed the bishops' statements as instigating the Civil War, which he hyperbolically deemed 'the greatest scandal in the history of Christendom ... we would spare nothing to have it exposed.' He added that '[a] crime like this delivers the hierarchy into our hands.'[138] In a letter to Father Canice, a republican Capuchin, de Blácam accused the bishops of siding with perjury and badness against truth and charity. The only way for Ireland to ever truly be free was for the people to revolt against the bishops as well as England or for the Church to purify itself and join forces with those in the right, i.e. republicans.[139]

Republicans in America also contributed to the debate, often demonstrating theories and solutions far more radical than those found in Ireland. James Brown of Lynn, Massachusetts criticised the republicans in Ireland for failing to act against the bishops, who were the real leaders of the anti-republican movement and whose actions proved them as bad as or worse than the traitors of the Free State government.[140] Rather than stand against the bishops, Brown claimed that republicans threw themselves at their feet, causing the English to laugh at them and the rest of the world to heap scorn upon them: 'If instead of fasting or praying you had issued a boycott against Italian domination in Ireland as well as the boycott of Orange Belfast, and refused to go to church until your prisoners were liberated, your jails would be clear in a week and perhaps in less time.' Once the power of the Church was broken, he theorised, the remaining dominating factors would tumble like a house of cards.[141]

Several chapters of the AARIR issued resolutions protesting against the pastoral. The Terence MacSwiney Council (New York) decried the hierarchy's use of spiritual rank to lend support to Ireland's traditional enemies. It was resolved that the Council deplored the actions of the hierarchy 'as being un-Catholic, anti-patriotic, and calculated to subvert their prestige as the moral teachers of the Irish people.'[142] The Padraig Pearse Council (Chicago) issued a resolution threatening to 'excommunicate' the Irish bishops for supporting the English and Free State.[143] In December, 1922, the Council issued a startling resolution attacking what it referred to as the 'Roman Cabal'; 'The Resolutions put Rome, the Irish Bishops, the Freak State and England in the same bed, chloroforming them.'[144] The signing of the Treaty had been an act of supreme spiritual treason by the Invisible Government of the Roman Cabal and Irish Bishops, who had plotted with the English to create the Free State. The Council maintained that the bishops of Ireland and the Roman Cabal had sold Ireland to England for a price; 'Judas sold Christ for thirty pieces of silver and then went out like a man and hanged himself. Would that the Roman Cabal and the Bishops of Ireland would do likewise.'[145] The only way for Rome and the bishops to make amends was to publicly announce their support for the Irish republic. Failing that, the Council decreed that it would take concerted action with Irish republicans in America to withdraw their spiritual allegiance from Rome and initiate their own Church in America. They also importuned the republican government in Ireland to make the same demands on Rome.[146] The new Reformation never took place on either side of the Atlantic, though examples like this indicate that, though Catholic republicans would never admit such a thing, Protestantism had made its mark on criticism of the episcopate.

The resolution, which was widely distributed throughout Britain and Ireland, even appearing in the *Irish Independent*, was attacked by the *Irish Catholic Herald* as 'fanatical and criminal ferocity and insanity'. In the opinion of the editors, though, it was the logical and inevitable outcome of the methods, principles, actions and words of those who were upholding the Irish republic.[147] After the resolution received further press coverage, Peter Gannon, president of the Pearse Council, repudiated the resolution, claiming that a similar resolution had been brought before the council by a small group but had died in committee. The publication, he claimed, was the work of enemies of the republican movement,[148] though there is no proof of this.

Knowing how important clerical approval was to the devout Catholics of Ireland, many republicans were busy criticising the political activities of Free State supporting clergy while they were equally eager to show clerical support for their own cause, thus demonstrating yet again their double standard for clerical involvement. The few newspapers sympathetic to republicans were filled with articles proving clerical approval of republicanism. Michael O'Flanagan regularly contributed to the *Roscommon Herald* as 'A Western Priest'. While in republican possession, the *Cork Examiner* reprinted most of Patrick Browne's political articles and pamphlets.

The Connachtman, a republican weekly, frequently took statements out of context in an effort to make the clerical speakers appear sympathetic to the republican cause. In the 28 January 1922 edition, the Archbishop of Baltimore, Michael Curley, was quoted as saying that England's position in Ireland was analogous to a man who had seized his neighbour's house and then offered to let his neighbour use some of the rooms on the promise of good behaviour. The article implied that Curley was opposed to signing the Treaty, despite the fact that he had informed Harry Boland that he should return to Ireland and urge de Valera to sign it. In an even more brazen episode of manipulating quotations, in mid-April the newspaper included an article on a sermon given by Bishop MacRory in Belfast: 'There are several things in [the Treaty] that I dislike very much, and if my opinion was asked about it before it was passed and before the country came to be divided, I should have objected strenuously to some of it.' Rather than quoting the statement in its entirety, or even offering a full summary, the newspaper leaves out MacRory's actual pro-Free State message, ending simply with his comment: 'I have the greatest respect for Mr. de Valera and the men and women with him. I deeply appreciate and respect their patriotism.'[149] The majority of episcopal statements, though, were simply omitted from the newspaper altogether, including the April pastoral and all Lenten pastorals, which other broadsheets commonly printed in their entireties.

APPEAL TO THE VATICAN

Having had no luck changing the minds of the Irish bishops, on 19 March 1923 Eithne MacSwiney wrote to the Cardinal Prefects in the Vatican. She stated that while the Church had no more loyal followers than those in Ireland, that '[c]itizens of the Republic [of Ireland] will never swear allegiance to England, and the Bishops of Ireland have no more right to issue in the name of the Catholic Church, an order to them to do so, than the Sacred Congregation would have to issue an order to the Citizens of Italy to swear allegiance to the Kaiser of Germany when he was in the zenith of his power.'[150]

Many Irish Catholics took it upon themselves to appeal directly to the pope, hoping that Pius XI would see the wisdom in reining in the bishops. One such petition informed his Holiness that '[o]ur grevious [sic] sin, in the eyes of our Bishops, is that we refuse to recognise as legitimate the usurping Government now functioning in Ireland',[151] intimating that a secular issue had taken on a religious quality simply because the bishops made it so. Documents such as this had to have attracted some degree of interest in the Holy See, but a letter of complaint against the bishops from several priests of the Dublin diocese no doubt raised many more eyebrows than could letters from small groups of the laity. The priests informed the Vatican of the situation in Ireland using the standard republican narrative. They then presented their complaint:

> We the undersigned Priests consider ourselves bound to inform the Holy See that we feel certain that the Irish Bishops are guilty of a dreadful wrong to a vast number of Irishmen and women, that they are the cause of woeful scandal, that they are endangering the salvation of many, and that they are inflicting a grievous wound on the Church of God.[152]

The only correct course of action, as they deemed it, was for the bishops to stand by impartially, rather than take it upon themselves to decide on a purely political matter, as they had done, thereby abusing their spiritual positions by refusing the Sacraments to republicans. The priests noted that while they had not been able to seek the support of priests from other dioceses for this document, they were certain that such endorsements would be many in number.[153]

The call for an official republican appeal to the Vatican had been made almost immediately after the issuing of the October pastoral. In a communiqué dated 16 October, the republican Dáil called for President de Valera to formally and emphatically protest as Head of State to the Vatican against the unwarrantable action of the hierarchy in presuming to pronounce an authoritative judgement upon the political questions Ireland faced 'and in using the sanctions of religion to enforce their own political views and compel acquiescence by Irish Republicans.'[154] Count Plunkett had approached de Valera on 12 October about the possibility of drawing up a petition on behalf of all republicans. He had already begun consulting priests about proper procedure for a plea to the pontiff. Before the month was over, the committee that would draw up the appeal had already been put together. It consisted of Dr. Patrick Browne, Count Plunkett and Dr. Hugh Ryan with Dr. Conn Murphy acting as secretary. Mary MacSwiney and Cait O'Kelly were also involved in the production of the document.

The writing of an acceptable document proved extremely challenging given the variety of opinions held by the members of the committee. On numerous occasions, Browne expressed concern that Plunkett's contributions would make the appeal unacceptable to the pope. He believed it would be better to have no appeal at all rather than one that was rejected by the Holy See.[155] O'Kelly informed Hagan that even after all the safeguards they had put in place to keep Plunkett's 'malign influence' out of the document, he still managed to alter it. It was only after she had received the English draft to be translated that she saw it was full of Plunkett's 'overstatements and "Republican" delusions'.[156] After a week's work with Browne and Murphy, she was able to reshape it closer to the original upon which the committee had agreed. In spite of this, Plunkett's status as a papal count made him crucial to the petition process. Though the other members of the committee certainly wished to keep his involvement minimal, they could not risk upsetting him.

Concern was so great about the pope's rejection of the appeal that de Valera refused to allow either his name or Austin Stack's to be attached to the document. His excuse was that he did not want the appeal to be misrepresented as political rather than religious.[157] However, given the concern of papal rejection that emanated from both Rome and Ireland, it appears de Valera was hedging his bets by maintaining an unofficial involvement. Plunkett had originally wanted all republican TDs to affix their signatures, but it was eventually agreed that generally prominent Catholics would suffice. However, there was continued pressure for de Valera to sign. Arthur Clery threatened to remove himself from the delivery deputation claiming that without the signatures of TDs, the appeal was coming from 'a few nobodies without any weight'.[158] Murphy suggested de Valera sign not as the president but rather simply as a Catholic. De Valera remained resolute and Clery eventually gave way. Hagan fully expected de Valera to sign and had even wanted him to be part of the deputation that delivered the appeal to the Vatican.[159]

Monsignor Hagan played a peripheral but important role in the appeal process. Murphy sent Hagan a draft of the appeal in late October asking for criticisms and suggestions. O'Kelly and Murphy displayed no reservations about sharing all details about the process of writing and delivering the appeal. Hagan's attitude towards the entire situation is difficult to judge. He clearly was of the opinion that no good could come from the appeal. In a letter to Borgongini Duca, Secretary of the Congregation for Extraordinary Ecclesiastical Affairs, Hagan urged the Church to take a 'neutral and procrastinating attitude'. Whether because he reflexively felt compelled to try to keep the Vatican out of Irish affairs,[160] or because he feared that the Holy See would oppose the republicans cannot be ascertained. However, he strongly urged inaction on the part of the Vatican:

> Any action, even a negative one, on the part of the Holy See, may easily lead to developments and complications gravely prejudicial to the interests of religion for many a year to come; and I feel confident that I am voicing the views of the great majority of the Irish Bishops in venturing to point out that that great majority would earnestly desire to see as little intervention as possible on the part of the Holy See in Irish political or semi-political affairs.[161]

The appeal that resulted from the committee's work, an eighty-seven page document, mostly appendices, was delivered on 17 January 1923 by Murphy and Clery into the hands of Cardinal Gasparri, the cardinal secretary of state. Along with three interviews with Gasparri, Murphy and Clery had an audience with Pope Pius XI. The document, while very respectful towards papal and Church authority, presented a case for Irish republicanism that incorporated most of the more mainstream arguments against the actions of the Irish bishops. The authors claimed that of the two rival governments in Ireland at present, only the republican one had been confirmed by the votes of the people. The Provisional Government had received its authority from an act of Parliament and the English government, whose power in Ireland rested solely on force. The English had sought to impose their will upon Ireland during the talks that resulted in the Treaty. The results were partition and the Provisional Government, dominated by the power of the English government. The Provisional Government, besides robbing the majority of their popularly elected government, engaged in fraud, violence and an unjust war against the legitimate republican government and the people who continued to fight for it.[162]

While the writers of the appeal recognised the bishops as guardians of the beliefs and morals of their followers and accepted their right to pronounce on matters of morality, the pastoral made declarations inconsistent with what the appeal writers described as the fundamental laws of Ireland and inflicted harm and penalties on many Irish Catholics as a result. The first of these fundamental laws was that Ireland was a nation, recognised by all outside powers, except England, and therefore possessed the right of self-determination. Ireland's unique nationality was undoubtedly accepted by all the signatories of the pastoral letter. The second law was Ireland's right, as a nation, to maintain its territorial integrity. This right had been universally recognised by theologians, Catholic philosophers, the consensus of the people and even Pope Benedict XV. The Treaty and ensuing Provisional Government acknowledged the partitioning of the island and the existence of an undemocratic government of Northern Ireland dominated by the English government. This Protestant-controlled government had already subjected Catholics to atrocious acts of violence, thievery and refusal of employment. Whereas the Provisional Government tacitly accepted the oppression of Catholics in the north, the republican government refused to recognise either the northern government or the partitioning of the island. In doing so, only the republicans have remained loyal to the sacred duty fighting for the citizens of a free and united Ireland. The opponents of the republic had acted tyrannically and illegally, thus depriving the republicans of using many of the essential elements of constitutional action in support of the republican cause, which defended the fundamental laws of the nation. Due to the importance of the cause, the writers of the appeal stated with profound regret that to accept the decisions of the pastoral letter and concede the authority of the Provisional Government would be to act contrary to moral law.

The hierarchy's legitimisation of the Provisional Government, aside from being out of accord with traditional Catholic practice, was the result of the bishops' confusion of political ideas. Throughout the pastoral the bishops failed to make a distinction between the Provisional Government and the Dáil. More than once they referred to the Dáil of the Provisional Government, which was, in fact, a non-entity. Whereas Dáil Éireann had been elected by a clear majority to defend the Irish republic, the Provisional Government had not been designed by the Dáil. It did not exist in Irish law nor in the Constitution of the Irish republic. It was a foreign invention and completely incompatible with the sovereign authority of Dáil Éireann. Thus, the Civil War resulted in large part due to the Provisional Government's suppression of the republican government as established by the second Dáil as well as the coalition government.

Prior to the issuing of the pastoral, the authors noted, the bishops had accepted that the question of the Treaty was a legitimate subject for deliberation and discussion and that all Irish were entitled to their opinions. Because of this, the bishops proclaimed that they would refrain from making public their own opinions. However, they did not follow through on this decree, but rather declared in favour of one political party and imposed spiritual penalties on those who disagreed with them. Furthermore, they argued, in issuing the pastoral, the Irish hierarchy acted without precedent or parallel in any other nation. Through decades of revolutions and civil wars in Catholic countries, these Irish bishops stood alone amongst bishops as judging, on an official level, the legitimacy of any government. Rather than imitating the sound Catholic practice of impartiality so well illustrated by Pope Benedict XV during the rise of Italian fascism, the Irish bishops showed favour for one party over another and imposed severe penalties on those who opposed them in these political affairs. As the pope himself noted during the political turmoil in Italy, he had many followers on both sides of the conflict and so it was his job to understand the perspective of belligerents on both sides and work towards the salvation of as many as possible, regardless of political inclination.

The appeal concludes with the writers informing the pope that the draconian measures the bishops had taken against Catholic republicans ran a great risk of damaging Catholicism in Ireland simply because they hoped to protect one government over another. The writers begged that the pope do whatever he deemed necessary to bring an end to these measures.

Most press outlets dismissed the appeal as insubstantial and standing no chance of changing the Church's opinions. Some papers, though, published scathing attacks on the republicans for having the audacity to go above the authority of the Irish Episcopacy. The *Irish Catholic Herald* had previously issued an acidly sarcastic 'translation' of the republican Dáil's statement announcing its request for an appeal; 'The Catholic Bishops of Ireland hold the wrong political opinions. They think the Irish voters are the State. They are using the sanction of religion to enforce their opinions – to stop us from enforcing *our* opinions by means of revolvers and dynamite.' It continued: 'Their conduct is unwarrantable, because it has no warrant from us – no authority at all except their own degraded commonsense and their wild idea that the Catholic Church ought to have some connection with the Ten Commandments of God.'[163] The next month, the *Herald* published a more reserved, yet ironical piece that stated that the sight of Irish Catholics appealing to Rome against the hierarchy was edifying. The author asked if new Church law in Ireland was to be that the hierarchy had less authority than a committee of Catholic laity. The whole situation was, according to the article, ridiculous and, perhaps ignorantly, a repudiation of Catholic principles.[164]

Episcopal responses to the appeal were varied. On 31 October, after learning of the forming appeal, Archbishop Gilmartin wrote to Murphy hoping that if both sides accepted the decision of the Vatican a truce could come about as a result. In his response, Murphy informed the archbishop that while he too hoped for an honourable peace, the committee's only job was the preparation and submission of an appeal for the 'removal of grievous spiritual penalties on a large number of Irish Catholics solely because of their political opinions and actions.' They had no intention of asking the pope to make a decision regarding the legitimacy of the competing governments. They believed the Vatican would acknowledge that such a political question lies 'outside the province not merely of the Irish Hierarchy, but even of the Church itself as a whole.'[165] In a separate letter, Gilmartin protested that the bishops had not condemned the notion of the republic, but rather the methods by which that republic was being sought.[166] Bishop Foley offered to answer the republicans' case if they presented it to him in thesis form, though nothing more came of this.[167]

Other bishops were much less conciliatory towards the appellants. Harty uncharacteristically gave little thought to the possibility of the appeal presenting a problem for the hierarchy: 'We shall easily deal with the appeal if the Holy See desires a reply.'[168] Morrisroe believed that it was in the hierarchy's best interests to safeguard against a Vatican statement against them by sending two bishops to have an interview with Gasparri and outline a list of Republican atrocities.[169] Byrne believed that people who refused to obey the bishops would also refuse to obey the Vatican, and even if it issued an *ex cathedra* pronouncement, it would not be obeyed.[170] Logue responded that all 'real' Catholics would listen to the pope and the 'bad people … can scarcely be going more to the devil than they are going at present.'[171] He questioned how the hierarchy was in any way connected to political actions. The only charge that could be brought against the bishops, he wrote, was that they lamented the state of the country, which had been bad, and had since worsened, warned the people against crime, which was their duty, appealed for peace and expected the people to obey the present government. Nevertheless, he believed the bishops should remain publicly silent on the issue for the present.[172]

Logue was much more distressed at the end of 1923 when he discovered that Donal O'Callaghan, Lord Mayor of Cork, and Conn Murphy had travelled to Rome to have an interview with Gasparri and push the case of the appeal further. He was very upset by the circumstances of the trip and wanted to know how two private gentlemen, without receiving authority from anyone in a position to give authority, could act as ambassadors and receive an audience with the cardinal secretary of state and even the pope to make charges against the bishops.

Furthermore, he wanted to know how this could happen without prior warning being sent to the bishops.[173] He had little to fear though. In keeping with the Vatican's policy of non-intervention, Gasparri made vague promises to the men and tried to get them back to Ireland as quickly as possible, and they appear to have been disappointed with the trip.[174]

CONCLUSION

Three months after the appeal was lodged with Cardinal Gasparri, Monsignor Luzio arrived in Dublin as an Apostolic delegate, prompting many to believe that the appeal had finally drawn the Vatican into the Irish problems. Little came from Luzio's trip, which is the subject of the next chapter, but heated emotions. The Vatican chose a policy of non-intervention and neutrality, fearing that taking either side would alienate Catholics in the opposition. Even after the pope studied the situation in Ireland and decided to remain silent, republicans continued to look to the Vatican for support against the bishops. In May 1925, de Valera wrote to Pius that the bishops continued to abuse their authority to further their preferred political policy. Because they acted under the auspices of the leadership of the Irish Catholic Church, the scandal was resulting in serious injury to the prestige of the Church. In their assumption to decide on the constitutional question, de Valera continued, the bishops often condemned republicans using language that cast aside Christian charity. They discriminated against priests who remained loyal to the republic while giving free rein to Free State supporters, many of whom used their pulpits as political platforms or as rostrums from which they could attack republicans. He concluded that for the Vatican to do nothing about the situation could only add to the belief that it was hostile to Irish liberty, the consequences of which could be disastrous.[175]

The bishops had succeeded in their primary goals: the Free State government was firmly established, and by offering its support, the Church maintained its control on issues it deemed vital, especially education and health care. The bishops were firmly entrenched as the moral leaders of Ireland, and it would be decades before their authority was again questioned by so large a percentage of their flock.

When faced with the choices Irish nationalism offered after the

Treaty, militant republicanism and the Free State government, the bishops had no real decision to make. Even if the bishops had not been prone to accepting the course of action that called for an end to violence, the republicans believed in their goal with religious fervour. They wrote and talked about it as if it had parallel importance to Catholicism. This was, of course, a threat to the power of the hierarchy. If the republic held an equally high or, worst of all, superior position to the Church, the bishops had competition in the form of republican leaders. The Free State government, on the other hand, was a seemingly weak government,[176] under siege and in need of strong support and intellectual and philosophical guidance. By supporting the Free State and by extension the will of the majority, the bishops were able to maintain their strong social influence.

The true extent of their influence is certainly debatable. Clearly many republicans were outraged by the bishops involving themselves in the national question, but it appears that this was primarily due to concern over how it would impact on the Irish people in general. Ernie O'Malley believed that the only real bearing the bishops' actions had was on public opinion; 'Those people who supported the Republican movement resented the abuse of clerical power to suit political ends, but Republicans already had their minds made up, and despite the clergy, the press, and the Provisional Government, their views remained unchanged.'[177] In a statement reminiscent of Fr. Dominic's rejection of Cohalan's 1920 excommunication order, Packie McCluskey, a divinity student at Maynooth wrote to his brother, an IRA Adjutant and prisoner of the Free State:

> ...by way of advice there is no need to ask you to do nothing which your conscience tells you is wrong and as long as you do that you need not fear the statement of the Bishops. You can act without sin if you can say for sure that the above statement does not apply to you ... It is well to say that what would be a serious mortal sin for one to kill a soldier, might not be for another at all.[178]

Despite displaying a poor theological understanding of Catholicism, statements like this, as well as those of priests sympathetic to the republican cause, alleviated most of the spiritual concern that remained in the movement. Tod Andrews credited Patrick Browne's presence with assuaging any feelings of guilt Andrews might have had disobeying the Church.[179]

Is there evidence, though, that the bishops' statements had the desired effect on the populace? In a short yet insightful essay, Joe Lee contends that the bishops' political power ultimately derived from the people's willingness to accept their authority.[180] In other words, the bishops were listened to because what they had to say synched up with what the majority already thought. Furthermore, the episcopal condemnation of militant republicans seems to have had virtually no effect on popular opinion. Lee is sceptical of the condemnation as helping to legitimate the Free State government in the eyes of the public. The republicans' parliamentary gains during the 1923 General Election show that people were still willing to vote for them,[181] despite the bishops' and clergy's harsh words. Though Lee does not mention them, Fianna Fáil's 1926 electoral success and 1932 win demonstrate that a mere ten years after they had been punished by the hierarchy, republicans were democratically granted the right to run the nation they had violently opposed, indicating that the people gave the bishops' condemnations little thought.

Nor do the actions of the Cumann na nGaedheal governments indicate that the bishops achieved a greater degree of influence because of their endorsement. Education, health care and sexual morality stayed firmly within their remit, but politically, the bishops were largely ignored by the ministers. As will be argued in Chapter 4, even regarding issues as important and debatably moral as the government's execution and internment policies, the bishops' concerns were politely tolerated but largely ignored. Chapter 5 hopes to illustrate that though the hierarchy was unified in its abhorrence of partition, the bishops were essentially powerless in the matter and resigned themselves to abiding by the Free State government's expedient course of action. The most pressing issue for the hierarchy, though, was the possibility of the loss of religious authority because of their belief that the Vatican desired to involve itself more directly in Ireland. The republicans' spiritual threat could be fought directly. The same could not be said about the activities of the Holy See.

NOTES

1. Walter McDonald, *Reminiscences of a Maynooth Professor*, edited by Denis Gwynn (Cork, 1967 edition), p.126.
2. UIM, MacCaffrey papers, 27/21/5, McDonald, Cornelius Mulcahy and James Donnellan to MacCaffrey, 3 May 1919.
3. Walter McDonald, *Some Ethical Questions of Peace and War with Special Reference to Ireland* (London, 1919), pp.31–51.
4. *CB*, January 1926.
5. Walter McDonald, *Reminiscences of a Maynooth Professor*, p.263.
6. For more on the bishops and the nationalist movements during World War I, see Jérôme aan de Wiel, *The Catholic Church in Ireland, 1914–1918: War and Politics*. His work on how the 1916 partition concept and the 1918 conscription crisis radicalised many within the hierarchy is especially insightful.
7. AAA, O'Donnell papers, Box 6, *Irish Bishops on English Rule*.
8. Ibid.
9. Ibid.
10. CCCA, Sinn Féin tracts, U105, 'Cork Sinn Féin Pamphlets: No. 2. "The Bishop of Limerick and the British Constitution"'.
11. AAA, O'Donnell papers, Box 6, *Irish Bishops on English Rule*.
12. ICDA, 1921, p.507.
13. CAA, Harty papers, interview with Harty, 22 April 1921.
14. Ibid.
15. Quoted in Emmet Larkin, 'Church, State, and Nation in Modern Ireland', *American Historical Review*, 80 (Dec. 1975), p.1272.
16. AAA, O'Donnell papers, Box 6, *Irish Bishops on English Rule*.
17. ICDA, 1921, p.507.
18. AAA, O'Donnell papers, Lenten letter, 1921.
19. Dermot Keogh, *The Vatican, the Bishops and Irish Politics*, pp.60–61.
20. See David Fitzpatrick, *Harry Boland's Irish Revolution*, pp.190–1.
21. NLI, O'Ceallaigh papers, MS 27,712 (3), quoted in Curran's memoirs.
22. CDA, Cohalan papers, Lenten pastoral, 1921.
23. David W. Miller, *Church, State and Nation in Ireland*, p.465.
24. CCCA, U149, Dominic to Seán Hegarty, 15 December 1920.
25. *Belfast Newsletter*, 23 December 1919.
26. *FJ*, 29 November 1920.
27. Ibid.
28. Ibid., 26 November 1917.
29. AAA, Logue papers, box 2, folder 9, R. Pope-Hennessy to Logue, 4 March 1920.
30. IER, February 1920, 'Pronouncement of the Irish Hierarchy at a General Meeting held at Maynooth on Tuesday, January 27'.
31. IER, November 1920, 'Statement Issued by the Cardinal Primate and the Archbishops and Bishops of Ireland on the Present Condition of their Country'.
32. AAA, Logue papers, political documentation, clipping from *IC*, December 1919.
33. IC, 10 October 1920.
34. Ibid.
35. See Michael Hopkinson, *Green Against Green*, pp.52–7.
36. CCCA, de Róiste papers, U271/A/41, de Róiste journal, 10 December 1921.
37. UCDA, de Valera papers, P150/1653, Memo by Collins, 16 January 1922.
38. UCDA, O'Malley papers, P17b/116, O'Malley interview with Browne.
39. UCDA, de Valera papers, P150/2902, Byrne to de Valera, 3 January 1922.
40. UCDA, Mary MacSwiney papers, P48a/192, MacSwiney to the Archbishops and Bishops of Ireland, 11 December 1921.
41. TAA, Gilmartin papers, Curran to Gilmartin, 1 January 1921 [misdated, actually 1922].
42. See David W. Miller, *Church, State and Nation in Ireland*, Chapter 18.

43. See Jérôme aan de Wiel *The Catholic Church in Ireland*, Chapter 6.
44. AAA, Logue papers, box 3, Logue to Walsh, 14 March 1919.
45. *II*, 9 December 1921.
46. Ibid., 10 December 1921.
47. David W. Miller, *Church, State and Nation in Ireland*, p.490.
48. ICR, Hagan papers, Logue to Hagan, 10 December 1921.
49. ICDA, 1923, p.538.
50. Dermot Keogh, *The Vatican, the Bishops and Irish Politics*, p.80.
51. CCCA, de Róiste papers, U271/A/41, de Róiste journal, 28 December 1921.
52. AAA, Logue papers, Cohalan to Logue, 30 June 1921.
53. *CE*, 2 January 1922.
54. Ibid., 3 January 1922.
55. ICR, Hagan papers, Harty to Hagan, 18 February 1922.
56. See Chapter 5 of this volume.
57. ICR, Hagan papers, Sean T. O'Kelly to Hagan, 11 April 1922.
58. *II*, 10 December 1921.
59. ICR, Hagan papers, Mulhern to Hagan, 6 January 1922.
60. ICR, Hagan papers, Fogarty to Hagan, 11 April 1922.
61. Quoted in Michael Hopkinson, *Green Against Green*, p.35.
62. ICR, Hagan papers, Mulhern to Hagan, 15 April 1922.
63. *CE*, 12 April 1922.
64. Ibid., 6 April 1922.
65. Ibid.
66. DAA, Byrne papers, Logue to Byrne, 15 April 1922; GDA, O'Doherty papers, Box 45, No. 38, Gilmartin to O'Doherty, 5 April 1922; GDA, O'Doherty papers, Box 45, No. 42, Rbt. Browne to O'Doherty, 21 April 1922.
67. UCDA, Desmond FitzGerald papers, P80/279, 'Statement Issued by the Cardinal Primate and the Archbishops and Bishops of Ireland on the present Condition of Their Country', 26 April 1922.
68. Ibid.
69. Ibid.
70. Ibid.
71. DAA, Byrne papers, Logue to Byrne, 5 April 1922.
72. DAA, Byrne papers, Harty to Byrne, 8 April 1922.
73. *CE*, 27 April 1923.
74. *WP*, 22 April 1922.
75. CCCA, de Róiste papers, U271/A/45, de Róiste journal, 5 July 1922; ICR, Hagan papers, O'Dea to Hagan, 18 March 1922.
76. CCCA, de Róiste papers, U271/A/43, de Róiste journal, 27 April 1922.
77. See Chapter 1 of this volume.
78. ICR, Hagan papers, Hoare to Hagan, 4 January 1922.
79. *CE*, 20 July 1922.
80. *WP*, 26 August 1922.
81. Ibid.
82. *CE*, 31 August 1922.
83. Ibid.
84. Ibid.
85. IT, 25 September 1922.
86. NAI, Department of An Taoiseach, Executive Council minutes, 14 October 1922, PG28(a).
87. Until further notification, all statements, opinions and quotations come from: UCDA, Andrews papers, P91/99, 'Pastoral Letter of his Eminence Cardinal Logue, the Archbishops and Bishops of Ireland, to the priests and people of Ireland'. There are multiple versions of the pastoral available, though revisions were very slight.
88. *FJ*, 14 October 1922.
89. *CE*, 12 October 1922.

90. *IT*, 11 October 1922.
91. *DWNTH*, 14 October 1922.
92. Emmet Larkin, 'Church, State, and Nation in Modern Ireland', *American Historical Review*, p.1273.
93. Quoted in *DWNTH*, 9 December 1922.
94. ICH, 13 May 1922.
95. *PP*, 30 April 1922.
96. Ibid.
97. Ibid.
98. UCDA, de Valera papers, P150/1653, 'Episcopal and Clerical Injustice: Grave Responsibility of Churchmen'.
99. Analysis is based on recurring phraseology and arguments from those documents known to have been his own.
100. AAA, O'Donnell Papers, box 5, 'An Irish Priest's Appeal'.
101. Ibid.
102. DAA, Curran papers, Columban na Banban, 'False Pastors', pp.41–2.
103. AAA, O'Donnell papers, 'Ghosts—Other Ghosts or The Priests and the Republic'.
104. Ibid.
105. Ibid.
106. Ibid.
107. GDA, O'Doherty papers, box 45, no. 51, Logue to O'Doherty, 2 November 1922.
108. AAA, O'Donnell papers, 'Ghosts—Other Ghosts or The Priests and the Republic'.
109. Ibid.
110. DAA, Curran papers, Columban na Banban, 'False Pastors', p.9.
111. UCDA, O'Malley papers, P17a/153, 'A Priest', 'Reply to the Pastoral issued by the Irish Hierarchy in October 1922'.
112. DAA, Curran papers, Columban na Banban, 'False Pastors', p.43.
113. UCDA, O'Malley papers, P17a/153, 'A Priest', 'Reply to the Pastoral issued by the Irish Hierarchy in October 1922'.
114. GDA, O'Dea papers, box 39, no. 203, JJ O'Kelly to O'Dea, 10 August 1922.
115. DAA, Curran papers, no. 204, Hagan to [unknown bishop], 22 August 1922.
116. ICR, Hagan papers, Curran to Hagan, 20 July 1922.
117. ICR, Hagan papers, O'Muireadaig to Hagan, 24 September 1922.
118. DAA, Curran papers, Hagan to Curran, 13 October 1922.
119. UCDA, de Valera papers, P150/2909, de Valera to Mannix, 6 November 1922.
120. DAA, Byrne papers, O'Connor to Byrne, 21 August 1922.
121. UCDA, de Valera papers, P150/1653, 'The Refusal of Absolution in Mountjoy: Questions that should be answered'.
122. UCDA, O'Malley papers, P17a/163, Frank Gallagher, 'The Bishops' Pastoral: A Prisoner's Letter to His Grace the Archbishop of Dublin', 12 November 1922.
123. Hopkinson agrees with this perspective, stating that the Army Executive had entered the war because it had been declared against them. Michael Hopkinson, *Green Against Green*, p.119.
124. UCDA, O'Malley papers, P17a/163, Frank Gallagher, 'The Bishops' Pastoral', 12 November 1922.
125. Ibid.
126. UCDA, Mary MacSwiney papers, P48a/195, Eithne MacSwiney to Byrne, 28 February 1923.
127. Désiré-Félicien-François-Joseph Cardinal Mercier (1851–1926): Archbishop of Mechelen, Belgium; known for staunch resistance to German occupation of 1914.
128. DAA, Byrne papers, O'Moore to Byrne, 11 October 1922.
129. DAA, Byrne papers, Kettle to Byrne, n.d.
130. DAA, Byrne papers, An Old Republican to Byrne, 16 October 1922.
131. UCDA, FitzGerald papers, P80/745, Mary MacSwiney to Byrne, 5 November 1922.
132. UCDA, FitzGerald papers, P80/745, Byrne to Mary MacSwiney, 8 November 1922.
133. UCDA, de Valera papers, P150/1653, 'Statement prepared by Count Plunkett on behalf of Republican women'.

134. GDA, O'Dea papers, box 39, no. 199, O'Daly to the hierarchy, 9 November 1922.
135. UCDA, de Valera papers, P150/1653, 'The Case for the Republicans of Ireland'.
136. Ibid.
137. UCDA, FitzGerald papers, P80/736, de Blácam to Sheehy-Skeffington, 27 July 1922.
138. Ibid.
139. UCDA, FitzGerald papers, P80/736, de Blácam to Canice, 27 July 1922.
140. NLI, Sheehy-Skeffington papers, Ms 41,178/40, James P. Brown to Hanna Sheehy-Skeffington, n.d.
141. Ibid.
142. GDA, O'Dea papers, box 39, Resolutions passed by the Terence MacSwiney Council of the AARIR, 22 October 1922.
143. KDA, Fogarty papers, Resolutions adopted by the Padraig Pearse Council of the AARIR, 14 October 1922.
144. KDA, Fogarty papers, Resolutions adopted by the Padraig Pearse Council of the AARIR, 9 December 1922.
145. Ibid.
146. Ibid.
147. *ICH*, 20 January 1923.
148. Ibid., 27 January 1923.
149. *The Connachtman*, 15 April 1922.
150. UCDA, Mary MacSwiney papers, P48a/195, Eithne MacSwiney to the Cardinal Prefects, 19 March 1923.
151. UCDA, Andrews papers, P91/98, Undersigned to Pope Pius XI (signatures missing), n.d.
152. UCDA, Mary MacSwiney papers, P48a/196, Undersigned priests of the Dublin Diocese to Pope Pius XI, (1922). Unfortunately, the signatures have been lost.
153. Ibid.
154. UCDA, de Valera papers, P150/1653, Dáil Communiqué, 16 October 1922.
155. UCDA, de Valera papers, P150/1654, Fr M. Kingston to de Valera, 7 December 1922.
156. ICR, Hagan papers, O'Kelly to Hagan, 12 December 1922.
157. UCDA, de Valera papers, P150/1654, de Valera to Murphy, 10 December 1922.
158. UCDA, de Valera papers, P150/1654, Murphy to de Valera, 12 December 1922.
159. UCDA, de Valera papers, P150/1654, Murphy to de Valera, 13 December 1922.
160. For more on this, see Chapter 3 of this volume.
161. ICR, Hagan papers, Hagan to Borgongini Duca, 13 November 1922.
162. Until further notification, all statements, opinions and quotations come from: UCDA, de Valera papers, P150/1656, Committee of Irish Catholics to Pope Pius XI. Translated from the French by Chris Davies and the author. See Appendix C for the petition, appendices omitted.
163. *ICH*, 2 December 1922. (Emphasis in original.)
164. Ibid., 20 January 1923.
165. UCDA, de Valera papers, P150/1654, Gilmartin to Murphy, 31 October 1922; UCDA, de Valera papers, P150/1654, Murphy to Gilmartin, 2 November 1922.
166. DAA, Curran papers, Gilmartin to Curran, 18 November 1922.
167.   UCDA, de Valera papers, P150/1654, Seumas O'Donovan to de Valera, 25 October 1922.
168. ICR, Hagan papers, Harty to Hagan, 30 December 1922.
169. GDA, O'Doherty papers, box 45, Morrisroe to O'Doherty, 23 January 1923.
170. DAA, Byrne papers, Byrne to Logue, 19 November 1922.
171. DAA, Byrne papers, Logue to Byrne, 22 November 1922.
172. DAA, Byrne papers, Logue to Byrne, 21 January 1923.
173. DAA, Byrne papers, Logue to Byrne ('Confidential'), 17 December 1923.
174. GDA, O'Doherty papers, box 46, no. 96, Hagan to O'Doherty, 17 November 1923. See the next chapter for more on Vatican policy.
175. UCDA, de Valera papers, P150/1927, de Valera to Pope Pius XI, 12 May 1925.
176. Perceived versus actual weakness of the government is touched upon in Chapter 4.
177. Ernie O'Malley, *The Singing Flame* (Dublin, 1978), p.172.

178. UCDA, Desmond FitzGerald papers, P80/342, Packie McCluskey to Edward McCluskey, 23 December 1922.
179. C.S. Andrews, *Dublin Made Me* (Dublin, 1979), pp.260–1.
180. J.J. Lee, 'The Birth of the Modern Irish State: The Larkin Thesis' in Stewart J. Brown and David W. Miller (eds), *Piety and Power in Ireland, 1760–1960: Essays in Honour of Emmet Larkin* (Belfast, 2000), p.149.
181. Ibid., p.153.

3

Rome Rule?:
Vatican Involvement in
Irish Affairs

In the early twentieth century, the Catholic hierarchy of Ireland arguably enjoyed more freedom from the Holy See than the bishops of any other predominantly Catholic nation. The ultramontanist Paul Cardinal Cullen, famed Archbishop of Dublin during the middle of the nineteenth century, had brought the Irish hierarchy under control and had realigned it to conform with the directives coming from Rome, but this was not to last. With the political influence bishops and clergymen gained by supporting Parnell, alongside the weaker leadership of Cullen's successor, Edward Cardinal McCabe, followed by the naming of outspoken nationalist William Walsh as Archbishop of Dublin in 1885, the Irish Church regained much of its independence towards the end of the century. Looking for a way of recovering authority over the Irish hierarchy, the Vatican chose to use the issues of boycott and the Plan of Campaign to remind the bishops of their duties to obey Rome. After the fact finding mission of Ignacio Persico in 1887, Pope Leo XIII issued *Saepe Nos*, the papal Encyclical against the Plan of Campaign, in 1888.[1] The bishops, most of whom had supported the Plan, resented Vatican interference in Irish affairs and fought the pope's decision, upsetting both Rome and London, while further cementing their place within the realm of nationalist politics. The Vatican's plan failed and the bishops found their position stronger than it had been in recent memory.

Over thirty years later, the Encyclical of 1888 was an unpleasant memory for Irish nationalists, including the bishops, who knew what sort of complications could arise from Vatican involvement in Irish affairs. During the war for independence, there was widespread belief that English influence would create an atmosphere of hostility to nationalist Ireland within the Vatican, and the fear was that the Holy See would issue a pronouncement on the Irish situation. The bishops faced the added possibility of Rome becoming interested enough in Ireland to send another delegate, possibly with the goal of establishing a permanent Vatican presence in Dublin, which would serve as a check on their power over the national Church and something against which they could not raise any complaint. For the Irish bishops, Rome was a useful ally, but one that threatened their hegemony if it became too interested in their activities.

Nor were all the members of the Free State's Executive Council, most of whom were devoutly Catholic, eager to see interest in Ireland emanating from Rome. Recognition to any degree from the Church would be a welcome boost to the state's legitimacy, but interference would run the risk of playing to Protestants' and unionists' fears of a Free State that took orders from the Vatican, and would ruin any potential reunification with the North. Cosgrave was wary due to his close friendships with many of the bishops, especially Archbishop Byrne and Bishop Fogarty, who was the president's frequent riding partner. Because of this, ministers had to be careful in the tack they adopted with the Holy See. Likewise, despite republicans' repeated appeals to the Vatican for its intervention and their welcome reception of Monsignor Luzio, it seems the opponents of the Treaty were just as doubtful of the Holy See involving itself in Irish affairs unless it was directly to benefit their cause. In short, it would appear that unionists' cries of an independent Ireland submitting to 'Rome Rule' were far from the mark. Irish Catholics maintained the strong independence that had frustrated the Vatican for centuries.

THE REPUBLICAN RECTOR

Monsignor John Hagan, rector of the Irish College, Rome from 1920 to 1930, played a large and important role in Vatican–Irish relations during this period. He was the Irish hierarchy's representative in Rome and was well-known amongst the Curia. He had regular audiences with Popes Benedict XV and Pius XI and Cardinal Gasparri, the cardinal secretary of state under both. He considered it his duty to keep the Vatican out of Irish affairs, especially those that were predominantly political; a mantle he had inherited from his predecessor, Monsignor Michael O'Riordan. He was passionately involved in the nationalist cause and considered it one of his primary duties to ensure that Ireland's welfare was not overshadowed in the Vatican by what he believed to be a large, powerful, anti-Irish English lobby. His primary concern was that this English agency had achieved a level of influence which made his job all the more difficult. In early 1921 he wrote about the Vatican: 'If an Irishman speaks or writes about happenings in Ireland, his words are discounted and set aside on the plea that they are those of a partisan; whereas the most violent Englishman or anti-Irishman is listened to with respect, and evidently his words do not fall on deaf ears.'[2]

His influence cannot be denied, but his thoughts, predictions and advice must be understood within the context of his biases and personality. An authoritative biography is yet to be written on Hagan.[3] However, his vast correspondence provides a fascinating and useful source from which to glean much of his character and outlook. The result of careful examination is a picture of a resolute separatist who maintained a near-paranoid fear of English influence, primarily through Cardinals Merry del Val and Gasquet, within the circles that directed Vatican policy on Ireland. His letters and published writings, including his many contributions to the *Catholic Bulletin* as 'Scottus' from his years as vice-rector, are peppered with theories bordering on the conspiratorial about England's steady attempts at using the Vatican to end popular support for the Irish fight for independence. He believed the English were trying to use the love and reverence that Irish Catholics had for their religion against their national aspirations. If they could convince the Vatican to speak against Irish nationalism, the movement would be deflated and countless supporters would abandon it.[4] Unfortunately for him, his theories of English domination within the corridors of the Vatican do not withstand close academic scrutiny.

If one takes Hagan at his word regarding English influence in Rome, there is little doubt that the Vatican's British–Irish policy was practically dictated by London. However, his bias against England coloured his every political thought. Also, Hagan was prone to pessimism and his statements were often on the verge of histrionic. Hagan's vice-rector, Michael Curran, often displayed a more objective, less pessimistic grasp of the state of diplomatic struggles going on within the Holy See. He was certain that prior to early 1920, the Irish nationalist movement had received no positive promotion in Rome. However, through the hard work of Hagan and the naming of Donato Cardinal Sbarretti, who served as Prefect of the Sacred Congregation of the Council, as Cardinal Protector of the College, English domination of attitudes towards Ireland dissipated.[5] This did not mean that Curran looked upon the struggle as won. He believed that many men in important positions within the Vatican were strong English supporters, including Cardinal Gasquet, his private secretary, Dom Philip Langdon, OSB and Cardinal Merry del Val, all of whom had grown up in England and maintained close ties with their native country. This was hardly an optimistic picture, but it was substantially more positive than Hagan's, who wrote to Archbishop Harty that there were only four cardinals to whom they could look for sympathy, with two potentially sympathetic cardinals, and this among all the cardinals in the Vatican. The rest, he claimed, were pro-English.[6]

Curran, too, was perhaps sometimes prone to an overly-glum perspective regarding Ireland's influence within the Vatican. Dermot Keogh theorises that both men flattered the English lobby with more power than it actually had, and that the English actually maintained a healthy respect for Irish influence in Rome.[7] In large part, ironically, this was due to the influence exerted by Hagan and Curran, but the Holy See's apparent openness to Irish entreaties also contributed to English concerns. Count Plunkett claimed that he had a private audience with Benedict XV in 1916 which lasted for nearly two hours. During this meeting, Plunkett informed the pope that an uprising had been planned and that the men and women of the executive pledged the republic to the fidelity of the Holy See. The pope, according to Plunkett, gave his Apostolic Benediction to those who were facing death for Ireland's liberty.[8] Again, at the beatification of Oliver Plunkett, Count Plunkett met with Benedict, and the pope congratulated him on representing the republican cabinet.[9] If Plunkett's accounts are accurate, then it would appear that the Irish separatists enjoyed the sympathy of Benedict XV. Hagan, though, generally discredited displays like this. He claimed that most people in Rome were full of words of sympathy for Ireland, but these words were rarely followed by positive actions.[10]

Plunkett's pre-Rising meeting with the pope went almost completely unnoticed at the time, but resurfaced in 1933, causing concern among some within the English Catholic circles. In late May 1933, the *Irish Press* published a statement by Plunkett describing his private meeting with Benedict and the papal blessing issued to the men of the Rising. The story quickly made it into *The Times* of London, causing a great deal of consternation for retired diplomat and devout Catholic Sir Esme Howard. Howard wrote to his cousin, the former Lord Lieutenant of Ireland, Lord FitzAlan, that Plunkett's statement could greatly affect the position of the Catholic Church in England if it became widely believed in Protestant circles. It could give rise to the rumour that the pope had supported the Rising and lead to waves of anti-Catholic propaganda. Howard asked Monsignor Bernardini, Cardinal Gasparri's nephew, to contact the retired cardinal secretary of state with the request that an official denial be issued in the *Osservatore Romano* which could then be forwarded to *The Times* and the English Catholic papers.[11]

The denial was issued a week later, though Gasparri refused to attach his name to it, claiming that as he had not been referred to in Plunkett's statement, it was not proper for him to do so.[12] It was a good example of Gasparri's diplomatic skill, as it stated quite plainly that Benedict had not blessed the Rising. However, it failed to mention the blessing imparted upon the men, which had been Plunkett's contention all along. Given Gasparri's penchant for carefully selected words, it is quite probable that Plunkett had, in fact, secured Benedict's blessing for the people involved in the Rising, and that the denial was worded so as to appease the English Catholics while avoiding the need to lie.[13]

Despite Howard's deep concern for the scandal that could arise from Plunkett's statement, FitzAlan was much less worried. Now that the issue had been addressed, he preferred to cease drawing attention to the whole affair, hoping that it would be forgotten. Plunkett, in his estimation, was deemed an eccentric joke, even by the Irish. Any additional action would just play into the hands of those in the press who were opposed to Catholicism.[14] Judging from the lack of any further press attention, FitzAlan was correct. However, this brief tempest in a teapot is important because it highlights the concern some English Catholics felt about the position of their Church, highlighting that it did not enjoy the strength feared by the Irish.

The position of the English Catholic Church was also a concern of Cardinal Gasquet, who, according to Hagan, was one of the principal opponents of Irish nationalism in the Curia. Shane Leslie, Gasquet's admirer and biographer, described the Cardinal's feelings towards Irish politics and Monsignors O'Riordan and Hagan as those of bewilderment.[15] Contrary to Hagan's fears of Gasquet's desire to keep Ireland firmly connected to Britain, Ireland was of little concern to him. Nor did Gasquet's actions indicate that he was opposed to Irish national aspirations. He was a close friend of former Vicar General of the Franciscans, Fr. David Fleming, whose Irish nationalist sentiments were well-known. He even recommended to Benedict in April 1916 that Archbishop Walsh of Dublin should be elevated to the rank of cardinal to make the Irish Catholics content.[16] Given Walsh's strong, public nationalist feelings, this was not the manoeuvre of a man who was vehemently opposed to self-government for Ireland.

Gasquet had virtually been the sole British representative in the Vatican prior to the foundation of the British mission in December 1914.[17] His pro-British stance during the war also angered Irish nationalists. Gasquet's relations with Fleming were severed, and students of the Irish College no longer saluted him. Through this, though, Benedict continued to look to Gasquet to act as an umpire for the English Church, which the pope found truly puzzling.[18] Though Leslie fails to mention Ireland falling under Gasquet's remit, O'Riordan obviously believed this to be the case; a suspicion he passed on to Hagan.

As Leslie's complimentary account of Gasquet's Vatican career shows, he was a rather powerful individual who enjoyed the close confidence of Benedict XV. However, his voice was loudest during the war, when he feared that Britain's enemies were gaining an advantage in influence. After the war ended, Gasquet, a scholarly man who suffered ill-health for most of his life, was able to return to his academic work, which he did with relish as the Vatican's archivist and librarian. With this, British representation suffered a setback and his involvement in the Vatican's international policy virtually ended, though his Irish critics did not comment upon this occurrence or its impact on Irish representation, which was significantly strengthened.

Aside from Gasquet, Cardinal Merry del Val was roundly regarded by Irish nationalists as another of their most vehement adversaries in the Vatican. Merry del Val retained close ties with his native country despite living elsewhere since his teenage years. He had been called upon to offer his expertise on the English Church during Pius X's papacy, and Benedict XV described him as: '*Multo Inglese!*'[19] Just as Irish fears of Gasquet's involvement were greatly exaggerated, so too were those of Merry del Val's influence, which had virtually disappeared with the elevation of Benedict. As cardinal secretary of state, Merry del Val had excluded della Chiesa's name from the cardinal list several times before Pius X placed it there himself. Less than four months after his elevation to cardinal, della Chiesa became Pope Benedict XV, and Merry del Val was no longer cardinal secretary of state. Part of this was due to Benedict's desire to focus on international diplomacy and his move away from Pius X's anti-modernism campaign, of which Merry del Val had been one of the prime movers, and Benedict had been one of the potential victims. Christian charity aside, the sometimes acrimonious relationship of the two men undoubtedly played its part. As a final act of degradation, Benedict asked Merry del Val to vacate his rooms.[20] This was not a man who had any real say in Vatican policy on Britain and Ireland.

*   *   *

Once the Anglo-Irish Treaty was signed and ratified, Hagan became reticent about discussing his political views with those who did not share them. In a rare display of forthrightness, he told Archbishop Gilmartin that he was disappointed with the Treaty; '[W]hile it is so satisfactory in most things of a substantial nature, it is attended by the galling limitations which though they mean very little in fact are all-important as symbols.'[21] However, he would have difficulty voting either way because of the divisions within the Dáil, the people of Ireland and most importantly the army. In his opinion, the fighting men should have the last word. Like so many other republicans, Hagan clearly adhered to a Rousseauian view of democracy – some have more of a right to be heard than others.

The rare instances when the bishops allowed themselves to discuss Hagan's political philosophy show that some of them were concerned that their representative in Rome was unsympathetic or possibly even opposed to their own views. Cardinal Logue expressed such concerns after receiving a letter from Cardinal De Lai in which De Lai cited a confidential conversation between an Irish bishop and a religious about the political affiliation and ideas of Hagan. During the conversation, the bishop terminated all discussion of the matter when he stated plainly that Hagan did not represent him in Rome.[22] According to Logue, De Lai found this to be in accord with many others' attitudes towards Hagan and wanted an answer from the Primate regarding the level of confidence the Irish hierarchy had in their rector.[23] Logue stated that even Pope Benedict had been disturbed by Hagan's involvement in Irish politics. During an audience, the pope informed Logue that there had been strong opposition amongst many cardinals in the Curia against granting Hagan a prelature, and Benedict was concerned about the incongruity of an ecclesiastical college being made a political centre. Logue, himself, expressed disapproval of the fact that every time he had stayed in the Irish College as a guest he found that it was constantly frequented by Sinn Féin delegates.[24]

Archbishop Byrne agreed with Logue that Hagan was not in political sympathy with the hierarchy, and as a result the bishops were left bereft of much of the assistance the rector of the Irish College was in a favourable position to give. He could have provided the help they so needed during the recent difficulties, but Hagan's political outlook prevented this to a large degree. Having said that, Byrne believed Hagan had not acted contrary to the wishes of the bishops since the issuing of the October pastoral. He theorised that if called upon, Hagan would even be prepared to carry out the interests of the bishops if that was their desire.[25] It does not seem that Byrne was eager to test his theory.

Bishop Cohalan, who was also concerned about Hagan's political leaning, wrote to the rector in early 1924 to express his feelings. He informed Hagan that both he and Curran were regarded throughout Ireland as the Roman agents of the republicans and not of the bishops. As they were the official agents of the hierarchy, this was unacceptable; 'I think you ought to be on the Bishops' side, or so neutral and non-political that you could not be quoted in opposition to the Bishops. You are doing yourselves a good deal of harm.'[26] It was believed by some that Hagan's republicanism all but exterminated his chances of receiving a bishop's hat, though he stated on several occasions that if nominated, he would refuse to accept.

Undoubtedly some of Hagan's unpopularity among the Roman Curia was a result of his aggressive attitudes and actions, which some-times were known to rankle even his allies. One of the four cardinals

Hagan believed to be sympathetic to the Irish cause, Vincenzo Vannutelli, Dean of the College of Cardinals, had refused to interfere on Terence MacSwiney's behalf during the Lord Mayor's fatal hunger strike. Hagan never forgave Vannutelli for this and, as a result, never again invited him to any function at the Irish College.[27] He was even more caustic towards perceived enemies. In 1920, a man named Leonard Hawksley politely requested some information from Hagan so that the College could be entered into a publication recording the British residents in the Roman area. Hagan scathingly replied that he did not concern himself with whether or not the College was entered into the publication as it was not a British college. Furthermore, he believed that the intention was for the creation of a league of some variety, which he bluntly proclaimed he had not the remotest intention of joining.[28]

Even after the Free State was fully operational, Hagan continued his Anglophobic activities. In a letter to Gilmartin, he mentioned a sum of money which had been sent from Tuam to be lodged to the pope. Hagan wrote that he would do this at his first convenience, but only after King George had left the city. He thought the pope would command him to pay his respects to the monarch and he was not prepared to do this.[29] In early 1922, he proudly informed Archbishop Gilmartin that he was carrying on Monsignor O'Riordan's attitude toward all British representatives in Rome by refusing to cultivate any relationship with them. This, he said, displeased the Vatican.[30]

Hagan took every opportunity to proclaim his Irishness, which as a non-Irish speaking cleric living in Rome, whose connections to Ireland had, since 1904, been limited to vacations, personal communication and relations, and what he read in newspapers, generally took the form of defiant Anglophobia. This same pattern can be seen with others, including Archbishop Mannix, another republican-sympathising cleric whose vocation had limited his connection to his native country. Both men fit into the category of the Irish abroad who, according to Bishop Mulhern, were least qualified to dictate terms to those in Ireland.[31] The safety of distance allowed their principles to guide their thoughts and actions because they did not have to deal with the violence and strife for which their principles were responsible.

Even if the British had possessed the strong influence within the Holy See which Hagan feared so much, the relationship between

Ireland and Britain was complicated enough that objective outsiders working in the Vatican would still have been anxious to avoid involvement. On the one hand, the Vatican was reticent about speaking out against Great Britain. It was one of the most powerful and stable nations in post-war Europe, if not the world, and to risk upsetting it would be diplomatically foolish. Doing so could also indirectly harm the Catholic Church in England and the largely Irish Catholic Church of Scotland. On the other hand, pressuring the Catholics of Ireland to acquiesce to the demands of a Protestant state could prove equally disastrous. It could result in another case of the hierarchy speaking out against the pronouncements of the Church and the Catholics of Ireland following their local leaders over those in Rome, as had been the case to a large extent in 1888.

FEAR OF ROMAN INTERFERENCE

The threat of Vatican involvement in Irish affairs was always present in the thoughts and rumours of nationalists. Archbishop Clune of Perth, while visiting Europe from 1920 to 1921, had interviews with Pope Benedict XV, Cardinal Merry del Val, and Monsignor Cerretti, during which he ascertained 'beyond any shadow of doubt' that a pontifical document was ready to be issued on the Irish situation: 'Though on the surface it was to condemn violence on each side equally, the real purpose seems to be contained in the remark of Card. Merry del Val, that it was time to remind the Irish people that there was such a thing as the fifth Commandment.'[32] Clune was convinced that the document would be detrimental to, potentially even disastrous for nationalists. Hagan described the potential papal letter as one that was designed not to be an open condemnation of Sinn Féin; 'it was rather to condemn deeds of violence on all sides, but in substance it would be taken by both friend and enemy, to be a death-blow aimed at Irish aspirations.'[33]

Clune and Hagan agreed that the best Benedict could do regarding the Irish situation was issue a document demanding a public investigation, made up of an international tribunal, into the acts of violence. They argued that the people of Ireland would be satisfied with this action and the British government could not reasonably object. To combat Merry del Val and the alleged English domination of the Vatican's attitude regarding Ireland, they also felt that there needed to be a constant pro-Irish presence in the Vatican, preferably an intelligent and multi-lingual bishop. He should be sent as a plenipotentiary and furnished with all necessary authorisations to speak and act for the Irish hierarchy.[34] The two men agreed that they, along with sympathetic men like Bishop Amigo of Southwark and Archbishop Mannix, could affect the necessary influence when called upon, but to counter the constant presence of Anglophiles an equally constant Hibernophilic presence was crucial. As Hagan stated once the perceived threat of a papal condemnation of violence had abated: 'For the moment the danger is over, but seeing how swiftly opinions can be changed, it would be unwise to close one's eyes to the possibility of thunder and clouds gathering at any moment.'[35]

Such a storm appeared on the horizon in October 1921 when Pope Benedict and King George communicated via telegrams regarding the re-opening of negotiations regarding affairs in Ireland. The exchange between the two leaders was little more than a formality, but it caused the resurfacing of republican fears that the Vatican's policies were guided by the pro-British lobbies. Benedict's wire stated very plainly: 'We rejoice at the resumption of the Anglo Irish negotiations and pray to the Lord with all our heart that he may bless them and grant to your Majesty the great joy and imperishable glory of bringing to an end the age long dissension.'[36] The King's response was as simple and formulaic as the Pope's: 'I have received the message of Your Holiness with much pleasure, and with all my heart I join in your prayer that the Conference now sitting in London may achieve permanent settlement of the troubles in Ireland, and may initiate a new era of peace and happiness for my people.'[37]

Irish reaction to the telegrams is highly intriguing. On the one hand, no harsh words could be found for the pope's wire. Despite the fact that Benedict's language granted George all authority and responsibility over the situation, Hagan described the wording of it as harmless, possibly even good.[38] His only concern was the absence of a telegram to the Irish, which made him suspicious that British interests were involved in Benedict's wire to the King for their own propaganda purposes; a suspicion he shared with Seán T. O'Kelly as well as many in Ireland.[39] It was believed that George's response had been inspired by unionist press baron Lord Beaverbrook and drawn up by Bishop Cowgill of Leeds.[40] A memo prepared during the Anglo-Irish peace conference noted that while the absence of a papal telegram to the Irish people was an unfortunate step that allowed for misunderstanding, the substance of the telegram was not offensive to the Irish cause at all.[41] Conversely, furore was raised in the republican camp over George's telegram. Liam de Róiste described the British telegram as 'being intended manifestly to befog the Irish people and the world',[42] and de Valera took great offence at what he perceived to be the king's inference of Ireland as a subject nation.[43]

Seizing the moment to further proclaim Ireland's independence, de Valera sent a telegram to the pope on behalf of the Irish nation. Rather than engage in the single sentence style exchange of Benedict and George, de Valera sent a four paragraph piece that thanked the pope for his interest and paternal regard in the welfare of the Irish people. He criticised the ambiguities of the King's telegram, adding that the troubles were not 'in' Ireland, but rather between the two nations, and that the Irish people did not owe allegiance to the British King. He informed the pope that the Irish people longed to be at peace with the British, 'but the same constancy through persecution and martyrdom that has proved the reality of our people's attachment to the faith of their Fathers proved the reality of their attachment to their natural freedom, and no consideration will ever induce them to abandon it.'[44]

De Valera recognised that this move may have been a disconcerting one to members of the British government, but he felt that it was necessary.[45] He believed that the British had to be taught that propaganda stunts of this nature would not be allowed to pass unchallenged. Without being openly critical of the pontiff's telegram, de Valera expressed the primary fear it had roused in republican ranks; 'We cannot expect the Vatican to recognise us, but we have a right to expect that it will not go out of its way to proclaim its denial of recognition as it did by addressing King George alone as if he were the common father, so to speak, of both disputant nations.'[46] De Valera, like Hagan and O'Kelly, believed that the Vatican's telegram was inspired by British sources and that, while it might not have been intended to be damaging to the cause of Irish republicanism, its recognition of the struggle as a purely domestic one for the monarch implicitly pronounced judgement against the Irish independence movement.[47]

Whether or not British representatives had used their influence to get the telegram issued, it was clear to Curran that the cardinal secretariat of state was very pleased with itself and believed it was coming to the rescue of the negotiations for peace and was certain that its action would be met with applause on both sides.[48] That this was not the case caused concern, resulting in Vatican officials asking Hagan how they could remedy their gaffe. The Vatican did not repeat the mistake in December, when, upon receiving news of the signing of the Treaty, it issued telegrams of congratulations to both King George and President de Valera. Along with the Luzio visit, this demonstrates that the Vatican's policy towards Ireland was designed with the best of intentions and to be beneficial to all sides. However, those involved in the planning and execution were ignorant of the repercussions their actions would have, especially with an Anglophobic rector telling people in Ireland that the English were always the architects.

* * *

The greatest fear was of the possibility of a representative of the Vatican being assigned to Ireland. Apostolic delegates and nuncios were common throughout the world, but many in Ireland, especially the majority of bishops, were opposed to the prospect of a Church authority responsible directly to the Vatican amongst them. Despite Hagan's protestations as late as March 1923 of receiving no news of Monsignor Luzio's mission, he had informed Bishop MacRory at the close of 1921 of the possibility of an Apostolic delegate being assigned by Rome. In his response, MacRory stated that he refused to believe such rumours and would pray that nothing more would come of them as such a delegate would do only harm.[49]

The day after Achille Cardinal Ratti's elevation to the papacy, Hagan warned about the possibility of a representative of the Vatican being sent to Ireland. In a letter to Archbishop Byrne, Hagan theorised that the re-appointment of Gasparri as cardinal secretary of state by the new pope, Pius XI, meant that the policy of extending diplomatic relations with new states would continue. He expected that an Apostolic visitor would be appointed who would eventually be promoted to nuncio. Further countering his later claims of ignorance, he went so far as to predict that the visitor would be Luzio, who, if an official from Rome had to be appointed, was 'the best of a bad lot by long odds'.[50] Keogh has convincingly shown that Hagan was all but certain that Pius and

Gasparri were bent on installing a permanent Vatican delegate in Dublin. They were backed, he believed, by Luzio for reasons of a personal nature. In other words, Hagan was convinced that Luzio was vying for the position.[51] In Hagan's opinion, the British government was as eager to see a nuncio in Dublin as the Vatican. The Vatican wanted representation in the British Isles, but a nuncio in London would wound English scruples. Dublin was, therefore, an ideal choice. A representative could serve as a semi-diplomatic mouthpiece for the British when necessary and would be an ideal agent for keeping unruly clergymen in line.[52]

Like Hagan, Curran believed that the real purpose of Luzio's mission was to pave the way for an Apostolic delegation. Hagan was convinced that many in the Free State government, including George Gavan Duffy, then Minister for Foreign Affairs, and a man he deemed to have 'the brain of a sparrow', wanted a representative in the Vatican.[53] Curran went one step further in theorising that the Free State government was eager for a Vatican representative in Dublin. It would allow for the government to receive the recognition the ministers were craving, and he was even of the opinion that some of them had been angling for this mission.[54] Curran believed Logue would try to use the delegate to condemn the republicans, while they, in turn, would seek a condemnation of the bishops' censures. Also, the British government would try to use the delegate as a replacement for the Irish bishops, who, since the conscription crisis, could not be counted on for their support.[55] As long as Ireland was tied to England, Curran argued, a permanent delegation would generate nothing but suspicions in Ireland. It would be seen as the puppet of the English hierarchy, or, worse yet, English politicians. He surmised that if a delegate was sent, no one outside London and Rome would be happy 'and the next generation of Irishmen, lay and ecclesiastical, will not be praying for the churchmen and republicans who called in, or caused to come in, the outsider.'[56]

Hagan and Curran were justified in noting the diplomatic aspirations of the new papacy, though any pessimistic concerns were largely unfounded. Ratti had served as Apostolic visitor, later nuncio, to the newly independent post-war Poland and was known for his affinity for stimulating the Church's diplomatic relations and his openness to accepting democracies more than his papal predecessors. This meant that there was strong potential for the Vatican to want to strengthen relations not just with Ireland but also with Britain. However, Pius XI's decision to maintain Gasparri as secretary of state worked against any supposed anti-Irish machinations on the part of Merry del Val, as the two men maintained a strong rivalry. Merry del Val's English sympathies were easily offset by the secretary of state's and pope's internationalist outlooks.

Cardinal Logue's support for a papal representative in Ireland caused concern among the many clerical opponents to the idea, and by November Hagan was more concerned than ever that a Vatican appointment of a representative to Ireland was an inevitability. He urged Byrne to write a letter to Pius XI or himself as the rector, the hierarchy's mouthpiece, explaining matters as they stood in Ireland. Failure to do so, especially when taking into consideration the upcoming appeal against the bishops' October pastoral,[57] could result in the appointment of a delegate. Worse yet, if a delegate was appointed, the appealers could proclaim that they had drawn blood against the bishops, 'and moreover a cute Italian may find it an easy way of ingratiating himself into public favour by making his first step to consist in suspending or revoking the provisions contained in the recent Episcopal pronouncement.'[58] He reiterated these feelings in a letter to Bishop O'Donnell written the same day. His concerns were much more detailed than they had been in the missive to Byrne. He had heard that the pope was on the verge of issuing a strong pronouncement on the situation in Ireland, though he failed to discuss any details; 'More definite still is the news of the projected appointment of an Apostolic Delegate, so definite indeed that the name of Luzio is a matter of gossip in interested circles.'[59] Perhaps Hagan considered Luzio to be 'a cute Italian'.

Cardinal Logue's welcome to a papal delegate in Ireland was predicated on the notion that he was only to be assigned temporarily and only to gather information on the present situation in Ireland.[60] In this matter he differed from most of the other members of the hierarchy who, like MacRory, believed that a papal representative could not help the situation, regardless of the limitations placed upon him. Hagan was perfectly willing to assert to the proper Vatican authorities that the Irish bishops were not in favour of the Holy See getting involved in the Irish situation, 'but as long as Armagh is knocking at the other side of the door my words are not likely to carry great weight.'[61]

Bishop O'Donnell, ever the diplomat, met with Byrne regarding the issue, then travelled to Armagh where he met with Logue. He informed Hagan that Logue, who had closer and more regular contact with the Holy See than anyone else in Ireland, was convinced that any pronouncement from the Vatican would be helpful to the bishops and their pastoral.[62] This misguided optimism on the part of Logue probably partially explains his disappointment with the Vatican's representative's attitude when he arrived four months later. Hagan later thanked O'Donnell for this information and stated that the Vatican had decided to again remain aloof from the Irish situation. In fact, according to Bishop Amigo, it had been looking for any decent excuse to stay out of Ireland. However, as usual Hagan warned of the possibility of future papal interference if pressure on the Holy See renewed.[63] That interference was just a few months away, and no one was prepared for the tension it created.

MONSIGNOR LUZIO'S MISSION

In early March 1923, Hagan reported back to Ireland that he had heard a few weeks previously that Luzio would soon be sent 'for the purpose of bringing the warring leaders together and making peace.'[64] Indicative of the Irish bishops' lack of uncritical support of the Holy See, Bishop O'Doherty deemed the idea of a peace mission as 'ludicrous … There *must* be some other motive behind his mission, unless people there have gone crazy.'[65] Hagan reiterated his now well-worn suspicions that the mission was not simply one of peace. His greatest concern was the news he received from his Vatican informant that the real purpose of Luzio's mission was to ascertain whether there would be great objection on the part of the clergy or laity to a delegation of a permanent nature.[66] This was the news Hagan was sending back to the Irish bishops. In his usual style, Hagan portended Vatican involvement in Irish affairs as problematic and something which must be fought:

> Should [Luzio's trip] mean the establishment of a Delegation, I need not say that it bodes no good for the future of the country; but on this head I do not think there is need for me to say much to you, except that the only thing that can impede it will be the uncompromising attitude of a united hierarchy; and I am not so sure that this can be counted on.[67]

With news like this coming from Rome, it is no wonder the bishops greeted Monsignor Luzio so coldly. It is fascinating, though, that Cardinal Logue, a man who had been pushing for Vatican involvement against the wishes of his fellow Irish ecclesiastics, was far from welcoming when the Apostolic delegate arrived.

When on 7 March the *Freeman's Journal* reported that the Vatican was sending Luzio on a special mission to Ireland to extricate the Irish bishops from their difficulties with republicans, Logue refused to comment. He claimed that rumours had been floating around Rome for ten months but he had heard nothing of any mission. On 15 March, the *Freeman* interviewed Logue who again stated that he had not been given any prior indication of Luzio's visit and that, like the Irish public, he had only been made aware of the mission with the press release of the previous day. In fact, Logue had been privy to rumours coming out of Rome that a delegation was to be sent, but he dismissed these as typical. If there was to be a representative of the Vatican sent, he surmised, surely Cardinal Gasparri would have made mention of it in one of his many letters.[68] Once Luzio's mission had been made public, it was common knowledge among clerical circles that the Cardinal 'must feel a bit put out' that Gasparri did not send word of Luzio's visit.[69] Given Logue's pride, this is something of an understatement. Combined with Hagan's ominous predictions, these factors were probably what initially soured Logue on the mission.

According to Luzio, the Vatican intentionally kept the mission a secret from the Irish hierarchy,[70] though he fails to explain the logic behind this move. However, given the examples of communications between themselves and Hagan dating as far back as 1921, those with access to such information could not have been surprised by the mission or even the delegate himself. Their displays of ignorance were little more than public protest at the attempts of Vatican officials to keep Luzio's mission a secret. Logue, as he publicly admitted, had been privy to repeated reports of Luzio's pending delegation for months, but his wounded pride at the lack of official announcement from Rome undoubtedly caused him to feign ignorance.

It was quickly seen that any Vatican representation was done independent of the wishes of the hierarchy.[71] The repeated protestations of ecclesiastics that they were caught unaware of the mission as recorded in the newspapers only served to strengthen this perception, resulting in the belief that their authority was being trumped by the Holy See. As one priest reported: 'To the man in the street the visit means that the Pope was doubtful of the theology of the Joint Pastoral and he sent his man over to find out whether the Republican appeal against it should be upheld!!!'[72] Whether this was true or not, such public images were harmful to the bishops' authority and this was undoubtedly one of the primary reasons they did not welcome Luzio upon his arrival.

The bishops' first public display of indignation came on 15 March in the form of an interview with 'a distinguished city priest' who the *Catholic Bulletin* believed, probably accurately, to be a mouthpiece for the hierarchy.[73] He declared that Luzio was not coming as a matter of state, as that would have required activity between the Free State government and the cardinal secretary of state's department. With this stroke, the Irish Catholic Church began the campaign to reduce the importance and meaning of Luzio's mission. To further reinforce the prerogative of the bishops to speak on Irish issues, the priest speculated against Luzio's interfering in their decisions. When asked to comment on the probable outcome of Luzio's mission, he responded:

> I do not know why you should ask that question. The Irish Bishops have pronounced. That is the law of the Church. Here in Ireland they are the Church. It may be possible that there may be additional affirmation of the law of the Church, but I do not know why that should be necessary. But if *Monsignor Luzio is coming here on business of State* he is coming to make perfectly sure of the facts.[74]

In the same issue, the *Freeman* reported that an unnamed Church authority described Luzio's mission as 'purely private and unofficial ... The law of the Church is that the Irish Bishops are supreme, and that the Bishops of any country, speaking as a body, are supreme in matters of dogma as a teaching authority, and you may take it that this mission is one to make sure of certain facts and not to upset or interfere with the jurisdiction of the Irish Hierarchy.'[75]

Keogh is of the opinion that Luzio found it extremely difficult to understand the cold reception he received.[76] On the contrary, his report demonstrates that he had rationalised the problems using his limited knowledge. He postulated that the secrecy with which the Vatican had acted had been interpreted by the bishops and the Free

State government as a lack of respect and served, particularly in the case of the bishops, to create a hostile atmosphere against him.[77] This, coupled with the dissemination of what he believed to be exaggerated and possibly erroneous information by Gasquet's secretary, Dom Philip Langdon, made Luzio admit: 'in such a situation it is easy to imagine the coolness and suspicion with which the Bishops received me. Even my closest friends were trying to avoid me.'[78] He obviously was unaware that Hagan had also caused concern with his talk of a permanent delegation.

* * *

Salvatore Luzio arrived in Ireland on 19 March to very little fanfare. He considered Armagh his first port of call, and so paid a visit to Logue almost immediately upon arrival to Ireland. Logue received him kindly, but told him that he was expected to bring approval from Rome for the bishops' actions in relation to the October pastoral, and therefore to reject the appeals made by the Republicans. '[Luzio] answered that that was not [his] mission, but that [he] did not believe that the Holy See would ratify the Bishops' decision on the legitimacy of the government of the Free State, since in doing so it would enter into a political question in which it did not wish to be involved.'[79] He further upset Logue by requesting that he join him in a mission to the republican leadership. With the Cardinal's noted disapproval of the republicans and their methods, this was a foolish mistake and one of two tactical blunders, according to Keogh, from which Luzio's mission never recovered.[80] At this same meeting, Luzio requested a letter of introduction from Logue to persons of influence, especially Cosgrave. Astonishingly, Logue responded that he did not feel he had authorisation to do so. At this point, Luzio was aware that he did not find himself in a favourable environment.

Luzio appears to have limited himself to visiting the more important members of the hierarchy and those men with whom he had personal ties. This is supported by Patrick Browne, who recalled in an interview that Luzio had ignored all the bishops except the few who had been on staff with him at Maynooth.[81] Upon arriving at the Archbishop's Palace in Drumcondra, the visitor found Byrne to be as indignant towards the mission as Logue. Demonstrating an almost Gallican degree of independence, Byrne very respectfully informed Luzio that the Holy See should not concern itself with these matters, because for politics in Ireland there was the Free State government, and for religion, there were the Bishops, neither of which needed unwanted mediation. Luzio summed up his interactions with the Archbishop simply with: 'I had lost.'[82] Keogh credits Byrne's attitude in large part to what the Archbishop felt was an insult on the part of Luzio. Despite using the Shelbourne Hotel as a base during his mission, Luzio had not visited Byrne until after his trip to Armagh.[83] It is difficult to believe that a mistake as trivial as this could have been more influential to the outcome of Luzio's mission than the points discussed above regarding rumours and the insult of secrecy.

Archbishop Gilmartin met with Luzio in early April but did not comment beyond saying that the visitor had already met with prominent republican leaders and was preparing to meet with government leaders shortly.[84] Bishop O'Donnell finally met with the monsignor in mid-April. He had wished him all success in his mission of peace from the onset, but he was not optimistic.[85] By this late stage in Luzio's trip, he believed that doing anything beyond collecting information would prove difficult.[86] Harty had been the sole voice in the hierarchy that found Luzio's involvement encouraging and potentially beneficial. He had expressed hope that Luzio could help resolve a situation that was nowhere near reaching a settlement.[87] Even after the government and bishops soured on Luzio's intervention, Harty apparently still welcomed his assistance.

Aside from the examples discussed above, one of the most striking aspects of hierarchical attitudes towards the Apostolic delegate is the deliberate reluctance to articulate their opinions or reactions. Apart from very occasional letters and press statements delivered through an intermediary, the majority of bishops remained silent on the issue of Luzio's trip. This is not altogether surprising, however. Primarily, their lack of communication with Luzio, generally due to his decision not to call upon them, coupled with his almost complete public silence, left many of them in the dark. They knew little about his trip or his intentions. They made little attempt, though, to learn anything for themselves. Keogh states that the bishops engaged in an almost complete boycott of Luzio,[88] but that is probably too strong a term for episcopal relations with the delegate.

Unlike the episcopal snubbing of Archbishop Mannix during his 1925 visit,[89] the bishops had no choice but to display reserved courtesy towards the Vatican's representative. Mannix came of his own accord and he had the option of declaring his visit as unofficial, but Luzio was ordered to Ireland by Pius XI, and so any affront against the Monsignor was an insult against the Church itself. The bishops were not at all pleased that the Vatican was suddenly taking an interest in the Irish Church. There was general concern that Luzio might not give his or the Church's full support to the recent hierarchical backing of the Free State government. They were also motivated by the possibility of his calling for a nuncio. However, they could not criticise Luzio or work against him for fear of the repercussions emanating from Rome. As a result, for the most part the bishops did little other than hope the issue would resolve itself in their favour.

This is evident in the lack of Irish diocesan archival sources on the subject of Luzio's trip. The bishops wrote very little to each other about the matter, and even more telling is the lack of communication between bishops and Hagan. For several members of the hierarchy, Hagan was a valuable and trusted correspondent regarding all matters. He was in regular communication with most members of the hierarchy and was the recipient of many letters from Gilmartin, O'Donnell, Mulhern, Fogarty and MacRory, many of which displayed levels of openness and friendship that are rare among the guarded missives of bishops. Yet, despite the fact that the number of letters arriving in the rector's post did not diminish during Luzio's trip, only a handful from bishops mention the visitor, and then only a few of those with anything more than a passing reference. It seems that, despite their concerns about Luzio's trip and possible implications for their control of the Irish Church, they had very little to say on the matter. Secondly, as the unofficial representative of the Irish hierarchy in Rome and the primary source of ideas and rumours circulating through the Vatican's halls, Hagan would have been the natural choice for correspondence even of those who were not close to him. Logue is a perfect example. His letters to the rector demonstrate a formal, business-like relationship between the two men, and as has been shown he was not completely trusting of Hagan's political orientation, but in his letters to Hagan he was perfectly open regarding the Luzio affair. Even the Cardinal had little to say about Luzio once the mission was underway.

Patrick Murray contends that the Free State government and most bishops viewed Luzio's trip primarily as a republican event through which the Vatican gave the forces of anarchy a wholly unacceptable moral respectability and constitutional status.[90] As the discussion below will hopefully demonstrate, when pertaining to matters of the government, this statement is perfectly apt. However, Murray's joining of the two groups into this overarching statement oversimplifies the concerns of the hierarchy. Many bishops did share such complaints with the government, but it simply cannot be argued that this was their first and foremost concern. With rumours floating around of an expected nunciature, as well as the possibility of Luzio speaking against their October pastoral, the bishops were bracing for potential damage to their authority from the one source against which they could not fight back.

THE FREE STATE VERSUS THE VATICAN

Before Luzio arrived in Ireland, as the press tried to make sense of the surprise thrust upon the island by Rome, the *Freeman* referred to Luzio's trip simply as that; 'It is evidently not a "mission," much less a delegacy, and, least of all, a political excursion.' Surely the hierarchy and/or Government would have received proper consultation in accordance with Rome's strict etiquette.[91] However, the *Freeman* attempted to remain optimistic. It declared that if the Vatican required a first-hand account of the situation in Ireland it could not choose a better man than Luzio. His keen, legal mind would not be captured by political sophistry, by which the paper clearly meant the rhetoric of de Valera.[92] The next day, a Vatican statement on the visit was published. The statement assured the Irish that '[Luzio's] errand has not the permanent or definite character of a mission, but aims rather at providing the elements necessary to enable the Holy See to choose the most opportune line of conduct, with a view to hastening the pacification of Ireland.'[93] Foreshadowing the critical manner with which it covered the visit a month later, the *Freeman* stressed the point that the statement was only semi-official and that this was the first time the Vatican had admitted that the visit was not made for personal reasons.

During the first half of his trip, the press and government were relatively silent regarding the visitor. Until the middle of April, Luzio received scant press coverage beyond the occasional update of his location. Partially this was also due to the seeming innocuousness of his trip. Luzio, himself, was largely to blame as well. He refused to discuss his mission with reporters. There was an element of paranoia to this silence. He was convinced that he was being watched around the clock, to the degree that 'a person sent from England' booked himself into the same hotel. Fearing that this unwanted attention was intended to catch him 'at foul play', Luzio 'always beat a gentle path'.[94]

It was only on 18 April that coverage turned critical of Luzio. On that day, the *Freeman* announced that as they understood the matter Luzio's mission had ended, an interestingly timed declaration given that Free State delegates sent to petition the Vatican for the termination of the mission did not even arrive in Rome until 22 April, and any statements that Luzio had a mission to the government were unfounded. He had not provided the proper credentials and the cardinal secretary of state had not informed the Free State of his coming, which is exactly what would have been expected had the mission been intended to be in any way political. Luzio would make a disastrous mistake if he gave countenance to the attempts of the republicans to use him to gain status and 'to be placated by agreements and compromises made over the people's heads and behind the people's backs'.[95]

The visitor dismissed the *Freeman's* article regarding the matter of credentials. Before leaving Luzio had been given a pontifical letter by Cardinal Gasparri, as well as a letter signed by Gasparri addressed to Logue. The latter, which the *Freeman* published on 23 April, informed the Primate that Luzio was being sent to Ireland to gather information on the unusual conditions as well as to facilitate peace.[96] Luzio saw the article for what it was: a government press statement;[97] 'The truth of the matter is this: that the Free State government wanted the Vatican to address the letters directly to them, thinking that in doing so, the Holy See would be seen to support the decision of the Bishops, recognizing it as the legitimate government, and that afterwards, the Republicans would cease their campaign.'[98]

Luzio was in Ireland for over three weeks before he made an effort to have an audience with any members of the Free State government. Whether this move was a diplomatic gaffe or an orchestrated manoeuvre was left out of his report, but it was widely regarded as a slap in the face of the government. More insulting yet, he had spent a great deal of this time meeting with prominent republican leaders, many of whom were wanted criminals who had been denied the sacraments and excommunicated by the pronouncements of the bishops. On 11 April, Luzio finally visited Cosgrave in an unofficial capacity, presenting no credentials and deeming the meeting as a necessary courtesy. Luzio described the reception he received as kindly and believed that Cosgrave, unlike some other ministers was disposed to peace by negotiation, understanding perfectly that in this way a lasting peace could be made, while peace after the devastation of the enemy would be momentary and ephemeral since the republicans would disturb it again as soon as they had the means.[99] However, shortly after this meeting, relations between the monsignor and the Free State government soured. So much so, in fact, that when Luzio requested a second unofficial interview with Cosgrave he was refused.

It was not until Luzio's secretary, Canon Conry, spoke with the press on the afternoon of 16 April that the Free State government decided that action must be taken. Conry said that the monsignor would intervene in the Civil War when a sufficient number of public bodies requested he do so. He said that Luzio 'would go in as Pius 11th' who had told him to leave himself free for peace once he had settled the ecclesiastical matter that drew him to Ireland, which was the October pastoral.[100] This statement was confirmed by Luzio himself on several occasions. In an interview published in the 7 April issue of the *Freeman*, Luzio states that he would support any movement which gave a promise of peace, provided the desire for his intervention was clearly expressed by the people. After Conry's announcement, Luzio was quoted in the *Irish Independent* as saying that he was now free to devote his services to the interests of peace, and in this capacity he would be representing the pope. He said that his services would be at the disposal of all who desired peace, regardless of political convictions.[101] According to his report, this was one of the primary reasons he was sent to Ireland. Luzio boastfully reported to Gasparri that he understood the political situation very well after several days, a statement most historians of the Civil War would find humorous. In his mind, 'the Free State army, aided as it was by England, had already virtually subjugated and defeated that of the Republic, and that it was only a question of months before it would end in a complete rout.' At the same time, 'given the stubbornness of the republicans until their army was totally defeated, they could still, through various means, bring about carnage and immense destruction.' As a result, he felt compelled to intervene in the conflict as a desire to avoid this.[102]

Patrick Hooper, editor of the *Freeman's Journal*, informed Seán Lester, who worked in the Department of External Affairs and had formerly been news editor of the *Freeman*, that Luzio's action of inviting local authorities to appeal to him would likely prolong trouble. Lester stated that '[t]he general feeling seems to be that if the Government is not to find itself in a predicament with the Irish people apparently appealing outside the authority of that Government, some action should be taken.'[103] With sentiments like this circulating throughout Dublin, the Government decided that the time for action had come, though they needed little convincing. Kevin O'Shiel, circulated a memorandum stating that 'designing and imprudent advisers' were trying to use Luzio's position to force the Government into calling a truce with the republicans and opening up parleys with de Valera. While some of these people were said to be foolish but well-meaning, others were in sympathy with de Valera and were probably acting under his directions, since their conspiracy was on the verge of collapse. He was undoubtedly trying to improve the terms of settlement for his party. The plan seemed to be to send representatives to local bodies and have them request Luzio work for peace.[104] O'Shiel contended that should Luzio agree to engage in these manoeuvres 'at this late stage in the day it will be tantamount to an act of gross discourtesy to the Irish Government, in so much as he had refused to recognise the lawful Government of the Land to which he had come as an Envoy from perhaps the greatest world power, and had endeavoured to engage whilst in that country, on a line of policy in direct conflict with the policy of the *de jure* and *de facto* Government.'[105]

Before receiving O'Shiel's memorandum, on 17 April, the Executive Council agreed that a letter should be drawn up and submitted to Cardinal Gasparri pointing out that Luzio had come to Ireland solely to settle an ecclesiastical matter, but was now 'endeavouring to interfere in the domestic affairs of the country without having sought or received permission from the Government'. Furthermore, the letter was to point out that his actions encouraged the forces of disorder at a time when they were near their nadir, both in terms of strength and morale.[106] The letter, dated one day after the *Freeman* had announced that Luzio's mission had ended, stated that the Government learned that once Luzio had disposed of his ecclesiastical duties he got in touch with some of the rebels 'against this Government and indeed against the social and moral order'.[107] These rebels, Cosgrave informed Gasparri, had attracted lawless and criminal elements, as well as those of noxious moral, social and political theories. Moreover, the Government's forces, having waged a long and steady campaign against these rebels, had overcome the enemy 'and the revolt has now almost burnt itself out, leaving but dying embers soon to be quenched, if not encouraged to flame again by hopes foolishly aroused of achieving some even partial success.'[108]

Unfortunately, the letter continued, Luzio's intervention in the political affairs, without ever officially presenting himself to the Government as authorised by the Holy See to intercede in Ireland's political matters, gave renewed strength to the irregular forces and supporters. This fact, coupled with his clerical position and his previous ecclesiastical mission, gave his actions 'a special character. The consequence is that the embers of revolt are not allowed to die. The unskilled hand of a man who has no real knowledge or understanding of the affairs of this country is fanning into continued life the destructive fires with which he should not meddle.'[109] Cosgrave wished the cardinal secretary of state to know that the circumstances of Luzio's visit 'are in the highest degree embarrassing to the Government in its onerous work of restoring peace and order' and so that serious mischief may not result from his actions, they urged the pope to recall Luzio once his ecclesiastical business was completed. The letter finished with a flourish, noting: 'In the meantime [Luzio's] intervention in the domain of politics or rebellion cannot be countenanced by [Cosgrave's] Government.'[110]

Armed with a copy of this letter, Seán Murphy arrived in Rome on 22 April. His mission was to convince the Vatican to recall Luzio immediately. He and Marquis MacSwiney met with Cardinal Gasparri on Tuesday 24 April. The Free State representative complained that Luzio's visit, in addition to the republican appeal against the bishops and the Vatican's failures to contradict grave statements published in the Irish press regarding this appeal, could foster the impression the Vatican was giving undue consideration to the republicans' claims. Luzio had even planned to attend a republican meeting at Count Plunkett's house, and it was only through occupying Plunkett's house and preventing the meeting that the government had saved the Vatican from being compromised internationally.[111] Gasparri listened intently and told the men that he would see the pope immediately, returned after some time and informed them that Luzio's ecclesiastical business was finished and that he would be recalled immediately. It was only two weeks later, on 6 May, that Luzio departed Ireland. Why his superiors did not recall him immediately, as they said they would, is intriguing and hints that perhaps Gasparri was only paying lip service to the Free State's concerns.

A REPUBLICAN SYMPATHISER?

Throughout the controversy, the *Catholic Bulletin* had supported Luzio's mission and had endeavoured to defend the monsignor from the harsh treatment he received in the *Freeman* from the middle of April on, though one has to consider that in this its editor, P.T. Keohane, was as eager to lambaste the *Freeman* and the government's censorship of the press as he was to support Luzio. The *Bulletin* reported that 'the visit of His Excellency demonstrated the will of the Irish people for the establishment of an honourable peace. The Irish people, despite the absence of a free press, rose to the occasion and made it plain that they desired the intervention of Monsignor Luzio for the achievement of their earnest desire.'[112] However, the article declared that the government, which defended its existence by claiming to be the manifestation of the democratic will of the people of the twenty-six counties, had refused to listen to the people and had done everything in its power to block Luzio's efforts; 'No official explanation has so far been made as to why the will of the Irish people in this matter was not complied with. They have been refused a request without a word of justification or palliation from anybody in authority. We doubt if a more glaring example of contempt for the desire of the people was ever placed on record.'[113]

Luzio's appraisal of the opposition to peace talks was even more damning than that of the *Bulletin*. Despite receiving 'hundreds and hundreds of telegrams, letters and agendas' calling for peace and proposing that he act as an intermediary, Luzio found that several Free State ministers, especially O'Higgins, as well as England and the hierarchy all looked upon his involvement and his mission 'less than favourably'. He was, fittingly enough, most shocked at the attitude of the bishops in regarding the public's voice on the matter of peace as non-existent and therefore not to be heard.[114] While he made no mention of democratic principles, he presented the situation as one of those in power unjustifiably suppressing a minority and keeping the nation in a state of war when peace was so desired. Luzio's presence had been rejected by the ministers and the bishops and he seems to have become quite bitter towards them. His attitude was also influenced by the reception he received in republican circles. Republican influence can be read in the fact that, in his report, he described these people as those who 'desired, as the Irish have always done, the complete freedom of their native land.'[115] Keogh contends that with no real assistance from the hierarchy or Free State government, Luzio inevitably fell prey to the designs of the anti-Treaty politicians.[116] However, Luzio was moved more by the rank and file republicans who turned to him for support and re-assurance than their political leaders, though he displayed great respect for them as well.

Many on the republican side flocked to Luzio shortly after his arrival, and most were delighted at the warm reception they encountered and the sympathetic ear he seemed to possess. Mother Stanislaus of the Loreto Convent described Luzio as quiet but very approachable; 'It is a comfort to think we are not utterly abandoned and that the Holy Father is mindful of his "erring" children.'[117] Sister Mary O'Daly wrote to Hagan: 'When I saw Mgr. Luzio in Dublin he gave me the impression that he realized the justice of our cause – the Irish Republican cause; he said among other things that he believed the Republicans to be the better of the two parties. Told me to send those Republicans who were refused absolution to him.' In her opinion, this act of his was very powerful. For a representative of the Holy See to accept tacitly that republicanism was not contradictory to the Church made it 'a just fight and not displeasing to almighty God.'[118] Sean T. O'Kelly's wife, Cait, described Luzio as very kind and patient, adding that it required patience to sit and understand, or even pretend to understand the republicans' grievances. She failed to see the point, however, of airing complaints to Luzio. 'I can't imagine myself that Mgr Luzio came to Ireland to console the Republicans and the down trodden.'[119] While he was still engaged in his mission, she heard rumours that he was actually a republican sympathiser, but she accredited this to his fair-mindedness. Regardless of his political sympathies, she was convinced that Luzio was eager for peace and he believed a free election would settle the whole matter. Once there was peace, there would be no use for the sacraments to be used as a weapon and they would cease to be a state monopoly.[120]

The only prominent republican who defied this line of thinking was Patrick Browne. He challenged the notion that Luzio was as sympathetic to the republican cause as was believed. While it was true, Browne argued, that he did not agree with the actions of the bishops, he had refrained from urging the pope to speak against their statements in order to allow them to save face.[121] Judging from the voluminous amount of republican correspondence praising Luzio months after his mission, it would appear Browne did not convince many people of his hypothesis. In an interview with Ernie O'Malley years later, Browne seemed to have changed his attitude toward the monsignor. He told O'Malley: 'Luzio was a consolation to the Republicans, as he was very nice to them.'[122]

De Valera was very much convinced of Luzio's sympathetic attitude, and he saw it as the primary reason so many thronged to him. He had had one interview with the monsignor during which they discussed matters generally. De Valera was pleased to say that the views Luzio expressed during their meeting 'were the proximate cause of my recent public offer. If peace is the outcome you certainly will have more than a share in bringing it about.'[123] When he did not feel obligated to resort to flattery, de Valera expressed fondness for Luzio, but he believed the visitor had succumbed to the peacemaker's temptation of pressuring the weaker side to give in though he should have stood rigidly for impartial justice.[124]

The manner in which the bishops were perceived to fight against Luzio's mission provoked anger and indignation from many on the republican side. After Luzio had returned to Rome, de Valera reported to Hagan that while he was in Ireland, he had received 'scant courtesy from the Bishops'.[125] From the information he had gathered of late, Hagan believed that Cardinal Gasparri was very upset with the bishops for what he felt was the cold shoulder they exhibited to the Papal delegate.[126] Keohane hoped that Pius XI would not take umbrage at the indifference and discourtesy shown to his representative by the bishops and especially the government. He worried that the Orangemen and Freemasons would have a good laugh over the whole affair.[127]

This would prove to have a lasting impact on the delegate. It was rumoured by several sources that during one of his less guarded moments, Luzio stated that he had not encountered a single Irish bishop but rather dozens of popes.[128] Most importantly, episcopal treatment of the delegate undoubtedly caused him to include in his report the highly critical passages about them and their control of the Irish Church.

The government's attitude towards Luzio was also heavily criticised. Cait O'Kelly described Luzio's treatment at the hands of the government as brutal.[129] Art O'Muireadaig, a young seminarian finishing his studies in Quebec, proclaimed that '[i]t was scandalous. Imagine the "Draper's Curate" Bill Cosgrave requiring Credentials from the Holy Father's Representative.'[130] Many believed that the Free State's attitude was caused by their desire to eliminate, rather than pacify the republican threat; 'The Free State people are settling themselves in their armchairs and do not intend to be disturbed by any clamours for peace. They are not at home to any peacemaker whether he be an archbishop or a papal legate.'[131] Similarly, de Valera announced that the Free State ministers were moving 'heaven and earth' to secure themselves in power.[132]

This kind treatment by republicans was due, in large part, to the belief that the treatment Luzio had received at the hands of the bishops and government made him more sympathetic to their cause. As explored previously, there was a strong element of Fenianism contained within post-Treaty republicanism, which made reliance on the clergy and even the Vatican unpopular. Patrick Browne, who had a strong self-interest in promoting clerical involvement in politics, wrote that neither bishops nor even the pope had the right to pronounce with any certainty on the matter of Irish politics; 'We will not submit the political question to the Pope. We do not take our politics from Rome.'[133] During the preparation of the formal appeal to the Vatican, Conn Murphy wrote to Archbishop Gilmartin that the appeal committee had no intention of asking Pius XI to settle the political question: 'We are of opinion that the decision of such a question of political fact will be acknowledged by the Holy See to lie entirely outside the province not merely of the Irish Hierarchy, but even of the Church itself as a whole.'[134] In his report, Luzio noted that the republicans had made numerous appeals to the pope to use his good judgments to intervene, but never with the intention of having the Holy See decide the political question.[135] Years later, Mary MacSwiney informed Rev Dudley

Fletcher that it would not have mattered if the pope had approved of the Treaty. She and her fellow republicans were not going to cease their demands for Ireland's freedom.[136] These examples would seem to indicate that had the Apostolic delegate been less approving of republicanism, his reception within the movement might have been as chilly as it was elsewhere.

Given the opportunity to play the diplomatic card, de Valera sent Luzio a letter indicating the disappointment he felt that the monsignor was leaving Ireland: 'I regret particularly that your leaving should be under circumstances which make it probable that your feelings are those of just resentment at the public discourtesy shown to the representative of the Holy Father and the personal injustice done to you as well.'[137] De Valera thought that if Luzio had been able to stay longer he would have seen that the people of Ireland retained their old reverence for the Holy See as well as their innate politeness 'and that the attitude of a certain churlish press and certain politicians is not characteristic of them.' Undoubtedly Luzio had noted from the attitudes of local assemblies that the people did not see his visit as an intrusion and that they longed for peace. His coming provided them with a chance to voice their wishes.[138]

The Neutral IRA, an organisation founded by Florrie O'Donoghue and Seán Hegarty composed of, according to O'Donoghue's estimates, twenty-thousand pre-truce IRA members, that sought to bring together the opposing sides in a truce to allow for political compromise,[139] sent Luzio a letter thanking him for his efforts at establishing peace. It was his presence that had largely contributed to the feeling of pacification made evident during the final days of his mission; 'The ordinary people who are not interested in politics, but who were very anxious for peace, looked instinctively to the Representative of the Holy Father to act as mediator.' Though Luzio was attacked and his actions misrepresented by the government and the press as interfering in purely Irish political affairs, the Neutral IRA assured him these attacks did not represent the people as a whole.[140] Michael Comyn, who had acquired some notoriety as a republican legal adviser, wrote to Luzio to congratulate him on his mission. Though his efforts seemed to have been for nought, when he had arrived Ireland was 'a nation of angry men engaged in mutual destruction. There did not seem to be any thought, or any hope, of peace.'[141] Luzio, though, stood like a rock and with the authority of the pope delivered a message of love and an appeal for peace and charity and it was this that had brought the country within reach of peace. Comyn claimed that the harsh coverage Luzio's mission received in the Irish newspapers served to represent the magnitude of his task and the greatness of his achievement. By conveying the love of the pope to all the people of Ireland without distinction, Luzio had 'won an enduring place in the hearts of Ireland's youth'.[142]

Contrary to the glowing accounts sent to Luzio by Comyn and the Neutral IRA, Fr Patrick Walsh, senior secretary to Archbishop Byrne, summarised the mission as accomplishing nothing and Luzio as eager to escape from the Irish climate and politics.[143] A man who signed his letter simply as 'Daniel' informed Hagan that he had learned that '[Luzio] was very disappointed and stated he would never come to Ireland again.'[144] The Italian Consul, who hosted Luzio during a tribute to the musician Professor Esposito on 16 April, reported that the monsignor had already deemed his mission a complete failure.[145] Dr. Michael Sheehan, Coadjutor Archbishop of Sydney, felt for Luzio. He believed from the beginning that the mission would inevitably end in failure, and as he thought the Vatican did not pardon failure, Luzio's chances of further advancement were extinguished. Sheehan was even more concerned about Luzio's personal welfare; 'I had a letter from the poor man some time ago. He seems to be cut to the heart.'[146] After Luzio had been recalled, Bishop O'Donnell expressed pity for the visitor.[147]

In fact, popular perception was that Luzio was disappointed with the results of his mission and was displeased with the treatment he received courtesy of the bishops and government. Hagan wrote to Mannix that it was known in Rome that Luzio was very bitter against the Free State Ministers, especially Kevin O'Higgins and Desmond FitzGerald, 'and that he has formed a higher idea of the Republicans as a body and individually than of their opponents.' Hagan's theories were rarely closer to the mark than they were in this instance. Luzio had developed a severe disliking of O'Higgins. He described the Minister as 'arrogant and fanatical' and hoping to annihilate the republicans because they had killed his father. He also referred to the 'Republican government' as the 'more religious, preferring the ancient and genuine Catholic faith of the Irish people'. Cosgrave had chosen eighteen Freemasons, by which he had to mean Protestants, for the Senate, and article eight of the Constitution guaranteed equality of religion, 'something which seems incredible in Catholic Ireland! And to think that this is the government supported by the ecclesiastical hierarchy.'[148]

In his report to Cardinal Gasparri, however, Luzio was very positive regarding his impact on the ending of conflict. He wrote that he believed he had assumed his duties 'perfectly regarding cooperation leading to peace'. He had attempted to induce de Valera to end hostilities and re-enter peace negotiations, and that was exactly what had happened. Furthermore, he pointed out, he had included in his report the letter from de Valera declaring that it was Luzio's arguments which persuaded him to end hostilities and make a peace proposal. Rather than admitting defeat, Luzio proclaimed 'it will be in no small part due to me if this peace is concluded.'[149] Perhaps his spirits rebounded after his 16 April confession of failure, or perhaps he was merely trying to save face. How much of this was posturing will likely remain unknown, but it ran counter to popular consensus both in Ireland and Rome. If Hagan is correct, it also did not impress Gasparri. He believed that '[Luzio] will be made the scapegoat, even though St Michael himself could have accomplished little.'[150]

For weeks after Luzio had returned to Rome, there were hopes within the republican community that the delegate who had been so open and kind to them would sway the Vatican into action vindicating the republicans and their complaints against the hierarchy. However, the Vatican's continued silence regarding Ireland left many disgruntled, and fears arose that the end result would be damaging to the Church. While travelling in Ireland, Michael Curran reported to Hagan that '[t]he prestige of the Secretariate [sic] of State is below zero. The whole situation here is ludicrous if it were not so tragic. The indignation of the republicans in Dublin against the Church (Local and Universal) over the denial of the sacraments is intense and will remain for many a long day.'[151] That indignation came across strongly in a letter sent to Hagan in November of 1923. The writer states: 'it seems to me that the Church is doing its best to alienate us, and we cannot hope to remain for ever unaffected by the actions of the Catholic Hierarchy, not only in Ireland but in America and indeed in Rome itself.'[152] In her opinion, feelings in Ireland were fast growing among republicans that if the Church did not want them that they could survive without it. So far, people had talked privately and given up their religion without publicising it, but if a movement of this sort went public, Ireland could become more anti-clerical than France.[153] P.J. Roughneen of Kiltimagh, Co. Roscommon was of the belief that the visit had not improved the status of the Vatican or the bishops in the eyes of the people and from a religious standpoint it was a 'failure and a blunder'.[154] Years later, a person writing as 'MacDara', the Christ-martyr hero of Patrick Pearse's 'The singer', informed Bishop Michael Browne of Galway, who, as professor of moral theology at Maynooth, had been a quiet republican sympathiser during the Civil War, that it had been a pity that Pius had sent Luzio instead of 'another Rinuccini'.[155] MacDara was distraught that Luzio had allowed himself to be browbeaten by the bishops, but was thankful that he had failed to influence the pope.[156] Obviously, even more than a decade after the event, Luzio's recommendations remained unknown to the majority of Irish Catholics.

Hagan also deemed the mission a mistake. The Vatican had not shown approval of the October pastoral, but once they had sent Luzio to investigate, it was incumbent upon them to make a pronouncement. The lack of a statement could be taken as a virtual endorsement of what the bishops had done. He was of the opinion that the people in the cardinal secretariat of state did not agree with the actions of the Irish hierarchy, but as it was pleasing to England, they did not dare interfere.[157] Once again he was demonstrating his belief that the British had undue influence in the Vatican because of the increased diplomatic power they enjoyed after the First World War. A memorandum from Cork which found its way onto Hagan's desk helped convince him that the republicans had already begun to feel ignored by the Church. The document urged the Holy See to reconsider the appeal and the findings of the visitor and to raise its voice in protest and defence for the suffering while there was time, and before the people formed the belief that Gasparri was willing to sacrifice every Irish interest rather than risk upsetting England.[158]

The Vatican's failure to act, though, was in no way attributable to Luzio's submitted report, which, with the recent opening of the papers of Pius XI's papacy, has for the first time been made accessible to the public.[159] The visitor's conclusions were highly critical of the actions of the hierarchy. He referred to the October pastoral as 'less than prudent … But the worst thing was that of having wished to mix the Sacraments with a questionable political issue, to reach a decision on which they had neither authority nor certain information'.[160] The bad situation started by the bishops was further aggravated by their clerical supporters, who, in order to show themselves as zealous, took things to the extreme, not only refusing confession to those republicans who had fought and facilitated the use of violence, but also to those who had never been involved in politics but who had only republican ideals. He portrayed the actions of the bishops as potentially detrimental to the Irish Church, because were it not for the 'profound piety of the Irish people', he believed 'that Ireland would have witnessed the defection of thousands from the Catholic Church.' Contrary to the belief that he had not strongly urged the pope to act, Luzio reported that it was necessary to rectify the abnormal situation in Ireland immediately, especially since hostilities had ceased and thus the reason given up to the present of the opposition being guilty of opposing with force a legitimate government, as the bishops described it, no longer applied: 'And it is also necessary to prohibit the Bishops entirely from taking part in politics, as this has always brought disastrous consequences for the ecclesiastical authorities and for the religion.'[161] Finally, he advised that a permanent delegation, described as vital to the region, be installed in Ireland, regardless of the wishes of the bishops.

Nor had the Vatican intended to remain silent. At the outset of his mission, Luzio was informed that the pope wanted him to determine whether the publication of a letter would be advisable. Pius XI hoped that this action on his part would help pacify the Catholics of Ireland.[162] Luzio discussed the possibility of such a letter with Logue and Byrne, both of whom were vehemently against it. He was finally persuaded that publication of such a letter would worsen the situation. As the letter stated that the pope could form no exact opinion, this would serve as detrimental to the legitimacy claims of the Free State government and it would embarrass the bishops.[163] This was the conclusion at which Luzio had arrived before he began to feel victimised by the government and bishops. However, in his report, he noted that due to de Valera's peace proposals a pontifical letter would not have much effect.

THE VATICAN RETREATS

Upon Luzio's departure from Ireland, the Free State government continued its manoeuvres to outflank the republicans. The day Luzio announced he was returning to Rome the Executive Council decided that Cosgrave should send a telegram to Cardinal Gasparri thanking him for the manner in which he dealt with the situation.[164] In the telegram, Cosgrave wished Gasparri to express appreciation to Pius for the evidence of the Holy See's undiminished affection for Ireland, 'whereby the embarrassment caused by the manner of the Right Rev. Monsignor Luzio's intervention in our affairs has been brought to an end and Monsignor Luzio has been able to take his departure without further difficulties ensuing.'[165]

The real push came in the form of Desmond FitzGerald's visit to Rome from 29 April through 9 May. Despite rumours within the republican camp that FitzGerald had been sent to apologise on behalf of the Free State government for its behaviour towards Luzio,[166] Marquis MacSwiney explained to Under Secretary of State Pizzardo that FitzGerald had come to express the gratitude of the president and the cabinet for the prompt action taken by the pope regarding the Luzio affair. Pizzardo was 'particularly cordial and showed much anxiety to repair the harm that had been done by Mgr. Luzio's visit'.[167]

FitzGerald also pushed on the Vatican's attitude towards the republicans who had presented the appeal in January. In a meeting with Gasparri the same day, he referred to the arrest of Dr. Conn Murphy by Free State forces. This had been one of the primary reasons Fitz Gerald had been sent to Rome. After discussing the issue with Byrne, the Executive Council came to the conclusion that the pope did not have proper knowledge of the case, and so the government sent FitzGerald to correctly inform the Vatican.[168] He assured Gasparri that the government had ample reason for arresting Murphy and raised a complaint about the Vatican's telegram to Archbishop Byrne calling for an intervention to secure his release. Gasparri informed FitzGerald that the telegram was in no way an order; it left the question completely at the discretion of Byrne. It was sent due to numerous telegrams received from Ireland and the United States stating that Murphy had been imprisoned for his trip to Rome.[169] FitzGerald assured the Cardinal that this was certainly not the case, and it allowed him the opportunity to bring up the bad impression created in the Free State by the Vatican's attitude towards Murphy and Arthur Clery during their appeal trip.

According to press reports in Ireland, Gasparri had met with the two men in January and had promised that the Sacred Congregation would study the matter of the October pastoral once Gasparri had obtained the information he required from Logue. The fact that these reports remained un-contradicted by the Vatican had, according to FitzGerald, caused alarm among the majority of Irish Catholics, who also supported the government; 'Their political convictions remained unshaken but the apparent consideration shown by the Vatican to the enemies of the established Government and its apparent indifference to the express public declaration of the Bishops had been a source of grave scandal and disedification to them.'[170] When added to the feelings elicited by the Luzio visit, the Catholics of Ireland were being forced to think that the Vatican believed the reports coming from anti-Free State forces in the United States, Australia and Ireland.[171]

In the opinion of FitzGerald and other Free State ministers, the Apostolic benediction sent to Conn Murphy, who had gone on hunger strike while in prison, was another example of the damage the Vatican could inflict on Irish affairs unless it chose its actions more carefully. It appears many who supported the Free State were genuinely upset at the rumoured benediction given to Murphy. Liam de Róiste wrote in his diary that this action 'would seem to indicate that the Vatican has repudiated the declaration of the Irish Bishops that Irregularism is immoral!'[172] FitzGerald told Gasparri of the anxiety caused to the Government at which time Gasparri displayed a sense of perturbation at the unintended results of Vatican involvement. He stated that the actions of the Vatican had been misinterpreted. He stated that the benediction had not been sent to Murphy, and Luzio was sent merely to aid the Government during the time when the Vatican believed elections were to occur. An internal note from Under-Secretary of State Francesco Borgongini Duca affirms that the telegram had not been sent.[173] However, nowhere in Luzio's report is anything mentioned about Irish elections.

It is interesting that Cardinal Gasparri was so apologetic and accommodating to the representative of the Free State and that he was apparently so eager to smooth any possible tension that existed between the young state and the Church. When confronted, Gasparri told FitzGerald that Luzio's role had been one of supporting the government during the upcoming elections. However, had this been the case, it would have been only logical that Luzio would have been ordered to present credentials to Cosgrave at the onset of his mission in order to gain state recognition and possibly even appreciation. One would also expect to find mention of elections somewhere in his report. It appears instead that Luzio's mission was designed to be an unstructured study and that the visitor was encouraged to work for peace. In the 21 April issue of the *Freeman*, a Press Association representative in Dublin was authorised to say the following by Luzio: the pope did not dream of interfering with the political affairs of Ireland; 'He merely intended to exercise an act of Christian charity, which he believes is not foreign to his duties ... But if, for some reason or other, such an act of charity becomes inopportune or not welcome, the Holy Father and Monsignor Luzio have not the least desire to obtrude where their intervention is not necessary or wanted.'

Without an adequate knowledge of the personal and ideological bitterness that had developed in Ireland during the Civil War, the Vatican was caught completely unprepared for the backlash to what it believed was simply an investigation by the Catholic Church into the reported turmoil of one of the most Catholic countries in the world for the good of its followers. Salvatore Luzio's naïve attempts at working for peace in a country he had known quite well demonstrated that even those previously familiar with the island, who had not lived through the last few years, possessed a mentality that was not compatible with those who were attempting to pacify and lead the Free State as they saw necessary. Compromise and negotiation were unwelcome regardless of their source; a theme that is examined in greater detail in the next chapter.

The highest echelons of the Vatican were definitely not ready for the reactions to their involvement in Irish affairs. The quickness with which they reversed their positions in the face of Free State annoyance and their seeming inability to commit to the positions they took indicate that they had approached the situation with nowhere near the level of caution and sensitivity which was required. Moreover, the men who were responsible for formulating the Vatican's policy on Ireland clearly did not understand the nuances of the Irish situation. The pope had on occasion attempted to use his high office to effect peace first between Britain and Ireland and later between the warring factions within Ireland. During all attempts he found that his offers were rebuffed by one side or the other as beneficial to the opposition. The results were first that the Vatican attempted to tread more lightly to do the least harm while achieving the maximum benefit, and finally exhaustion with the Irish situation and a desire to avoid it altogether. Despite constant rumours among Irish circles that the Vatican was anxious to get involved in their affairs, this was, in fact, the Vatican's first and last foray into Irish politics during this turbulent period. The failed attempts and the jockeying for a pontifical blessing or condemnation from people concerned with politics rather than religion soured the pontiff on allowing himself to speak to the faithful in Ireland on issues which he considered important. It appears that the leadership of the Church, especially Pope Pius XI, had had enough of the difficulties of getting involved in Ireland, and in fact wanted to hear no more about it.[174]

Four years later, the British representative to the Holy See reported that in the wake of the papal condemnation of *Action Française*, Pius XI was enacting a policy of withdrawing the Church as far as possible from the political arena. He had personally forbade the creation of a Catholic political party in Mexico. Furthermore, 'any tendencies on the part of the clergy to mingle politics and religion beyond the prudent limits laid down by the Holy See will be severely suppressed. The Vatican formula in respect to those limits is that the Church only comes into direct contact with politics when politics threaten the altar or the family.'[175] This episode points to two possibilities regarding the Irish affair. Firstly, it seems to suggest that while the Vatican never actually condemned the Irish bishops for their Civil War era statements and actions, the odds of Pius doing so were much greater than his supporting them. The pontiff was clearly opposed to the mixing of religion and politics, and as the bishops did not feel the need to defend their actions, the majority of materials presented to Vatican authorities argued that they had, in fact, combined the two. Secondly, his condemnation of *Action Française* demonstrates that he would have condemned the republican movement if he actually felt the need to do so. It would seem that the ending of armed hostilities gave the Holy See the excuse it desired to excuse itself from speaking on Ireland.

With an outside source of authority threatening to involve itself in the power struggle occurring within the Free State, those who had the strongest claim to legitimate authority were loath to see any involvement that did not further legitimise their position. Given the Vatican's seeming neutrality and desire for peace in Ireland without concern for the struggle between Treaty supporters and opponents, the Free State government's opposition to Luzio's trip is logical. The hierarchy's opposition, though, can only be explained as an attempt to maintain control of the Catholic Church in Ireland, regardless of the Vatican's wishes, as well as the result of the bishops' alliance with the Free State government. The Vatican had not endorsed the October pastoral and had, instead, agreed to receive republican delegations on two separate occasions, regardless of the wishes of the Irish hierarchy. This was an embarrassment to the bishops and damaged their authority over their Church and the morality of their treatment of republicans. The morality of the bishops' actions, though, suffered an even greater blow due to their silence in the face of the Free State's questionable treatment of republican prisoners.

NOTES

1. See Emmet Larkin, *The Roman Catholic Church and the Plan of Campaign in Ireland, 1886–1888* (Cork, 1978); Patrick O'Farrell, *Ireland's English Question: Anglo-Irish Relations, 1534–1970* (London, 1971). For a newer study, which includes more on the British element of the Vatican's activities in late nineteenth-century Ireland, see Ambrose Macaulay, *The Holy See, British Policy and the Plan of Campaign in Ireland, 1885–93* (Dublin, 2002).
2. AAA, Logue papers, Hagan to 'My Dear Lord' [recipient unknown: letter forwarded to Logue], 25 January 1921.
3. See Dermot Keogh, *The Vatican, the Bishops and Irish Politics*; Dermot Keogh, *Ireland and the Vatican*; Patrick Murray, *Oracles of God*, pp.195–210. My thanks to Vera Orschel, former archivist of the Irish College, Rome, for her help with better understanding Hagan.
4. TAA, Gilmartin papers, 'Church and State in Ireland'.
5. NLI, O'Kelly papers, Ms 27,712 (3), Curran memoirs.
6. CAA, Harty papers, Hagan to Harty, 14 February 1921.
7. Dermot Keogh, *Ireland and the Vatican*, pp.5, 8.
8. If Plunkett's daughter is to be trusted, not only did the count speak to the pope about the Rising, but he also communicated with as many bishops as he could, warning them that something was going to happen, asking that they not denounce it. NLI, Geraldine Plunkett Dillon papers, Ms 33,731/1, Geraldine Plunkett Dillon notes.
9. NLI, Sheehy-Skeffington papers, Ms 41,212/25.
10. CDA, Harty papers, Hagan to Harty, 14 February 1921.
11. CRO, Lord Howard of Penrith papers, D HW 9/23/2, Howard to FitzAlan, 3 June 1933.
12. CRO, Lord Howard of Penrith papers, D HW 9/23/2, Howard to FitzAlan, 10 June 1933.
13. Jérôme aan de Wiel also believes that Plunkett was successful in getting Benedict's blessing for those who partook in the Rising but not the Rising itself. Jérôme aan de Wiel, *The Catholic Church in Ireland*, p.86. For the translated text of the denial, see *The Times* (London), 10 June 1933.
14. CRO, Lord Howard of Penrith papers, D HW 9/23/2, FitzAlan to Howard, 19 June 1933.
15. Shane Leslie, *Cardinal Gasquet* (London, 1953), p.237.
16. Ibid., p.247.

17. Ibid., pp.212–13.
18. Ibid., p.208.
19. NLI, O'Kelly papers, Ms 27,712 (3), Curran memoirs.
20. Shane Leslie, *Cardinal Gasquet*, p.190.
21. TAA, Gilmartin papers, Hagan to Gilmartin, 1 January 1922.
22. According to the minutes of the 15 January 1924 Standing Committee meeting, the bishop was Robert Browne of Cloyne, who also stated that the bishops were ashamed of Hagan. GDA, O'Doherty papers, box 46, no. 88.
23. DAA, Byrne papers, Logue to Byrne, 17 December 1923.
24. Ibid.
25. DAA, Byrne papers, Byrne to Logue, December 1923.
26. ICR, Hagan papers, Cohalan to Hagan, 16 January 1924.
27. NLI, O'Kelly papers, Ms 27,712 (4), Curran memoirs.
28. ICR, Hagan papers, Hagan to Hawksley, 11 April 1920; ICR, Hagan papers, Hagan to Hawksley, 20 April 1920.
29. TAA, Gilmartin papers, Hagan to Gilmartin, 26 April 1923.
30. TAA, Gilmartin papers, Hagan to Gilmartin, 11 January 1922.
31. GDA, O'Doherty papers, box 45, no. 19, Mulhern to O'Doherty, 10 February 1921. Mulhern was referring to a letter sent by the *Association des Etudiants Irlandais* asking the Irish hierarchy to offer their public support for the Dáil. There is no reason to believe that his attitude would have changed since.
32. AAA, Logue papers, Hagan to Logue, 24 January 1921.
33. AAA, Logue papers, Hagan to Logue, 25 January 1921.
34. Ibid.
35. AAA, Logue papers, Hagan to Logue, 24 January 1921.
36. RA, PS/PSO/GV/C/K/1702A/78, Benedict to George, 18 October 1921.
37. RA, PS/PSO/GV/C/K/1702A/78, George to Benedict, 18 October 1921.
38. ICR, Hagan papers, Hagan to 'My Dear Lord', 18 October 1921.
39. ICR, Hagan papers, McKenna to Hagan, 1 November 1921.
40. CCCA, de Róiste papers, U271/A/40, de Róiste diaries, 5 November 1921; NLI, O'Kelly papers, Ms 27,712 (3), Curran memoirs.
41. ICR, Hagan papers, memorandum on the history of de Valera's telegram to the pope, n.d.
42. CCCA, de Róiste papers, U271/A/40, de Róiste diaries, 27 October 1921.
43. ICR, Hagan papers, Fogarty to Hagan, 23 October 1921.
44. Ronan Fanning, et al. (eds), *Documents on Irish Foreign Policy*, vol. I (Dublin, 1998), no. 171, Telegram from de Valera to Pope Benedict XV, 20 October 1921, pp.282–3.
45. Ibid., p.288, no. 174, Extract from memo from de Valera to Griffith, 22 October 1921.
46. Ibid.
47. Ibid.
48. NLI, O'Kelly papers, Ms 27,712 (3), Curran memoirs.
49. ICR, Hagan papers, MacRory to Hagan, 3 January 1922.
50. ICR, Hagan papers, Hagan to Byrne, 7 February 1922.
51. Dermot Keogh, *The Vatican, the Bishops and Irish Politics*, p.109.
52. ICR, Hagan papers, Hagan to Byrne, 7 February 1922.
53. Ibid.
54. AAA, Logue papers, Curran to 'My Dear Lord Archbishop', 14 March 1923.
55. Ibid.
56. Ibid.
57. See Chapter 2, pp.87-91.
58. ICR, Hagan papers, Hagan to Byrne, 13 November 1922.
59. ICR, Hagan papers, Hagan to O'Donnell, 13 November 1922.
60. DAA, Byrne papers, Logue to Byrne, 22 November 1922.
61. ICR, Hagan papers, Hagan to Byrne, 13 November 1922.
62. ICR, Hagan papers, O'Donnell to Hagan, 25 November 1922.
63. ICR, Hagan papers, Hagan to O'Donnell, 2 December 1922.

64. AAA, Logue papers, Hagan to 'My Dear Lord', 8 March 1923.
65. ICR, Hagan papers, O'Doherty to Hagan, 6 March 1923 [misdated 1922]. (Emphasis in original.)
66. AAA, Logue papers, Hagan to 'My Dear Lord', 8 March 1923.
67. Ibid.
68. DAA, Byrne papers, Logue to Byrne, 22 November 1922.
69. ICR, Hagan papers, Miller to Hagan, 21 March 1923.
70. Vatican City, A.E.S., Inghilterra, Posizione 167, fascicolo 14, 'Relazione Della Missione in Irlanda di Mons. Luzio Salvatore' (hereafter 'Relazione'), Translated by Mike Hodder.
71. ICR, Hagan papers, R to Hagan, 16 March 1923.
72. ICR, Hagan papers, Roughneen to Hagan, 25 April 1923.
73. *CB*, 'Far and Near', 1923, p.347.
74. FJ, 15 March 1923. (Emphasis in original.)
75. Ibid.
76. Dermot Keogh, *The Vatican, the Bishops and Irish Politics*, p.113.
77. Vatican City, A.E.S., Inghilterra, Posizione 167, fascicolo 14, 'Relazione'.
78. *'Stando così le cose è facile immaginare con quale freddezza e diffidenza fui accolto dai Vescovi. Anche gli amici più intimi cercavano di sfuggirmi.'* Ibid.
79. *'Risposi che di ciò non avevo nessun incarico, ma che non credevo che la S. Sede ratificasse la decisione dei Vescovi sulla legittimità del governo dello Stato Libero perchè avrebbe così risoluto una questione politica in cui non vuole intrometrtersi.'* Vatican City, A.E.S., Inghilterra, Posizione 167, fascicolo 14, 'Relazione'.
80. Dermot Keogh, *The Vatican, the Bishops and Irish Politics*, p.113.
81. UCDA, O'Malley papers, P17b/116, O'Malley interview with Patrick Browne.
82. Vatican City, A.E.S., Inghilterra, Posizione 167, fascicolo 14, 'Relazione'.
83. Dermot Keogh, *The Vatican, the Bishops and Irish Politics*, p.113.
84. ICR, Hagan papers, Gilmartin to Hagan, 11 April 1923.
85. ICR, Hagan papers, O'Donnell to Hagan, 21 March 1923.
86. ICR, Hagan papers, O'Donnell to Hagan, 16 April 1923.
87. ICR, Hagan papers, Harty to Hagan, 21 March 1923.
88. Dermot Keogh, *The Vatican, the Bishops and Irish Politics*, p.113.
89. See Chapter 1, p.56.
90. Patrick Murray, *Oracles of God*, p.191.
91. FJ, 15 March 1923.
92. Ibid.
93. Ibid., 16 March 1923.
94. Vatican City, A.E.S., Inghilterra, Posizione 167, fascicolo 14, 'Relazione'.
95. FJ, 18 April 1923.
96. Ibid., 20 April 1923. The letter is dated 9 March 1923.
97. Keogh argues the same point. Dermot Keogh, *Ireland and the Vatican*, p.19.
98. Vatican City, A.E.S., Inghilterra, Posizione 167, fascicolo 14, 'Relazione'.
99. Ibid.
100. Ronan Fanning, et al. (eds), *Documents on Irish Foreign Policy*, vol. II, no. 60, Seán Lester to Desmond Fitzgerald, 16 April 1923, p.84.
101. II, 16 April 1923.
102. *'l'esercito dello Stato Libero, aiutato com'era dall'Inghilterra, aveva già virtualmenta soggiogato e vinto quello della Repubblica, ed era solo questione di mesi perchè avrebbe finito collo sbaragliarlo intieramente...che data l'ostinatezza dei repubblicani prima che il loro esercito fosse del tutto sbaragliato dovevano ancora per vari mesi succedere delle carneficine e delle distruzioni immense.'* Vatican City, A.E.S., Inghilterra, Posizione 167, fascicolo 14, 'Relazione'.
103. Ronan Fanning, et al. (eds), *Documents on Irish Foreign Policy*, vol. II, no. 63, Seán Lester to Desmond Fitzgerald, 17 April 1923, p.87.
104. Ibid., p.87, no. 64, Memo from Kevin O'Shiel, 19 April 1923.
105. Ibid.

106. NAI, Dept. of An Taoiseach, G2/1, C.1/85, Minutes of Executive Council meeting, 17 April 1923.
107. Vatican City, A.E.S., Inghilterra, Posizione 167, fascicolo 14, Cosgrave to Gasparri, 19 April 1923.
108. Ibid.
109. Ibid.
110. Ibid.
111. Ronan Fanning, et al. (eds), *Documents on Irish Foreign Policy*, vol. II, no. 73, Seán Murphy's report on the Mission to Rome, 26 April 1923, p.99.
112. *CB*, 'Far and Near', 1923, p.354.
113. Ibid., pp.354–55.
114. Vatican City, A.E.S., Inghilterra, Posizione 167, fascicolo 14, 'Relazione'.
115. '*come sempre hanno desiderate gli Irlandesi, la piena libertà della propria nazione.*' Ibid.
116. Dermot Keogh, *The Vatican, the Bishops and Irish Politics*, p.115.
117. ICR, Hagan papers, Mother Stanislaus to Hagan, 4 April 1923.
118. ICR, Hagan papers, SM O'Daly to Hagan, 26 April 1923.
119. ICR, Hagan papers, Cait O'Kelly to Hagan, 9 May 1923.
120. ICR, Hagan papers, Cait O'Kelly to Hagan, 13 April 1923.
121. DAA, Curran papers, Columban na Banban. 'False Pastors', pp.46–7.
122. UCDA, O'Malley papers, P17b/116, O'Malley interview with Patrick Browne.
123. Vatican City, A.E.S., Inghilterra, Posizione 167, fascicolo 14, de Valera to Luzio, 30 April 1923.
124. ICR, Hagan papers, de Valera to Hagan, 19 May 1923.
125. Ibid.
126. ICR, Hagan papers, Hagan to Mannix, 5 November 1923.
127. ICR, Hagan papers, Keohane to Hagan, 27 April 1923.
128. Peadar O'Donnell, *The Gates Flew Open* (London, 1932), pp.44–5. Keogh notes that the story may be apocryphal but that it was probably not far from Luzio's thoughts. Dermot Keogh, *The Vatican, the Bishops and Irish Politics*, p 263, n.78.
129. ICR, Hagan papers, Cait O'Kelly to Hagan, 9 May 1923.
130. ICR, Hagan papers, O'Muireadaig to Hagan, 26 September 1923.
131. ICR, Hagan papers, Seamus to Denny, 24 March 1923.
132. ICR, Hagan papers, de Valera's statement, 23 June 1923.
133. UCDA, Andrews papers, P91/99, Columban na Banban [Patrick Browne], 'Reply to the Pastoral Issued by the Irish Hierarchy in October 1922'.
134. UCDA, de Valera papers, P150/1654, Murphy to Gilmartin, 2 November 1922.
135. Vatican City, A.E.S., Inghilterra, Posizione 167, fascicolo 14, 'Relazione'.
136. UCDA, Mary MacSwiney papers, P48a/190, Mary MacSwiney to Fletcher, 28 February1929.
137. Vatican City, A.E.S., Inghilterra, Posizione 167, fascicolo 14, de Valera to Luzio, 30 April 1923.
138. Ibid.
139. Florence O'Donoghue, *No Other Law* (Dublin, 1986 edition), p.288. For more, see Bill Kissane, *The Politics of the Irish Civil War*, pp.139–41, 146–7.
140. Vatican City, A.E.S., Inghilterra, Posizione 167, fascicolo 14, Neutral IRA to Luzio, 3 May 1923.
141. Vatican City, A.E.S., Inghilterra, Posizione 167, fascicolo 14, Comyn to Luzio, 30 May 1923.
142. Ibid.
143. ICR, Hagan papers, Walsh to Hagan, 23 May 1923.
144. ICR, Hagan papers, Daniel to Hagan, 8 June 1923.
145. Dermot Keogh, *The Vatican, the Bishops and Irish Politics*, pp.117–18.
146. ICR, Hagan papers, Sheehan to Hagan, 15 December 1923.
147. ICR, Hagan papers, O'Donnell to Hagan, 15 June 1923.
148. '*superbo e fanatico…è molto più religioso il Governo repubblicana che professa l'antica e genuine fede cattolica del popolo Irlandese…Cosa che sembra incredibile nella cattolica Irlanda! E dire che questo è il governo sostenuto dalla gerarchia ecclesiastica.*' Vatican City,

A.E.S., Inghilterra, Posizione 167, fascicolo 14, 'Relazione'.

149. *'che si deve a me in massima parte se questa pace viene conchiusa.'* Ibid.
150. TAA, Gilmartin papers, Hagan to Gilmartin, 26 April 1923.
151. ICR, Hagan papers, Curran to Hagan, 24 June 1923.
152. ICR, Hagan papers, C ni G to Hagan, 5 October 1923.
153. Ibid.
154. ICR, Hagan papers, Roughneen to Hagan, 25 April 1923.
155. Giovanni Battista Rinuccini (1592–1653), papal nuncio to the Irish Confederation, 1645–9. Initially, Rinuccini proclaimed that his mission was to support Charles I against the Parliamentarians and to secure religious freedom for Catholics. He denounced the First Ormond Peace of March 1646 and excommunicated all Confederates who supported it. As newly-elected president of the Confederate Supreme Council, he called for an attack on Dublin. He denounced the treaty with Inchiquin in 1648, but found that most Confederate generals supported it. Upon his return to Rome, he found Innocent X highly critical of his conduct in Ireland.
156. MacDara, 'The bishop of Galway on national affairs', Mary MacSwiney papers, UCDA, P48a/228.
157. ICR, Hagan papers, Hagan to Mannix, 5 November 1923.
158. ICR, Hagan papers, Memorandum, November 1923.
159. See Appendix D for the full report, appendices excluded.
160. *'poco prudente...Ma il male maggiore però fu quello di aver voluto mischiare i Sacramenti con fatto politico disputabilissimo per la cui decisione non avevano nè dati certi'.* Vatican City, A.E.S., Inghilterra, Posizione 167, fascicolo 14, 'Relazione'.
161. *'Ed è anche necessario che venisse assolutamente proibito ai Vescovi di prendere parte in politica, giacchè ciò ha portato sempre delle conseguenze disastrose per l'autorità ecclesiastica e per la religione.'* Vatican City, A.E.S., Inghilterra, Posizione 167, fascicolo 14, 'Relazione'.
162. Ibid.
163. Ibid.
164. NAI, Dept. of An Taoiseach, G2/2, C.1/99, Minutes of Executive Council meeting, 5 May 1923.
165. Ronan Fanning, et al. (eds), *Documents on Irish Foreign Policy*, vol. II, no. 78, Cosgrave to Gasparri, 8 May 1923, pp.103–104.
166. ICR, Hagan papers, Cait O'Kelly to Hagan, 9 May 1923.
167. Ronan Fanning, et al. (eds), *Documents on Irish Foreign Policy*, vol. II, no. 79, Joe Walshe's Report on the Mission to Rome, 9 May 1923, p.104.
168. NAI, Dept. of An Taoiseach, G2/1, C.1/89, Minutes of Executive Council meeting, 21 April 1923.
169. Ronan Fanning, et al. (eds), *Documents on Irish Foreign Policy*, vol. II, no. 79, Joe Walshe's Report on the Mission to Rome, 9 May 1923, p.105.
170. Ibid.
171. Ibid.
172. CCCA, de Róiste papers, U271/A/49, de Róiste diaries, 21 April 1923.
173. Vatican City, A.E.S., Inghilterra, Posizione 167, fascicolo 14, 'Relazione'.
174. ICR, Hagan papers, Hagan to Mannix, 5 November 1923.
175. UCDA, Blythe papers, P24/184, Odo Russell to Austen Chamberlain, 18 April 1927, forwarded to Kevin O'Higgins.

4

The Politics of Desperation?: Executions and Hunger Strikes

Damn the Dead! When will they cease to infect both Irish and English with their mortality?[1]

M ichael Collins's death on 22 August 1922 is regarded as a major turning point in the Civil War. Charles Townshend, Colm Campbell and Michael Hopkinson attribute an increased level of bitterness and violence to Collins's death, with Hopkinson arguing that his death led to the government's increased ruthlessness, culminating in reprisal executions.[2] John Regan contends that his death allowed the civilian element of the government to push through hard-line measures Collins and Mulcahy had previously blocked,[3] such as the Army Emergency Powers Resolution and the Special Powers Act, which gave the government powers of indefinite internment without trial and gave military courts the right to impose the death penalty on civilians.

The studies of the Civil War produced in the 1980s tend to explain the government's actions after Collins's death by highlighting its weaknesses. Charles Townshend, Michael Hopkinson and Jeffrey Prager all argue that the government's use of force was caused by its desire to stabilise itself and terminate the threat of strong republican opposition.[4] Dermot Keogh theorises that while more experienced politicians would have perhaps acted otherwise, the Free State leaders, uncertain that the state could withstand the republican threat, acted as they believed necessary.[5] More recent works, particularly those of David Fitzpatrick, Peter Hart and Bill Kissane posit that the Free State acted the way it did towards the republicans at this time because with superior military strength and widespread popular support, it had the necessary power to quickly suppress the republican movement using methods the British had unsuccessfully utilised.[6] Rather than showing concern about the stability of the state, the government's actions seem to have been viewed as the most expedient way of ending the conflict through show of force and demoralisation of the opposition. According to Regan, the elevation of civilian ministers after Collins's death allowed them to fulfil their desire to not just defeat opposition to the civilian government but to defeat it in such a way that there could never be reconciliation between the civilians and militarists.[7] This does not indicate weakness, but rather governmental strength and confidence with the ranks of the Cabinet. They were not fighting for the survival of the state per se, but for their vision of the state.

The government of late 1922 was definitely stronger and more established than it had been just months prior. Many, though, still perceived the Free State as weak, and the government used this perception to its advantage. Organisations craving stability were prepared to grant the apparently weak executive greater latitude in the hope that strong actions would benefit the Free State in the long run. This perception allowed the government to achieve ends via means that otherwise would have been unavailable to it. This is evident in its overall treatment of republican prisoners. Through its execution and internment policies, the government greatly reduced the republicans' morale and will to continue the struggle. By allowing the hunger strikers of October – November 1923 to fail of their own accord, the government won the battle of wills and terminated hunger striking's effectiveness as a tool of protest. The government's strength was evident in its maintaining a hard-line stance even after Denis Barry died. These moves severely deflated the militant republican movement, and did so on the government's terms. These moves were, in essence, the government demonstrating to the public as well as the international audience that perceptions of weakness had been wrong.

Cabinet relations with the Catholic bishops during this period are indicative of both the latitude that was granted to the government and how the ministers used this to pursue what otherwise would have been very unpopular programmes. Realising that the bishops were concerned by the 'weak' state of the government, the ministers took the opportunity before them of playing off episcopal fears, knowing that they could carry out their preferred course of action with impunity and the bishops would offer only quiet, private protest. In other words, they could ignore the bishops temporarily to pursue their goals as ruthlessly as they deemed necessary to bring order and stability to the country.

The bishops produced virtually no public criticism of the Free State government during this period. Despite internment of thousands of untried Irish citizens, seventy-nine official government executions and reports of several unofficial deaths at the hands of Free State forces, hundreds if not thousands of reported acts of brutality committed by the state's forces and allowing two uncharged prisoners to starve themselves to death, the bishops remained remarkably silent. The reason for this was not necessarily their political leanings, though in some instances this was the case, or a callous disregard for republican lives. Some bishops, especially Archbishop Byrne, Bishop O'Donnell and even Cardinal Logue to a lesser degree, worked diligently to secure an end to executions and release of hunger strikers. As Dermot Keogh notes, the 'secret role played by some of the bishops will come as a surprise to many who hold to the popular view that the hierarchy virtually acted as a "State Church".'[8]

Keogh's contention is undoubtedly correct. However, questions are raised by the bishops' 'secret role'. If the government was engaged in activities which those particular bishops found morally questionable, perhaps even repellent, why did they retain the veil of secrecy even after their private attempts at influencing government policy achieved little if anything at all? Does this not, in fact, coincide with the contention that they were the heads of a *de facto* 'State Church' that conformed to government wishes, albeit with a degree of quiet criticism? An arguably more important issue is that only 'some of the bishops' displayed qualms about the treatment of prisoners, at least to the degree of commenting upon the situation, even in confidence. If the government's tactics were questionable enough to be confronted by Logue, Byrne and O'Donnell, how could the members of the hierarchy who said absolutely nothing justify their silence? Were republicans right in accusing the bishops of abiding by a double standard?

The hierarchy had aligned itself with the Free State government and had used religious authority to attempt to persuade, cajole and even threaten republicans into rejection of a continuation of the armed struggle.[9] When their chosen side engaged in activities that were questionable according to the very tenets of their faith, the bishops faced something of a crisis. They were certain that the government was not strong enough to survive without their unflagging and uncritical support. In their opinion, were they to show that they disagreed with any aspect of Free State policy, Irish Catholics would begin to question its legitimacy. There was also the fact that they did not want to lend any credibility to the militant republican cause, and by making a public showing of sympathy they would do just that. Despite their high-sounding rhetoric, it is difficult to see this episode as little more than the bishops' succumbing to the advantages of *realpolitik*.

EXECUTIONS

From the start, the government's execution policy was intended as a means of breaking the republican movement's determination to continue armed opposition to implementation of the terms of the Treaty. Given that the hierarchy so determinedly stood by the government even while executions were taking place, it is imperative that the government's justification for its actions be discussed. Failure to place such questionable tactics in the proper context would deprive any analysis of episcopal actions of the necessary degree of objectivity and would serve little purpose other than to parrot the complaints and grievances of republicans.

According to General Mulcahy, executions of republicans were justifiable because anything that would shock the country into realising the gravity of taking human life was warranted at that moment. He informed the Dáil that he was convinced that unless very stern measures were taken, the Free State would not throw back the tide of lawlessness, lust and loot that some mad political leaders had stirred up in their train.[10] Kevin O'Higgins explained the 17 November executions of John Gaffney, Peter Cassidy, James Fisher and Richard Tuohy, four average, unknown republican soldiers, as wisely calculated to demonstrate the government's determination to prevent the killing of the nation. Nothing particular about the four men distinguished them from the thousands of others leading the nation to death, he said, implying that all enemy combatants faced the same potential end. He reiterated that this was an extreme measure that had, in essence, been forced upon the government. It had 'entreated, coaxed and compromised, and went beyond the safety line in compromising' in the hope of averting the disaster of war. When force was finally decided upon, it tried simply to wear its opponents out; 'we tried to show them the futility, the wantonness, and the waywardness of the whole thing, and we tried to conduct this fight with a minimum expenditure of human life on both sides.' Given the situation the Free State now faced, O'Higgins concluded his remarks by stating: 'There was just one alternative to the policy we are now carrying out ... and that is to abdicate; and to say to the British signatories to that Treaty "we are not able to carry it out," and to let this country go down in dishonour and futility.'[11]

The government's determination to overwhelm their opponents was displayed with even greater intensity with the 8 December executions of Four Courts leaders Rory O'Connor, Liam Mellows, Richard Barrett and Joe McKelvey as a reprisal for the murder of Seán Hales and the attempted murder of Pádraic Ó Máille. As both Campbell and Hopkinson note, there was never any pretence of the executions being carried out under either the Army Emergency Powers Resolution or the Public Safety Act.[12] Therefore, their legality is highly dubious, though this seemed of little concern to the Executive Council. Ernest Blythe justified the reprisals by comparing them to standard executions. The Military Courts were not legalised by the Dáil, he said; 'They for their operations depend upon military necessity, and the executions carried out under the sentence of those Courts are justifiable only because of military necessity. The executions carried out this morning can only be justified on grounds of military necessity.'[13] While defending the government's actions, O'Higgins told the deputies: 'There are no real rules of war. They may be written in a book; they may get lip service from philanthropists. When war breaks out they are more honoured in the breach than in the observance.'[14] He defended the state's forces' activities, no matter what, because '[t]he safety and preservation of the people is the highest law. It is at any rate the only law, for laws are not made or written down in a book to guide men when a state of war exists, for war is anarchy, and there are no rules and no laws to guide men.'[15]

The executions highlight the fact that, in the words of the ministers, 'the Government was hardening in its determination to use *every possible means* for the speedy and complete suppression of crime and disorder in the country.'[16] O'Higgins was, without doubt, the strongest advocate of utter ruthlessness in the Cabinet. His hawkish stance can be summed up in one chillingly simplistic line: 'we must kill the active Irregular, tackle the passive Irregular, make friends with the rest.'[17] His close ally, Patrick Hogan, shared a similar outlook. Hogan's mentality was such that he warned Cosgrave in January 1923 that two more months like the previous two would see the end of the Free State itself. However, this attitude did not indicate a fear of the government's weakness. Rather, Hogan was convinced that the war could be won easily, provided the government went about it properly. He called for a short-term policy of the execution of republicans with a machine-like regularity because the people thirsted for strong, ruthless measures.[18] Legal adviser Kevin O'Shiel presented an equally bloodthirsty memo, calling for the government to step up its usage of violence. He informed the president that the government could win the fight if it continued along the present lines, but at the cost of the nation and potentially opening the way for Bolshevism. The way to avoid a Pyrrhic victory was by increased use of force.[19]

Despite the belief that Cosgrave was one of the more moderate members of the government and an opponent of unrestrained violence, it is made clear by his own writings that he personally felt that force was the only way to succeed in securing a permanent end to militant republican resistance. In his letters to Archbishop Byrne, Cosgrave adopted a very moderate tone, but in a letter to Mulcahy, his real feelings came across unfiltered: 'I am coming to the conclusion that if we are to exercise clemency at any time, it can only be of use to us *when the irregulars crave it.*'[20] Having the final say in the Dáil debate on the executions of the Four Courts leaders, Cosgrave accused republicans of engaging in a 'diabolical conspiracy' against the state; 'There is only one way to meet it, and that is to crush it and show them that terror will be struck into them.'[21] It would be enlightening to discover how much of Cosgrave's conclusions were the product of influence by O'Higgins, Hogan and O'Shiel.

The government's reliance on its strength and extra-legal responses can also be seen in its responses to rumours and accusations of illegal executions by Free State forces. Unofficial, non-sanctioned executions by its own forces, especially the Criminal Investigation Department (CID) were problematic for the government. Official records of these executions are nonexistent. Due to their illegality this is expected, but it makes the study of them all the more difficult. O'Halpin estimates that perhaps as many as one hundred and fifty republicans were murdered while in custody or while supposedly evading capture, a favourite excuse for cause of death. Most of these murders were committed in hot blood after engagements or as calculated reprisals for republican acts.[22] The best known example of such an execution was that of Noel Lemass, older brother of the future Taoiseach. After the ceasefire had been called, Lemass was abducted in daylight in Dublin by a number of plainclothes men. His body was discovered in the mountains outside Dublin in October. From the condition of the corpse it was suspected he was probably tortured and executed by a headshot.

News of the discovery of Lemass's body and subsequent accusations were common in the daily newspapers in late 1923. Indicative of popular conceptions of the activities of Free State forces, it was assumed before the coroner's inquest that the murderers were connected to the army and possibly the CID. O'Halpin asserts that the automatic blame placed upon Oriel House, even when it had nothing to do with an act, was a consequence of its own atrocious reputation.[23] The inquest found there to be reason to implicate Free State forces, causing one TD to question Kevin O'Higgins as to when a full judicial enquiry into the evidence of the case would be undertaken.[24] O'Higgins, who had little regard for the majority of CID men,[25] all but dismissed the entire incident. He stated that he wanted to clarify that the opinion expressed by the jury that armed forces of the State were 'implicated in the removal and disappearance of Noel Lemass from the streets of Dublin', was entirely unsupported by evidence. Also, as the coroner's inquest constituted a judicial enquiry in itself, there was no machinery for any further enquiry. Not completely ruling further action out, he said that if any sufficient evidence was found which could connect individuals to the crime, the appropriate court proceedings would be instituted.[26] These killings were almost surely done independently of government policy. The Cabinet did not approve of such methods, but, as O'Higgins's responses to pointed questions show, they appear to have been less than enthusiastic about bringing the culprits to justice. Cosgrave and his ministers were so intent on restoring social order, discipline and respect for the rule of law, that they were willing to accept ruthlessness within their own ranks. Though the CID was an acute embarrassment to the government, the ministers were not prepared to curb its excesses,[27] nor, it seems, to contend with the paradox of re-establishing the rule of law by circumventing and ignoring that very law.

The government's execution policy also displayed a large measure of cynicism. Ernest Blythe admitted years later that there had been some fear in the Cabinet that some 'cracked judge' might order Childers's release during his appeal, and that one or two ministers were of the opinion that after a judge had discharged the *habeas corpus* application Childers should be executed before any further application could be made to another judge.[28] Desmond FitzGerald's acknowledgment that Childers's possession of a firearm was merely the technicality that justified his execution allows for questions to arise about the entire execution policy.[29] How many others were executed with ulterior motives? Colm Campbell argues that the death sentences handed down from military committees were often more a matter of strategy than legality. Also, the fact that executions were geographically spread so as to increase their impact signifies that justice was not always the government's primary concern.[30] This can be seen in a memorandum circulated to the Executive Council by O'Higgins in which he calls for executions in every county because a Dublin-centred policy would have little psychological effect on the rest of the Free State.[31]

The policy of ruthlessness was extended to the degree of opposing attempts to ending the war. Towards the end of December 1922, the Executive Council decided that safe conduct could not be given for those who wished to travel between groups of irregular leaders for the purposes of negotiating towards a peace settlement.[32] Hogan's memo called for the government to commit to a policy of complete victory over the republicans. Anything less would leave the real issues unresolved.[33] Again in April the Council discussed the many requests they had received urging that the government negotiate with republicans with a view to arranging a peace settlement; 'It was agreed that the interests of the country would not be served by the Government's entering into peace negotiations with the Irregulars whose power was now definitely broken.'[34] De Valera believed that the government had adopted this attitude with the intention of destroying the republican organisation, thereby eliminating any sort of constitutional opposition. In his many letters to Archbishop Byrne and Bishop O'Dea, Conn Murphy implied this as well, noting time and again that his daughter, recently incarcerated, had committed no crime and was simply engaging in the democratic process as the hierarchy had urged the republicans to do. According to Murphy, the government, using the bishops' pronouncements as its justification, was systematically dismantling the Sinn Féin network by arresting constitutional republicans with impunity.[35]

It would appear that the government's actions against republicans were less about its own weakness and more about that of its opponents. Hopkinson contends that the executions could not have decided the war because there was no prospect of a republican victory by that time.[36] Inspired by the aggressive attitudes of Hogan, O'Higgins and O'Shiel, the other members of the government were won over to the idea that the best way to finish off the militant republican opposition and appease the populace, which was becoming disgruntled at the prolonged war, was swift and ruthless action. Executions marked the pinnacle of this strategy, though it also created a multitude of problems for the government and its supporters. The Catholic bishops, especially, faced harsh criticism because they maintained an awkward silence throughout the period of executions.

THE BISHOPS' INVOLVEMENT

Following the well-publicised executions of November and early December of 1922, episcopal silence was not received well by many throughout Ireland and the Irish communities abroad. Aside from the many telegrams and letters pleading for their intervention, the bishops were subject to more hostile communications as well as public denunciations. Hagan, who, it must be remembered, was a staunch republican and opponent of Cosgrave's government, reported to Bishop O'Donnell:

> Many letters reach me, containing statements to the effect that the executions would never have been possible had the Bishops not given their official corporate sanction by the October Pastoral; and great stress is laid on the silence observed with regard to the execution of Mellows and his companions. How far this may be true or partially true I am unable to say; but I think in all justice it is a pity that there was not some public expression of what I believe to be the Episcopal mind on the Mellows incident.[37]

One such letter was from Seán T. O'Kelly's wife, Cait. She rhetorically asked if the government would have dared to execute prisoners but for the October pastoral, and she wondered how its writers felt about the executions.[38]

Disbelief at episcopal silence towards executions began with the death of Erskine Childers on 24 November 1922.[39] Before his execution, Childers, a member of the Church of Ireland, requested the right to speak with either Fr. Patrick Browne of Maynooth or Fr. Albert Bibby, one of the Capuchin friars who had been present at the Four Courts. Despite promising to speak only of spiritual matters, Childers's request was denied, and so he sought solace from Rev. Edward Waller, a Protestant minister he had known since childhood.[40] In 'False Pastors', Browne refers to the quiescence of the bishops during the executions of Childers and the Four Courts leaders as the blackest stain on the Irish priesthood since the coming of St. Patrick. In this regard he holds Byrne to be the worst of the bunch.[41] This was due, in large part, to the belief that Byrne had refused Childers access to Browne. The rumour of Byrne's involvement appears to have been relatively widespread. A man named Denis Moran displayed his shock that Byrne had been responsible for the refusal of Childers's spiritual request. Moran was glad that a Protestant had attended to Childers and thus saved his soul from the tortures which Byrne had prepared for it,[42] a strange theory given that Tridentine Catholic doctrine stated that the only way for a Protestant to gain entry to Heaven was through conversion during life or purgation after death. This allegation against Byrne cannot be verified though. The *Catholic Times* believed that officials of the Free State were responsible for the refusal.[43] The rumour fit into the republican narrative of their persecution at the hands of the bishops, however, and the denial of the sacraments and religious comforting prisoners faced as a result of their refusal to abandon their republican principles. A letter writer named Allen offered his sarcastic congratulations to the Irish hierarchy on their efforts to kill Catholicism in Ireland through excommunicating all republicans at the instigation of the Provisional Government, followed by acquiescing in the condemnation and death of political prisoners deprived of their rights of visitation or religious comfort, clearly inferring Childers: 'I would now suggest that the Church goes a little further to complete the *orgies* by making a Sacred Feast of the Victims' bodies.'[44]

The 8 December reprisal executions of Four Courts leaders set off a new wave of anger and indignation from republicans. Cosgrave's government received the brunt of this, and not just from republicans. Labour TDs and the British press were shocked that untried and unconvicted men who had been in prison for months at the time of Hales's murder were executed for the actions of others. Many republican sympathisers also turned their disappointment and anger against the bishops, heavily chastising them for their continuing silence, seen as complicit acceptance of the government's policy, which was questionable in terms of morality and even legality.

After a series of civil letters between Dr. Conn Murphy and Bishop Thomas O'Dea, primarily focusing on the imprisonment of Murphy's daughter and his belief that the bishops' October pastoral was the government's justification for it, Murphy's final instalment encapsulates the anger and bitterness felt by many republicans towards the bishops. He was most aggrieved that they seemed to remain inactive as men were killed for the actions of others; 'You have condemned as murder the killing of Free State troops in open conflict, but you have maintained an appalling, cowardly silence in the face of the coldblooded murder of defenceless prisoners like Rory O'Connor, Liam Mellowes, Barrett and McKelvey.'[45] Unsurprisingly, there is no record of O'Dea ever responding to this letter and the correspondence between the two men appears to have ended.

Mary Walsh of Dalkey expressed to Archbishop Gilmartin her sense of disappointment at the hierarchy's silence: 'The frightful crime of the Official murders committed as a "reprisal" on the Feast of the Immaculate Conception [8 December] by the Murder Ministers whom Your Grace and the other members of the Hierarchy delight to honour brought not one word, not a whisper of condemnation from any episcopal palace.' Worse than the deaths of the Four Courts leaders were the seventy-nine official executions and one hundred and ten prisoner deaths at the hands of government forces, who 'have been left to their fate without a protest or even an appeal for mercy from the Catholic Hierarchy, who, on the contrary, have lost no opportunity, collectively and individually, of buttressing up the power of the Official Murderers.' No doubt, Walsh noted, the bishops were too remote from the people to see the consequences befalling Ireland as a result of their own unnatural and unchristian action, an old Fenian criticism of the clergy that could have come from the pen of John O'Leary. The people of Ireland had once believed that a priest would work unceasingly to save one soul, but that belief has been shattered by the last year:

> 'her best and bravest denied the Bread of Life, slandered and traduced from the pulpit, left without spiritual consolation in the prisons and on the hillsides when facing death, while a campaign of glorification of infamy and injustice, of Might against Right, has been embarked upon by the entire Irish Church.'

Informing Gilmartin that the letter had been composed in sadness and shame rather than anger, she writes: 'With a full sense of the seriousness of what I say I assert that the entire blood guilt of the recent struggle is on the hands of the Irish Hierarchy who have honoured and upheld the perjurer, the traitor and the murderer, and who then add to their terrible guilt the mean vice of hypocrisy.'[46]

Never ones to shy away from conflict with the hierarchy, the MacSwiney sisters wrote to Archbishop Byrne in the months following the executions of the Four Courts leaders. Mary wrote the day of the executions, stating that if the bishops did not publicly condemn the Free State's actions, '[w]e can draw no other conclusion than that you do approve ... and we count you guilty of this blood.' If more executions were performed, and MacSwiney believed they would be, and the bishops did not speak against them, the results would be detrimental for Ireland. The hierarchy, she claimed, had already strained republican belief in the ecclesiastical sense of justice to the breaking point.[47] A few months later, her sister Annie, writing again about the executions of the Four Courts leaders, told Byrne: 'To your eternal shame, Your Grace, it will always be remembered that no word of protest passed your lips when the revolting crime was committed under the personal supervision of Richard Mulcahy.'[48]

As unpleasant as writings of this nature were, they pall in comparison to some of the letters sent from abroad, which often contained disturbingly belligerent views. John McCann of New Bedford, Massachusetts, informed Archbishop Gilmartin of his shock at the fact that Liam Mellows was denied the sacraments before his execution because he refused to repent for his republicanism. McCann had become convinced 'that Ireland is the last stronghold of Medieval Clericalism ... My view of the Catholic Church since these events have happened in Ireland, have [*sic*] undergone a considerable change for the worse'.[49]

T.J. Wallace, also writing from the United States, accused the bishops of reducing the Irish people to slavery while making a mockery of the Catholic faith. They had remained silent while the Free State murdered its prisoners. There were traitorous bishops in the United States as well, Wallace wrote, but they could not turn Irish-born Catholics into serfs; 'The Klu Klux Klan [sic] is going to take care of them soon; and besides they are going to the Irish nation to look after you traitors, and us Irish will simply look on.'[50] Clearly feeling that the threat of the KKK was not enough, Wallace concluded by writing '[b]ut remember Devalera [sic] was too easy with you and the murder gang and all Free State traitors when he did not riddle all of you traitors with bullets the same as Russia did when the Polish Catholic priests and the Bishops when [sic] into that country to intrigue against that government.'[51]

Wallace's letter is Shakespearean in quality when compared to the missive written by James Crowe of Fort Collins, Colorado. He postu-lated that 'Ireland alwys [sic] known as the Island of traitors most foul daming [sic] traitors and the traitor Cursed Bishops has [sic] alwys [sic] been a dam [sic] curse to the Irish to try to hold the people under England.' Due to their complicity in allowing the continuation of what Crowe believed to be unfair treatment of republicans, he stated that 'all the Daming [sic] gangs of so called Bishops ought to be in hell years ago with the Freak staters hell was made for.' To right the situation in Ireland, Crowe believed that the Irish of the United States and other countries ought to go to Ireland and take all Free Staters and bishops far out in the ocean and 'let them down clean ... i [sic] would rather have the hand of the devil conferm [sic] my Children as the hand of the foul Bro [sic] Britiners [sic] Bishops in Ireland.' He concluded that if God did not damn the bishops for their actions, He was not Crowe's God.[52]

Clearly, Crowe did not represent the voice of educated Irish-Americans. However, letters like those from McCann, Wallace and Crowe prove that by continuing their self-imposed silence, the bishops incurred the wrath of people across the globe, and not just Ireland. Further proof can be found in a statement from a Dublin diocesan priest who was in California at the time. He wrote that whereas the Irish in America had strongly been in favour of the Free State at first, now many were offering sympathy and support to the republicans due to the executions, 'the news of which arouses resentment among even the most moderate.'[53]

As was so often the case, the bishops were publicly silent in regard to the government's execution policy, but a few hierarchy members were actively engaged in working to stop the killings. Bishop O'Donnell, a close friend of Childers, was grievously hurt by the execution. Both he and Cardinal Logue were against the government's policy, though they only said so in private.[54] O'Donnell, though, also personally intervened in an attempt to save his friend's life. Rumours circulated that he attempted on numerous occasions to stop executions, validating in the minds of many republicans their belief that he was one of the few bishops deserving of their unqualified respect. Archbishop Harty, who exerted a great deal of effort throughout the period working to bring about peace, asked Byrne to use his influence to halt the executions. Even Bishop Cohalan, who had shown no discernible sympathy for republicans, allowed his secretary, Fr. Tom Duggan, to work to halt the executions while attempts at peace were made. Despite contemporary popular opinion that Byrne remained aloof, amongst the bishops, he was the most involved in trying to terminate the executions. Basing his assertion on an interview with Bishop Patrick Dunne, who had acted as Byrne's secretary at the time, Dermot Keogh contends that Byrne's intervention probably caused the government to use more discrimination in its execution policy and that no more prisoners were executed as 'reprisals' after Byrne's meeting with the ministers in December 1922.[55]

In his many letters to Cosgrave, Byrne saved his most severe language for the topic of reprisal executions. Immediately after the executions of O'Connor, Mellows, Barrett and McKelvey, he wrote to Cosgrave that 'the policy of reprisals seems to me to be not only unwise but entirely unjustifiable from the moral point of view. That one man should be punished for another's crime seems to me to be absolutely unjust.' As proof that the hierarchy were concerned about the stability of the government, Byrne noted that '[s]uch a policy is bound to alienate many friends of the Government, and it requires all the sympathy it can get.'[56] Again, in March 1923, when Duggan attempted to negotiate a termination of executions, Byrne backed the plan and again suggested to Cosgrave that the government cease executing prisoners while Duggan attempted to bring about peace.

Cosgrave was politely defiant towards Byrne; 'If there were a reasonable inference or deduction that Peace were likely to result we would certainly stop these extreme measures.'[57] Captured correspondence, the president argued, showed that pressure from the Free State forces was felt in most areas, and the more it was exercised the greater the desire for peace: 'A real peace can only come from good military results, and we feel it would be much better that they would be beaten in the field which they selected.'[58] Cosgrave wrote that he was sure it was unnecessary to assure Byrne that the government would not exercise severity but that some show of it or pretence might be necessary in view of the large number of prisoners, which numbered over ten thousand at the time. They posed a serious problem in the minds of the government and 'are so ridiculous in their notions that they might want some thousand different peace arrangements.'[59] Due to Cosgrave's attitude, it is difficult to agree with Keogh's contention that Byrne played a major role in the ending of reprisal executions and reducing the number of executions altogether. From their correspondence, it would appear that this marked the nadir of Byrne's influence over the president. Some were of the opinion that this was a general trend within the government. Hagan informed Bishop O'Donnell: 'I am inclined to believe that some of the more notable Free State leaders are not disposed to listen to representatives even from the Bishops.'[60]

Despite negative connotations connected to the concept of 'reprisal' the government was not averse to implementing it even after Byrne had expressed his outrage. Kevin O'Shiel argued to Cosgrave that reprisals were necessary: 'Furthermore it must be recognised that by their [republican] tactics and the projects they pursue the same faction has placed itself outside the pale of civilization,' he wrote '*and must be dealt with by means not usually* (but *de facto* in times of special stress, occasionally) adopted by civilised Governments. I am alluding of course to reprisals, which can I believe be defended on theological grounds, and which were systematically practiced during the Catholic ages.'[61] Clearly, Byrne's interventions did not have the serious impact on all members of the government that Bishop Dunne believed they had had, a fact proven by the continuation of reprisal executions. Contrary to Dunne's conjecture, reprisals did not end in December 1922. Michael J. O'Donnell of Letterkenny reported that Free State troops executed four republican prisoners in west Donegal as an act of reprisal for the actions of their comrades.[62] In April 1923, Archbishop Gilmartin reported that after Republicans attacked a Free State post in Tuam and killed three soldiers, six republican prisoners were executed as a consequence.[63]

Perhaps the most shocking aspect of episcopal attitudes towards the execution policy was the seeming indifference displayed by the majority of bishops. Aside from Byrne, Harty, Logue and O'Donnell, there appears to have been virtually no concern about the government's actions. For example, Gilmartin offered absolutely no comment on the executions of six prisoners for the deaths of three soldiers; he simply reported it as a local occurrence. In his 1921 Lenten pastoral, Bishop Cohalan had informed his listeners that the execution of Cornelius Murphy, not to be confused with Dr. Conn Murphy, solely for possession of a revolver and ammunition 'was a shocking, savage business'. However, in 1923, following the execution of Erskine Childers for the exact same offence, Cohalan uttered no words of condemnation of the Free State authorities. In fact, despite the fact that most death sentences imposed by Free State military courts were for possession of arms without proper authority,[64] Cohalan had nothing to say on the matter. Surely the latest round of executions were just as shocking, savage and worthy of public condemnation.

Another of Cohalan's sermons was the subject of controversy in late May 1923. During a Confirmation Mass, Cohalan told the congregation: 'Some people complain of the number of prisoners in the jails. The military might have adopted a different plan of campaign, under which there would be fewer in the jails, but more in the graveyards of the county. But they have preferred to take prisoners, and the number of killed men is comparatively very small.'[65] The IRA O/C of Prisoners, on behalf of those men and women in Cork jails, wrote a scathing letter to Cohalan the next day, calling his sermon an 'incitement to murder'. The officer attempted to scold Cohalan:

> It is appaling [sic] to think that the altar of God is turned into a political and partisan platform from which we give free run to our personal opinions leaving them open to be interpreted by the uneducated as the Word of God. That you should go further and imply that the Imperial F[ree].S[tate]. troops were very lenient for not shooting all that stood for Irish Independence and that we should be very grateful for having been flung into evil-smelling foul gaols; instead of being summarily executed, is outrageous.

That you should moreover, have chosen for audience little children, many of whose relatives are doubtless imprisoned is unprecedented.

He then expanded his accusations to the hierarchy as a whole: 'You have chosen to become the champion of a murderous policy which leads us to believe what we have for some time suspected – that the campaign of executions received the tacit approval if not the official sanction of the Bishops of Ireland.'[66] This particular situation never gained any traction, primarily because Cohalan's speech was, overall, very positive and discussed the great possibilities laid out before the nation. This was not one of Cohalan's hyper-critical statements against republicans, though it shows his relative indifference to the situation republican prisoners faced.

Keogh speculates, probably accurately, that while the Standing Committee could have issued a statement, it was doubtful that Byrne could have got much support from the episcopal bench for his broader objections to the executions.[67] Given that Byrne had described the reprisal policy as 'absolutely unjust' and 'entirely unjustifiable from the moral point of view', widespread episcopal silence and even the possibility of opposition to a statement against this policy seems inexplicable. As a result of this inactivity, many republicans believed that not only had the religious leaders placed themselves firmly within the Free State camp, but that they were willing to turn a blind eye to illegal and immoral activities emanating from that camp. In the minds of these men and women, the bishops had become nothing more than political actors in the guise of religious leaders.

HUNGER STRIKES

Building on the precedent laid out by the suffragette movement in both Ireland and Britain, Irish nationalists had used hunger striking with a notable record of success for the past decade, during which at least 1,000 men and women took part in over fifty strikes.[68] Famous nationalists such as James Connolly and Francis Sheehy-Skeffington had secured release from prison by refusing to eat. In April 1920, approximately fifty prisoners in Mountjoy jail began a hunger strike demanding prisoner-of-war status. The episode is memorialised in Frank Gallagher's *Days of Fear*, the 1928 publication that was purportedly the diary he kept while on strike in 1920. Though critical readers must remain sceptical about how authentic it is to the original document, Peadar O'Donnell, author of his own memoirs of hunger striking, calls it of great value to students; sincerely and convincingly written.[69] Gallagher believed, like most of the others, that the government would not allow them to die, especially after the death of Thomas Ashe by forced feeding in 1917. The strikers were convinced that once the government realised that the prisoners were striking in earnest, they would back down and grant their demands. By the ninth day, as Andrew Bonar Law announced that the strikers would be allowed to die if that was their wish, the prison governor was quietly offering the leaders political status for all prisoners. However, their resolve had hardened and they now demanded immediate release. The next day, their demands were granted and the men were freed.

Hunger striking had proven an effective weapon against the Free State government as well. Immediately after her arrest in November 1922, Mary MacSwiney began a hunger strike that was to last twenty-four days. The Free State government had resolutely stated that no hunger striker would be freed, and yet their resolve broke and MacSwiney was unconditionally released. In fact, prior to October 1923, all republican hunger strikes against the Free State ended with release of the prisoners.[70] However, these strikers were predominantly women and none were well-known republican soldiers with a record of attacking Free State troops. In late September 1923, though, Dan Breen went on strike while in Mountjoy demanding unconditional release, and after seven days was released to the Eccles Street nursing home in a very weak state.[71] Though his strike did not receive enormous press coverage, it received mention in the dailies and was used as a rallying point for republicans. This marked the first unconditional release of a renowned republican combatant and had to be an embarrassment for the government as well as a morale destroyer amongst Free State forces. These were the examples upon which the strikers of October 1923 placed their hopes. So often the British and Free State governments had, after a mock show of strength, abandoned their hard line stance and capitulated.

Even when demands were not met, hunger striking could prove to be a very potent weapon. The most famous example of this was the hunger strike of Terence MacSwiney, the Lord Mayor of Cork, who died in Brixton prison on 25 October 1920 after refusing food for a remarkable seventy-four days. MacSwiney's strike received immense international publicity and elevated him to the position of one of the most celebrated martyrs of the Irish war for independence. However, after MacSwiney and two others died, the strike was called off and no more were attempted against the British government, demonstrating that once the government finally became intransigent, hunger striking lost its effectiveness as a practical tool and became solely one of propaganda, a lesson the Free State government seemed to learn only after the Civil War had ended.

An argument could be put forward that the ministers of the Free State government had learned a great deal from the Anglo-Irish War. While true that no more hunger strikes were attempted after October 1920, public support for the British regime had dissipated, so that no more strikes were needed. British intransigence had come at the wrong time. By quietly releasing republican hunger strikers during the Civil War, the government avoided rallying opposing forces around any new martyrs in the vein of Terence MacSwiney. Their newfound mettle of October 1923 was partially the result of the end of large-scale republican military operations and a guarantee by republican leaders to adopt legitimate forms of opposition. In essence, the government could act strongly because the opposition was severely weakened and no longer willing to fight.

Terence MacSwiney's death also made hunger striking a matter of moral debate. The Standing Committee of the Irish bishops had stated in 1917, during the original republican hunger strikes in Mountjoy that any deaths of the prisoners were the responsibility of the government. They showed their support when many members of the hierarchy participated in Ashe's funeral, marking the first time Irish bishops had taken part in a Fenian funeral.[72] As far as the hierarchy was concerned, the matter was settled, though Irish clergy and theologians continued debating the issue. During the strike of April 1920, Frank Gallagher was visited by Fr. O'Carney, who scolded him for attempting suicide and assured Gallagher that he would refuse absolution to any man still striking on the ninth day. Gallagher was of the opinion that O'Carney's moral standards were affected by his political views.[73] During the MacSwiney hunger strike, though, the issue of voluntary starvation was not treated so simplistically. Few clergymen were prepared to argue that MacSwiney's determination and self-sacrificial dedication to the cause of Irish nationalism were merely suicide.

Fr. P.J. Gannon's article defending hunger striking in the September 1920 issue of the Jesuit journal *Studies* was treated as an authoritative text of the period. Written while MacSwiney was still on strike, Gannon asserted that refusing to take food for the purpose of killing oneself is indeed sinful: 'But no hunger-striker aims at death. Quite the contrary; he desires to live. He aims at escaping from unjust detention, and, to do this, is willing to run the risk of death – a very different frame of mind.'[74] Even if he carried it to its fatal conclusion, he was still not seeking death. His object was to bring pressure of public opinion to bear on his unjust aggressor to secure his release and advance a cause for which he might face certain death in the field. Borrowing the argument of Francisco Suarez that sacrificing oneself for another is not sinful, Gannon wrote: 'If charity towards a single individual be held an adequate reason for not eating and thus sacrificing life, it would seem that love of one's country, which is really charity towards the millions of one's countrymen, constitutes a far more valid excuse for neglecting the positive precept of life.'[75] Gannon's article became widely read and generally respected, and as will be shown became the basis of much of the republicans' argument in favour of their hunger strike three years later. Ironically, Gannon, who was still publishing articles, was an outspoken opponent of the republican movement at that point.

Nor was the Catholic Church unified in its support behind MacSwiney. In 1920, Cardinal Gasquet wrote to Cardinal Secretary of State Gasparri from London that MacSwiney's strike should be condemned by the Holy See as it was causing much injury to religious feeling in England.[76] Like so many of their religious counterparts in Ireland, English Catholics had come to see the affair as a political rather a religious one. From Monsignor Curran's memoirs, though, it appears papal condemnation was never a serious threat. Curran, who was then Archbishop Walsh's private secretary, had discovered that Cardinal Giorgi, Cardinal Penitentiary, was of the opinion that hunger striking was morally justified and wanted to refer the case to the Sacred Penitentiary rather than the Holy Office, as was possible according to Church Law, so that he could express his opinion on the matter. His opinion, though, never clearly appeared in print. Giorgi had little about which to worry. The Assessor of the Holy Office, its chief theologian and executive officer, Monsignor Lottini, strongly upheld the morality of MacSwiney's strike, and so it was almost certain that condemnation by the Holy Office would not take place. It was only in 1930 though, while entertaining Archbishop Kelly of Sydney at dinner, that Curran was told by Cardinal Cerretti that Benedict XV had suffered much anxiety over MacSwiney's hunger strike and was determined to do all he could to avoid a decision. He was particularly anxious not to involve the Holy Office and wanted to keep the matter between MacSwiney and his confessor.[77] In the end, Benedict even granted MacSwiney a papal blessing as his death approached.

Much to the consternation of Cardinal Gasquet and most likely Cardinals Bourne and Merry del Val, the Irish bishops, as well as Bishop Amigo of Southwark, fully supported MacSwiney during his strike. Bishop Cohalan, who visited MacSwiney in Brixton and presided over his requiem Mass along with seven other bishops, stated publicly that everyone admired MacSwiney's heroic sacrifice. His death had drawn the attention and sympathy of the world to the cause of Irish freedom.[78] This is not to say that he embraced hunger striking as an assured beneficial weapon, quite the contrary. In the same letter in which he praised MacSwiney, Cohalan asked the prisoners in Cork gaol who were still refusing food to end their strike. If the strike was not called off, he believed, these men would die without impressing on the world more than had already been impressed. Continuance would only lead to the waste of human life. The morale of the nation could be maintained without the useless sacrifice of valuable lives.[79] The hierarchy had supported hunger strikers throughout the Anglo-Irish War and even endorsed hunger striking as a legitimate weapon in the case of Terence MacSwiney. With the onset of the Civil War, however, their public stance changed and they castigated republican hunger strikers as engaging in acts of suicide.

Interestingly enough, the first striker to draw their criticism was Mary MacSwiney, who began hunger striking for unconditional release in early November 1922, as she believed her imprisonment to be illegitimate and knew of no more effective protest.[80] Bishop Cohalan, the same man who supported Terence during his hunger strike towards the same ends and for the same reasons, informed his flock from the pulpit that Mary was guilty of the crime of self-murder. According to

MacSwiney, when her friends questioned Cohalan how he could condemn her actions after praising her brother for his sacrifice, '[h]e replied "Bishops can make mistakes sometimes".'[81] Though his statement seems to imply that he had been wrong in supporting Terence MacSwiney's popular hunger strike, he did not explain himself further. As was often the case during this period, Cohalan publicly expressed the most severe attitude amongst the hierarchy, most of who chose to remain silent. There is no reason to doubt, however, that they fundamentally agreed with their colleague in Cork.

Two of the MacSwiney sisters sought to point out the inconsistencies in the bishops' attitudes towards hunger striking. Annie sent a letter to Pope Benedict XV informing him that while he had sent a papal blessing to Terence in 1920 as he neared his death, Mary, 'dying in Dublin 1922 for same cause in same way, refused Sacraments because she will not take oath that is not meant to be kept.'[82] Eithne released a statement a year later pointing out that the men engaged in hunger strike were fighting for the republic, just as Terence had done, using the same weapon he had used. Though Terence's death had been labelled a suicide by some people, the actions of the Irish bishops and priests, as well as the pope, proved that he certainly was not; 'It is hardly necessary to point out that the Bishops and Priests of Ireland could hardly pray and express reverence and admiration for suicides, nor would the Holy Father The Pope bestow a special Blessing on a suicide.'[83]

While Terence MacSwiney's hunger strike has received a great deal of scholarly attention,[84] the problematic strikes of the Civil War are rarely invoked. Even when they are, explanations for changes in episcopal attitudes are insufficient. James Healy, one of the few scholars to examine those hunger strikes in detail, insists that the seeming reversal of Cohalan's mentality was nothing of the sort. Rather, it displays the fact that Cohalan did not view all hunger strikes as equal. Some were justifiable while others were not, and those that were not were most easily condemned as suicide.[85] Healy, though, fails to offer any further insight into what he sees as the complexities of Cohalan's views, never offering further details on his theory of Cohalan's dichotomous view of hunger strikes. How he could praise one MacSwiney and condemn another for the same act, or how he would preside over a solemn requiem Mass for Terence while refusing Denis Barry's remains into any church in his diocese remains unexplained.

Pádraig Corkery offers a better explanation, claiming that Cohalan's views towards hunger striking had undergone a drastic change during those years. His stance towards them during the war for independence had been a reluctant acceptance of their legitimacy as a weapon of resistance provided they contained proportionate reason. In other words, Terence MacSwiney's strike was acceptable because the benefits were immediate and weighty.[86] By the time Denis Barry died, Corkery postulates, Cohalan had given serious deliberation to the subject of hunger striking and changed his attitude completely. The proof of this, he finds, is in Cohalan's use of the language of suicide.[87] Whereas he could have employed his old theological framework and stated that this strike was not moral under the circumstances, he chose instead to refer to it as a suicide. Corkery's argument is more sound that Healy's, but it is still unsatisfactory. Like Healy, Corkery shies away from allowing for politics impacting on Cohalan's views. Further deliberation may have caused him to switch to the language of suicide, but it was only once the republicans were striking against the Free State that Cohalan even considered criticising hunger striking. Furthermore, his letter to the *Cork Examiner* stating, in effect, that republicans could not openly oppose the decrees of the bishops and then protest when the bishops did not cooperate, in this instance referring to his having refused Barry's body into a Cork diocesan church, shows that his decisions were not simply guided by theological re-examination.[88]

During Mary MacSwiney's hunger strike, Cohalan's actions sometimes contradicted his strong pronouncements against her. Like Archbishop Byrne and, to a degree Cardinal Logue, Cohalan attempted to act in a way beneficial to republicans while appearing to maintain unwavering support of the Free State government. According to Liam de Róiste, by the final week of her strike, Cohalan stated that he was willing to take responsibility for her if she was released. A few days later Cohalan said that he would use his influence to secure her release on humanitarian grounds. At the same time he proclaimed in his sermon that she could not receive the sacraments because she was committing suicide.[89] De Róiste offered no explanation for this paradoxical behaviour, but given the level of indignation among the Cork population at MacSwiney's continued imprisonment, perhaps Cohalan was simply bending to popular pressure. Undoubtedly he was influenced by a requisition for release signed by such prominent Corkonians as Professor O'Rahilly,

Daniel Corkery and de Róiste himself, who demonstrated his lack of regard for MacSwiney by referring to her as a 'monomaniac' in his journal.[90]

Mary MacSwiney's hunger strike was something of a cause célèbre. Many groups, including several branches of the Irish Self-Determination League, Sinn Féin's British organisation, sent letters of protest to President Cosgrave and Archbishop Byrne, who as Archbishop of Dublin was responsible for spiritual affairs of some of the largest and symbolic prisons in the Free State, including Mountjoy and Kilmainham, regarding the continued imprisonment of MacSwiney. The Central Branch (London) of the ISDL informed Byrne that they were humiliated that Mary's brother had received better treatment at the hands of the English than she did in her own country. They called upon him to insist on the application of Christian principles and end the present system of brutality.[91] As her strike drew on and reports appeared in the press that she was weakening, several more branches of the ISDL appealed to Byrne to not allow MacSwiney to die without the sacraments of the Church that were granted to Terence. A woman named Elizabeth Moran informed Byrne that no other bishops in the world but those in Ireland would dare to stand between God and His children at the hour of their death.[92]

These angry letters were the result of Byrne's continued silence on the subject of MacSwiney's strike and requests for the sacraments, which had been denied her by the prison chaplain. This was a calculated manoeuvre by Byrne, who refused to give public interviews or make public statements on the subject to keep his name from being used for republican propaganda. He saw two aspects under which hunger strikes could be considered – the political point of view and as a means of forcing the government to release prisoners. He decided that neither were any of his business.[93] This did not mean, though, that he actually stayed aloof from the matter. While he remained publicly silent, he was very engaged in attempting to resolve the situation. In communications with Cosgrave, Byrne remained steadfast that it would be a grave mistake for the government to allow MacSwiney to die as a result of hunger striking, and therefore she should be released. He admitted that he had no great sympathy for MacSwiney personally and none politically, but she was a woman, and an untried and unconvicted prisoner. Therefore, the government would not be absolved of the taint of inhumanity, even if she died by her own refusal to take food. Further-more, she was the sister of Terence and as such would be identified with him as a martyr apotheosis.[94] Cosgrave responded that while he respected the Archbishop's views, it would be impossible to release MacSwiney. He justified this stance not with a direct accusation against MacSwiney, but an imprecise allegation against the female sex in general: 'Your Grace may not be wholly cognisant of the prominent and destructive part played by women in the present deplorable revolt against the definitely expressed will of the vast majority of the Irish People, and against those sacred principles upon which civilization and even Christianity itself is founded.'[95] He accused MacSwiney of being largely responsible for the prevailing anarchy and crime, but never elaborated on this statement. Perhaps he felt that given her reputation, no elaboration was necessary.

The attitude of Cosgrave towards female republicans seems to have been especially antagonistic throughout the duration of the war. In a plea for Byrne's intervention, the sister of one of the girls on hunger strike in April 1923 asked him to approach Cosgrave about freeing the prisoners, who had demanded their release. Byrne agreed to do what he could, but added that his powers in such matters were small.[96] He wrote to Cosgrave:

> Don't you think the Government has the rebellion sufficiently in hand without allowing [the hunger strikers] to die even through their own fault? I am aware of the Government view as to the machinations of women in the movement but even at the risk of being tiresome and perhaps illogical I would put in a strong word for a gesture of clemency in regard to these women. There is no doubt their deaths would cause a wave of sympathy through the country.[97]

In conclusion, he stated that the Free State government was strong enough not to make war on women. Cosgrave replied that Byrne would have observed that real success did not attend the government's efforts until particular attention was directed at women, 'who operated with impunity in every possible way'.[98] He continued his seemingly para-noid view of female Republicans: 'Our experience is that those in arms against us are opposed to any limitation imposed by any government and the more serious opposition comes from the women, who apparently are a law to themselves.'[99] The government might have been strong enough not to make war on women, but clearly Cosgrave was not.

THE HUNGER STRIKE OF OCTOBER – NOVEMBER 1923

With the end of armed hostilities, many on the Republican side had resigned themselves to accepting their defeat. The thousands of internees faced their indefinite detention with a sense of necessary compliance. They had been handily defeated and the Free State government showed no signs of rehabilitating them. This attitude was evident prior to the general election held on 27 August 1923, in which most Republicans feared they would suffer a routing at the hands of Cumann na nGaedheal. However, by winning forty-four seats to the government's sixty-three, a feeling of renewed hope spread through the movement. Republicans believed that, despite the attitude of the Church and press, the people were still supportive of their efforts. This recharging undoubtedly restored the prisoners with a vigour that had been absent for months and probably helped cause the September Mountjoy riot and the hunger strike that began in October. They believed that the same people who voted for them would use the strike as a rallying point, back them fully and the government would be forced to succumb to popular pressure.[100]

This pressure was evident in the form of multiple petitions calling for release of the internees. Over the course of the autumn of 1923, local government organisations throughout the island passed resolutions calling for the immediate and oftentimes unconditional release of all political prisoners.[101] The newspapers reported almost on a daily basis several county councils, urban councils or rural district councils, spread across the Free State, which passed resolutions of this nature, and very rarely did such motions fail. The reasons given for these resolutions consisted of a standard list: the ambiguity of 'political prisoner' status, no justification for holding internees after the calling of the ceasefire, financial hardship faced by families whose primary sources of income were locked away, the cost to the government of maintaining so many internees, and the likelihood of increased bitterness and possible retribution if the prisoners continued to be held. Patrick Hogan, Labour TD for Clare, told the Dáil that he was in possession of a memorial signed by thirty thousand Clare residents calling for the release of political prisoners: 'I would suggest to the Ministry that the little heed they give to the voice of public opinion, as expressed by public bodies and by public plebiscites,' he added 'would explain the little heed that has been given to this Parliament in certain quarters.'[102]

The government's high-handed attitude to public bodies was evident in the language of ministerial responses to resolutions calling for release of internees. O'Higgins responded to the Clonmel Number 2 Rural District Council's resolution calling for the release of prisoners with a letter stating that release would constitute a danger to the country. Furthermore, as long as arms were hidden throughout the country with the express object of challenging the principles upon which all civilised states must rest, the question of release was difficult 'and cannot be approached in the light-hearted and irresponsible spirit of your Council's resolution'.[103] On 28 October, the Cork Corporation unanimously voted to request that the government take immediate steps for liberation of the political prisoners in the interests of peace and good feelings. Mulcahy responded that while these concepts were serious concerns of the government, 'Surely, your Corporation may in time consider it its duty to offer to those charged with the grave responsibilities of securing these blessings more serious-minded and effective assistance towards that end than that of unreasoned telegrams.'[104] The second piece in *The Times*, it should be noted, had been submitted by the Ministry of Defence for publication. In other words, the government was demonstrating that it was not backing down.

Two other incidents most likely contributed to the change in internees' attitudes. On 12 October, the Catholic bishops of the six-county area issued a statement complaining of unequal treatment of Northern Catholics by the Protestant-dominated government.[105] They criticised the termination of proportional representation in local elections, gerrymandering, the education system, which they considered anti-Catholic, the oath of allegiance to the King and Northern Government, and the disregard for Catholics' rights as evidenced by the treatment of Fermanagh and Tyrone in the boundary issue. This statement, intended solely for criticism of the six counties, became a propaganda weapon for republicans eager to highlight the discrepancies in the bishops' opinions. Multiple speakers asked why the oath of allegiance in the Free State was acceptable while the oath in the North was not. Surely, they told their audiences, the bishops did not have the political under-standing to be able to distinguish the nuances that separated the two. Also, the body of Noel Lemass had only recently been found. Though official accusations against government forces would only come weeks later at the inquiry, republicans used the discovery of the body as proof of government criminality from the time of the finding of the body and as a way of inciting popular opposition to the government's tactics.

The combination of optimism due to these occurrences and feelings of helplessness caused by fear of indefinite detention caused conditions within the jails and internment camps to worsen. In mid-September 1923, shortly after Dermott MacManus replaced Paudeen O'Keeffe as deputy governor of Mountjoy, a row broke out between the prisoners and authorities that changed the nature of prisoner treatment in the jail. Mulcahy reported in the Dáil that the prisoners mutinied after bolts and padlocks were installed on their doors.[106] Ernie O'Malley believed that the problem was that the authorities were attempting to treat the republicans like regular prisoners.[107] The internees objected, using extreme measures. They destroyed prison property as tempers flared in the jail offices and extra troops were called in to prepare for difficul-ties. When the prisoners were called out of their cells, they refused, leading to hosepipes being used against the men on the bottom landing and troops dragging prisoners from their cells, and in the case of the upper landing, throwing them down the stairs.[108] Upon arriving back at Mountjoy after a brief stay in Arbour Hill, Peadar O'Donnell found that the authorities had intensified their attempts at forcing republican prisoners to adhere to regular prison regulations.[109] This was due, no doubt, to the fears raised by the riot. The result was increased prisoner discontentment. With the belief that release was not likely prisoners be-came more and more convinced that extreme measures were necessary.

The new regulations exacerbated the longstanding problem of internees' allegations of cruel treatment at the hands of the jailors. In September 1922, republican prisoners at Kilmainham complained to Seán Ó Muirthile, the governor. They claimed that they had been denied the right to receive visitors and that the food was inedible. They demanded that their own cooks have the right to prepare their meals and that a representative of the prisoners be present at the censoring of parcels. These, they claimed, were basic rights that even the English had granted. They lamented the fact they were treated worse by their fellow Irishmen then they had been under the Black and Tans. They threatened that they would not tolerate this treatment for much longer and that 'a tragedy is imminent such as startled Dublin when Tomas Ashe was done to death striving for these same rights which his death won from the British for all Republican prisoners afterwards.'[110]

By October 1923, republican claims of cruel and inhuman treatment were widespread. A report from (republican) Dáil Éireann pointed out several allegations of cruelty, including prisoners manacled in the basement for over a fortnight, men driven into their cells at 7pm by rifle fire, deprivation of parcels, letters and recreation and hospital patients deprived of exercise. Given that the systemised cruelty the prisoners faced reached its height in mid-October, the statement claimed, the men who started the hunger strike did so feeling that the only choice they had was a slow death.[111] Acting President Patrick Ruttledge wrote that:

> [n]ot content with depriving their victims of liberty the new tyrants have, with the zeal of the imitator, sought to outdo their masters in the infliction of suffering and humiliation on defenceless prisoners. Having exhausted every means of protest to no avail, and seeing the treatment meted out to them grow daily more barbarous, the prisoners have been forced to adopt the last dread course open to them, and are now on hunger strike. This strike ends with release or death.[112]

Headquarters of the IRA sent a document to members of the medical profession calling their attention to inhuman conditions in several prisons; 'Such conditions and treatment are certain to injure prisoners mentally and physically, and that such should prevail with the cognisace [sic] of the "Free State" authorities is a disgrace to a Christian Country and a crime against humanity.'[113]

Despite republican allegations of cruel treatment meted out by Free State authorities, overall treatment of internees appears to have been very good. Prior to the September riot, most jails and internment camps had been run effectively as prisoner-of-war camps, a fact that the Red Cross confirmed after visiting several camps.[114] Despite destruction of property, constant escape attempts and a general disregard for Free State authority, the government allowed republican prisoners leeway that regular prisoners would never be granted. Punishments were meted out for failure to comply with rules, including shutting off of gas to the cells, reduction or stoppage of parcel delivery and alleged episodes of torture, but prisoners were allowed to fraternise and organise themselves complete with leaders, and jail authorities were even prepared to deal with prisoners through these leaders. Peadar O'Donnell admitted that even when in solitary confinement in Finner Camp in County Donegal he began to forget he was a prisoner.[115] Aodh de Blácam wrote to Professor Alfred O'Rahilly that during the two months he had been a prisoner, he had been treated as well as circumstances allowed with the exception of one savage week.[116] Given this relatively cooperative relationship between internees and jailors, the enforced strictures that came into effect in September undoubtedly caused a rise in conflictive attitudes within the internee communities.

According to the republican leaders within Mountjoy, the hunger strike began on Sunday, 14 October, and by the following Wednesday 458 of the approximately 500 prisoners across three sites were on strike, demanding immediate and unconditional release.[117] Accurate information was slow in disseminating throughout society. Initially the *Irish Times* reported that approximately 300 prisoners were striking. The next day, the *Times* was using an unreferenced quotation that this was the 'biggest hunger strike in history' and that 380 men were now refusing food.[118] At a concert held on 17 October in connection with the Sinn Féin Ard Fheis, it was announced that 440 men were on hunger strike. On 19 October, the Re-organising Committee of Sinn Féin announced 'on reliable authority' that 1,301 prisoners at Tintown No. 3 Camp had joined in on the hunger strike since the eighteenth.[119] On 22 October, the Re-organising Committee announced that the total number of strikers had risen to 7,280, and the next day they reported that with the addition of approximately 1,000 prisoners at Haretown Camp, the total number of hunger strikers was approximately 8,200 across ten separate gaols and internment camps, making it the largest hunger strike in Irish history, though this number is most likely inflated.

Scholars who have examined the strike have produced conflicting figures for it. Healy believes the number to be approximately 8,000. Biggs puts the number at approximately 7,800. Fallon finds the number to be 5,000, though this estimation is, by most accounts, inadequate. IRA headquarters informed members of the medical profession that at least 7,407 prisoners were striking on 23 October, though this figure is only a total for eight camps.[120] This final number, though, seems to exaggerate the extent of the strike. The most accurate data appear to come from the reports received twice a day by the Executive Council. According to the government's information, the largest the strike ever got was on 23 October, when between 7,439 and 7,196 men and women in twelve camps were on strike.[121] The total number of prisoners who engaged in hunger strike at some point during the months of October and November was 7,618, though this number was never achieved all at once.[122]

Attempting to explain the motivations of over 7,000 hunger strikers would be academically irresponsible. Michael Kilroy, O/C of the prisoners at Mountjoy, released a statement declaring that the prisoners had resorted to hunger strike as a result of the Free State's tactics to break their passive resistance. Despite the 'voluntary' nature of the strike, most strikers, quite likely, began and ended the strike under orders or were subjected to the moral conscription that Peadar O'Donnell noted in which many were unwillingly swept. This would explain why so many abandoned the strike so quickly. By 2 November, 3,442 men had abandoned the strike while only forty men and women took it up independently in the same period. As O'Donnell stated, he encountered many who wanted to merely flirt with being on hunger strike. In his mind, that was not possible – 'A powerful force like hunger won't be toyed with.'[123]

However, there was a minority of vocal ideologues who have left a record of their thoughts and arguments which offer a great deal of insight into their actions. Of fundamental importance to their entire argument was their belief in the illegitimacy of the Free State as an institution. To the men and women who refused food in October 1923, the Free State and its government were the newest iteration of British attempts to control the island. With this in mind, they viewed theological justifications for the 1920 hunger strikes as equally applicable to their own struggle. Fr. Gannon's article in *Studies* was referenced on several occasions, including by Monsignor Michael Curran, vice rector of the Irish College in Rome, who though a republican supporter, chose, like his superior, Monsignor Hagan, to stay relatively silent on the matter of the October 1923 strike.

When seeking justification for their actions, republican hunger strikers did not look solely to theological experts, though their writings indicate that morality was their primary concern. The best known works on this are the writings of Ernie O'Malley. O'Malley had arrived at Mountjoy in a weak state having capitulated to Free State forces after multiple gunshot wounds. While still recovering, he joined in on the strike and, going against the wishes of doctors and fellow republicans, he refused food until the strike was called off. His memoirs, *The Singing Flame*, offer some insight into his hunger strike, but the book was written decades later. For a less filtered perspective, the letters he wrote while on strike are indispensable.

In reading the letters, one sees that O'Malley was obsessed with the spirituality of the nation and the republican movement. For him, the strike was a spiritual exercise, one which highlighted the importance of suffering:

> Frank [Gallagher] and I last night discussed the spiritual side of the strike. One felt it impossible to have carnal thoughts or to sin, though of course one knew how imperfect was their fervour. The equity of God is wonderful. He takes from the body to add to the spirit. I understand the spiritual side of suffering now.[124]

The suffering of the strike was a spiritual gain, and O'Malley became convinced that until the Irish people experienced a degree of spiritual suffering, they would lack the spirituality to create the Irish nation as it truly deserved to be. Well into the strike, he informed Erskine Childers's widow, Molly, '[t]he country has not had, as yet, sufficient voluntary sacrifice and suffering and not until suffering fructuates will she get back her real soul. The people are all right but need the driving force and they will suffer.' [125] O'Malley's lack of religious fervour just a few years later suggests that perhaps these were his attempts at rationalising his support of the losing side.

Frank Gallagher is another important source for the motivation of idealistic hunger strikers. While he wrote mostly political propaganda during the 1923 strike and was opposed to it from the start, his journal of the 1920 Mountjoy strike offers many insights into his mentality. Aside from the occasional episodes of delusion and paranoia, such as when he was convinced that hundreds of men with red eyes were attempting to steal his cup of water, Gallagher's journal entries show a mind that was guided almost solely by spirituality. He stated that he was not prepared to die for a people or the earth. However:

Ireland is something else ... Ireland is the dead and the things the dead would have done ... Ireland is the living and the things the living would die for ... Ireland is the Spirit. ... It is the tradition of the laughing courage of men upon whose heads the pitch-cap has been placed by fiends. ... It is the tradition of undefeat ... of indomitable failure ... of love for an ideal as strong as the love of the Apostles for Christ as He quivered upon the Cross. ... The crucifixion of Ireland is interminable and so her apostles are innumerable. ... Ireland is justice, is truth ... That Ireland with the Christ-like spirit which God breathes into subject peoples ... *that* Ireland I am willing to die for; I wish, I long to die for.[126]

For the benefit of the nation and to prove the sincerity of the republicans and the truth of their national doctrine, Gallagher was prepared to die joyfully to give the people proof.[127] This desire for death for the good of Ireland was briefly questioned when Gallagher considered that God may have been opposed to their cause. Even if this was the case, he was prepared to face the anger of God and suffer in his soul for the freedom of the Irish people. He then realised that God must be with them. For Gallagher, God is truth and liberty is part of truth. The saints died to profess God. It cannot be wrong to die to profess liberty.[128]

As the sister of Terence MacSwiney, Mary's thoughts and writings on hunger striking carried a certain amount of influence among those for whom her militant republican intransigence was not a problem. In her samizdat piece 'A Hunger Striker's Opinion of the Weapon from a Moral Standpoint', MacSwiney built an argument, borrowing largely from Gannon's 1920 article, to prove not only that hunger striking was not, as Bishop Cohalan had stated, suicide, but also that it was a powerful moral weapon in line with the teachings of Jesus Christ. She quoted John 15:13, 'Greater love than this no man hath, that a man lay down his life for his friend' and posited this as divine justification for hunger striking as a moral weapon in the fight for freedom; 'In all ages the man who lays down his life voluntarily for his country, his friend, for his religion above all, has been venerated. He can show no greater love. We note that Our Lord does not specify any particular method of laying down his life. No way is specially praised, none is condemned.'[129] Contrary to Cohalan's statements, willingness to lay down one's life for a good purpose is not the same as taking one's life, she contended. Hunger strikers are not desirous for death, any more so than a soldier bravely going into battle desires it. Fasting, in itself, is not an evil act; it is generally a meritorious act. While death is a possible effect of a hunger strike it is not a necessary effect. There is another possible and more probable effect: the release of the hunger striker and the consequent triumph, to that extent at least, of the protest against unlawful authority.[130]

* * *

As was his wont, Archbishop Byrne remained publicly silent regarding the October hunger strike. However, he wrote to Cosgrave in late October asking him to reconsider allowing the hunger strike to continue. Displaying a practical understanding of the situation, he stated that the war had ended and republican leaders had declared that they would adhere to constitutional methods. In Byrne's opinion, any death by hunger strike would be 'a downright calamity for the country'. No government however strong could afford to let thousands die for a political cause. It would cause such revulsion as to shake the very foundation of the state.[131] Like Byrne, Cardinal Logue worked quietly to terminate hunger strikes. He had sent a telegram to the Executive Council in November 1922 urging for the release of Mary MacSwiney and other female prisoners, only to be rebuffed.[132] Again, in October 1923, he wrote to Byrne that he expected trouble over the hunger strike. He had already had three women to see him about it 'and one of them was very wild'.[133] As the mass strike neared its conclusion, Logue expressed his displeasure at the intransigence regarding the hunger strike displayed by both sides of the political fray. After receiving a request for intervention from Madame O'Rahilly, he responded that he had no authority in the matter and could not see how he was even involved. He added that it was not his wish for anyone to go on hunger strike or die from it, and closed by informing her that if he had his wish, all uncharged and untried prisoners would be released.[134] The very fact that this telegram was reprinted in the *Irish Times* indicates that Logue was not quite as private as Byrne in expressing his displeasure.

Around the same time, Logue expressed himself even more publicly with a published appeal. In it, he admitted that republican prisoners had suffered severely: 'I sympathise sincerely with them; and were it at my disposal I should have the prisons emptied, and the concentration camps emptied before Christmas.' His chief anxiety was the danger to the health, lives and salvation of those on hunger strike, which he deemed 'foolish, ineffective, and of very doubtful morality'.[135] Contrary to Mary MacSwiney's contention that the sacrifice of life that the strikers were prepared to offer was in line with the teachings of Christ, Logue argued that for this to be true a cause needs to be universally and unanimously acknowledged as sufficient to justify the sacrifice. In other words, the Cardinal was attempting to reaffirm his moral superiority over people who had, time and again, chosen to see their cause as one that transcended the authority of the hierarchy. He earnestly appealed to those on hunger strike to abandon it and to find a more reasonable and lawful means of protesting for their liberation. He also urged the Government, 'who declare their readiness to liberate those untried and unconvicted prisoners, not to do things by halves and by driblets, thus prolonging the agony.' [136] While not complimentary to the republican side, Logue's appeal marked the only public episcopal criticism of the government during this period.

Addressing a crowd in Sackville Street days after the hunger strike had ended, Maud Gonne announced that it was largely through the intervention of Cardinal Logue and Bishop O'Donnell that the strike had been called off.[137] Frank Aiken had alerted prisoners the week before that Logue 'has gone the whole hog in demanding the release of all untried prisoners.'[138] Given the antipathy that had existed between Logue and the republicans, especially since the October pastoral, and Logue's previous refusals to show any public sympathy for the republicans, his statement was indeed an amazing document. It is probable that the aged Cardinal, who would not live another year, felt that as long as he maintained a strong pro-government and stability façade, he could work to help even those against whom he often railed. Furthermore, with the cessation of violence, he thought that the republicans should be given the opportunity to reincorporate themselves into society. It is equally interesting that the republicans, who had so vigorously continued to criticise the hierarchy for its political stances, were suddenly willing to abide by one of Logue's requests. It is arguable that they used Logue's intervention to abandon the strike with what dignity they could salvage. Sinn Féin released a statement pointing out that while the clergy had no right to enter the political sphere, Logue's pastoral was an appeal of a religious nature and devoid of any seed of bitterness. As a matter of saving face, the statement ended with a parting criticism of the clergy: 'The sooner political bitterness is dropped by our bishops and priests, the better. Then there will be no attacks on either side.'[139]

Not all bishops were willing to help the strikers, even in secret. Bishop Thomas O'Doherty, recently transferred from Clonfert to Galway made a rare display of harsh aggression aimed at the republican movement in a letter to Hagan. The republicans, he noted, were calling for the unconditional release of prisoners and have bombarded the bishops with appeals for intervention. If they were truly beaten as they confessed they were, he asked, why did they not surrender the bombs and arms which were being used to demoralise and terrorise decent people. During the elections, some even declared that the war would be renewed at the first possible opportunity; 'In face of all this I, for one, have no sympathy with the outcry.' Regarding the appeals for episcopal help, all he had to say was: 'They come well from the crowd that have tried to blacken the Bishops in Ireland and all over the world!' The bishops were keeping silent, but if they did speak O'Doherty was sure they would all say let the hunger strikers strike until they accepted the very reasonable terms of the government. The republicans had demoralised the people and half-ruined the country and could not be released on their own terms.[140]

Facing this major crisis, the Executive Council stood firm. As before, Cosgrave's letters are filled with rhetorical intransigence. Unlike past episodes though, the government's display of obduracy was more than mere words. Its attitude had hardened and it was prepared to actually allow for casualties to achieve victory: 'We had the matter of the hunger strike under consideration during the week and came to the conclusion that we could not give way', Cosgrave informed Archbishop Byrne, 'This view is so fixed in our minds that I believe each minister would prefer to leave public life altogether rather than yield.'[141] Cosgrave would be sorry to learn of any hunger strike-related deaths, but if he had any responsibility whatsoever, on no account should a single one be released save when the ordinary machinery of the state operated to secure it. Also, contrary to Byrne's fears, he believed that there would be some strike casualties but that they would have the opposite effect of that espoused by Byrne. On numerous occasions, the government had offered 'a clean slate' and every time these offers have been spurned. 'I am myself perfectly satisfied that generosity or mercy is thrown away on those people.'[142]

The government's obstinacy in the face of this hunger strike was inevitable. In a way, the size of the strike made the government's course of action easier than it would have been had the strike been small. Small-scale strikes were difficult because the strikers, being few in number, provided a personal axis around which attention could revolve. The striker could be portrayed as a victim facing an entire government for his or her principles. Release of strikers in these conditions could prove to be huge propaganda victories for the republicans and even demoralising acts for Free State forces, yet the government knew that allowing any of a small group to die would prove disastrous. The situation was drastically different with over 7,000 political prisoners striking for immediate release. The government had no choice but to stand firm and wait for the strike to flounder. To do otherwise meant releasing a potential opposition force in possession of weapons caches deposited throughout the country. Furthermore, release of the strikers, even over a period of time, would function as a propaganda tool for the republicans, who could claim to have achieved a large victory, while serving to highlight the government's weakness in the face of opposition. Even if the government was as sure of itself as its rhetoric indicated, giving in on this occasion would be sheer folly.

Unlike with small strikes, death was not a mitigating factor in the minds of the Free State leaders. They were not concerned that they would have to face widespread casualties despite the large number of strikers. Cosgrave had indicated as much when he wrote that the government expected a few deaths.[143] Death by voluntary starvation was extremely rare and required a mentality that most political prisoners did not possess, a fact of which the Free State government and all but the most idealistic prisoners were aware. Including Thomas Ashe's death by forced feeding, a total of four prisoners out of approximately 1,000 had died due to hunger strike. The government had only to bide its time and wait for the weaker strikers to abandon. Once the process started, the whole scheme would inevitably collapse. To maintain a façade of strength and put behind them the embarrassment of the release of all hunger strikers to date, including well-known republicans Mary MacSwiney and Dan Breen, the government was prepared to let the strikers of October 1923 go without food until their resolve was broken and they terminated the strike.

The government's obstinacy proved correct. By the evening of 3 November, only 1,531 remained on strike, with the Hare Park strike collapsing that day. The next evening saw the number of strikers down to 671. A steady stream of men continued to abandon the cause until only 328 remained a week later. Few gave up from then on until 21 November, when the strike at Tralee jail collapsed.[144] By then, though, Denis Barry had died and the strike was in its final hours. Barry died on 20 November after thirty-four days of refusing food. Andrew O'Sullivan died after striking for forty days on 23 November, the same day that the strike was called off. At the bitter end, 221 strikers remained.[145]

When theorising on why the hunger strike failed, Ernie O'Malley wrote: 'There is not enough spirituality in our movement – that is what beat us here and I'm sure also in other gaols, so we have another lesson in humility to learn.'[146] Despite the defeat, the strike had been worth it to O'Malley, who was convinced that it had allowed him to pray and think more fervently than before. Most republicans, though, whether in prison or not, were just glad it was over, and that hints at the real reason the strike failed. Peadar O'Donnell was less philosophical in his analysis of the failure. For him, continuing the strike once the initial break up was found to be large and widespread was a mistake and showed a weakness of leadership in the prisoners. Once it became a relatively small cadre, the strike changed in its whole meaning; 'Instead of being a burst from the jails it became an attack on the stubborn resistance of the mass whom we now began to break into new divisions; the relatives of those who had "given in" and those who were "sticking it out".'[147]

When Barry's remains were finally released by the government, Bishop Cohalan refused to allow them in any Cork diocesan church until Bishop Foley of Kildare had verified that Barry had received Last Rites. Even after Sinn Féin had received written confirmation from Foley that Barry had in fact received Last Rites, Cohalan refused to allow his body entry into his parish church. The Cork branch of Sinn Féin released a statement relaying this information. The statement concluded:

'We shall make no further comment here on His Lordship's

action. The present and the future will judge him standing at the foot of the Graves, where the hungerstrikers lie buried, and contrast His Lordship's action three years ago and to-day. The wonder will be all the greater when men reflect that his action was taken as Representative of the unchanging and unchangeable Church.'[148]

Cohalan justified his actions by pointing out that while he regretted that he had to deny Barry a Christian burial, he was merely enforcing Church law, and had his own brother taken the same course as Barry, he would have treated his burial the same way. Expecting conflict over the fact that Barry had received Last Rites but was being refused a Christian burial, Cohalan noted that few people are denied absolution on their deathbeds. However, in the sphere of external public social order in the Church, to allow Christian burial after certain crimes requires some proof of repentance, and a man who deliberately determined to starve to death shows no sign of repentance. Demonstrating that he still believed republican actions necessitated whatever punishments were available to the bishops, Cohalan concluded with: 'I feel bound to do it [refuse Christian burial], especially on account of the challenge to the Church.'[149]

Unsurprisingly, Mary MacSwiney took up the challenge of replying to the Bishop of Cork with a statement that invoked her brother and Cohalan's changing attitude over the course of three years:

> Could anything prove more clearly that the Bishop of Cork is not acting in accordance with Catholic teaching in his treatment of Comdt. Denis Barry than the fact that all he says about hunger striking in this statement, if true to-day, must have been equally true three years ago, when he officiated with all the honour that the Church can pay to a faithful son, at the obsequies of another hunger striker.[150]

Interestingly, though, her greatest outrage was due to a section of Cohalan's statement that accused her of having opposed the Easter Rising and of gambling with her brother's life when he was on hunger strike. 'She encouraged Terry to continue the strike. She never believed it would go to a fatal end. She thought he would be released, and that she would share in a sunburst of cheap glory.'[151] MacSwiney's written response belied her indignant rage at her bishop's characterisation of her. She intermittently petitioned the Vatican to summon Cohalan before an ecclesiastical court for the next nine years, finally accepting that no action would be taken when a Monsignor Ribberi informed her that the Vatican could not hear cases that had an evident political bearing.[152]

*   *   *

Internment had been a strategic weapon of the government, but indefinite imprisonment, except of the prominent leaders, had never been considered. Contrary to republican propaganda, the government had been releasing prisoners in a steady stream, with eight hundred gaining freedom the week ending 13 October 1923.[153] As part of the government's show of determination, release of all prisoners on hunger strike had been suspended as of 26 October, even if they had been recommended for release. Prisoners who came off the strike, though, were released upon signing the standard form promising to abstain from illegal activities against the state. Cosgrave mentioned in his letter to Byrne that numerous strikers were already giving up without winning any concessions from the government.[154] He saw that the numbers kept dropping. The government appears to have been confident that this would continue and the Free State Publicity Bureau made sure that the daily newspapers gave a running account of how many people came off the hunger strike.

Once the strike had virtually ceased, the government began releasing large numbers of prisoners again, with five hundred gaining freedom during the week ending 10 November. The Publicity Bureau, proving that the government was not eager to keep a large number of citizens in jail, released information showing that on 1 July 1923 there were 11,316 prisoners, whereas on 17 November that number had been reduced to 6,834.[155] By 23 November, the last day of the strike, the total number of prisoners was down to 6,124, with 2,303 having gained their freedom during the period of the strike.[156] Widespread releases continued and when Seán T. O'Kelly was released in mid-December, he theorised that the remaining 3,500 prisoners would be released by Christmas, with the possibility that de Valera would even be freed early the next year.[157] The government did not operate as quickly as O'Kelly predicted, but 1,500 prisoners were all that remained in early January of 1924, though it was then expected that the leaders would be held for substantially longer, which proved true.[158]

Even Kevin O'Higgins was of the opinion that the internees should be released at the first opportune moment. Before the strike collapsed, he informed Cosgrave that he believed that Christmas should be seized upon as a time to reduce the number of internees down to 2,500, with the government announcing that it would adopt a policy of releasing five to seven hundred internees every month if the general attitude and conduct throughout the Free State warranted it. What was important, though, was that large-scale releases could not synchronise with the hunger strike or even follow too closely after it. To allow such would associate the two in the minds of the prisoners and the general public, thereby justifying and vindicating the hunger strike policy.[159]

The government was determined to defeat the republican opposition, but it was not intent on exterminating it altogether. Its refusal to release or even negotiate with the few hundred strikers who remained at the end, though, shows that internment would end on the government's terms. A last-minute display of clemency would have been a popular move, but it would have run counter to the government's intentions of destroying hunger striking as an effective weapon of protest, and the plan seems to have been successful. In relation to concurrent hunger strikes in Northern Ireland, which will be briefly examined in the next chapter, the governor of the Londonderry prison would report to Home Affairs (Northern Ireland): 'The firm attitude adopted by the Ministry during the hunger strike of October 1923, in not giving way in one single instance, sounded the death knell to the Sinn Féin policy of demanding release unconditionally.'[160]

O'Halpin remarks that the ministers handled the entire hunger strike with considerable skill. They allowed the republicans to make all the moves, therefore all the mistakes.[161] The argument that the government lost any advantage it had gained when it refused to release the prisoners after the collapse of the strike, he says, would only be apt were there evidence that softer treatment would have diluted the militancy of the detainees. Instead, he believes that the government's policy towards republican internees after the war, while ungenerous, 'was amply justified both by circumstances and by events'.[162] The collapse of the strike was the last straw for most prisoners, who saw the futility of resuming armed resistance. Equally importantly, the handling of the strike underlined for the majority of republicans the power and political authority of the Free State government. Softening their stance just as they were gaining the grudging respect of their opponents would have been a grave mistake on the part of the ministers.

CONCLUSION

In the end, the strike backfired on the republicans. Despite the personal victories it allowed for some, it did little good for the republican movement. Cait O'Kelly, who had been negotiating for a pre-Christmas release through an intermediary, blamed the end of the strike for the government's hardened stance on release of internees, though at the time of her writing she remained hopeful that the government would not scrap the terms to which they had unofficially agreed.[163] Termination of the strike without achieving any of their goals also left republicans more dispirited than they had been at the close of armed resistance. One man informed Hagan that whatever impetus the republicans had received from the elections, the end of the strike had been a distinct loss to their cause.[164]

The collapse of the strike could not even be propagandised as successfully garnering popular support back into the republican camp. As has been pointed out in many books on the Civil War period, the Irish people suffered from war-weariness even before the outbreak of the Civil War. After the war, with the fighting finally over, people wanted to get back to their lives. Therefore, when the hunger strike broke out in October, the public showed little interest in the matter. Mary MacSwiney's strike of November 1922 had caused widespread indignation against the government, surpassing the expectations of the government or even Cumann na mBan, which had organised the protest movement.[165] With each successive strike, public interest dwindled, and though interest rose with the October 1923 strike, considering the number of people on strike, the number of protests was minimal.[166]

Even with the announcement that Denis Barry had died, public outcry was almost non-existent. As expected, republicans made use of Barry's death for propaganda purposes, but few people seemed to care. His funeral was well-attended, but there was no increase in anti-government sentiment afterward, a marked difference from what occurred after the funerals of Thomas Ashe and Terence MacSwiney. The government had waited nervously for public reactions to Barry's death, uncertain how the public would respond. The lack of a public outcry, coupled with Cohalan's refusal to allow Barry's remains in a Cork diocesan church reaffirmed in the minds of the ministers that their actions were widely accepted as the correct course to take. Public reactions seem to have validated Hogan's belief that the people craved strong, ruthless measures.

Perhaps worst of all from the republican perspective, there was the perception that the hunger strike had greatly strengthened the government party.[167] The Provisional Government had been viewed as weak, especially after Collins's death deprived it of his popular and commanding presence, but the Cosgrave government emerged from the struggle seemingly stronger and with a greater public mandate than the 1923 General Election had indicated they possessed. The ministers believed in the strength of their own government and acted with a pragmatic ruthlessness they thought to be most expedient in ending the republican opposition to their leadership. Reactions to the execution policy and the government's handling of the hunger strike of October – November 1923 proved to the Free State's leaders that they had the support of the public and the relatively uncritical support of the Church.

Remarkably, though a section of the hierarchy secretly acted to end the executions and reintegrate republicans back into Free State society, most bishops remained completely silent and uninvolved. Even those who did act never openly criticised the Free State government, despite displaying clear moral opposition to the treatment of prisoners. That they felt compelled to speak so forcefully against republicans for 'moral outrages' and yet not against the government for actions which they felt to be similarly outrageous indicates that political considerations played a larger role in their decision-making process than they were prepared to admit. The political expediency of the bishops' actions had a large impact on the thousands interned by the Free State government, but this palled in comparison to the hundreds of thousands of Catholics in the six-county area who found their lives changed forever by partition. Once again, despite initial outspoken opposition to the founding of a Northern Irish state, the hierarchy aligned itself to the Free State playbook and accepted the 'temporary' exclusion of Northern Catholics from the Free State with minimal complaint given the severity of the situation.

NOTES

1. Oliver St John Gogarty, *As I Was Going Down Sackville Street*, p.133.
2. Michael Hopkinson, *Green Against Green*, p.179.
3. John Regan, *The Irish Counter-Revolution*, p.106.
4. Charles Townshend, *Political Violence in Ireland* (Oxford, 1984), p.372; Michael Hopkinson, *Green Against Green*, p.89; Jeffrey Prager, *Building Democracy in Ireland*, p.66.
5. Dermot Keogh, *The Vatican, the Bishops and Irish Politics*, p.100.
6. David Fitzpatrick, *The Two Irelands*, p.132; Peter Hart, *The IRA at War, 1916–1923* (Oxford, 2003), p.15; Bill Kissane, *The Politics of the Irish Civil War*, pp.3–9, 82–4.
7. John Regan, *The Irish Counter-Revolution*, p.125.
8. Dermot Keogh, *The Vatican, the Bishops and Irish Politics*, p.4
9. See Chapter 2.
10. *Dáil Debates*, vol. 1, 17 November 1922, Military Executions.
11. Ibid.
12. Colm Campbell, *Emergency Law in Ireland, 1918–1925* (Oxford, 1994), p.167; Michael Hopkinson, *Green Against Green*, p.191.
13. *Dáil Debates*, vol. 2, 8 December 1922, Mountjoy Executions.
14. Ibid.
15. Ibid.
16. NAI, Dept. of Taoiseach, G2/1, No. C1/13, Executive Council Minutes, 20 December 1922. (My emphasis.)
17. UCDA, Mulcahy papers, P7/b/96, Memorandum from O'Higgins, January 1923.
18. UCDA, Mulcahy papers, P7/b/96, Hogan memo, 11 January 1923.
19. UCDA, Mulcahy papers, P7/B/101, O'Shiel to Cosgrave, 1 February 1923.
20. UCDA, Mulcahy papers, P7/B/101, Cosgrave to Mulcahy, 25 January 1923. (Emphasis in original.)
21. *Dáil Debates*, vol. 2, 8 December 1922, Mountjoy Executions.
22. Eunan O'Halpin, *Defending Ireland: The Irish State and Its Enemies Since 1922* (Oxford, 1999), p.35.
23. Ibid., p.14.
24. *Dáil Debates*, Vol. 5, 12 December 1923, Inquiry into the Case of Noel Lemass.
25. Colm Campbell, *Emergency Law in Ireland*, p.185.
26. *Dáil Debates*, vol. 5, 12 December 1923, Inquiry into the Case of Noel Lemass.
27. Eunan O'Halpin, *Defending Ireland*, pp.13–14, 29.
28. UCDA, Andrews papers, P91/86, Tod Andrews's notes.
29. John Regan, *The Irish Counter-Revolution*, p.112.
30. Colm Campbell, *Emergency Law in Ireland*, pp.214, 222.
31. UCDA, Mulcahy papers, P7/b/96, Memorandum from O'Higgins, January 1923.
32. NAI, Dept. of An Taoiseach, G2/1, No. C1/13, Executive Council Minutes, 20 December 1922.
33. UCDA, Mulcahy papers, P7/b/96, Hogan memo, 11 January 1923.
34. NAI, Dept. of An Taoiseach, G2/1, No. C1/84, Executive Council Minutes, 16 April 1923.
35. GDA, O'Doherty papers, box 45, no. 57, Murphy to O'Dea, 31 January 1923.
36. Michael Hopkinson, *Green Against Green*, pp.191–2.
37. AAA, O'Donnell papers, Hagan to O'Donnell, 26 March 1923.
38. ICR, Hagan papers, Cait O'Kelly to Hagan, 12 December 1922.
39. Childers's life and problematic execution have received a substantial amount of attention. See Frank Gallagher, 'Erskine Childers: a study in serenity' in *Irish-American Review*, (1) 1939, pp.193–201; Michael McInerney, *The Riddle of Erskine Childers* (Dublin, 1971); T. Cox, *Damned Englishman: A Study of Erskine Childers, 1870–1922* (Hicksville, NY, 1975); Andrew Boyle, *The Riddle of Erskine Childers* (London, 1977); and B. Wilkinson, *The Zeal of the Convert* (Gerrards Cross, 1978). The only substantial study since then is Jim Ring, *Erskine Childers* (London, 1996).
40. Máire Cruise O'Brien, *The Same Age as the State* (Madison, WI, 2004), p.67; UCDA, Andrews papers, P91/98, Tod Andrews's notes.

41. DAA, Curran papers, Columban na Banban [Patrick Browne], 'False Pastors', p.45.
42. DAA, Byrne papers, Denis Moran to Byrne, 26 November 1922.
43. UCDA, Andrews papers, P91/98, Tod Andrews's notes.
44. DAA, Byrne papers, D. Allen to Byrne, 27 November 1922. (Emphasis in original.)
45. GDA, O'Doherty papers, box 45, no. 65, Murphy to O'Dea, 28 February 1923.
46. ICR, Hagan papers, Walsh to Gilmartin, 30 September 1923.
47. DAA, Byrne papers, Mary MacSwiney to Byrne, 8 December 1922.
48. DAA, Byrne papers, Annie MacSwiney to Byrne, 28 February 1923.
49. UCDA, Mary MacSwiney papers, P48a/196, John McCann to Gilmartin, 17 June 1924.
50. KDA, Fogarty papers, T.J. Wallace to Fogarty, 4 July 1925.
51. Ibid.
52. KDA, Fogarty papers, James B. Crowe to Fogarty, 14 April.
53. DAA, Byrne papers, John Dunn to Fr Dunne, 25 May 1923.
54. DAA, Byrne papers, O'Donnell to Byrne, 26 November 1922.
55. Dermot Keogh, *The Vatican, the Bishops and Irish Politics*, pp.98, 100.
56. DAA, Byrne papers, Byrne to Cosgrave, 10 December 1922.
57. DAA, Byrne papers, Cosgrave to Byrne, 18 March 1923.
58. Ibid.
59. Ibid.
60. AAA, O'Donnell papers, Hagan to O'Donnell, 26 March 1923.
61. UCDA, Mulcahy papers, P7/B/101, O'Shiel to Cosgrave, 1 February 1923. (Emphasis in original.)
62. ICR, Hagan papers, Michael O'Donnell to Hagan, 22 December 1923.
63. ICR, Hagan papers, Gilmartin to Hagan, 11 April 1923.
64. Colm Campbell, *Emergency Law in Ireland*, p.209.
65. *CE*, 23 May 1923.
66. UCDA, Mary MacSwiney papers, P48a/196, O.C. Prisoners to Cohalan, 24 May 1923.
67. Dermot Keogh, *The Vatican, the Bishops and Irish Politics*, p.99.
68. George Sweeney, 'Irish Hunger Strikes and the Cult of Self-Sacrifice', *Journal of Contemporary History*, Vol. 28, No. 3, (1993), p.424. For analysis of nationalists' use of hunger strike prior to the Treaty, see Seán McConville, *Irish Political Prisoners, 1848–1922: Theatres of War* (London, 2003), pp.718–37.
69. Peadar O'Donnell, *The Gates Flew Open* (London, 1932), p.213.
70. The release of Conn Murphy was allegedly due to his signing the document promising not to support armed resistance to the government, though he claimed he never signed the document.
71. *IT*, 24 September 1923.
72. Charles Townshend, *Political Violence in Ireland*, p.316.
73. Frank Gallagher, *Days of Fear* (London, 1928), pp.83–4.
74. P.J. Gannon, SJ, 'The Ethical Aspect of the Hunger-Strike', Studies, 9 (September 1920), p.450.
75. Ibid., p.452.
76. NLI, Sean T. O'Ceallaigh papers, Ms 27,712 (3), Curran memoir.
77. Ibid.
78. *CE*, 11 November 1920.
79. Ibid.
80. UCDA, De Valera papers, P150/1653, 'Miss MacSwiney's Statement', n.d.
81. Ibid.
82. UCDA, Mary MacSwiney papers, P48a/196, Annie MacSwiney to Pope Benedict XV, 1922.
83. UCDA, Mary MacSwiney papers, P48a/196, Statement of Eithne MacSwiney, 1 November 1923.
84. Older works include J.J. O'Kelly, *A Trinity of Martyrs: Terence MacSwiney, Cathal Brugha, Austin Stack* (Dublin, 1947); and Dominic O'Connor, O.F.M., 'Terence MacSwiney' in *Capuchin Annual* (1942), pp.337–42. For more modern pieces, see Francis Costello, *Enduring the Most: The Life and Death of Terence MacSwiney* (Dingle, 1995); Seán McConville, *Irish Political Prisoners*, pp.735–55; and Kevin O'Gorman, 'The hunger strike of Terence MacSwiney' in *Irish Theological Quarterly*, 58 (1993), pp.114–27.

85. James Healy, 'The Civil War Hunger-Strike – October 1923', *Studies*, 71 (September 1982), pp.218–19.
86. Pádraig Corkery, 'Bishop Daniel Cohalan of Cork on Republican Resistance and Hunger Strikes: A Theological Note', *Irish Theological Quarterly*, 67 (2002), pp.121–2.
87. Ibid., pp.122–23.
88. *CE*, 28 November 1923.
89. CCCA, de Róiste papers, U271/A/47, de Róiste journal, 21 November 1922 and 24 November 1922.
90. De Róiste claims that he urged for her release on multiple occasions out of Christian charity. He also describes her as someone whose feelings have been less than charitable towards him. CCCA, de Róiste papers, U271/A/47, de Róiste journal, 16 November 1922.
91. DAA, Byrne papers, Irish Self-Determination League (Central Branch, London) to Byrne, 16 November 1922.
92. DAA, Byrne papers, Elizabeth Moran to Byrne, 26 November 1922.
93. DAA, Byrne papers, private note on hunger strikers, n.d.
94. DAA, Byrne papers, Byrne to Cosgrave (draft), n.d.
95. DAA, Byrne papers, Cosgrave to Byrne, 18 November 1922.
96. DAA, Byrne papers, Byrne to Mary O'Kelly, 17 April 1923.
97. DAA, Byrne papers, Byrne to Cosgrave, n.d.
98. DAA, Byrne papers, Cosgrave to Byrne, 19 April 1923.
99. Ibid.
100. Peadar O'Donnell, *The Gates Flew Open*, p.193.
101. See Bill Kissane, *The Politics of the Irish Civil War*, pp.126–50.
102. Dáil Debates, vol. 5, 16 November 1923, Prisoners on Hunger-Strike.
103. *IT*, 16 October 1923.
104. Ibid., 29 October 1923.
105. See Chapter 5, p.205.
106. Dáil Debates, vol. 5, 31 October 1923, Treatment of Prisoners.
107. Ernie O'Malley, *The Singing Flame* (Dublin, 1978), p.242.
108. Peadar O'Donnell, *The Gates Flew Open*, p.184.
109. Ibid., p.186.
110. NLI, Piaras Beáslaí papers, Ms 33,915 (11), Oscar Traynor, Tom Barry, Seán Priondargas, Thomas Hanrahan and Seán MacEntee on behalf of the Republican prisoners to Seán Ó Muirthile, 8 September 1922.
111. AAA, O'Donnell papers, box 6, (Republican) Dáil Éireann, Roinn an Chraoibh-Sgaoileachain, n.d.
112. AAA, O'Donnell papers, box 6, (Republican) Dáil Éireann, Oifig an Uachtarain to the Presiding 112. Chairman and Delegates, Ard Fheis, 16 October 1923.
113. PRONI, Home Affairs, HA/32/1/120, Conchubar Ua Luasaigh (Conor Lacey), Director of Medical Service, Statement made by the IRA GHQ to members of the medical profession, 23 October 1923.
114. Republican spokesmen complained that the Red Cross intervention had been one-sided. Prisoners were not interviewed and some of the camps with the most complaints were overlooked. See Colm Campbell, *Emergency Law in Ireland*, pp.229–30.
115. Peadar O'Donnell, *The Gates Flew Open*, p.175.
116. DAA, Byrne papers, de Blácam to O'Rahilly, 14 October 1922.
117. UCDA, O'Malley papers, P17a/43, Mountjoy Gaol hunger strike leaders to Archbishop Byrne, 17 October 1923. The total number of prisoners in any one site is difficult to gauge due to steady arrivals and releases.
118. *IT*, 17 October 1923.
119. Ibid., 20 October 1923.
120. James Healy, 'The Civil War Hunger-Strike – October 1923', Studies, p.213; Michael Biggs, 'The Rationality of Self-Inflicted Sufferings: Hunger Strikes by Irish Republicans, 1916–1923' Working Paper Number 2007–03, Department of Sociology, University of Oxford; Charlotte Fallon, 'Civil War Hungerstrikes: Women and Men', *Éire-Ireland*, 22

(Autumn 1987), p.88; PRONI, Home Affairs, HA/32/1/120, Conchubar Ua Luasaigh (Conor Lacey), Director of Medical Service, Statement made by the IRA GHQ to members of the medical profession, 23 October 1923.

121. Two hundred and forty-three prisoners came off the strike during the course of the day.
122. UCDA, Blythe papers, P24/192, Reports on the progress of the hunger strike.
123. Peadar O'Donnell, *The Gates Flew Open*, p.197.
124. Richard English and Cormac O'Malley (eds), *Prisoners: The Civil War Letters of Ernie O'Malley* (Dublin, 1991), p.66.
125. Ibid., p.48.
126. Frank Gallagher, *Days of Fear*, pp.56–7. (Ellipses in original.)
127. Ibid., p.161.
128. Ibid., p.126.
129. UCDA, de Valera papers, P150/1653, Mary MacSwiney, 'A Hunger Striker's Opinion of the Weapon from a Moral Standpoint'.
130. Ibid.
131. DAA, Byrne papers, Byrne to Cosgrave, 28 October 1923.
132. NAI, Dept. of An Taoiseach, G1/3, Executive Council minutes, 15 November 1922.
133. DAA, Byrne papers, Logue to Byrne, 27 October 1923.
134. IT, 17 November 1923.
135. AAA, Logue papers, Political: General Documentation, 'Internees. Cardinal Logue and Their Detention. Hunger-Striking' (newspaper unknown), n.d.
136. Ibid.
137. IT, 26 November 1923.
138. UCDA, O'Malley papers, P17a/43, Aiken to the prisoners on hunger strike, 19 November 1923.
139. Sinn Féin statement in CE, 20 November 1923.
140. ICR, Hagan papers, O'Doherty to Hagan, 29 October1923.
141. DAA, Byrne papers, Cosgrave to Byrne, 28 October 1923.
142. Ibid.
143. Ibid.
144. UCDA, Blythe papers, P24/192, Reports on the progress of the hunger strike.
145. Ibid.
146. Richard English and Cormac O'Malley (eds), *Prisoners*, p.58.
147. Peadar O'Donnell, *The Gates Flew Open*, p.203.
148. UCDA, Mary MacSwiney papers, P48a/196, 'The Burial of Comdt. Denny Barry', Cork.
149. Sinn Féin, 29 November 1923.
150. UCDA, Mary MacSwiney papers, P48a/197, Cohalan, 'The Burial of Denis Barry', n.d.
151. UCDA, Mary MacSwiney papers, P48a/232, [Mary] MacSwiney's Reply [to Cohalan's statement on Barry's burial], 28 November 1923.
152. UCDA, Mary MacSwiney papers, P48a/197, Ribberi to MacSwiney, April 1932.
153. *IT*, 21 November 1923.
154. DAA, Byrne papers, Cosgrave to Byrne, 28 October 1923.
155. *IT*, 21 November 1923.
156. UCDA, Blythe papers, P24/192, Reports on the progress of the hunger strike.
157. ICR, Hagan papers, O'Kelly to Hagan, 19 December 1923.
158. ICR, Hagan papers, O'Donnell to Hagan, 4 January 1924.
159. UCDA, Blythe papers, P24/193, O'Higgins to Cosgrave (Personal and strictly confidential), 15 November 1923.
160. PRONI, Home Affairs, HA/32/1/46, memo from Governor of Londonderry Prison. [FM Stuart], 13 February 1925.
161. Eunan O'Halpin, *Defending Ireland*, p.43.
162. Ibid., p.44.
163. ICR, Hagan papers, Cait O'Kelly to Hagan, 25 November 1923.
164. ICR, Hagan papers, Roughneen to Hagan, 8 November 1923.

165. Charlotte Fallon, 'Civil War Hungerstrikes: Women and Men', *Eire-Ireland*, p.78.
166. Ibid.
167. ICR, Hagan papers, Roughneen to Hagan, 8 November 1923.

5

The Problem of Partition: Pragmatism versus Principle and the Six Counties

The attitude of contempt and derision towards Partition changed remarkably within twelve months, or so, and this political fickleness will be one of the most difficult problems for historians to solve.[1]

Prior to the Civil War, hierarchical and clerical involvement in politics in the areas of Ireland where Catholics were the majority caused a minimum of politico-religious conflict. The same was not true in the northeast of Ulster, where Protestants outnumbered Catholics. Ulster Protestants had feared the influence of the Catholic clergy on their followers for much of the nineteenth century, and *Ne Temere* (1908) and *Quantavis diligentia* (1911), papal pronouncements on the issues of mixed marriage and civil courts, caused further consternation at the Catholic Church's involvement in politics. Worse, though, according to Ulster Protestants, were the Irish bishops' responses to the statements, which were, according to Mary Harris, defensive justifications aimed at co-religionists rather than the concerned Protestants.[2] They were proof that the leaders of the Irish Catholic Church were not interested in incorporating members of other faiths into a Home Rule Ireland.

Harris's work discusses the northern bishops' alliance with the nationalist movement and their close involvement in the attempts to defeat partition. She acknowledges that as the leaders of the Catholic Church, they ensured that the Church played a very large role in how northern Catholics responded to the initial establishment of Northern Ireland as well as their relations with the state for several decades. She also recognises that the bishops successfully linked together nationalist politics with Catholic educational and social concerns. Though she hints at it, the piece of the puzzle she leaves out is that by extending their grasp from educational and social issues to the broader political issues, the Catholic bishops of the north contributed significantly to creating and perpetuating the political divisions along sectarian lines. They had been largely responsible for the electoral pacts of 1918 between Sinn Féin and the Irish Party that allowed for maximum representation of northern Catholics.[3] By addressing the northern government's treatment of the nationalist minority entirely as a religious issue, the bishops helped solidify the Catholic-nationalist alliance in the minds of the unionists, further cementing in their minds the notion of northern Catholics as internal enemies.

Considering their confrontational attitude toward the unionists and the northern state, the bishops displayed a paradoxical attitude towards partition. Once the Treaty was approved, the bishops allied themselves with the Free State government and were not prepared to publicly oppose it in any regard, even the matter of partition. Despite their rejection of the existence of Northern Ireland and their denouncements of the northern government's anti-Catholic agenda and its complicity or even active engagement in sectarian violence, they pragmatically followed the Free State line. As was the case with many of their activities in the temporal sphere, this was, and still is to a great degree, an under-analysed matter of the bishops allowing expediency to trump principle.

For the bishops, the issue of partition was not an easy one. A decade of vehement anti-partitionism, with northern bishops not only providing some of the loudest voices against the proposal but even organising and leading anti-partition groups, ended with a formal acceptance of the Free State government and, by extension, the creation of the six county area. Their endorsement of the Free State was not an automatic acceptance of partition, and despite the setback for Irish unity, the hierarchy continued to work against partition, always possessing the naïve belief, like so many of their nationalist and even British contemporaries, that the northern state was a temporary necessity that would inevitably be absorbed into the rest of Ireland. The seeming lack of continuity of their thoughts and actions did not go unnoticed by the republicans, who used the bishops' endorsement of the Free State government as proof that the bishops had placed politics even above their own religious calling or the welfare of their flocks. Had republicans dedicated any sizeable amount of time or energy to challenging the hierarchy on this matter, they would have found that they could have possessed the moral high ground in a propaganda battle, which was their coveted location on all fronts against the Church leaders. Had they done so, however, they would have found a largely indifferent audience in the south.

Though theoretically opposed to partition because it resulted in the termination of Irish unity and allowed the British to maintain a presence on the island, republicans failed to demonstrate the passion for the northern question that would be expected with the loss of six counties from their hallowed republic. There were several reasons for this. Partially, it was due to there being so few northern republicans, or even people who displayed republican sympathies. A large percentage of the local Catholic population displayed hostility to their movement and a desire to defeat it, and Protestants were almost unanimously in opposition. There was also a strong prejudicial element to how southern republicans treated the six counties. Many republicans wanted to avoid the north altogether, feeling that even its Catholics were a sectarian, possibly unwelcome element in the new Ireland, a prejudice they shared with many Free State supporters.[4] Those southern republicans who were at all concerned about the issue still placed it below the fight for the republic which would subsume any aberrant Protestant-controlled state created by the British once the fight was won in the south. This was another case of some republicans giving priority to lofty, impracticable ideological goals rather than focusing on the matters at hand.

EARLY HIERARCHICAL ATTITUDES TO PARTITION

Episcopal opposition to partition originated with the idea of partition itself. Among the northern bishops, Patrick O'Donnell, then Bishop of Raphoe, stood alone as one who was prepared early on to accept some form of partition as inevitable, though he opposed any form that included any of the five counties he deemed nationalist, in other words, those counties in which Catholics were in the majority. In 1913, while still the Irish Party's strongest clerical advocate, he wrote to John Redmond: 'There is no length to which any of us would refuse to go to satisfy the Orangemen at the starting of our new Government, provided Ireland did not suffer seriously, and provided also the Nationalist minority in the N.E. did not suffer badly.'[5] At the opposite end of the spectrum was Bishop McHugh of Derry.

Charles McHugh receives little mention in the other chapters of this book because, aside from partition, he remained relatively non-political. However, he was a fervent opponent of partition who reflected the northern nationalist sense of embattlement more authentically than did O'Donnell.[6] McHugh was implacably opposed to any form of partition. He was the driving force behind the Anti-Partition League and the Irish Nation League. In May 1917, McHugh led the drive to get a petition of protest signed throughout the country by men and women of all classes and creeds. On 8 May, his petition appeared in the *Irish Independent*. It proclaimed that while there had been an immense amount of individual protest to the idea of partition, there was no national movement. To this end, people were urged to send their names for subscription to the petition:

> Our requisition needs no urging. An appeal to the National conscience on the question of Ireland's dismemberment should meet with one answer, and one answer alone. To Irishmen of every creed and class and party the very thought of our country partitioned and torn as a new Poland must be one of heart-rending sorrow.[7]

The signatories of the letter included eighteen Catholic archbishops and bishops, three Church of Ireland bishops and several prominent laymen. It is interesting to note that all northern bishops except O'Donnell signed the letter. He told McHugh that to sign would be to oppose the county option on the lines of the 1914 Amending Bill. He was opposed to partition, but would accept the 1914 Bill if there was no alternative.[8] Unfortunately for McHugh, his petition was soon over-shadowed by the Irish Convention, to which he had been invited but refused to attend on the grounds that he would not even discuss partition. Following the announcement in 1920 that Lloyd George was working to pass a Home Rule bill that would result in a partitioned Northern Ireland, McHugh was one of the proposal's first and harshest critics. Framing the northern conflict entirely in a religious context, he wrote: 'in the present case, there is more at stake for us in this corner of Ulster than purely national rights; for the interests of religion and our position as Catholics are inseparably connected with any proposals that may be put forward for the solution of the Irish problem.' He stated that the Catholics of the north were prepared to share in the fates and fortunes of their fellow countrymen, 'but, to become serfs in an Orange Free State carved out to meet the wishes of an intolerant minority, to this we will never submit.'[9] A month later, in a letter written to the *Derry People*, he stated that after perusing the Government of Ireland Bill he had come to the conclusion that it should rather be called 'A Bill for the permanent Partition and plunder of Ireland and the enslavement of her people in the interest of Great Britain.' McHugh could find no reason for the coercion of Fermanagh, Tyrone and Derry City other than that Catholics were no longer accorded full civil rights, and should those areas be forced into the partitioned area, they must 'declare their determination to remain united with that part of Ireland whose aspirations and sympathies are identical with their own.'[10] Indicating an antagonistic, yet very definite allusion to accepting a modified form of partition, McHugh added that if Carson wanted to establish a Protestant colony, thus continuing the religious bickering which had been so characteristic of the north's past, let him confine his attention to those areas where he could claim a majority of co-religionists.

Cardinal Logue engaged in his usual private protestations, hoping that his influence could sway powerful members of society to help the northern Catholics. In a letter written to the chief secretary about police attendance at Mass, Logue used the opportunity to chastise the Crown forces for their treatment of Catholics. He was especially appalled at the prospect of government-sanctioned arming of Orangemen in the northeast, leaving Catholics defenceless. The only thing that could prevent outright massacre, the cardinal stated, was the mercy of God: 'However it is in pursuit of a policy which has for generations lain at the root of the misgovernment of Ireland, the fostering for political ends of a small minority of the population to the prejudicial neglect and even unfair treatment of the majority.'[11]

The years between his above letter to Redmond and the 1920 Act had had a great impact on O'Donnell's thinking. After his falling out with Redmond and subsequent disillusionment with the Irish Party, O'Donnell had witnessed the acceptable county-option partition change into an attempt to coerce all of Ulster into partition and finally the six-county proposal, which he deemed absurd. Having taken the British government's proposals of 1914 in good faith, O'Donnell became extremely bitter when the six-county option took centre stage. '[H]owever little the bulk of the English population may realise it, Ireland is ruled and treated to day by the ruling class in England in the same spirit that dictated the Plantation of Ulster in the seventeenth century.'[12] To him, the proposal simply did not make sense; 'The unfairness of partition ought be judged from the fact that no matter how narrow the ring fence was made the proportion of Nationalists to Unionists within it would be larger than the proportion its Unionist population bore to the inhabitants of the rest of the country, or even to the Nationalists alone in the rest of Ireland.'[13]

Early the next year, O'Donnell was so opposed to the Northern Irish state that he actually saw bloodshed and chaos in an advantageous light. He believed that the violent state of affairs throughout the island could potentially have the positive effect of delaying the opening of the northern parliament.[14] Whereas during the Irish Convention he had been prepared to grant unionists and even northern unionists disproportionate representation under Home Rule, he now believed that northern unionists did not warrant such. Furthermore, he hoped that Nationalists and Sinn Féiners would unite in the north, potentially delaying the opening of the northern parliament until the Council of Ireland had met and hopefully ended the need for a Belfast government.[15]

Of all the northern bishops, Joseph MacRory of Down and Connor faced the most precarious difficulties in dealing with the creation of the northern state, to which he was passionately opposed. As the episcopal overseer of Belfast's Catholic population, he had intimate knowledge of the violence committed by government forces against his people. He also faced the inevitable seclusion of his flock from the majority of Catholics in Ireland. Unlike McHugh's, MacRory's diocese did not stand a chance of unification with the south unless the Northern Irish state collapsed. This forced him to adopt a more pragmatic opposition to the northern state than bishops who were confident that their dioceses, or at least parts of them, would be transferred by a Boundary Commission which was to be created should the six counties opt out of the Free State.

In August 1920, MacRory joined with Seán MacEntee, Denis McCullough, Frank Crummey and Fr. John Hassan to form the Belfast Boycott Committee. The aims of the committee were to inflict economic harm on the six-county area by shutting off trade from the rest of Ireland in retaliation for the damages imposed on northern

Catholics, get the expelled workers back to their jobs, and to prevent partition by demonstrating to the northern business community their dependence on the rest of Ireland for trade. They petitioned the Dáil to institute a vigorous boycott on Belfast goods and Belfast-oriented banks throughout the rest of Ireland in retaliation for the war of extermination waged against northern Catholics. MacRory went even further. Whenever the boycott came under fire from critics who claimed that it was doing more harm than good to the intended beneficiaries, he defended it and said that if Ulster unionists persisted in refusing to come to terms with the rest of Ireland it might be necessary to arrange a boycott of northern manufacturers by Catholic countries abroad.[16]

The critics were correct, though, and both the 1920 and 1922 boycotts backfired, further cementing the commercial ties between the northeast and Britain, thus making Irish unification less economically viable. Paul Bew has estimated that as little as ten per cent of northern businesses were affected by the boycott in the economic sense, making it little more than a gesture made for political consumption.[17] Ernest Blythe, Free State Minister of Finance, spoke against the boycott, arguing convincingly that the only sector of northern business a boycott could have any real impact on was distribution, and as the government controlled a large portion of its revenue through customs and excise, it could not tolerate any irregular and disorderly method of importation.[18]

The remarks of the bishops of the Free State regarding partition are most remarkable not for their substance, but for their non-existence. Very few spoke out as individuals, and those who did seemed to do so only as an aside. Bishop Kelly of Ross, the hierarchy's financial expert, said in 1920 that a northern state would be inherently unstable because of a large working class. There would no longer be the 'preponderating proportion' of landowners over proletarians that the island at large enjoyed and made for a conservative Ireland.[19] Bishop Cohalan told his flock that the Union and unionism were dead, and that many in the northeast were looking to the south for commercial and political union, though he failed to offer reasons for believing so.[20] Neither man demonstrated any anger at the treatment of northern Catholics but rather seemed to view the situation with cold objectivity, which, for Cohalan at least, was a drastic change from his statements on the state of affairs in the Free State.[21]

The exception was Bishop Fogarty of Killaloe, whose strong nationalist feelings have been dealt with above. In a pastoral issued during the war for independence, Fogarty blamed the anarchy and Cromwellian ferocity rampant throughout Ireland on the British ministers and others who organised and headed the revolt of the Belfast Orangemen. He theorised that they hoped by their terrorist techniques 'to break the spirit of Ireland and compel her through sheer exhaustion to accept quietly the "Partition" harness cut and made for her by the Orange leaders.'[22] Fogarty's intense disapproval of partition was evident in 1918, when he wrote that '[t]he authors of that criminal and cowardly surrender will never be forgiven in Ireland.'[23] When the plenipotentiaries returned in 1921 with their agreement, Fogarty was oddly silent regarding the issue of partition.

As a unified body, the hierarchy had opposed partition since the plan offered in 1916, which had been endorsed by Redmond and Devlin, both of whom believed it to be temporary.[24] The bishops issued two statements in 1920 which covered the topic of partition. The first, in January, only briefly made mention of it, stating that the true way to terminate the historic troubles and establish friendly relations between England and Ireland to the advantage of both was to allow an undivided Ireland to choose its own form of government. By October, with sectarian violence resurgent in Belfast and the unionists of the six-county area firmly intent on maintaining their separation from the rest of Ireland, the bishops issued a statement that was very critical of the British attitude toward partition. The bishops wrote that carnage of sectarian riots on a vast scale was being allowed to run its course in Ulster. In no other part of Ireland was a minority persecuted, hinting at the fair treatment Catholics in the twenty-six counties were granting their Protestant neighbours: '[P]erhaps recent sad events may, before it is altogether too late, open the eyes of the people of England to the iniquity of furnishing a corner of Ulster with a separate government, or its worst instrument, a special police force, to enable it all the more readily to trample under foot the victims of its intolerants [sic].'[25] Using logic that would become one of the standard arguments of opponents to partition, the bishops claimed it was not hatred of coercion but partiality for the northeast that drove British interest in partition. Ulster must not suffer under a Dublin parliament but all of Ireland must be coerced for the sake of the northeast.[26]

IMPACT OF THE TREATY

As discussed in Chapter 2, the Anglo-Irish Treaty of December 1921 changed the entire debate in the minds of the hierarchy. While no bishop spoke against the Treaty, three of the six northern bishops were conspicuously absent from the rota of its initial public supporters. Bishops O'Donnell and Mulhern, both of whom had resigned themselves to accepting some temporary form of partition, chose to remain silent, as did McHugh, whose opposition to partition has been thoroughly discussed. The most fervent Treaty supporter in the hierarchy was Cardinal Logue, who feared northern/Protestant domination over Catholic interests, especially education, so much that he famously said that he would rather remain under Westminster for another fifty years than be placed under a northern government.[27] Despite this, he was an unwavering supporter of the Treaty and had pushed his fellow bishops to offer their weighty endorsement of the document before it had even been approved by the Dáil. This demonstrates the conflict the northern bishops faced. They wanted peace, but realised that it came at the price of partition. Harris theorises that Griffith allayed the bishops' concerns regarding the northeast when he informed Bishops McHugh and O'Dea that the necessary safeguards would be inserted into the Treaty and built their hopes up regarding the Boundary Commission.[28] However, the bishops' statements following the signing of the Treaty do not indicate that their concerns were completely dispelled, but rather that as they supported the creation of the Free State, they felt they had no alternative but to hope for the best. A good example can be found in the words of Bishop O'Sullivan of Kerry, who, as has been discussed,[29] was one of the more vociferous critics of opposition to the Treaty. Though he would not admit it in public, he was so opposed to partition that he preferred to see the Treaty rejected than the country divided.[30] His fears had certainly not been put to rest.

Bishop MacRory, who publicly supported the Treaty, had an attitude towards partition that was complex and seemingly contradictory at times. He wrote at the beginning of 1922 that the Treaty was a poor settlement for the Catholics of the six counties, whom, he feared, would find themselves in a difficult situation for the next few years.[31] He was frightened, due to information he had received from one 'who knew much', that a rejection of the Treaty could result, in the six counties, in the arrest of all the leaders of Sinn Féin, and perhaps even, according to another source, that the possibility existed that all citizens would have to declare a pledge of loyalty or they would be shot.[32] Personally, he refused to recognise the northern government or to take any part in affairs relating to it. However, he also believed that the Free State's policy of non-recognition was a mistake and would leave northern Catholics to fight alone. Displaying hope that the entire partition debacle could be ended promptly, he urged the Free State government to attempt to get Craig into the Free State as soon as possible.[33] These were his thoughts when among friends and away from the observation of the media. When before a public audience, MacRory's message was altogether more fiery and uncompromising.

In public, MacRory was a dedicated opponent to the northern government. Both he and Logue refused invitations to the opening of the northern parliament. MacRory said he would not signify special approval for an institution which was set up in defiance of the determined wishes of over eighty per cent of the Irish nation.[34] During his 1922 Lenten pastoral, the Bishop of Down and Connor spared no vitriolic word for the treatment of Catholics at the hands of Northern Ireland's political leaders, though he limited his disapproval to 'a few unscrupulous political leaders and a comparatively small number of very young men.'[35] It was definitely a sectarian issue in his opinion. Catholic dock workers had taken the blame for their co-religionists and, contrary to the articles put out by the unionist press, Catholics were entirely guiltless of acts of arson. These words masked the private thoughts of a man who remained unsure of how best to react to the new state. The paradoxical nature of MacRory's relations with Northern Ireland was typified by an occurrence in 1929. Queen's University, Belfast conferred an honorary LL.D. on MacRory, who was then cardinal. Though he refused to attend the ceremony, he did not refuse the degree itself.

In several ways, Bishop Mulhern's deliberations on the problem of the north represented the seemingly contradictory thought process of other bishops, and even many lay nationalists, who were opposed to partition but supportive of the Treaty that recognised it. Immediately after he read about the Treaty in the papers, his newfound enthusiasm lapsed due to the clauses relating to the six counties. Upon talking to others, though, his fears of what would happen if the Treaty was not accepted got the best of him. Despite his refusal to publicly speak on the Treaty immediately after its signing, Mulhern was a supporter, and as the situation in the north grew more deplorable in his mind, he came to be a stronger advocate both of the Free State and recognition of the northern government. Like so many others, he was hopeful that the creation of the Free State would bring about the quick demise of Northern Ireland.[36]

Throughout the early months of 1922, Mulhern remained convinced that the only obstacle to an end of problems in the six counties was unity within the ranks of nationalists. It became increasingly clear to him that the primary responsibility for the state of the north rested squarely on the shoulders of de Valera, who belonged in a lunatic asylum according to his former friend and admirer.[37] When de Valera communicated with Mulhern about the bishops condemning recent Belfast horrors, Mulhern responded that he along with his northern colleagues placed the blame on de Valera and his party, though he later admitted that thinking about murders made him grow heated.[38] He privately admitted that de Valera and the republicans were not solely at fault; that both sides had let the north down.[39] This was a feeling that was shared by McHugh, who admitted that he had no faith in the Provisional Government, especially in regard to their Ulster policy.[40] In April 1922, Mulhern remained convinced that unity was the cure for Irish ills. He believed that what they had at present was actually better than a full measure of freedom: 'Time will level down difficulties, and even the much-neglected N. East situation will solve itself after a short trial.'[41] Even in late June, he was still advocating nationalist unity as a cure-all,[42] though the assassination of Henry Wilson and the ensuing Civil War rather changed matters.

The bishops' confidence in a quick disestablishment of Northern Ireland was fed by the articles and speeches of Treaty supporters. In an article of the *Free State*, Desmond FitzGerald argued that while Ulster should not be coerced to join the twenty-six counties, the Provisional Government now had 'the power to make it worth Ulster's while to join with the rest of Ireland.'[43] The next month, Seán MacCaoilte wrote that the Treaty presented Ulster with a position which, with time, must become untenable. By leaving the rest of Ireland, Ulster would be making a decision that pressed severely on its economic life, so that surrender to national unity would be the only means to prevent financial and economic paralysis.[44] The Devlinite *Irish News* assured its readers that 'there is a probability, amounting to a certainty, of killing partition if all the people who dread and abhor it assert and exercise their right to vote.'[45] These examples demonstrate the wishful thinking propounded by most nationalists, and even some republicans. They were convinced that the northern unionists were guided solely by materialistic concerns and by dangling an economic carrot before them, southerners could tempt them into unity. This was a comforting thought to nationalists, as it allowed them to place blame purely in the unionists' camp while dismissing the seriousness of the division between themselves and their northern adversaries.[46] It also granted them a self-ascribed sense of moral superiority, as they were fighting for convictions rather than material gain.

*   *   *

The pastoral of April 1922, which is discussed at length in Chapter 2 for its criticisms of continued republican resistance to the Provisional Government, featured some very harsh words aimed at the northern government, with the bishops engaging in bursts of exaggeration as was so often the case. They stated that contrary to the best interests of the nation, peace and progress, part of Ireland had been partitioned 'apparently to give us a specimen of model government. If that government is to be judged by results, it must rank more nearly with the government of the Turk in his worst days than with anything to be found anywhere in a Christian State.'[47] Catholics had been denied their natural rights for twenty months and faced savage persecutions hardly paralleled by even the bitterest sufferings of the Armenians.[48] The authorities had responded to these attacks with nothing but empty promises, while all able-bodied Protestants were supplied with arms to harass Catholics.[49]

Their June pastoral, which primarily discussed the atrociousness of attacks on Protestants within Free State territory, repeated many of the same accusations against Belfast, dedicating two pages to biting criticism of the northern government. The bishops proclaimed that there was no government in the north for Catholics, again relying on the Turkish-Armenian comparison. The ruthless arson attacks and episodes of murderous slaughter, they proclaimed, had driven thousands of Catholics out of Belfast. Ultimate responsibility, though, rested in London. The British government had been warned about the dangers of handing over power to a section of the people remarkable for their intolerance. Now they were exaggerating the crisis by paying the sectarian police force, not to dispense justice, but to engage in unbridled bigotry; 'The deadly effect of partition has been to ruin Ireland.'[50]

In October 1923, the hierarchy issued another statement criticising the northern government's treatment of its Catholic population: 'It is doubtful whether in modern times any parallel can be found for the way in which the Catholic minority of the North of Ireland is being systematically wronged under the laws of the Northern Parliament.'[51] Their grievances were broken down into four main points: proportional representation in local elections had been eliminated while gerrymandering constituencies to give unionists majorities had become commonplace, an education system which deprived Catholic schools and teachers of the same rights granted to their Protestant counterparts, an oath of allegiance prescribed for all those paid by the government with an attempt to even impose the oath on priests who served as chaplains and teachers, and an utter disregard on the part of the government for the rights of Catholics as best illustrated by the attitudes of the leading ministers on the boundary question in regard to Tyrone and Fermanagh. The time had come, the bishops announced, when northern Catholics must resolve to lie down no longer and organise openly and along constitutional lines.[52]

As would be expected, republicans took umbrage at this ecclesiastical statement, especially regarding the issue of the oath. At a meeting in Upper Sackville Street a few days later, many speakers wondered why the bishops were prepared to criticise the oath of allegiance required in the north, yet they were perfectly willing to accept the oath imposed by the British on the Free State. There were multiple protestations against the lack of sympathy displayed by the bishops towards southern Catholic republicans, especially when compared to their outcries in favour of their northern co-religionists.[53] At the Sinn Féin Ard Fheis the next week, Conor Maguire put forward a motion that the bishops' document should officially be disapproved. The feelings against the actions of the hierarchy escalated during the affair and by the time of the passing of various resolutions, a multitude of episcopal actions were condemned, and for good measure the delegation agreed to send a copy of the resolutions to the pope.[54]

REPUBLICANS, PARTITION AND THE BISHOPS

The *Plain People*, which so regularly expressed disappointment and shock at the way millions of Irish had abandoned the republican cause, maintained an extra-severe criticism of the widespread acceptance of partition. In this regard, the hierarchy fell victim to the *People*'s attacks frequently. In April 1922, shortly after the April pastoral, the paper informed its readers that the bishops had deserted them and the army, which had remained true to the republic, re-imposed the Belfast boycott and placed the welfare of expelled and persecuted Catholics of Belfast before the license to outrage of Craig's murder gang.[55] The writers were unrepentant about the violence committed against the Orangemen and the northern state. They knew it was the work of the IRA and they saw it not as rebellion against the state, but the continuation to drive the English from Ireland.

The hierarchy's June 1922 pronouncement was the subject of much criticism by the paper. Catholics of the six counties, the writers theorised, were somewhat puzzled by the bishops' statement. They wholeheartedly condemned partition, however, they called upon the people to support the party which championed the Treaty of which partition was a feature. To the lay mind the issue was uncomplicated, the writers simplistically suggested; people were either partitionists or anti-partitionists. They could not, unlike the bishops, condemn partition while railing against republicans, the sole organisation that refused to recognise it.[56]

Those republicans looking to the Vatican for support were also quick to highlight the disparity between the bishops' previous opinions on partition and their newfound appreciation for a government which accepted partition, even if only as a temporary necessity. The appeal against the October pastoral presented to Cardinal Gasparri in January 1923 pointed out that in demanding allegiance to the Provisional Government, the bishops were guilty of issuing a decision that ran counter to the 'fundamental natural law' of preservation of Irish territorial integrity.[57] This law had been recognised, the appeal writers argued, by Catholic theologians and philosophers, general consensus and the opinions of peoples throughout the world. By accepting the partitioning of the island, the Free State government not only violated Ireland's territorial integrity but also exposed northern Catholics 'to the tyranny of savage organisations that have committed and continue to commit the atrocious acts of violence against the Catholic community.'[58]

The Protestant government of the north had even introduced an education bill that would prove detrimental to the Catholic faith. Though the bishops were vehemently opposed to this bill,[59] the appeal writers failed to mention this detail to the pontiff. Furthermore, they added, the previous statements of the bishops had shown them to be overwhelmingly opposed to partition, and yet their demands of allegiance to the Provisional Government, which recognised the northern parliament, contradicted their strong positions of only months before. This demonstrated a fundamental inconsistency in their outlook.[60]

In a document given to Monsignor Luzio, which he included in his report to Cardinal Gasparri, republicans pointed out that by using excommunication and denial of the sacraments to bind people to accept the Treaty, the bishops were, by extension, forcing people to accept partition and, it was inferred, Protestant domination over Catholics. The writers felt that the disparity between the bishops' pre-Treaty opinions and their current ones highlighted the immorality of their stance, and cited as proof several pre-Treaty quotes from bishops emphasising the importance of national unity and the heartrending sorrow that Irishmen would feel at the thought of partition.[61] Aside from this document, Luzio made no critical remarks about Northern Ireland or partition, mentioning the subjects only twice in his report.

Individual republican attacks against the episcopal opinion on partition, though, were scant when viewed in the context of total republican propaganda. Of the many anti-ecclesiastical pieces examined in Chapter 2, only a mere handful even made mention of partition or the bishops' attitude toward it. Few letters written to the bishops chastised them for their acceptance of partition. One notable exception was Cathleen O'Moore, who scolded Byrne for the bishops' reversal on the issue. By accepting the Treaty, she informed him, he and his colleagues were accepting partition and were, by extension, handing over northern Catholics to the mercies of Protestant bigots without protest.[62] Considering that in this one aspect the republicans had indisputable evidence of hierarchical pragmatism taking precedence over principle, it seems profoundly surprising that they did not incorporate this element into every publication released and speech made. By equating acceptance of partition with deficiency of principles, republicans would have gained an even stronger weapon in their fight for moral superiority over the religious leaders who had excommunicated them and referred to their stance as wrong and immoral, but they never really took full advantage of this opportunity.

The reasons for this blunder are unknown and subject only for educated speculation. The heated rhetoric used against the bishops and clergy in all other regards indicates that it was not respect for the men or positions that kept republican propagandists from going on the attack. As detailed in Chapter 2, the bishops faced a wide array of unkind language from individuals, organisations and republican press bodies, specifically for their involvement in the affairs of the nation. They were called cowards, traitors, West Britons and were compared to Judas. Father Peter Yorke had even declared that the bishops should be cast from the Church and denied Christian burial.[63] Yet such harsh words were rarely aimed at the hierarchy when the topic of the north was raised. Nor could republican barbs have been blunted by any episcopal volte-face regarding partition. While championing the Free State, they still decried partition and railed against Craig's government and its treatment of Catholics. It would seem that this sort of apparent hypocrisy was manna for republican propagandists. Why, then, did they not utilise it more than they chose to?

The answer seems to be that like the majority of Free State bishops and a large percentage of the population, republican propagandists chose to overlook Northern Ireland. Instead they focused on the principles of republicanism and the actions of the Free State government and its forces. Even someone as erudite as Patrick Browne largely bypassed the six counties. His 'Reply to the Pastoral issued by the Irish Hierarchy in October 1922' made constant reference to the Provisional Government as the 'Partition Government' and in doing so linked the bishops closely with the issue of partition. However, this was the extent of his criticism of their stance on partition. He made no direct attacks against them and, contrary to his usual tendency, did not use their earlier statements against partition to criticise them for their current official stance. It is probable that like so many other republicans, Browne simply did not concern himself enough with the north to occupy time on it exclusively. The Tipperary-born Maynooth professor rarely made mention of the north and seems to have concerned himself with the overall principled struggle rather than any one particular aspect of it, though pointing out the hypocrisy of supporting the Free State while opposing partition certainly should have appealed to his principle theme.

Men and women on both sides of the Treaty divide seem to have wanted to avoid discussing the wrench that the north threw into their idealised Catholic Gaelic Ireland. As the generation of Irish-Irelanders who were destined to be responsible for the founding of the Irish state, they were the first generation that had to fully come to grips with the separateness of the Ulster Protestant communities. The 'Black North' had been a place apart for a century,[64] but never before had the Catholics of the twenty-six counties had to deal with this concept as anything more than an abstract. The events of the recent past, though, forced reality upon them, and that reality did not synchronise with their message. Try as they might to promote Ulster as the most 'Irish' of the four provinces, containing as it did the sites of Saints Patrick, Brigid and Columcille, as well as the historic base of the O'Neills, neither republicans nor Free Staters could mask the fact that hundreds of thousands of Ulster's residents rejected Irish independence, Gaelic culture as promoted by the Gaelic League and the spiritual authority of the Bishop of Rome. Free Staters and republicans differed on their chosen means, but they desired the same ends. Allowing Northern Ireland to enter the discussion would have forced rhetoricians to acknowledge that the Ireland they were striving to attain was not the goal of all. Their over-generalisations regarding Ireland's nationalist desires would have been exposed for what they were. It would have also forced them to face up to the existence of violence and religious hatred in Ireland, a nation that was to be, with the severing of the Union, free of problems confronting Britain.

Another problem was that Catholic–Protestant conflict was not the only division; there was a marked rift between Catholics in the Free State and those in the north. The divisions within northern Catholic society have been well researched. Robert Lynch's work offers fascinating insights into the intra-group fighting and strained emotions, as does Tim Wilson's recent monograph.[65] The republican leadership's detestation of sectarianism and attempts to focus hostility towards England, while downplaying the importance of local rivalries, made their brand of nationalism less popular than Devlin's and the Hibernians', which was Ulster oriented.[66] Many local Catholics involved in the northern conflict identified less with a political or paramilitary organisation than with their preferred identity as defenders of the Catholic community.[67] Despite the IRA leadership's desires, their local operatives and forces in the six counties viewed the conflict as a sectarian one.

Many republicans in the north were convinced that they had been abandoned by their comrades in the Free State. One such woman expressed concern to Monsignor Hagan that the supply of republican propaganda in the six counties had dried up and she had come to believe that many of the so-called republicans were nothing more than twenty-six county 'Republicans' who saw the north as a problem and were quite glad to get rid of it.[68] Giving credence to her theory, Patrick Keohane was convinced that the republic had been lost in the south and west because too much attention had been paid to the north. He wrote that he had told many people he would let the north 'go to Hell as long as it served the Republic here', but he felt this attitude was acceptable because within twelve months the 'Northern *cormorants*',[69] or at least the businessmen among them, would be craving entry into the Irish state.[70]

A few within the ranks of republicanism even chose to accept partition, albeit either temporarily or hidden within nationalist rhetoric. One prominent republican who exhibited an evolving and, many argued, hypocritical attitude towards partition was Sinn Féin vice-president Father Michael O'Flanagan. Immediately after Asquith offered Home Rule to the twenty-six counties in 1916, O'Flanagan endorsed the offer and was the only prominent Sinn Féin member to do so, placing himself alongside the Irish Party's leadership and against, it should be noted, the Catholic bishops. Ulster unionists, he contended, had never given their love and allegiance to Ireland. Nationalists demanding the right to self-determination owed northern unionists the same right.[71] As he saw it, the way to solve the 'Ulster problem' was by addressing the real seat of trouble: the abuse of politics and religion for a confusion of ends. He believed that it was wrong to gather people under the banner of religion and then use that organisation to purely secular ends. His criticism was aimed especially at the Orange Order, the Ancient Order of Hibernians and those clergymen whose political involvement ensured that both sides of the political divide remained under ecclesiastical influence.[72]

O'Flanagan's notions were original and pragmatic amongst a party whose members either viewed partition with knee-jerk revulsion or feigned outrage masking actual indifference. Unfortunately, they were also momentary and by the second half of 1921 he had joined the ranks of those opposed to partition on ideological grounds. When fundraising for Sinn Féin in the United States, O'Flanagan repeatedly lambasted partition. He said that the concept of Northern Ireland was built upon a false interpretation of the idea of self-determination. A part of a nation, he argued, could not practice self-determination, and the case of Ulster was especially egregious because while the original motive had been to protect the Protestant northeast from coercion, Fermanagh and Tyrone were now being coerced.[73] O'Flanagan's opposition to partition and the existence of the northern state eventually earned him multiple orders of prohibition from entering the area from September 1925 to October 1938, with the order being restored in January 1939 for wanting to speak alongside Peadar O'Donnell.[74] He was one of only three Catholic clergymen who received such restrictions; the others being Fr. Peter Ward, who the northern government believed was involved with the Fermanagh IRA,[75] and Archbishop Mannix.

O'Flanagan's newfound opposition to partition did not sit well with nationalist opponents of the republicans. The *Derry Journal* blamed him for paving the way for partition when he went to London and spoke with Lloyd George shortly before Treaty negotiations. The paper found it ridiculous that O'Flanagan would include himself in the list of people who had defended the Republic since 1916 when he had harangued northerners to accept partition in that same year. In short, the *Journal* decried O'Flanagan's political involvement, exclaiming 'The nation has paid dearly for his dabbling in politics, and for his unforgivable blundering.'[76]

Like O'Flanagan, Arthur Clery initially favoured partition. Unlike O'Flanagan, though, Clery maintained his support of partition until his death in 1932. He regarded Ulster Protestants as entitled to the same rights of self-determination for which Irish nationalists were fighting, going so far in 1906 as to compare Irish nationalist attitudes toward Ulstermen to English attitudes toward the Irish.[77] Patrick Maume's work shows that Clery viewed partition as the best possible option for a peaceful resolution of the conflicting desires of the majority populations in the north and south. Class interests had kept many southern Protestants from embracing nationalism, he argued, but Ulster Protestants, who embraced democratic principles and the goals of the Land League, were opposed to the notion of Home Rule on national and religious grounds. While abandoning principles could bring the southern ex-landowners into the fold, no degree of abandonment could tempt the northern unionists in.[78]

Clery displayed an enlightened, though highly biased, understanding of northern unionists. Unlike most nationalists in the Free State, he did not see them as mindless bigots led by place-hunters. Rather, he understood that they adhered to a serious political movement, responding rationally to a distinctive set of loyalties and beliefs.[79] This is not to say that he admired them. Clery disliked Ulster Protestants severely, referring to them as the most criminal and least moral section of the population, as well as 'turbulent and bigoted aliens'. Ulster Catholics, it should be added, were only slightly less offensive in his regard, especially the Catholic residents of West Belfast.[80] His lack of affection for northern Catholics probably made granting northern Protestants the right of self-determination all the easier.

Éamon de Valera's track regarding partition ran counter to Father O'Flanagan's. Lord Longford and Terence O'Neill first postulated that it was the threat of partition in the 1914 Home Rule Bill, that led de Valera into politics, a contention that John Bowman accepts.[81] The problem, in de Valera's estimation, was entirely the fault of British guile. There was nothing to the religious divide, he said. Though the political divide in the north roughly corresponded with the religious divide, it was only due to exploitation by British statesmen that this issue remained a pressing one. In early 1918, he believed that Ulster unionists must take their place in Ireland's glorious traditions, he said, or stand out as an alien garrison, in which case there could be no peace. In 1919, he was still of the opinion that northern unionists must either abandon their misguided allegiance to Great Britain or leave Ireland altogether, by which he meant physical relocation. During this period, he fluctuated between supporting and opposing coercion as a means of bringing the north into a unified Ireland.[82]

A year later, after returning from the US, he had softened his attitude. T. Ryle Dwyer posits that while de Valera was willing to accept the north's secession, he remained anxious that his public image remained one of opposition.[83] By the time he submitted his Document No. 2 for consideration by the Dáil, his stance was practically identical to that of Free State supporters. His document dedicated its addendum to the topic of northeast Ulster:

> That, whilst refusing to admit the right of any part of Ireland to be
> excluded from the supreme authority of the Parliament of Ireland,
> or that the relations between the Parliament of Ireland and any

subordinate Legislature in Ireland can be a matter for treaty with a government outside Ireland, nevertheless, in sincere regard for internal peace, and in order to make manifest our desire not to bring force or coercion to bear upon any substantial part of the Province of Ulster, whose inhabitants may now be unwilling to accept the national authority, we are prepared to grant to that portion of Ulster which is defined as Northern Ireland in the British Government of Ireland Act of 1920, privileges and safe-guards not less substantial than those provided for in the Articles of Agreement for a Treaty between Great Britain and Ireland signed in London on December 6th, 1921.[84]

Free State supporters marvelled at this document, which essentially granted the north the same rights as did the Treaty against which de Valera and his comrades fought. Desmond FitzGerald pointed out that the Free State government agreed with de Valera that Ulster was not to be coerced, but the positive comparison ended there. Whereas Document No. 2 was described as a final word on matters, thus placing the north in a seem-ingly permanent state of limbo, the Treaty was merely an expedient document for the current state of affairs and did not set boundaries for Ireland's future.[85] In other words, the Free State's policy was fluid and offered a better chance for unification of the island.

SECTARIAN VIOLENCE

The bitter sectarian fighting of the 1920s has been discussed and analysed in several works.[86] There is no reason to repeat anything here but the most crucial elements. It cannot be argued objectively that the Catholics of the newly-created Northern Ireland were not subject to state-sponsored discrimination and violent reprisals for the actions of the IRA and militant opponents of the Belfast government. Violence in Northern Ireland began on 21 July 1920 with the expulsion of Catholic and socialist dock workers by the Belfast Protestant Association.[87] By the end of 1920 at least 73 people had been killed, 395 wounded and 9,631 'expelled workers' registered for relief, with countless families (both Catholic and Protestant) driven from their homes. These numbers, though, show disproportionate violence against Catholics.[88] Tim Wilson's research shows that the death rate in Belfast for Catholics during this period was 28.63 per 10,000 people, while for Protestants it was 6.30

per 10,000.[89] By September 1922, when sectarian violence trickled to a stop, 453 people had been killed, of which Catholics made up fifty-seven per cent.[90] All sections of nationalists, including MacRory, believed anti-Catholic violence during this period was part of a concerted plan on the part of certain elements in unionist establishment to clear the nationalist minority from Belfast.[91] As Tim Wilson notes, '[i]t says much for the atmosphere of prevailing fear that the killing of perhaps 0.29 per cent of the Catholic community in Belfast (267 persons out of 93,243) could be presented as its wholesale destruction.'[92]

There was no shortage of contemporary treatment of northern violence as if it were solely a sectarian crisis. Southern newspaper coverage of northern violence gave the impression of a pogrom, resulting in southern nationalists characterising Belfast unionism by sectarianism and mob violence.[93] The most exhaustive contemporary nationalist propaganda piece that detailed what was described as the crimes committed against the Catholic community was Fr. John Hassan's *Facts & Figures: The Belfast Pogroms, 1920–22*, which appears to have been written in conjunction with the Free State government.[94] Writing under the pseudonym G.B. Kenna, Hassan, in a style similar to Dorothy Macardle's *Tragedies of Kerry*, paid homage to the men, women and children who had suffered, as he portrayed it, at the hands of the northern government, Orange agents and their English overlords. While the English pushed for an anti-nationalist pogrom, Orange extremists attacked Catholics simply because of sectarian hatred. To strengthen his argument, Hassan cited attacks on Crown forces by Orangemen. As most of the forces attacked were Catholic, he concluded that the activities of the Orangemen were purely out of religious hatred.[95] He reserved a special disgust for an episode in which several disabled Catholic Crown soldiers recuperating in Craigavon military hospital received threatening letters. Further comment, he stated, was not needed 'when it is remembered that those to whom these threatening messages were addressed were invalid ex-soldiers who had fought for the same King and Empire to which their persecutors are so fond of paying tributes of lip loyalty.'[96] Hassan, it should be noted, almost completely avoided mentioning the IRA throughout his book, alluding instead to a harmless civilian Catholic population.

Hassan's piece was not an accusation against all northern Protestants, and he made efforts to show his appreciation for those who were not

involved in sectarian violence, though one wonders if these protestations of communal respect are rather for propagandistic consumption:
'There are many thousands of Protestants in Ulster who would thrill
with horror and indignation at the true story of what has happened in
Belfast and other places in the North-East. But they have not heard the
truth, and their Press will see to it that, so long as it suits a political
game, they shall not hear the truth.' He even dedicated the book to the
'many Ulster Protestants' who had always lived in peace and friendli-
ness with their Catholic neighbours.[97] These men and women were,
like those outside the province, deprived of the truth by the biased
Orange press. This press, he contended, was Orangeism's greatest
weapon. They had three daily papers with wide local and international
circulation. Northern Catholics, by comparison, had only Devlin's *Irish
News*, which, while 'bright and well-written', suffered from a small
local circulation and practically no international influence.[98] These
Orange papers often committed the travesty of blaming the victims of
violent crimes for those crimes, such as when two young men were shot
dead by the RIC and an unnamed news agency described the men as
RIC members murdered by Sinn Féin.[99]

Despite the protestations of MacRory, Catholics were not helpless
and were responsible for many killings, beatings and arson attacks. The
Altnaveigh massacre committed by IRA forces caused public disgust
equalling the killings of the McMahons in Belfast.[100] The kidnapping of
forty-two prominent unionists in response to the planned execution of
three nationalist prisoners shows that nationalists were just as capable
of large scale reprisal actions as their opponents.[101] In *A State Under
Siege*, Bryan Follis, though perhaps overly sympathetic to the government officials whose papers he utilised so thoroughly in his research,
contends that the B Specials were reacting to, rather than creating, 'a
situation which was clearly born of the IRA outrages and inter-communal
rioting.'[102] He cites, as examples of Catholic aggression, multiple acts of
violence by the IRA, as well as an incendiary campaign that resulted in
claims for compensation rising from £252,578 in April 1922 to
£794,678 the next month.[103] The Catholic *Tablet* placed responsibility
for murders on both sides of the political and religious divide; a level
of objectivity that no widespread publication in Ireland was able to
achieve.[104] Even Hassan attributed some of the violence to the Catholic
side, though only at most ten per cent of all cases, and then only as a

matter of self-defence due to inadequate military and/or police protection.[105] While Hassan's bias must be acknowledged, research by Peter Hart and Tim Wilson lends credence to the notion that Catholics were less likely to expel Protestants from their homes or kill Protestant women and children.[106] Given that fewer Protestants lived in Catholic areas than vice versa, it may simply have been a matter of having less opportunity.

*   *   *

Catholics felt themselves especially aggrieved by the treatment they received at the hands of the northern government's police services. Special outrage was reserved for treatment meted out to hierarchical figures. On at least four separate occasions, Cardinal Logue and Bishop O'Donnell were stopped by Specials, who ordered the elderly men out of their automobile while it was searched. During the second instance, Logue remonstrated that he was on official business and had two firearms aimed at his head. The search during the third instance was so thorough that the Specials removed the air from the spare tyre and checked inside the wheel.[107]

Northern Catholics were appalled at the treatment of the Cardinal and his co-adjutor. It was seen that 'decent Protestants' were also upset at how the government forces had treated Logue, though, it was added, this was due to how the situation would work against them.[108] Several nationalist papers covered the affair in detail, remarking on the insulting manner in which the Specials had treated the prelate. The *Derry Weekly News* was especially indignant at the seemingly preferential treatment shown to Protestant ecclesiastics stopped by northern forces. The paper reported that the Bishop of Derry and Raphoe for the Church of Ireland, the Right Rev. Dr. Peacocke, was stopped near Glenties. His attaché case was searched and he was asked what other bags the car contained. The sentry took him at his word and he was permitted to proceed without further hassle.[109]

New fuel was added to the fire of northern Catholic indignation over the summer of 1922 when Church of Ireland prelates Dr. D'Arcy of Armagh and Dr. Grierson of Down and Connor, along with Dr. Lowe, Moderator of the Presbyterian General Assembly, and Rev. W.H. Smyth, President of the Methodist Conference, issued a statement which laid out their beliefs regarding the troubles in the north. They were of the opinion that the violence was not the result of religious strife but rather politics. This was proven, they contended, by the fact that there had been efforts to paralyse the northern government. Furthermore, in their opinion, the government had shown itself to be impartial in its efforts to put down the illegal use and carrying of arms. They proclaimed that they and their people had done everything in their power to prevent the struggle from becoming a religious one. The men expressed their profound regret about the reprisals that had been engaged in by their followers. They assured their audience that services and meetings had been held to denounce murder and to warn against reprisals. Regarding the topic of religious discrimination, they felt that the northern government had shown in many ways its earnest desire that Catholics should have full share in public and private life in Northern Ireland.[110]

Fr. Patrick Gannon, author of the 1920 article defending Terence MacSwiney's hunger strike and a staunch supporter of the Free State, was incensed by the document and wrote a scathing rejoinder that set the tone from the title, 'An Amazing Document', which received Archbishop Byrne's stamp of Imprimatur for publication, thus ensuring that his statements were in keeping with the approval of his superiors, accusing the eminent Protestant leaders of getting their facts solely from the Belfast loyalist press. Where, Gannon enquired, were the gangs of Catholic gunmen mentioned in the statement when Catholics were being expelled from their jobs and homes? The signatories forget to mention that horrible deeds done by Catholics had only come after the systematic bombing of Catholic homes and quarters and attacks on individuals for over four months.[111] They asserted that there had been an effort to paralyse the northern government, but the pogroms against Catholics were in operation for a full year before the northern government came into being.[112] He found it strange that Catholics would set out to paralyse a non-existent government in Belfast, where they were outnumbered three to one.[113] In arguing this point, Gannon conveniently overlooked the Ulster provisional government established in July 1914 with Carson as prime minister, as had been approved by the Ulster Unionist Council the year before. Even if it was argued that this government never truly gained sovereignty, it cannot be denied that the boycott and IRA campaigns had been designed to cripple the northern economy and paralyse the province's infrastructure, before and after the founding of Craig's government. Perhaps the Protestant prelates should have used the word 'state' instead of 'government', but this does not excuse Gannon's nitpicking.

The Protestant leaders said that they had done all they could to keep violence from turning religious. Perhaps pedantically so, Gannon took this to mean that they were content to let it stay political. He asked why they were not doing all in their power to stop it altogether. He took special affront to the idea that the northern government had shown a desire to include Catholics. He acidly asked if this was done by suppressing every local assembly in which they were a majority. By keeping expelled workers out of work? By raiding homes at every hour of the day looking for phantom IRA men?[114] As an example of Catholic incorporation into the state, he examined the police. Despite the fact that the Craig–Collins Pact had called for one-third of all northern police to be Catholic, almost the entire force remained Protestant.[115] Gannon failed to include that many Catholic organisations and clergymen were actively discouraging their members from joining the Ulster Special Constabulary and the Royal Ulster Constabulary.

In spite of Gannon's caustic tone and occasional sophistic reliance on insignificant details there is some credence to the questioning of the government's desire to incorporate Catholics into the state. Despite an arguably justifiable mistrust of the Catholic population, which had openly refused to recognise the existence of the northern government, what is remarkable is not the suspiciousness against the Catholics, but the absence of magnanimity or generosity and the government's lack of determination in luring the Catholics into incorporation or at least acquiescence.[116] A good example of this can be seen in the case of the calls to appoint a Catholic to the advisory committee for internees. Despite the fact that all but five internees were Catholics, none of the members of the committee established to hear their appeals were. W.B. Spender, former UVF commander, head of the civil service and a strong critic of the anti-Catholicism demonstrated by many within the government, had received calls for a Catholic to be placed on the committee. Richard Megaw, Dawson Bates's parliamentary secretary, wrote that after careful consideration, the appointing of a Catholic was not possible. Due to the confidential nature of the information to which the committee was privy, only the most exceptionally loyal of men could be appointed. Furthermore, 'the organisation of the R.C. Church, and the number of its confessors trained in inquisitional work who are actively engaged in the campaign against our Govt. increases the difficulty' and the ministry had not been successful in finding a candidate. The one Catholic barrister they had approached, a unionist named Raymond Burke, declined. Demonstrating to an even greater degree the anti-Catholic paranoia Harris has found to be common among northern unionists, Megaw added that it must be remembered that at the general election, 'Sinn Féin and Nationalists under the auspices of the Church combined forces to make our Govt. impossible and practically all Roman Catholics in the six counties threw themselves into the movement.'[117]

Sectarian conflict was not the rule throughout the north. Catholic businessmen, especially, sought for reconciliation of the two groups. They desired that their leaders accept the northern government for the betterment of the Catholic community and an opportunity for it to partake in the north's industry and commerce. In March 1922, James Lichfield, of the Northern Irish Civil Service, informed Thomas Jones, Lloyd George's private secretary, that the best way to overcome the conflict was by working with businessmen rather than politicians.[118] Many Catholics and Protestants were eager to co-operate as they generally had done for many years. Tim Wilson has shown that even during the height of the troubles, most of the six counties enjoyed peace and co-operative inter-communal relations.[119] In April 1922, Catholic and Protestant religious authorities of Belfast met and drew up a manifesto which was read from pulpits at Sunday services. The document made five key points: all human life is sacred in sight of God, no person is justified in taking life to serve any end by unprovoked aggression or for sake of reprisal or vengeance, responsibility lies upon every Christian to use influence in his or her private and public life to restrain lawlessness and outrage and promote a spirit of good will, as Christians they were bound to recognise rights of others who differ in creed and/or politics to live lives in peace, they were responsible for good name of city and honour of common Christianity.[120] The local unionist paper in Enniskillen deplored the state of affairs; 'Anyone who would curse the Pope would not be a Christian. That sort of thing may savour of Sandy Row [in Belfast], but not of Fermanagh.' [121]

INTERNMENT AND HUNGER STRIKES

On 22 November 1921, security matters for Northern Ireland were handed over to the Ministry of Home Affairs. Dawson Bates, who was irrefutably bigoted against Catholics, began a constant and unceasing war against any form of dissent in the Catholic community.[122] Almost immediately, unionist authorities called an end to the truce that had come about as a result of the cessation of hostilities between nationalists and British forces, due, in large part, to the resumption of IRA activities along the border. After several chaotic months, which included the kidnapping of forty-two unionists and the escalation of hostilities triggered by the Clones battle between A Specials and the IRA,[123] Bates informed the members of the northern parliament that their government was at war with the IRA. Using words reminiscent of those of O'Higgins, he said:

> But do not let us be under any delusion. We are not going to get peace in a day. The only way we are going to get peace in this community is by breaking the power of the Irish Republican Army in the Six Counties and by insisting, so far as regards the administration of the law, that it be vigorously carried out. Justice will be fairly and impartially administered to all, irrespective of creed or class, and the distinction hitherto recognised by the Imperial Government shall cease the distinction between a political criminal and an ordinary criminal.[124]

Bates's Civil Authorities (Special Powers) Act was very similar to the Restoration of Order in Ireland Act, 1920 as well as the Free State's Public Safety acts, though much less severe than its Army Emergency Powers Resolution, which granted military courts and committees the power to impose death penalties on non-military individuals.[125] It was only after the assassination of William Twaddell, MP, in May 1922 that the government brought the Act into full operation. The night after Twaddell's death, Craig ordered all A and B Specials, who had been called up to full-time active duty, to arrest suspected IRA and Sinn Féin members throughout the six counties. Two hundred and eighty-two were arrested the first night, and arrests continued a second night, until the government announced 348 men were to be interned. As many as eighty more men were arrested by the end of June. A substantial number of the men were released after signing an agreement to keep the peace or agreeing to an exclusionary order to leave the six-county area. A total of twenty Protestants were arrested; all but five were released.

Though the order had been to arrest IRA and its allied associations, most prisoners were constitutional nationalists and Free State supporters, with republicans making up a small minority. Denise Kleinrichert contends that, despite knowing a great deal about the IRA's northern hierarchy, the government selectively chose local Catholic leaders with no connection to the republican movement for internment.[126] She sees this as proof of the government's attempts to obliterate political opposition. However, the government's actions were not totally unjustifiable, at least when viewed in the contemporary perspective. It is worth remembering that in May 1922, both pro- and anti-Treaty organisations were still calling themselves Sinn Féin and were still attempting to come to agreeable terms, as demonstrated by the Collins–de Valera election pact, which was not well received amongst Ulster unionists. Prior to the start of the Civil War, telling the opposing sides apart was incredibly difficult, especially as both sides shared a mutual opposition to the northern government.

Paul Bew contends that by the spring of 1922 there was belief in the south and especially in the north that a civil war was inevitable, but the conflicting sides appeared to be lining up as nationalist versus unionist. Church of Ireland Archbishop Gregg of Dublin publicly aired his concern that the rival states in Ireland seemed to be headed for conflict.[127] On top of that, the northern government was well aware of the Free State government's attempts at damaging the northern government in the hope that the northern state would collapse. In a meeting with Arthur Balfour, Craig said that the South had voted £100,000 for propaganda and 'were dexterously spreading lies all over the world'.[128] While elements of the programme, such as funding northern Catholic schools that refused to accept state money,[129] were public, elements such as Collins's arming of the northern IRA with weapons given to the Free State by the British were meant to be secret, but Lynch believes that unionist authorities in Belfast were well aware of his involvement as well as that of other members of the Provisional Government.[130] If this is true, Craig would have viewed Free State supporters as enemies equal to the actual soldiers and republicans who had sworn to continue the fight against the existence of Northern Ireland. According to the perspective of the northern government, it faced an internal enemy that was determined to topple not just the current government but the very structure of the state, and that enemy was receiving support from the highest echelons of the Free State government. Craig and his ministers had witnessed what Sinn Féin and the IRA had done to Imperial rule in the twenty-six counties, and they knew that some of the most powerful men in the movement, namely Collins and his cohort, had turned their attention northward. Faced with this situation as well as rampant unemployment and the travails which accompany it, there is little reason to wonder that the state interned its perceived enemies. The Free State government, after all, was doing the same thing and on a much larger scale, but because the northern government was composed entirely of Protestants and those subjected to punishment were almost all Catholic, the issue was treated as a religious one. As an official government policy, this appears to have been untrue, but the anti-Catholic biases of many with briefs of authority allowed sectarianism to penetrate into much of the government's activities.

* * *

The majority of arrested men were interned on the *Argenta*, a former emergency vessel for the American war effort that had been declared unseaworthy. Shortly before midnight on 20 June, 273 men were taken on board. Conditions on the ship were notoriously appalling; worse even then the usual state of Northern Irish prisons, which, during his month-long incarceration in Derry in 1924, de Valera found to be the worst he had experienced in Britain or Ireland.[131] The food was a constant source of complaint. The five doctors interned declared the meat unsuitable for consumption and the vermin problem was partially attributed to the poor quality of bully beef and biscuits.[132] As bad as conditions were, Robert Lynch theorises some of the poorer elements of the IRA seem to have preferred internment to living in the extreme poverty and unemployment to which they were accustomed,[133] though this supposition seems highly unlikely.

As a result of conditions, hunger strikes were a regular occurrence on the *Argenta*. Most were commenced by small bands of internees and never got beyond the threat stage, and those that did lasted no more than one meal 'and a request was always made later for the meal which had been missed.'[134] This routine proceeded until 25 October 1923, the third anniversary of Terence MacSwiney's death, when 131 internees on board went on hunger strike, claiming that in the twelve months and more they had been held no charges had been brought against them. Four days later, sixty-five men in the Larne workhouse joined the strike, though equally notable is that 108 refused to join.[135] The maximum was reached on 2 November, when a total of 269 men were on hunger strike. Mass abandonment began the next day. By 11 November, all but one individual had given up the strike, and he finally abandoned it after seventeen days. The governor of Londonderry Prison proudly noted that only six men had had to be transported to the prison hospital, and Shewell at Home Affairs reported that no internee had to be released on conditions of health due to the strike.[136] It was, in short, an unmitigated failure.

From the beginning, the Belfast government dealt with the strike severely, looking to quash it before the situation got out of hand. The governor of Belfast prison reported that it was obvious to him that a large number of the strikers were forced by their leaders to join: 'Several have told me that they did not want to go on hunger strike, but were made to and are now afraid to take food. One, who is now taking food, is afraid to leave his cell until he goes back to Larne.'[137] He did believe, however, that at least thirty per cent were prepared to see the strike through, though most believed they would be released before they would be allowed to die. If the government yielded to their demands, he theorised, it would not be possible to hold interned prisoners in the future and they could even see similar troubles with ordinary prisoners.[138] To this end, the strikers were isolated from the other prisoners and transported. There were also reports of strikers being handcuffed and beaten by Specials,[139] though evidence is unsurprisingly scant. Once sent to Belfast or Londonderry, the strikers often found themselves subjected to solitary confinement and further harassment by the guards. In retrospect, the governor of Londonderry prison insisted that the government's firm stance during the strike had brought an end to Sinn Féin's policy of demanding unconditional releases.[140]

The strikers also faced the disheartening reality of an apathetic Catholic community. Devlin's *Irish News* ran reports of two separate meetings being held in support of the strikers and as means of protesting the continued imprisonment of the uncharged men. The first meeting, held in Armagh and presided over by Monsignor Ward, was described as 'largely attended'. Those present unanimously passed a resolution calling for immediate and unconditional release of the prisoners as continued internment was, in their opinion, 'contrary to all sense of justice, and absolutely inconsistent with the spirit of humanity and good-will.'[141] Contrary to this glowing report, the Inspector General reported to Home Affairs that '[t]he general public took little or no interest in the proceedings, which passed over almost unnoticed. There were only about 30 people present and the meeting lasted half an hour.'[142]

The second meeting, held in St. Peter's Club, Divis St, Belfast, was much better attended. Even the government had to admit that approx-imately four hundred people were present, including seventeen Catholic clergymen. Archdeacon Convery, parish priest of St. Paul's presided over the meeting. He gave an emphatic speech calling for the immediate and unconditional release of the internees, who were being denied the same rights to which the subjects of any civilised government were entitled – 'They had committed no crime except that of loving their country, and they were now pining in the internment camp at Larne, or suffering the pangs of hunger in the jails of Belfast and Derry, and on the *Argenta*. They might die as far as the Northern Government was concerned.'[143] The resolution passed with only one dissention. The dis-senter, a republican named William Shaw, requested that reference be made to the thousands of prisoners in the Free State suffering the same fate. Interestingly, the chairman refused the request as, he claimed, the meeting had been called for a specific purpose.[144]

While glossing over the larger meeting, the District Inspector reported that it was believed that ninety per cent of northern Catholics were opposed to the internees going on hunger strike, and, he added rather fantastically, even their release on such grounds: 'There was little or no excitement observed amongst the Roman Catholic population over the hunger strike, except amongst a few of the immediate friends of the internees; and so far, the action of the Government in not releasing them appears to have excited little comment.'[145] One exception was Bishop MacRory, who on numerous occasions attempted to attract as much attention as possible to the plight of the internees. On 4 November he sent a telegraph to the *Manchester Guardian* asking that the paper give publicity to the 130 men going without food in protest of up to seventeen months of internment without charges preferred against them.[146] Shortly thereafter, he was the first of thirteen signatories, which included Convery, Devlin and the ex-Mayor of Derry, of a letter of protest sent to Stanley Baldwin, Craig and Cosgrave. The letter stated that the men were arrested with no charge and had endured long and distressing confinement on the convict ship and in internment camps. One hundred and fifty had gone on hunger strike as a protest against this detention without charge or trial.[147] The men being held were Catholics, the writers pointed out, 'and the Catholics in the "Northern" area regard their detention in the circumstances as one more proof of the partisan and bigoted spirit of Sir J. Craig's Government.' The letter concluded with a call to release the men without degrading conditions pressed upon them.[148]

Over 7,000 men and women interned in the Free State were on hunger strike at the time this letter was written, and yet Cardinal Logue was the only bishop who gave any semblance of disapproval of the government's treatment of the men, and that was countered by equal criticism of the strikers themselves.[149] Even MacRory, who was so actively involved in fighting for the northern internees, never once spoke on behalf of those in the twenty-six counties. Why the divergence? The answer seems to lie in expediency. MacRory supported the Free State government, and so, like the other members of the hierarchy, he refrained from publicly criticising it for fear of swaying opinion against it. However, matters regarding the six-county area were different. Without the constraint of trying to shield the government, he could take strong oppositional stances. He was still opposed to the idea of the Belfast government as a matter of principle, and his harsh criticisms of its internment policy were aimed at discrediting it in the eyes of the British while working to help his followers. It seems a shame that the men interned in the Free State did not enjoy the same level of his support due to political inconvenience.

Nor did the plight of interned Catholics in the north receive any noticeable support in the Free State. On the night of 5 October, a contingent of 'prominent Ulster men' that included Captain Jack White, labour leader Jim Larkin, who, though a Liverpool native had strong ties to Ulster, and IRB notables Denis McCullough and Dr. Pat McCartan met in the Mansion House in Dublin to protest against harassment of nationalists in Northern Irish prisons and to demand their release. Despite this impressive line up, the room was less than half full. Councillor William

Paul accused the Free State government and the hierarchy of failing to defend the Catholics of the north, thereby allowing Craig and his government to do what they wanted. McCartan, in an impassioned speech, said it would not be through de Valera or Cosgrave that unity would be achieved. There was no use protesting prisoners in the north while there were still prisoners in the south. Acquire unconditional release for those in the Free State, he demanded, and then work could begin on the situation in the north. Rather than blaming the government for the situation, he told his audience that they should work to get rid of the hate and dissension that had plagued the country for the last year.[150]

While an inconsequential meeting at the time, and one that has received no apparent historiographical attention, this collection of men shows how different the northern crisis was when compared to the Civil War raging throughout the rest of the island. As a member of the Dáil, McCartan had been the final, albeit grudging supporter of the Treaty. McCullough served as the Dáil's Special Commissioner to the United States in 1922 and was elected TD for Donegal as a Cumann na nGaedheal candidate in 1924. At the opposite end was Jim Larkin, who vocally opposed the Treaty from the beginning. Both he and White, though, were more interested in socialist issues than Ireland's political status. While men of opposing opinions were at each others' throats elsewhere, these disillusioned northerners/sympathisers focused their attention on Ulster and sought to garner attention for their cause, though they did so in vain.

There is also the matter of how internment and the failed hunger strikes affected the Catholic community. Again, one would postulate that if the government had been planning the whole affair for months with the intention of destroying nationalist morale, as Kleinrichert contends,[151] the ministers would have taken all necessary steps to magnify the impact of internment on the northern Catholics. In fact, nothing of the sort happened. Public reaction to internment was minimal and was notable at the final releases in 1924 by its absence.[152] This is not to say that the community was entirely apathetic. The northern edition of the *Irish Catholic Herald* ran many articles on internment describing the *Argenta* as '[a] Floating Death-trap' and comparing the treatment meted out to the internees as worse than that of British soldiers in German prisoner-of-war camps.[153] The *Derry Weekly News* theorised that the true purpose behind the prison ship was to provoke reprisals so that the British might be scared out of ratifying the treaty and accepting the constitution: 'Possibly, probably,' the paper pessimistically noted 'they will succeed.'[154] However, unlike in the Free State, where hundreds of municipal organisations were calling for the release of the internees, very few councils and public bodies made a similar request in the north. Of notable exception was the Newry Urban Council, which, in November 1923, called upon the release of the internees as further holding had to be the result of a desire for revenge or leverage used for a boundary agreement.[155] Undoubtedly, gerrymandering of local government and Belfast's use of putting councils under administration had reduced the number of nationalist bodies, but even within their dwindling numbers, protest was sparse.

What is difficult to comprehend is why the bishops, especially those in the north, did not fight more on behalf of their fellow Catholics. Given that they had no loyalty to the state, why did they not speak against internment more? Why were their statements criticising government-sponsored prejudice against Catholics not more severe? By refusing to participate in Lord Londonderry's education commission they had effectively silenced themselves on their favourite topic, and by showing relative restraint they passively granted Craig's government a degree of legitimacy. MacRory remained an intractable spokesman for northern Catholics in keeping with his unofficial position as their primary advocate, but he stood alone. There are several possibilities for why this was the case.

One issue may have been the potential Pandora's Box that could have been opened had they chosen to speak on the northern internment policy. Speaking against the injustice of imprisoning a few hundred untried men would have raised expectations that they also address the thousands of untried prisoners being held by the government they had so fervently endorsed. Rather than run the risk of facing this hurdle, their silence may have been a practical means of avoiding this potentially disastrous subject. Fear seems to have been another of their prime motivating factors. An example of this can be seen in their attitude towards the oath demanded of those who received payment out of the state's coffers, including priests and members of religious orders who acted as chaplains and teachers. The bishops were categorically against allowing this, and Logue promised to do what he could to prevent it.

Nothing came of this though and the hierarchy advised that the oath be taken for fear of losing seminaries.[156] By summer 1922, Mulhern was quietly in favour of recognition of the northern state, fearing that a continuation of the current stance would result in Newry being staffed for a generation with Orange officials.[157] Now that the northern bishops were the religious leaders of the minority, they no longer had the strength of the populace behind them that had previously given their voices such resonance in the fight against Crown forces. Unable to speak on behalf of the majority of the state's citizens, the bishops faced a new challenge and it took several years for them to properly adjust. Without the majority of the population as their support base, it would appear, the bishops did not know how to oppose the tactics of the northern government, nor were they prepared to engage in the level of confrontation that was necessary.

ACCEPTANCE OF PARTITION

The establishing and running of the Boundary Commission demon-strated the political naïveté and lack of experience of both the Free State ministers and the Catholic hierarchy. The first mistake the nation-alists made in regard to the restructuring of the border was the wording of the Treaty itself, which, through their ignorance, the plenipoten-tiaries had allowed to remain vague:

> ...a Commission consisting of three persons, one to be appointed by the Government of the Irish Free State, one to be appointed by the Government of Northern Ireland, and one who shall be Chairman to be appointed by the British Government shall determine in accordance with the wishes of the inhabitants, so far as may be compatible with economic and geographic conditions the boundaries between Northern Ireland and the rest of Ireland, and for the purposes of the Government of Ireland Act, 1920, and of this instrument, the boundary of Northern Ireland shall be such as may be determined by such Commission.[158]

Each side could interpret article twelve as they desired. Nationalists stressed the need for the border to comply with the wishes of the inhab-itants, while unionists paid closer attention to the economic and geographical conditions. As Joe Lee has pointed out, definitions for crucial words like 'inhabitants' and 'wishes' were absent, thus open for further interpretation.[159]

The Free State government was in no hurry to initiate the Commission. The Civil War had turned all attention away from the north and Collins's assassination deprived northern nationalists of their strongest champion in the Free State. Once Collins was dead, none of the southern ministers were particularly interested in attending to northern matters. Primarily through the influence of Cosgrave and Blythe, the Free State government adopted a policy of co-existence with the northern regime much to the chagrin of northern nationalists, especially those of Fermanagh, Tyrone and Derry City, all of which hoped to become incorporated into the Free State. Blythe had previously advocated a policy of urging northern Catholics living in the Free State to return to their homes and prepare to fight or at least be prepared to help fill the jails. Those young men who remained in the south should have little sympathy shown to them, he wrote.[160] Not only did the Free State government not want to have to contend with the northern crisis but it appears that some within the government did not even want to have to deal with its victims.

Northern Catholic resentment against this inactivity was obvious when, in May 1923, a delegation of thirty AOH members from the six counties travelled to Dublin to meet with Cosgrave. They were received, instead, by future Boundary Commissioner and County Antrim native Eoin MacNeill. During the three-hour interview, MacNeill was asked about taking seats in the northern parliament. He answered that they knew best what to do; 'he would not advise them to break their pledge given in 1921' though personally he was not going to sit.[161] He also refused to commit himself to the setting up of the Boundary Commission, stating that the Free State government would have nothing to do with it until an election took place. He said that the Commission would be set up in due course, but that it was in the hands of the Imperial Government. The delegates left disappointed with his evasive answers and feeling, according to the RUC report, 'that there will be no Commission set up, and that no sympathy may be expected from the Free State Government, at least as far as the Constitutionalists are concerned.'[162]

Cosgrave's government was banking on the collapse of the Conservative government in Westminster. It was believed that Bonar Law's government could not appoint an impartial chairman to the Commission which was, in Cosgrave's opinion, the very crux of the boundary question.[163] Even if it could, Dublin was convinced that London would be reluctant to compel Craig to abide by any decision which did not favour the north. The Free State ministers were quite content to wait to start the Commission until there was a more sympathetic government in power in London, and they were convinced that by ignoring the issue, Craig had done them a great service.[164] The bishops, too, were eager to see a change of government in London. Mulhern thought that the forthcoming general election of December had the potential to be of momentous importance in the boundary question, and could even lead to Irish unity.[165] After Labour's victory, many were hopeful of a quick resolution. O'Donnell remained sceptical of a positive result from the Commission but thought that the advent of a new government would work against partition. Mulhern became quite enthused that the matter would soon be resolved, but at the same time feared the possibility of the new government collapsing and the Tories returning and ending Fermanagh and Tyrone's chances of joining the Free State.[166]

With the end of the Civil War and the return to relative peace in the Free State, Cosgrave had become more sensitive to the pressure exerted by northern Catholics to initiate the Boundary Commission. On 26 April 1924, his government formally applied for the appointment of the Boundary Commission as laid out by article twelve of the Treaty. The Commission met from November 1924 until August 1925, with their first formal hearings taking place in April.[167] Their tours of the border areas attracted a lot of attention from both sides, each looking to present its case. The hierarchy and clergy were heavily involved in preparing and presenting the case for inclusion in the Free State, though it is interesting that while O'Donnell, McKenna, McHugh and Mulhern met with the Commission, only Mulhern, who was desperate to see Newry in the Free State, presented evidence in person. This was a pattern repeated by Catholic clergy of the disputed area. The Commission reported very few interviews with Catholic clergymen, and those that did take place often contradicted each other. The Parish priest in Magheramena Castle, County Fermanagh informed the commissioners that the Specials had occupied his house and done terrible damage, and that their arrival had marked the beginning of the local troubles. Conversely, Fr. Gorman of Rosslea had no complaints to register regarding the Specials. He said that they treated him and all local Catholics with civility and respect.[168]

The bishops had reason to remain confident regarding the decision of the Boundary Commission. The Free State government had been assuring them for years that their side would come away with the better deal. Collins had been so sure of the benefits the Commission would give to the Free State he admitted to Craig during one of their meetings leading up to their first pact that he expected almost half of the northern state to be transferred,[169] though this was probably partially bluster and Collins's attempt at psychological battle. Kevin O'Shiel, who headed the Free State's North-Eastern Boundary Bureau, predicted, as his minimal claim, more than 600,000 residents' transferral to the Free State: all of Counties Fermanagh and Tyrone, the southern portions of Counties Armagh and Down, and Derry city.[170] Even Blythe was of the opinion that the Treaty entitled the Free State to the acquisition of at least two and a half counties.[171]

By 1924, though, most members of the Free State government were aware before the Commission first met that it would end in failure and would simply strengthen partition and Craig's position. MacNeill had been chosen not for his negotiation skills but because he was the best candidate for a scapegoat.[172] Feetham, who due to Fisher and MacNeill cancelling each other out made all decisions virtually unilaterally, saw the Commission as a body intended to smooth the border while keeping Northern Ireland approximately the same size. To this end, the final judgment was that 286 square miles of the six counties be transferred to the Free State and 77 square miles of Free State territory were to go to Northern Ireland.[173] Craig had already threatened to resign if the Commission presented findings unfavourable to his government, and the Free State ministers knew that the people of the Free State would under no circumstances accept the transferral of any territory to the north. It would seem that their pessimism had been well-founded.

The Boundary Commission collapsed before its report could even be released. The report was leaked, undoubtedly by Fisher, to the *Morning Post* shortly before it was to be made public, causing outrage and protest on both sides.[174] MacNeill resigned from the Commission on the 20th, amidst a torrent of abuse from within the Free State, and from the Cabinet four days later. His prediction had indeed come true and the professor was never again politically active. Alongside MacNeill's political career also vanished nationalist hopes of reducing Northern Ireland to an economically unviable size. The quiet fears of many northern Catholics, who suspected that the Free State government would abandon them at the first opportunity for the betterment of the twenty-six counties, proved correct. The Boundary Commission did not turn out as they had hoped, leaving northern Catholics and especially the bishops, who had placed so much on the commission's outcome, wanting for a policy now that their worst-case scenario had come true.

CONCLUSION

Contrary to the hopes and wishes of all nationalists, the northern state proved not to be a short-term failed experiment. It became a stable entity that, after the summer of 1922, experienced lower levels of violence than the Free State would see for years. After 1923 there was not another sectarian murder in Belfast for ten years,[175] and the religious communities entered into a cold but relatively peaceful relationship. Anti-Catholic bigotry, however, was rampant throughout all sectors of the government and society. Catholics may not have faced any more gunfire and burnings, but they were still second-class citizens and would remain so for decades to come. The problem was the petty sectarianism that plagued Northern Ireland during the entirety of its self-government stemmed partially from the government and its support-ers regarding the Catholics as actual or potential traitors and treating them accordingly.[176] Though religious differences and sectarian violence had existed in the north for centuries, this political spin was the new-born product of the debate over partition and unionism's evolution into an Ulster-only phenomenon. Protestants saw Catholics as the enemy in the early days of the state because, for the most part, Catholics were the enemy. However, this internal enemy fear never disappeared, and so a justifiable paranoia became, over the years, an inexcusable remnant of a battle that had been fought and won.

The resulting situation was indeed difficult for the northern bishops. They had openly opposed partition and the northern state, but after 1925 that state was a matter of fact and if they were going to represent and fight for their co-religionists, they were going to have to deal with a government they had refused to accept. The Boundary Commission had been the last hope for many of them. When that hope disappeared, they faced the reality of having to formulate a programme that dealt not with a thirty-two county Ireland, but the six-county state in which they resided.

In February 1926, Cardinal O'Donnell formally announced that Northern Ireland was a fixed entity and its inhabitants had to take this into account. He told the crowd that he could not say what would have happened if Catholics and Nationalists had taken their seats in the northern parliament from the beginning: 'But what matters now is that the case be made in such a way as to be thoroughly understood, and that it be pressed by every legitimate means, with nothing but good feeling for our neighbours.'[177] With southern support diminished and the wreckage of the Boundary Commission swept under the rug, the northern bishops were finally forced to concede that partition was a fact, and one with which they would have to deal. O'Donnell seemed to be attempting to lead the Catholic population towards integration within the northern state, but his aspirations suffered a major setback in 1927 when he unexpectedly died and the pugnacious MacRory, who still refused to co-operate with the northern government, became the Archbishop of Armagh and Primate of All Ireland. MacRory's Belfast ghetto mentality permeated the actions of northern Catholics for decades, and sectarianism refused to disappear from either community.

In the final decade of his professional life, Ernest Blythe lamented the existence of the Nationalist Party in Northern Ireland. He regarded it as a sectarian institution and, as such, a bulwark of division which had been responsible for partition and had allowed it to continue. He yearned to see political parties that were rooted in genuine political and social issues rather than religious affiliation. Most importantly, he believed, northern Catholics had to cease their self-imposed segregation in politics and public affairs.[178] Though his statements were not aimed exclusively at the bishops and clergy, they could have been. In spite of their laudable efforts to protect their co-religionists, their close involvement and unwavering classification of government activities as sectarian rather than political played a large role in promoting the Catholic segregationist mentality that was blocking the way to co-operation, and possibly even, according to Blythe, Irish unity.

NOTES

1. 'Far and Near', *CB*, December 1923.
2. Mary Harris, *The Catholic Church and the Foundation of the Northern Irish State*, pp.14–16.
3. Ibid., pp.70–1. See also Eamon Phoenix, *Northern Nationalism: Nationalist Politics, Partition and the Catholic Minority in Northern Ireland, 1890–1940* (Belfast, 1994), pp.47–51.
4. Clare O'Halloran, *Partition and the Limits of Irish Nationalism: An ideology under stress* (Dublin, 1987), pp.58–9.
5. Quoted in Denis Gwynn, *The History of Partition, 1912–1925* (Dublin, 1950), p.63.
6. Eamon Phoenix, *Northern Nationalism: Nationalist Politics, Partition and the Catholic Minority in Northern Ireland, 1890–1940* (Belfast, 1994), p.11.
7. *II*, 8 May 1917.
8. AAA, O'Donnell papers, O'Donnell to McHugh, 4 May 1917.
9. *II*, 18 February 1920.
10. *DP*, 20 March 1920.
11. AAA, Logue papers, Logue to Chief Secretary, [undated but probably 1920].
12. AAA, O'Donnell papers, clipping from *The World's News*, 1920.
13. Ibid.
14. TCDA, Dillon papers, 6764/117, O'Donnell to Dillon, 19 March 1921.
15. Ibid.
16. Eamon Phoenix, *Northern Nationalism*, p.137.
17. Paul Bew, *Ireland: The Politics of Enmity, 1789–2006* (Oxford, 2007), p.424. For more on the boycott, see also D.S. Johnson, 'The Belfast Boycott' in J.M. Goldstrom and L.A. Clarkson (eds), *Irish Population, Economy, and Society* (Oxford, 1981), pp.287–307.
18. UCDA, Blythe papers, P24/70, 'Policy in Regard to the North-East', presented 9 August 1922. By the end of the 1920s, customs and excise accounted for 60–70 per cent of the Free State government's revenue. T.K. Daniel, 'Griffith on his Noble Head: The Determination of Cumann na nGaedheal Economic Policy, 1922–32' in *Irish Economic and Social History*, III (1976), p.59.
19. Quoted in Mary Harris, *The Catholic Church and the Foundation of the Northern Irish State*, p.34.
20. CDA, Cohalan papers, Lenten pastoral, 1921.
21. See Chapter 2, pp.70-1.
22. KDA, Fogarty papers, Fogarty pastoral, [no date but clearly written during Anglo-Irish War].
23. NLI, O'Ceallaigh papers, Ms 27,712(1), Fogarty to James O'Mara, 28 October 1918, quoted in Curran's memoirs.
24. Marianne Elliott, *The Catholics of Ulster: A History* (London, 2000), p.297. For more on the convention, see Mary Harris, *The Catholic Church and the Foundation of the Northern Irish State*, pp.52–5, and Eamon Phoenix, *Northern Nationalism*, pp.30–3.
25. *IER*, November 1920, 'Statement Issued by the Cardinal Primate and the Archbishops and Bishops of Ireland on the Present Condition of their Country (19 October 1920)'.
26. Ibid.
27. The issue of Protestant-dominated education was of great importance for the bishops of the North. For more on their opposition to Northern Ireland's education policy, see Mary Harris, *Catholic Church and the Foundation of the Northern Irish State* and Eamon Phoenix, *Northern Nationalism*.
28. Mary Harris, *Catholic Church and the Foundation of the Northern Irish State*, p.105; DAA, Byrne papers, McHugh to Byrne, 18 December 1921.
29. See Chapter 2, p.69.
30. DAA, Curran papers, Hagan to Curran, 8 October 1922.
31. ICR, Hagan papers, MacRory to Hagan, 17 January 1922.
32. ICR, Hagan papers, Mulhern to Hagan, 6 January 1922.
33. NAI, Dept. of An Taoiseach, G1/1, Minutes of the Executive Council, 30 January 1922.
34. Mary Harris, *The Catholic Church and the Foundation of the Northern Irish State*, pp.79, 93.
35. *II*, 27 February 1922.

36. ICR, Hagan papers, Mulhern to Hagan, 6 January 1922.
37. ICR, Hagan papers, Mulhern to Hagan, 22 March 1922.
38. ICR, Hagan papers, Mulhern to Hagan, 7 April 1922.
39. ICR, Hagan papers, Keohane to Hagan, 14 March 1922.
40. ICR, Hagan papers, McHugh to Hagan, 7 February 1922.
41. ICR, Hagan papers, Mulhern to Hagan, 7 April 1922.
42. ICR, Hagan papers, Mulhern to Hagan, 27 June 1922.
43. *FS*, 25 February 1922.
44. *FS*, 11 March 1922.
45. INBMN, 19 May 1921.
46. Clare O'Halloran, *Partition and the Limits of Irish Nationalism*, pp.45–7.
47. ICDA, 1923, p.603.
48. Donald Bloxham has shown that over one million Armenians died due to Turkish atrocities. Hundreds of thousands were deported or forced into concentration camps, women raped and orphaned children forcibly converted to Islam. By comparison, from 1918 to 1922, Ulster experienced 714 violent fatalities. Of course, contemporary Irish were ignorant of the true extent of the situation in the former Ottoman Empire. See Donald Bloxham, 'The Armenian Genocide of 1915–1916: Cumulative Radicalization and the Development of a Destruction Policy' in *Past & Present*, no. 181, November 2003, pp.141–191.
49. *ICDA* 1923, p.603.
50. *IER*, July 1922, 'Statement on the condition of the country adopted unanimously by the Archbishops and Bishops of Ireland, His Eminence, Cardinal Logue in the chair', pp.80–1.
51. *IT*, 13 October 1923.
52. Ibid.
53. Ibid., 15 October 1923.
54. Ibid., 18 October 1923.
55. *PP*, 30 April 1922.
56. Ibid., 25 June 1922.
57. UCDA, de Valera papers, P150/1656, Committee of Irish Catholics to Pope Pius XI.
58. Ibid.
59. See Mary Harris, *The Catholic Church and the Foundation of the Northern Irish State*, pp.196–200.
60. UCDA, de Valera papers, P150/1656, Committee of Irish Catholics to Pope Pius XI.
61. Vatican City, A.E.S., Inghilterra, Posizione 167, fascicolo 14, 'Quotations from Irish Bishops', contained within 'Relazione Della Missione in Irlanda di Mons. Luzio Salvatore'.
62. DAA, Byrne papers, Cathleen O'Moore to Byrne, 11 October 1922.
63. UCDA, Mary MacSwiney papers, P48a/216, Peter Yorke, 'Irish Bishops Usurp Papal Rights'.
64. Clare O'Halloran, *Partition and the Limits of Irish Nationalism*, pp.3–4.
65. Robert Lynch, *The Northern IRA and the Early Years of Partition, 1920–1922* (Dublin, 2006); Tim Wilson, 'Boundaries, Identity and Violence', D.Phil. thesis, vol. II, pp.218–27.
66. T.K. Wilson, *Frontiers of Violence: Conflict and Identity in Ulster and Upper Silesia, 1918–1922* (Oxford, 2010), pp.128-30.
67. Ibid., pp.130-31.
68. ICR, Hagan papers, Ni G to Hagan, 4 October 1923.
69. Merriam-Webster defines 'cormorant' as 'a gluttonous, greedy, or rapacious person', http://www.merriam-webster.com/dictionary/cormorant (accessed 10 June 2012).
70. ICR, Hagan papers, Keohane to Hagan, 14 March 1922.
71. *FJ*, 20 June 1916.
72. Denis Carroll, *They have fooled you again*, p.49.
73. Ibid., p.140.
74. PRONI, Home Affairs, HA/32/1/462, Issuing of prohibition of entry to Michael O'Flanagan under Regulation 23A of Civil Authorities (Special Powers) Act (Northern Ireland) 1922, 25 September 1925.
75. PRONI, Home Affairs, HA/32/1/525, List of the 31 Orders (under Regulation 23A – prohibition of entry into N. Ireland) in force, 1927.

76. *DJ*, 27 February 1925.
77. Patrick Maume, 'Nationalism and partition: the political thought of Arthur Clery' in *Irish Historical Studies*, xxxi (November 1998), pp.222, 230.
78. Ibid., pp.228–9.
79. Ibid., p.230.
80. Ibid., p.229.
81. John Bowman, *De Valera and the Ulster Question*, pp.6, 30.
82. Ibid., pp.31–9.
83. T. Ryle Dwyer, 'Eamon de Valera and the Partition Question' in O'Carroll and Murphy (eds), *De Valera and his Times*, pp.74, 77.
84. Ronan Fanning et al. (eds), *Documents on Irish Foreign Policy* vol. I, no. 218, 'Proposed Treaty of Association between Ireland and the British Commonwealth presented by Éamon de Valera to Dáil Éireann', p.370.
85. *FS*, 22 May 1922.
86. See Michael Farrell, *Arming the Protestants: The Formation of the Ulster Special Constabulary and the Royal Ulster Constabulary, 1920–7* (London, 1983); Eamon Phoenix, *Northern Nationalism*; Bryan A. Follis, *A State Under Siege: The Establishment of Northern Ireland, 1920–1925* (Oxford, 1995); Jim McDermott, *Northern Divisions: The Old IRA and the Belfast Pogroms* (Dublin, 2001); Richard English, *Armed Struggle: The History of the IRA, 1916–2002* (London, 2003); A.F. Parkinson, *Belfast's Unholy War* (Dublin, 2004); Robert Lynch, *The Northern IRA and the Early Years of Partition*; Timothy Bowman, *Carson's Army: The Ulster Volunteer Force, 1910–22* (Manchester, 2007).
87. Though this is generally regarded as the start of the troubles, Bardon has shown that 1919 through the first half of 1920 had experienced some sectarian violence. A riot in Derry in August 1919 was over fairly quickly but smaller scale incidents build up there in the spring of 1920, culminating in full-scale gun battles from the 18 to 23 June 1920 in which about 40 died. See Jonathan Bardon, *History of Ulster* (Belfast, 1994), p.469.
88. Eamon Phoenix, *Northern Nationalism*, p.89.
89. T.K. Wilson, 'The most terrible assassination that has yet stained the name of Belfast': The McMahon Murders in context', *Irish Historical Studies*, vol. xxxvii, no. 145, May 2010, p.89.
90. Marianne Elliott, *The Catholics of Ulster*, p.374.
91. Eamon Phoenix, *Northern Nationalism*, p.230.
92. Tim Wilson, 'Boundaries, Identity and Violence', vol. II, p. 239.
93. Clare O'Halloran, *Partition and the Limits of Irish Nationalism*, p.14.
94. Mary Harris, *The Catholic Church and the Foundation of the Northern Irish State*, p.127.
95. G.B. Kenna, *Facts & Figures: The Belfast Pogroms, 1920–22*, Thomas Donaldson (ed.), (1997 edition), pp.13, 62–3.
96. Ibid., p.72.
97. Ibid., p.12 and dedication page.
98. Ibid., p.33.
99. Ibid., p.40.
100. Wilson, *Frontiers of Violence*, pp.167-71.
101. Robert Lynch, *The Northern IRA and the Early Years of Partition*, pp.100–4.
102. Bryan A. Follis, *A State Under Siege*, p.94.
103. Ibid., p.98.
104. See, for example, issues of 11 February 1922 and 27 May 1922.
105. G.B. Kenna, *Facts & Figures*, p.51.
106. Peter Hart, *The I.R.A. at War*, pp.247–8; Tim Wilson, 'Boundaries, Identity and Violence', vol. II, p. 256.
107. ICDA, 1923, pp.570, 573–4.
108. ICR, Hagan papers, Illegible to Hagan, 11 June 1922.
109. DWNTH, 15 July 1922.
110. Quoted at length in Patrick J. Gannon, 'An Amazing Document', *IER*, July 1922, pp.1–2.
111. Ibid., p.4.

112. Use of the word 'pogrom' has been largely dismissed or at least highly qualified by Lynch and Wilson. See Robert Lynch, *The Northern IRA and the Early Years of Partition, 1920–1922* (Dublin, 2006); Wilson, 'The most terrible assassination that has yet stained the name of Belfast'.
113. Gannon, 'An Amazing Document', p.5.
114. Ibid., p.7.
115. Ibid., p.8.
116. Michael Laffan, *The Partition of Ireland, 1911–1925* (Dundalk, 1983), p.109.
117. PRONI, Home Affairs, HA/32/1/178, Memo from R. Megaw, 2 August 1922.
118. Thomas Jones, *Whitehall Diary, Volume III: Ireland, 1918–1925*, Keith Middlemas (ed.), (London, 1971), p.195.
119. Tim Wilson, 'Boundaries, Identity and Violence', vol. II, pp.308–15.
120. *The Tablet*, 15 April 1922.
121. Quoted in Tim Wilson, 'Boundaries, Identity and Violence', vol. II, p.331.
122. Robert Lynch, *The Northern IRA and the Early Years of Partition*, p.88.
123. Ibid., pp.104, 115.
124. *Debates of the Northern Irish Parliament*, 15 March 1922, vol. II, pp.57–8.
125. For more, see Colm Campbell, *Emergency Law in Ireland, 1918–1925*.
126. Denise Kleinrichert, *Republican Internment and the Prison Ship Argenta, 1922* (Dublin, 2001), p.62.
127. Paul Bew, *Ireland*, pp.434–5.
128. Thomas Jones, *Whitehall Diaries, Volume III*, edited by Keith Middlemas (ed.), p.208.
129. See Eamon Phoenix, *Northern Nationalism*, pp.189–91.
130. Lynch, *The Northern IRA and the Early Years of Partition*, p.119.
131. John Bowman, *De Valera and the Ulster Question*, p.84.
132. Denise Kleinrichert, *Republican Internment and the Prison Ship Argenta*, pp.84, 86–7, 92.
133. Robert Lynch, *The Northern IRA and the Early Years of Partition*, p.182.
134. PRONI, Home Affairs, HA/32/1/46, Drysdale to Bates, 16 January 1925.
135. Ibid.
136. PRONI, Home Affairs, HA/32/1/46, Report by F.M. Stuart, 13 February 1925; HA/32/1/46, E.W. Shewell, Draft report on internments, 18 January 1925.
137. PRONI, Home Affairs, HA/32/1/76, A.W. Long's report, 1 November 1923.
138. Ibid.
139. Denise Kleinrichert, *Republican Internment and the Prison Ship Argenta*, p.217.
140. PRONI, Home Affairs, HA/32/1/46, Report by F.M. Stuart, 13 March 1925.
141. *INBMN*, 3 November 1923.
142. PRONI, Home Affairs, HA/32/1/121, District Inspector to Secretary, Home Affairs, 5 November 1923.
143. *INBMN*, 8 November 1923.
144. PRONI, Home Affairs, HA/32/1/121, District Inspector to Secretary, Home Affairs, 12 November 1923.
145. Ibid.
146. *Manchester Guardian*, 5 November 1923.
147. *II*, 15 November 1923.
148. Ibid.
149. See pp.178-9.
150. *IT*, 6 October 1923.
151. Denise Kleinrichert, *Republican Internment and the Prison Ship Argenta*, p.20.
152. Robert Lynch, *The Northern IRA and the Early Years of Partition*, p.184.
153. *ICH*, 22 July 1922.
154. *DWNTH*, 24 June 1922
155. *ICH*, 10 November 1923.
156. ICR, Hagan papers, Mulhern to Hagan, 21 November 1923.
157. ICR, Hagan papers, Curran to Hagan, 19 July 1922.
158. Ronan Fanning et al. (eds), *Documents on Irish Foreign Policy*, vol. I, no. 214, 'Final text of the Articles of Agreement for a Treaty between Great Britain and Ireland as signed', p.358.

159. J.J. Lee, *Ireland, 1912–1985* (Cambridge, 1989), p.141.
160. *FS*, 10 June 1922.
161. PRONI, Home Affairs, HA/32/1/17, Ministry of Home Affairs report, 17 May 1923.
162. PRONI, Home Affairs, HA/32/1/17, District Inspector to Secretary, Home Affairs, 18 May 1923.
163. KDA, Fogarty papers, Cosgrave to Fogarty, 12 December 1923.
164. PRONI, Home Affairs, HA/32/1/17, District Inspector to Secretary, Home Affairs, 25 May 1923.
165. ICR, Hagan papers, Mulhern to Hagan, 21 November 1923.
166. ICR, Hagan papers, Mulhern to Hagan, 18 January 1924; Hagan papers, O'Donnell to Hagan, 18 January 1924; Hagan papers, Mulhern to Hagan, 15 April 1924.
167. For detailed accounts and analysis, see Ged Martin, 'The Origins of Partition' in Malcolm Anderson and Eberhard Bort (eds), *The Irish Border: History, Politics, Culture* (Liverpool, 1999), pp.57–111; Clare O'Halloran, *Partition and the Limits of Irish Nationalism*, Chapter 4; Margaret O'Callaghan, 'Old Parchment and Water: The Boundary Commission of 1925 and the Copperfastening of the Irish Border', *Bullán*, 4 (1999/2000), pp.27–55. For new analysis, see Paul Murray, *The Irish Boundary Commission and its Origins 1886–1925* (Dublin, 2011).
168. PRONI, Home Affairs, HA/32/1/16, Boundary Commission reports, 11 June 1925 and 20 June 1925.
169. Eamon Phoenix, *Northern Nationalism*, p.180.
170. Ibid., p.289.
171. UCDA, Blythe papers, P24/70, 'Policy in Regard to the North-East', presented 9 August 1922.
172. J.J. Lee, *Ireland*, p.147; For a thorough analysis of Eoin MacNeill's role in the commission, see Geoffrey Hand, 'MacNeill and the Boundary Commission' in *The Scholar Revolutionary: Eoin MacNeill, 1867–1945, and the Making of the New Ireland*, F.X. Martin and F.J. Byrne (eds), (Shannon, 1973).
173. Ged Martin 'The Origins of Partition' in Malcolm Anderson and Eberhard Bort (eds), *The Irish Border*, p.96; *Report of the Irish Boundary Commission, 1925*, Introduced by Geoffrey Hand (Shannon, 1969) is the completed report of the commission as submitted to the British government and offers a fascinating look at the thought process behind the creation of the final settlement. The transcripts of the Free State delegation's evidence hearing (Appendix A) are also extremely informative.
174. The diaries of Thomas Jones, Deputy Secretary to the Cabinet, are an excellent source on the political manoeuvrings, concerns and concessions that went into the finalising of the boundary, especially the meetings that took place between representatives of the Free State, Northern Ireland and Great Britain after the leaking of the Boundary Commission report to the *Morning Post*. See Thomas Jones, *Whitehall Diaries, Volume III*, edited by Keith Middlemas.
175. David Fitzpatrick, *The Two Irelands*, p.163.
176. Michael Laffan, *The Partition of Ireland*, p.109.
177. Quoted in Mary Harris, *The Catholic Church and the Foundation of the Northern Irish State*, p.173.
178. Daithí Ó Corráin, 'Ireland in his heart north and south', *Irish Historical Studies*, xxxv (May 2006), p.75.

Conclusion:
Fianna Fáil and the Bishops,
1926–1932

> We of the Fianna Fáil Party believe that we speak for the big
> body of Catholic opinion. I think I could say, without quali-
> fication of any kind, that we represent the big element of
> Catholicity.[1]

There is no debate that Liam Lynch's death marked the beginning of
the end for the military effort against the government. Once Frank
Aiken took over as Chief of Staff of the IRA it was only a matter of time
before the fight ended. Like so many others on the republican side, he
was aware of the futility of continuing the struggle. With his ascension
came the re-emergence of Éamon de Valera as political leader of the
movement. De Valera had indulged in spiritual rhetoric, especially during
the nadir of his power, but his behaviour both before and after the war
indicates the actions of a desperate man doing what was necessary to
maintain a semblance of control over or even relevance in a discordant
movement. The one thing that seemed to resonate with the masses was
the sacredness of their objective, and he gave the crowd what it was
looking for. However, as soon as he could, he resumed his favoured
approaches to achieving his goals: diplomacy and parliamentarianism.
With Aiken leading the military wing and de Valera in control of the
political offensive, there was little room left for the die-hard republican
ideologues who continued to preach freedom through bloodshed. The
reversion to Pearsian spirituality had been very temporary.

There was also the issue of demoralisation. That the battle had been
lost was bad enough, but the manner in which the Free State

handled the post-war period put the final nail in the coffin for the ideologues. The Free State ministers had learned much from the mistakes of the British government during the war for independence. As budding politicians and policy makers they were able to analyse the mistakes in British policy at the level of high politics, and as former fighters and prisoners they knew the weaknesses of the British military techniques and attempts at subduing Irish nationalism, such as the botched internment and reprisal policies. They used these lessons, as well as their knowledge of their former comrades-turned-enemies to the full extent. Through a ruthlessly efficient internment policy and emergency military powers acts, the Free State government demoralised republicans, both in camps and at large, who quickly lost the will to continue the fight and longed for the peace that so many of their fellow citizens had been crying for since the Treaty was signed.

Hindsight shows that the conflict between the republicans and the Church eventually and indirectly allowed for a smoother reconciliation of the former political adversaries. With the dumping of arms in May 1923, Cosgrave began the healing by allowing moderate republicans to travel a middle path between outright acceptance of the Treaty and armed insurrection against the state. The bishops may have been instrumental in these assuaging measures.[2] When de Valera finally led his followers out of the political wilderness, it was into a fully function-ing nation where Church and State shared a close, cordial relationship, a relationship de Valera strengthened by giving the Catholic Church the honour of being constitutionally recognised with a 'special position' as the religion of the great majority. This smooth transference was possible in part due to the Church's unwavering support of the Free State. Had the bishops joined in opposition to the Treaty, they could not have acted as moderators between the opposing sides. The bishops had said and written some harsh things about the republicans, but once de Valera was prepared to work within the system he had formerly virulently opposed, their lordships took to Fianna Fáil as prodigals who had finally given up their errant ways. When the party entered the Dáil in 1926, the bishops both welcomed the normalisation of political affairs and breathed a sigh of relief that the years of turbulence were at an end.

The platform laid out by Fianna Fáil also made the bishops' accept-ance of mainstream republicanism easier. Having left Sinn Féin, de

Valera was not confined by the strict tenets of the party's idealism. No longer did de Valera and his lieutenants have to focus their energies on appeasing the party faithful with rhetorical talk of a thirty-two county republic free of English influence. In fact, at the 1929 Fianna Fáil Ard-Fheis, the 'republic' was completely absent from the agenda.[3] Instead, the new party could work to create a legitimate political organisation with widespread, local support and a genuine socio-economic programme that would inspire those disillusioned with Cumann na nGaedheal, either because of their 'treaty betrayal' or their disappointing economic record, to vote Fianna Fáil. Though Fianna Fáil's detailed and attractive economic policy is undeniably important as a counter to Cumann na nGaedheal's reliance on civil war-era tactics and scaring voters with the spectres of communism and terrorism, the party's real triumph was to bring voters, especially those who had rejected the treaty, back to the polls. By 1938, nearly 76 per cent of eligible voters voted, and of those 52 per cent voted for the Republican Party.[4]

What made Fianna Fáil's socio-economic policies even more palatable for their lordships was the fact that they synchronised so perfectly with Catholic teaching. In 1931, to mark the forty year anniversary of Leo XIII's *Rerum Novarum*, Pius XI issued *Quadragesimo Anno*. Pius's encyclical laid out a social programme that emulated Leo's but incorporated changes he felt were necessary due to changes in the geopolitical and business models since 1889. In it, he reaffirmed the Church's commitment to private property, the incompatibility of the Church and socialism/communism, and the Church's devotion to helping Christians reconstitute the socio-economic model to eliminate free competition and increase social justice by providing the working class with a greater share of the fruits of their labours. Then and only then, Pius stated, would modern society be in a position to move toward social peace, reversing the ruin of souls inflicted by the demands of modern capitalism.

Just months after *Quadragesimo Anno* was published, Cosgrave brought forth a constitutional amendment bill that would grant the Free State government a set of severe Public Safety Bills designed to fight IRA violence, which had been on the rise since the organisation voted to resume its campaign against the Free State. By the late 1920s, IRA violence was enough of a threat for the Cabinet to ask the bishops to renew their condemnation of violence against the state in the form of a joint pastoral. As in the wake of O'Higgins's assassination, several ministers were very disappointed to find that the bishops' enthusiasm for defending the Cumann na nGaedheal government had waned to the point that though they were prepared to speak against the IRA, Saor Eire and left-wing groups as sinful and irreligious, the impassioned rhetoric of the Civil War was gone. Rather, the pastoral was 'studiously neutral' towards the government and failed to explicitly endorse the Public Safety Act.[5]

The bishops were much more open to working with Fianna Fáil and, therefore, politically neutral because Fianna Fáil was prepared to work with them. Days before the bishops' pastoral letter was circulated, de Valera travelled to Armagh to meet with Cardinal MacRory. During the meeting, de Valera laid out for MacRory Fianna Fáil's argument against the Public Safety Acts. By the time the two men parted company, the cardinal was content with Fianna Fáil's policies.[6]

On 14 October, de Valera and his chief lieutenants outlined Fianna Fáil's opposition to the Public Safety Bills along lines that coincided with the principles of *Quadragesimo Anno*. De Valera affirmed in the strongest possible language his party's commitment to the right of private property and the right of society to deal with relations between the community and individuals for the common good. As far as he was concerned, there was no immediate danger of these principles being undermined. The problems that the government wanted to terminate through the Public Safety Acts would not go away simply because the state was prepared to use more force:

> The way to deal with it is to deal with the conditions and see that people who are anxious to work will get work, that people who are entitled to have decent houses will get these houses, and organise the community to end the evils that are about them, and not simply to say there must be no movement of this sort in our midst, we do not want them. We may say that as much as we like. We may have as many laws to prevent it as we have Public Safety Acts and the rest here on the Statute Book. All the laws in the world are not going to prevent it unless you remove the causes.[7]

Two days later, Frank Aiken argued against passing the Public Safety Acts using Pius's own words from *Quadragesimo Anno*. He told the Dáil that he believed that if the government governed according to the principles laid out by the pope, it would be possible to establish a peace treaty honoured by all Irish and, quite possibly, a permanent peace settlement. At the end of the debate, Sean T. O'Kelly voiced his belief that what was necessary to deal with the current situation was not harsher laws, but the practising of Christian charity. Until the government based its policies on these principles, it could not and should not expect there to be any change of heart amongst the young men who stood for complete independence.[8]

At a time when the Vatican was encouraging Catholics to try to solve society's problems, Fianna Fáil used the same language to demonstrate their greater commitment to Catholic principles than Cumann na nGaedheal. Cosgrave and his deputies, as branded by their political opponents, were intent on bearing down on those who engaged in acts of violence because they believed these people needed to be dealt with forcefully. They were utilising the same mentality that had seen them through the Civil War – a fact underscored by the repeated and often unpleasantly aggressive references to 1922–3 made during the Public Safety Acts debates. While Cosgrave and his Cabinet were still locked in the Provisional Government mentality, Fianna Fáil and the voters had moved on. They sought modern solutions to peacetime problems. The Free State was a modern nation that faced social and economic problems at a time when the world's economy was in a terrible depression. Only Cumann na nGaedheal saw the violence of 1931 as a return to Civil War era mentality. As de Valera stated during the debates, 'if men are hungry they will not be too particular about the ultimate principles of the organisation they would join, if that organisation promises to give them bread.'[9]

Cumann na nGaedheal did not offer the sort of imagination and planning that Fianna Fáil could. While de Valera's party discussed how to overcome economic and social problems, Cosgrave's party pushed fear of communism, terrorism and the possibility of another civil war should the voters turn against them in the 1932 General Election. The voters did not believe the scare tactics and hype, and given the bishops' lack of involvement in the election, they seem to have become even less enamoured of Cumann na nGaedheal.

This was a process that had been in progress since almost immediately after the Civil War. Cumann na nGaedheal's reduction in popularity during the 1923 General Election showed the bishops that they still presided over a Church that was politically sharply divided. While Cosgrave's party won the largest share of votes with 39 per cent, Sinn Féin, which was still the party of excommunicants, received 27.4 per cent of the votes, surpassing everyone's expectations, and proving to the bishops that if they were going to lead a unified Church, they would have to bridge the gap between the two groups. Success would be found by removing themselves from the present political debate, an easy choice with the end of violence, and moving back into the realm of spirituality and morality. From 1924, the bishops defined their relation with the state through their involvement in the issues of sexuality and morality.[10] In 1923, the government had passed the first film censorship act. The next year, Cumann na nGaedheal turned their attention towards alcohol. By 1927, the government was eager to reduce the number of public houses. In 1929, Free State censorship became more entrenched with the establishment of the Censorship of Publications Board, to be chaired by a Catholic priest. At the same time, they banned sale of all birth control aids. A quick perusal of Archbishop Byrne's papers shows that his lordship always had advanced notice of the government's intentions, and that his feedback on bill drafts was always welcome. However, the relationship between the hierarchy and Cumann na nGaedheal was far from perfect. Starting in 1929, just as the Free State was preparing to celebrate the centenary of Catholic Emancipation, the convenient alliance that had marked the last five years of the Church–state relationship started to disintegrate.

Cosgrave had been anxious to establish diplomatic relations with the Holy See from the start of his presidency, but he was keenly aware of the strain this could place on relations with the bishops, who, as already demonstrated, were opposed to Vatican involvement in their affairs. In his mind, such a move would be intended solely to increase the international credibility of the Free State and was in no way a disciplinary measure against the hierarchy or wayward clergy.[11] By the end of the 1920s, with Cumann na nGaedheal's popularity slipping, Fianna Fáil serving as a genuine, and increasingly popular parliamentary opposition, and rising IRA violence provoking no comment from the bishops, Cosgrave began to realise diplomatic relations with the Vatican were essential to the survival of his government. The centenary of Catholic Emancipation would mark the perfect opportunity to inaugurate a nunciature.[12]

On 5 June 1929, Foreign Minister McGilligan informed the Dáil that the government was on the verge of exchanging diplomats with the Vatican. Speaking on behalf of Fianna Fáil, Sean T. O'Kelly raised objections for a variety of reasons. He was opposed to the idea that only the Free State rather than the entirety of Ireland would benefit from this relationship. He also demanded to know if the government had consulted either Archbishop MacRory or Byrne about this affair: 'I would be glad if the Minister would be kind enough to inform us whether these people were consulted and, if so, whether they are satisfied with the arrangement. If they are, so far as the Church is concerned I have nothing further to say.'[13] He received the answer he expected – silence.

Fianna Fáil, most likely with the aid of Hagan,[14] used the forthcoming nunciature to further improve their relations with the bishops. The government had tried to keep the negotiations with the Cardinal Secretary of State secret from the hierarchy; a preposterous notion given that the Vatican would certainly seek the opinions of the Irish bishops before installing a nuncio in Dublin. The way Cosgrave and his government handled the situation allowed Fianna Fáil to take full advantage and show the hierarchy that their party was the more receptive to the needs and wishes of the Church. Cumann na nGaedheal's remaining time in power would further allow Fianna Fáil several opportunities to convince the bishops that they were the true defenders of Catholicism in the Free State.

In late 1929, Bishop Collier of Ossory informed Minister for Justice Fitzgerald Kenney that the new law banning contraception was inadequate. Fitzgerald Kenney responded that greater restrictions were not possible at the moment. The next year, Cosgrave and his government faced hierarchical resistance to their efforts to tax clergy for more income than they were claiming. Cosgrave did a fine job of settling the squabble between the Church and the Revenue Commissioners, but not before Cumann na nGaedheal's image in clerical circles took a beating.[15] A year later, the government-created Committee on the Criminal Law Amendment Acts (1880–5) and Juvenile Prostitution reported that the degraded moral state of the nation was due to the influx of popular amusements without proper supervision or legal restraint. Dance halls, picture houses and the misuse of automobiles were all contributing to the ruination of Ireland's young girls. The Department of Justice was not receptive to the committee's findings, especially criticising the over-exuberance of the clergy who gave evidence.

These examples could not but show the bishops, guardians of Ireland's morality, that the Cumann na nGaedheal government were not as dedicated to guarding the souls of Irish citizens as they should have been. During the controversy over appointing Letitia Dunbar-Harrison, a Trinity trained Protestant, as librarian in Mayo,[16] Cosgrave finally became confrontational. He informed Archbishop Gilmartin that to discriminate against any Free State citizen on account of his or her religion would violate the state's fundamental principles; two weeks later, he wrote to MacRory that there were effective limits to the government's powers which existed in relation to certain matters if fundamental principles were not to be repudiated.[17] Again, Cosgrave avoided a Church-state crisis, but while he and his government were actively trying to keep from offending the bishops, de Valera and his lieutenants were courting the bishops and all clergy who were prepared to listen. These turned out to be enough to allow Fianna Fáil to portray itself as the more Catholic party. From 1932, it became quite clear that this was certainly accurate. While Cumann na nGaedheal had, at least according to religious leaders, moved towards secularism in an effort to be palatable to the Protestant minority, Fianna Fáil displayed an almost deferential attitude towards the Irish bishops – a vast change from their attitudes of a decade earlier.

Though such an enormous change of attitude initially seems highly unlikely, it was, in fact, perfectly understandable and points to the very reason why Fianna Fáil was created in the first place. Those Treaty opponents who followed de Valera into his anti-abstentionist party did so because they saw how unproductive spiritualising the fight for independence had been. Despite their best rhetorical efforts, the bishops, clergy and majority of voters had supported the Treaty. Proclaiming their superiority had not worked for the Fenians, it had not worked for Treaty opponents, and it would not work for those who resisted the continued existence of the Free State. De Valera had realised as much during the debate over the Treaty, and he directed his efforts to ensuring that he and Sinn Féin would not voluntarily marginalise themselves. Unfortunately for him, the gunmen and fanatics got the better of him in 1922. It was not until 1926 that he and those who thought like him were able to re-emerge into the political mainstream.

De Valera had never intended to go to war against the Catholic Church. The man who had seriously considered joining the priesthood remained a devout Catholic to his last breath. It seems that, even more so than Cosgrave, de Valera could not envision an Irish government that failed to account for the desires of the bishops and the moral and spiritual needs of Irish Catholics. Fianna Fáil was not a political party that incorporated Catholic doctrine because it was politically expedient, it was a party that fused Catholicism into its government because it believed it was right. When Sean T. O'Kelly stood before the Dáil on 5 June 1929 and told the deputies on the other side that he believed Fianna Fáil spoke for 'the big element of Catholicity',[18] he was utterly sincere.

* * *

Just as the landscape within republicanism changed greatly after the Civil War, so too was it modified within the ranks of the bishops. The changes to the benches served to alter the Church's relationships with both major political parties. Cardinal Logue, who had presided over the Irish Catholic Church for over thirty years, died in 1924. He was never as subtly political as Walsh or O'Dwyer and he generally relied on his episcopal brothers to craft the hierarchy's politically oriented statements.[19] He was a strong religious leader, but tended to follow when it came to politics. This allowed for the more outspoken among the hierarchy to formulate the Church's political policies during this unstable period. Logue's death led to Patrick O'Donnell's ascension, and none of the other bishops possessed his acute political mind. O'Donnell had been the Irish Party's chief religious backer. He had been close to both Redmond and Devlin. After Redmond's illness removed him from his leadership position during the Irish Convention, O'Donnell had become the *de facto* leader of the nationalist contingency at the Convention.

The bishop's close relationship to the Party came to an end, though, over partition. Like so many others, he believed the Party had sold out the northern Catholics with the 1916 partition agreement that incorporated Tyrone and Fermanagh into a Protestant dominated northern state. Having never been a Sinn Féin supporter, O'Donnell all but bowed out of politics. When he became Primate of All Ireland in 1924, his policies dictated hierarchical policies. Logue had never been active in politics, but was not averse to them. O'Donnell had been active and became disillusioned as a result. Rather than letting other bishops create hierarchical political policies, he kept the bishops from speaking on such matters. Bishops who wanted to speak on political matters were forced to do so alone. Even after Kevin O'Higgins was assassinated in 1927, O'Donnell kept the hierarchy from issuing a joint pastoral, though several bishops expressed their opinions individually.

The General Election of 1923 indicates that this was a trend that had begun when O'Donnell was still Logue's coadjutor. With the Civil War over and thousands of republicans interned in Free State camps, Cumann na nGaedheal fully expected to be able to count on the unified vocal support of the hierarchy. They were severely disappointed. What they found instead was that not only did the bishops not come out as a body to support them, but some even refused to support the party as individuals. There was concern amongst the bishops that Cumann na nGaedheal had not won over the hearts and minds of those who had opposed the Treaty, and they were nervous about further alienating themselves from Irish Catholics they had preached against, denied the sacraments and excommunicated.[20] The 290,000 voters who sided with Sinn Féin proved them to be right.

The hierarchy's unified political stance was further placed in jeopardy by the elevation of John Dignan to the Bishopric of Clonfert in 1924. In the speech Dignan gave at his anointment, he announced that he looked forward to the day when Ireland was a republic. He was, in essence, throwing his episcopal weight behind the recently defeated opponents of the Treaty, and his statement caused a stir throughout Ireland. Mulhern wrote that his public display of prophecy was dangerous, and Mannix subtly rejoiced that the Irish bishops could no longer claim solidarity. There were even rumours that Dignan might be deposed or degraded.[21] A reporter for the *Irish Independent* told Seán T. O'Kelly that he overheard Archbishop Gilmartin remark after the event that, as a result of the day's activities, he was finished consecrating bishops.[22] Dignan's elevation indeed marked the end of hierarchical political solidarity. Though Dignan and the rest of the bishops never publicly disagreed on matters of politics this can largely be attributed to the lack of public pronouncements regarding them.

O'Donnell's rise to the primature and Dignan's elevation to the episcopacy marked the beginning of a substantial change in the faces of the men who ran the Irish Catholic Church. Between the end of the Civil War and de Valera's rise to the premiership, thirteen bishops died or retired. Their replacements were generally younger and often had drastically different political sympathies, though none displayed the same outspokenness as Dignan during this period. The perspectives of the new bishops were notably different from those of their predecessors; their experience of the fight for Home Rule and independence was from a position where they could be less cautious and, like Dignan more outspoken in their nationalist sympathies. Furthermore, having not been in positions of national power during the Civil War, they did not carry the same emotional baggage in their relationships with republican leaders as did the older prelates. By the time Fianna Fáil came to power in 1932, they found that many of the men who made up the episcopal bench were relatively friendly, or at least neutral towards them; a vast improvement that could lead to normalisation of relations.

These events exaggerated the bishops' newfound political silence, but the end of the Civil War and the solidification of a native government meant that there was no longer a need for episcopal political activity in the twenty-six counties. The bishops' substantial influence had been used with great skill during the fight for Home Rule and after the rise of Sinn Féin. Even during Parnell's rule of the IPP, there had always been an undercurrent of agitation at Ireland's Catholics being ruled by Britain's Protestants, and the bishops' participation underscored this. Parnell's endorsement of denominational education had ensured that hierarchical support for the Home Rule movement was resolute, at which point the bishops became even more important to the Party's organisation. The rise of the Catholic Irish to leadership roles in the nationalist movement and the increased sectarianism caused by Ulster's vehement parochialised unionism made the bishops more integral to the movement. The hierarchy's opposition to republicanism during the Civil War combined remnants of this political activity, a desperate desire to see Ireland stabilised and concern over republicans' appropriating for themselves the language of morality and spirituality. With the war over, the state stable and firmly in the hands of devout Catholics, and the republicans pledging themselves to the constitutional process, there was no longer a need for the bishops to continue to act on behalf of the pro-treaty element.

The end result was a developing distance between Cumann na nGaedheal and the bishops. Cosgrave's party had felt betrayed by ecclesiastical inactivity during the 1923 election, but this merely marked the beginning of the Church's move away from partisan support. Despite the IRA's renewal of violence against the Free State starting in 1926, the bishops did not issue a joint pastoral until 1931. Many within Cumann na nGaedheal felt that the bishops had turned on them and were preparing themselves for what was becoming a foregone conclusion: Fianna Fáil's rise to power.

This was not the case in Northern Ireland, however, and in this regard the bishops failed to rise to the challenge of championing the rights of their followers in a Protestant-controlled state that adhered to a semi-institutionalised anti-Catholic bigotry until the end of the Stormont government in 1972. Much of this failure was due to the surprise death of Cardinal O'Donnell, who very well might have worked to integrate Catholics into the state. He was replaced by Joseph MacRory, whose lack of diplomatic skill and Belfast Catholic siege-mentality kept him from working with the northern government, further cementing the sectarian divisions for two more decades.[23]

Ecclesiastical failure in the north was also due to an inability to adjust their tactics to the new situation. Catholic bishops of the six counties were no longer the religious leaders of the majority against an unpopular government, as they had been during the fight against the Crown. Catholics were one-third of the state's population, and the majority of the remaining population was in favour of the status quo. Exaggerated accusations in pastoral letters intended to incite public furore no longer worked. Furthermore, many of the bishops were as cowed by the northern government as their followers. They viewed the situation as helpless and feared that the government was willing to punish any outspokenness with penalties against the Catholic Church.

* * *

In *Culture and Anarchy in Ireland*, F.S.L. Lyons remarked: 'It is difficult, after a lapse of more than half a century, to capture the mood of mingled hope and bitterness with which in 1922 the Irish Free State began its career as an independent nation.'[24] Like most other incestuous armed struggles, the Irish Civil War contained more bitterness than hope. Fear, desperation and mutual incomprehension of the motives of former comrades magnified the ill-will between the two camps and dragged many men and women, who would have otherwise been able to remain above the fray, into the impassioned struggle to determine Ireland's, or at least the twenty-six counties' fate. Into this category can be placed the unified hierarchy of the Catholic Church of Ireland. Having emotionally invested themselves in the separatist movement over the previous half decade, especially after the collapse of the IPP, and facing the prospect of a self-governing state in which they would be granted a great deal of authority, the bishops were incapable and unwilling to remove themselves from the political debate. As a result, they spoke against members of their own Church in a way they had not since the denunciation of Fenianism.

Fenianism, though, had been an underground phenomenon. Fenian supporters were not great in number, and the bishops had acted much as they did whenever they condemned a secret society. Anti-Treaty republicanism was altogether different. With a support base of approximately one-quarter of the Free State population and a political philosophy that, unlike Fenianism, did not, as a rule, attempt to exclude clerical influence, republicanism had a greater claim to immunity from clerical criticism than either Fenianism or post-split Parnellism. However, as far as the bishops were concerned, separatist support of a violent struggle against a *de facto* and *de jure* Catholic-dominated, native government relegated Treaty opponents to the realm of misguided fools or worse. The more the republicans resisted the Free State government and the statements of the bishops, the more severe ecclesiastical condemnation of them grew.

Naturally, the bishops defended their involvement in the struggle after the Treaty as a matter of guiding the members of their Church down the path of correct moral action. Republicanism, per se, was not erroneous, but the methods by which its goals were being sought were. In taking this line, the bishops attempted to dress their actions in the clothing of religion and thus stave off accusations that they had become political actors. This would also allow them to appear to remain above the conflict, but their words, both public and private, betrayed their emotional involvement. To understand this process requires a critical analysis of their motives and an unbiased examination of their ultimate goals in supporting the Free State so adamantly while faced with a strong opposition minority and an uncomfortably aloof Vatican.

The bishops' words and actions prove that both a desire to maintain authority and a powerful political instinct played important roles in their decision-making processes during the Civil War and in the immediate aftermath. Their lordships' reactions to the Vatican's involvement in Irish affairs, and especially their treatment of Monsignor Salvatore Luzio demonstrate that they were reluctant to voluntarily reduce their own clout, even if that meant disregarding the wishes of the Holy See. Though they repeatedly protested against republican accusations that their policies contained ulterior motives that did not coincide with the welfare of the Catholics of Ireland, the lack of ecclesiastical public protestation against reprisal executions and internment by the Free State versus the condemnation of Northern Ireland's internment policy demonstrates that their public admonishments were reserved for those whom they did not choose to support with their weighty influence.

It is a well-established fact that the bishops were not a monolithic bloc in terms of political outlook, but during this turbulent period, they were able to maintain a unified front. This was due primarily to their widespread acceptance of the Treaty. As essentially conservative men whose main political goals were peace and stability, their endorsement of militant republicanism against a native, essentially Catholic, government was never a possibility. Republicans never expected otherwise. What they did not anticipate, though, was the level of episcopal opposition to their movement. Nor were they prepared for the level of personal antagonism emanating from the hierarchy against their leaders, especially Éamon de Valera, who was never again on good terms with his former friends, Bishops Fogarty and Mulhern. The personal nature of the fight, in that respect so similar to the struggle between the rival political factions, made it all the more bitter and more difficult to overcome once peace and stability had been restored.

However, it is impossible to eliminate the possibility of fear as a motivating factor for either side. Neither Sinn Féin nor the Irish hierarchy were able to view the situation before them without a belief that Ireland was on the cusp of slipping away from them, either back into British control or into a bloody, chaotic war. Having come so close to achieving something akin to their professed goal, neither side was prepared to allow for the worst-case scenario to unfold without a fight.

For the republicans, this meant taking up arms against former comrades, defying the wishes of the majority of their fellow citizens and even risking damnation of their souls. For the bishops, all of whom were to some degree nationalists, it was a matter of speaking against a sizeable minority of their flock and taking drastic measures that could turn some away from the Church forever. They had to accept that they were endorsing policies that allowed for internment, execution of untried prisoners, and indefinite partition of Ireland with the six counties placed under an obviously anti-Catholic government. None of this could have been particularly palatable for any of them, and it is no wonder, therefore, that quite so many were eager to abandon involvement in politics the moment they felt it was safe to do so.

Their motives for backing such policies, especially given their attitudes towards Fianna Fáil only a few years later, point to fear of what would happen should they abstain from involving themselves. Given that both sides of the nationalist division were led by young men and women who had come into political maturity after the fall of the Irish Political Party, the bishops represented the elder generation, the voice of moderation and reason. To allow impassioned, naïve, untested people to lead Ireland into chaos without the aid of their years of experience would be more irresponsible than to remain above the conflict. This was a case when O'Leary and Kickham got it completely wrong. The bishops and elder clergy were the more experienced in terms of politics, and they felt that it was the lesser of two evils to participate now for the benefit of Irish Catholics not just of the present but future generations. It seems that Fenianism had permeated Irish politics so completely that even the hierarchy now utilised the same framework for their activities.

Whether or not the bishops had any affect on the outcome of the Civil War and its immediate aftermath will be a matter of speculation and argument for a long time to come. What is evident, though, is that a slender percentage of the Irish population sympathetic to the republican cause never truly forgave the Church for its involvement in the fight against those who opposed the Treaty. Those who remained militantly opposed to the Free State, even after de Valera led Fianna Fáil into the Dáil were often especially vitriolic. In the 1962 *Wolfe Tone Annual*, 80-year-old former Sinn Féin TD Brian O'Higgins reminded his readers that, '[o]ver two hundred "Authorised" and "Unauthorised murders" were committed by those in power, but they were hailed by the Bishops as the saviours of their Country, while their clean-hearted victims ... were denounced as robbers, looters, and hooligans who were not worthy of Christian Burial.'[25] However, even some in Fianna Fáil remained estranged from the bishops; it was the strong leadership of de Valera that allowed the party to appear monolithically pro-Catholic.[26] The fact that Lemass and the post-de Valera party were so quickly prepared to move beyond the party–Church alliance that had been the hallmark of Irish government from 1932 through the end of de Valera's time as Taoiseach suggests that this strain of mentality had been growing for quite some time.

NOTES

1. Sean T. O'Kelly, Dáil Debates, 5 June 1929.
2. Tom Garvin, 1922: *The Birth of Irish Democracy* (Dublin, 1996), p.175.
3. Richard Dunphy, *The Making of Fianna Fáil Power in Ireland, 1923–1948* (Oxford, 1995), p.137.
4. English, *Radicals and the Republic*, p.100. See also Richard Dunphy, *The Making of Fianna Fáil Power in Ireland, 1923–1948*, pp.141–4.
5. Regan, *Counter-Revolution*, p.291.
6. Ibid., p.301.
7. Dáil Debates, 14 October 1931.
8. Dáil Debates, 16 October 1931.
9. Dáil Debates, 14 October 1931.
10. Regan, *Counter-Revolution*, p.285.
11. Keogh, *Vatican, Bishops and Irish Politics*, p.127.
12. For a detailed account of the Catholic Emancipation centenary celebration, see Gillian McIntosh, 'Acts of "national communion": the centenary celebrations for the Catholic Emancipation, the forerunner of the Eucharistic Congress' in Joost Augusteijn (ed.), *Ireland in the 1930s: New Perspectives* (Dublin, 1999), pp.83–95. For the government's efforts to establish diplomatic relations with the Vatican, see Keogh, *Vatican, the Bishops and Irish Politics*, pp.134–57.
13. Dáil Debates, 5 June 1929.
14. Keogh, *Vatican, the Bishops and Irish Politics*, p.144.
15. A more detailed account of the matter can be found in Keogh, *Vatican, the Bishops and Irish Politics*, pp.161–3.
16. See Keogh, *Vatican, the Bishops and Irish Politics*, pp.166–77.
17. Ibid, pp.174–5.
18. Dáil Debates, 5 June 1929.
19. For more on Logue's involvement in the nationalist movement, see John Privilege, *Michael Logue and the Catholic Church in Ireland, 1879–1925* (Manchester, 2009).
20. John Regan, *Irish Counter-Revolution*, p.285.
21. ICR, Hagan papers, Mulhern to Hagan, 4 June 1924; Hagan papers, Mannix to Hagan, 10 June 1924; Hagan papers, Murphy to Hagan, 11 June 1924.
22. ICR, Hagan papers, O'Kelly to Hagan, 17 June 1924.
23. Proof of his tactlessness can be seen in a speech he gave in 1931 wherein he informed his audience that the Church of Ireland was not part of the Church of Christ.
24. F.S.L. Lyons, *Culture and Anarchy in Ireland, 1890–1939* (Oxford, 1979), p.147.
25. UCDA, Andrews papers, P91/98, Tod Andrews's notes.
26. See Whyte, *Church and State*, pp.40–49.

Appendix A:
Biographical Notes

Peter Emmanuel Amigo (1864–1949) – Born in Gibraltar to a flour merchant. Educated locally until sent to St. Edmund's, Ware at fourteen, then St. Thomas's Theological College, Hammersmith. Ordained in 1888. Became parish priest of St. Michael's, Stepney in 1901. Appointed Bishop of Southwark in 1904 due to influence of newly elevated Archbishop Bourne, with whom he later had a falling out. Became active in the Irish situation after the end of World War I and worked to expose the acts committed by Black and Tans. Supported Terence MacSwiney during his hunger strike.

Richard Dawson Bates (1876-1949) – Born in Strandtown, Belfast to a solicitor and clerk of the crown and peace for Belfast. Educated at Coleraine Academical Institution. Admitted as solicitor in 1900. Secretary of Ulster Unionist Council, 1905–21. Organised Ulster Covenant of 1912. Active in Ulster Volunteer Force and took part in Larne gun-running, 1914. Believed in fighting home rule from purely Ulster point of view. Helped set up Ulster Special Constabulary, 1920. Elected to Northern Ireland Parliament in 1921 for East Belfast. Minister for Home Affairs, 1921–43. Did not cooperate with conciliation committee established under Craig-Collins pact. Responsible for Civil Authorities (Special Powers) Act. Planned resistance to likely outcome of Boundary Commission. Knighted in 1921; made baronet in 1937. Refused to conduct important business by telephone as long as Catholic telephonist was employed in 1934. Resented by nationalists and criticised by some unionists as incompetent.

<u>Piaras Béaslaí</u> (1881–1965) – Born in Liverpool. Educated by Jesuits. Left England in 1904. One of the founding members of the Irish Volunteers. IRB member and helped Brotherhood infiltrate Gaelic League. Became vice-president of League. Fought in Easter Rising. Rose to rank of Commandant General in the IRA. Editor of *An tOglách*. Sinn Féin TD for Kerry East, 1918–21; for Kerry-Limerick 1921–23. Supported Treaty. Director of publicity for IRA. Did not stand for 1923 general election. Retired from politics and dedicated himself to literature. Wrote several novels, plays, essays and translations into Irish. Founder and president of An Fainne. Wrote the first biography of Michael Collins, published 1926.

<u>Pope Benedict XV</u> (1854–1922) – Born Giacomo Paolo Giovanni Battista della Chiesa in Pegli, Italy. Mother descended from family of Pope Innocent VII. Awarded a doctorate of law from the University of Genoa in 1875. Ordained in 1878. Awarded doctorates in theology (1879) and canon law (1880) from the Pontifical Gregorian University, Rome. Served as secretary to papal nuncio to Spain from 1882 to 1887, and then as assistant to Cardinal Secretary of State from 1887 to 1901. Elevated to Archbishop of Bologna in 1907 and Cardinal in 1914. Elected Pope in 1914. Maintained neutrality of Vatican during World War I while calling for peace.

<u>Francesco Cardinal Borgongini Duca</u> (1884–1954) – Born in Rome. Educated at the Pontifical Roman Seminary. Awarded doctorates in theology and canon law. Ordained in 1906. Professor of Theology at the Urban College of Propaganda, Rome, 1907–21. Official in the Sacred Apostolic Penitentiary, 1909–17. Pro-Secretary of the Congregation for Extraordinary Ecclesiastical Affairs, 1921, and Secretary from 1922. Co-wrote the Lateran Treaty. First papal nuncio to Italy in 1929. Appointed titular Archbishop of Heraclea in 1929 and cardinal in 1952.

<u>Francis Alphonsus Cardinal Bourne</u> (1861–1935) – Born in London to a Post Office worker and Catholic convert and a Dublin-born mother. Educated at St. Cuthbert's College, Ushaw, St. Edmund's College, Ware, St. Thomas's Seminary, Hammersmith, St. Sulpice, Paris and the University of Louvain. Ordained in 1884. Appointed Coadjutor Bishop

of Southwark in 1896, and Bishop in 1897. Appointed Archbishop of Westminster in 1903. Elevated to Cardinal in 1911. He desired self-government for Ireland but wanted to maintain its ties to the Empire.

Patrick Browne [Pádraig de Brún] (1889–1960) – Born in Tipperary to a teacher and shopkeeper, both strong Fenian supporters. Moved to Grangemockler soon after. Educated at Rockwell, Holy Cross College, Clonliffe, University College Dublin and the Irish College, Paris. Ordained in 1913. Received doctor's degree in mathematics from the University of Paris, Sorbonne, 1913. Also studied in Goettingen. Professor of Natural Sciences and Mathematics at Maynooth, 1914–1945. President of University College Galway, 1945–59. Served as a Senator of the National University of Ireland, and Chairman of the Council of the Dublin Institute of Advanced Studies, Director of An Chomhairle Ealaion (the Arts Council) after his retirement from UCG. Brother-in-law of Seán MacEntee and friend of several notable republicans, including Seán MacDiarmada and Éamon de Valera. Helped write appeal to the Vatican against October Pastoral. Wrote republican poetry under his own name and propaganda pieces under many pseudonyms. Arrested by CID in February 1923 at republican headquarters in Dublin, causing severe embarrassment for Maynooth and the hierarchy.

Cathal Brugha (1874–1922) – Born Charles William St John Burgess in Dublin to an art importer. Educated at Colmcille School and Belvedere College. Joined Gaelic League, 1906; became branch president, 1909. Joined Irish Volunteers at foundation, 1913; in charge of advanced party during Howth gun running, 1914. Vice-commandant of 4th Dublin brigade (South Dublin Union) during 1916 Rising. Elected to Sinn Féin executive, 1917. Elected TD for Waterford, 1918. Elected speaker of First Dáil, 1919. Minister of defence, 1919–22. Opposed Treaty. Fatally wounded in gunfight with Free State forces at Granville Hotel, Dublin. Known for his enmity towards Mulcahy and especially Collins.

Edward Joseph Byrne (1872–1940) – Born in Dublin. Educated at Belvedere College, Holy Cross, Clonliffe, the Royal University and the Irish College, Rome. Ordained in 1895. Served as vice-rector of the Irish College, Rome, 1901–4. Curate of the Pro-Cathedral, 1904–20.

Appointed Auxiliary Bishop of Dublin in 1920. Elevated to Archbishop in 1921. Attempted to negotiate peace settlement alongside Lord Mayor O'Neill in 1922 and worked quietly for the release of hunger strikers in 1923. Widely regarded as a cautious nationalist who preferred to exert his influence without fanfare. Responsible for holding of Eucharistic Congress in Dublin in 1932.

Bonaventura Cardinal Cerretti (1872–1933) – Born in Comune de Bardono, Italy. Educated at Spoleto Seminary, Pontifical Gregorian University and the Royal University, Rome. Ordained in 1895. Staff member of Cardinal Secretariat of State, 1899–1904. Secretary to Apostolic delegate to Mexico, 1904–1906. Auditor in Apostolic delegation to United States, 1906–1914. Elevated to titular archbishop in 1914 and appointed Apostolic delegate to Australia. Served as Secretary of the Roman Curia for Extraordinary Church Affairs, 1917–21. Served as papal nuncio to France, 1921–5. Elevated to Cardinal in 1926. Served as the Prefect of Apostolic Signatura, Roman Curia from 1931.

Robert Erskine Childers (1870–1922) – Born in London, but orphaned as a child and raised by an uncle in Co. Wicklow. Educated at Haileybury College and Trinity College, Cambridge. Fought on British side in Boer War. Wrote *The Riddle of the Sands* (1903). Became advocate of Irish Home Rule around 1910. Responsible for Howth gun running in 1914. Joined Royal Navy as Intelligence Officer at outbreak of First World War. Director of Publicity for First Dáil in 1919. Represented Irish Republic at Versailles conference in 1920. Appointed republican judge for Dublin in 1920. Adviser to the Irish Bulletin. First Secretary to the delegation of plenipotentiaries responsible for the Treaty. Opposed the Treaty. Editor of *Poblacht na h-Eireann* after arrest of Mellows. Arrested in November 1922 by Free State forces and executed for possession of an illegal firearm, a pistol given to him by Michael Collins. Father of Erskine Hamilton Childers.

Arthur Clery (1879–1932) – Born in Dublin. Father joined Indian Bar after mother suffered a breakdown. Educated at Catholic University School, Clongowes Wood and University College, Dublin. Practiced law but had to supplement income through journalism. Regular contributor to *The Leader* and *New Ireland Review*. Became part-time professor of property law at UCD in 1912. Joined Volunteers in 1914. Served as Eoin MacNeill's defence council at his court martial following 1916 Rising. Appointed to underground Supreme Court by Austin Stack in 1920. Opposed Treaty. Participated in drafting appeal to Vatican against October pastoral. Elected to Dáil for National University seat as an independent republican in June 1927, beating MacNeill. Did not contest September 1927 election. Acted as occasional legal adviser to both Fianna Fáil and Sinn Féin. Active in Society of St Vincent de Paul and An Rioghacht, which promoted Catholic social doctrine and which became a Catholic Social Services Conference.

Patrick Joseph Clune (1864–1935) – Born near Ruan, Co. Clare. Educated at St. Flannan's College, Ennis. Ordained in 1886. First served in New South Wales until 1893. Served throughout England and Ireland from 1895 to 1898. Became superior of Redemptorist seminary in Wellington, NZ in 1905. Appointed Bishop of Perth in 1910, elevated to Archbishop in 1913. Served as Archbishop of Perth from 1913 to 1933. Worked to bring about peace between Ireland and Great Britain during his visit in 1920–1921. His nephew was shot dead by Crown forces in an 'escape' attempt in Dublin Castle.

Daniel Cohalan [also Coholan] (1858–1952) – Born in Kilmichael, Co. Cork. Educated at local National School, classical school, St. Vincent's, Cork and St. Patrick's Maynooth. Ordained in 1882. Professor at St. Finbarr's. Served as Chaplain to Crown Forces, 1884–1885. Professor of Moral and Dogmatic Theology at Maynooth, 1886–1914. Appointed Auxiliary Bishop of Cork in 1914. Appointed Bishop of Cork in 1916. In 1916 acted as a mediator between the Cork Volunteers and the British military authorities. Presided over Tomás MacCurtain's funeral Mass, and visited Terence McSwiney shortly before his death. Issued decree of excommunication on all who continued to perpetrate violence in December 1920. Regular contributor to the *Catholic Bulletin* until 1918. Uncompromising, doctrinaire Catholic who referred to Protestant faiths as 'unlawful.'

Michael Comyn (d. 1952) – Born in Ballyvaughan, Co. Clare. Educated at Lancaster College, Preston College and University College, Dublin. Called to the bar in 1898. Appointed King's Counsel in 1914. Served as legal adviser for the republican movement. Defended Thomas Clarke and Erskine Childers. Senior counsel for republican government and IRA prior to Treaty. Unsuccessfully ran for the Dáil in 1923 as a republican. Elected to Senate in 1928, 1931 and 1934. Elected Leas-Chathaoirleach of the Senate in 1934. Vacated his seat in 1936 to become a Circuit Judge. Dedicated himself to phosphate mining after retiring.

Michael Joseph Curran (1880–1960) – Born in Dublin. Educated at Christian Brothers School, Holy Cross, Clonliffe and the Irish College, Rome. Ordained in 1904. Appointed Assistant-Diocesan Examiner of Dublin. Appointed secretary to Archbishop Walsh in 1906. Hid de Valera in the gate-lodge of the Archbishop's palace in 1919. Appointed vice-rector of the Irish College, Rome in 1919, and rector in 1930. Resigned in 1938. Appointed parish priest of Greystones in 1938. Named a Protonotary Apostolic of the Roman Curia in 1939. Parish priest of the Church of the Holy Family, Dublin from 1947. Fervent nationalist but avoided political discussions.

Aodh Sandrach de Blácam [né Blackham] (1890–1951) – Born in London to Ulster Protestant parents. Joined London Gaelic league. Moved to Ireland in 1915 and wrote for *Enniscorthy Echo*. Converted to Catholicism. Publicist for Sinn Féin during war for independence. Opposed Treaty. Founder member of Fianna Fáil. Member of Fianna Fáil Sub-Committee on Partition, 1938–39. Member of Fianna Fáil Ard Chomhairle (National Executive) until 1947, when he defected to Clann na Poblachta. Unsuccessfully ran for Dáil for Louth in 1948. Director of Publicity for Ministry of Health from 1948. Wrote for the *Irish Times* and the *Irish Press*, often under pseudonym 'Roddy the Rover.' Wrote many nationalist pieces including: *Towards the Republic* (1919), *What Sinn Fein Stands For* (1921), and the anti-partitionist *The Black North* (1938).

Gaetano Cardinal De Lai (1853–1928) – Born in Malo, Italy. Awarded doctorates in Theology, Philosophy and Canon and Civil Law from the Pontifical Roman Seminary. Ordained in 1876. Elevated to Cardinal in 1907. Served as Secretary of the Sacred Consistorial Congregation from 1908 to 1928. President of one of the two subcommissions for the codification of canon law. President of the commission for the reorganization of the Roman Curia, 1908.

Liam de Róiste (1882/3–1959) – Born in Tracton, Co. Cork. Founder of Celtic Literary Society. Chairman and secretary of Gaelic League in Cork. Founder and secretary of Colaiste na Mumhan. Founding member of the Irish Volunteers. Took part in march to Macroom, Easter, 1916. Sought by Black and Tans, who killed Fr. O'Callaghan at de Róiste's house when he could not be found. Chairman of first Sinn Féin meeting in Cork. Elected for Sinn Féin to first Dáil for Cork City, 1919; Cork Burrough in 1921 and 1922. Elected Leas Ceann Comhairle. Supported Treaty. Entered third Dáil as pro-Treaty Sinn Féin but changed affiliation to independent during course of term. Did not contest 1923 election. Stood for Cumann na nGaedheal for Cork Burrough seat in 1927 but lost. Co-founder of the Cork Industrial Trading Corporation. Secretary and Director of the Irish International Trading Corporation. Noted diarist.

John Dignan [also Duignan] (1880–1953) – Born in Ballygar, Co. Galway. Educated at Esker, Loughrea and St. Patrick's, Maynooth. Ordained in 1903. President of St. Joseph's College, Ballinasloe from 1904 to 1915. Served as curate and parish priest, 1915–24. Appointed bishop of Clonfert in 1924. Opposed Treaty. First bishop to support republican goals. Chairman of the Committee of Management of the National Health Insurance Society from 1936 to 1945. Produced Dignan Report (Beveridge Plan) in 1944. Known as a strong-willed man who inspired either intense loyalty or disliking. Upon first meeting him, Logue put his hands up and jokingly said 'I surrender.'

Thomas Joseph 'Desmond' FitzGerald (1888–1947) – Born in London to Irish parents. Moved to Brittany in 1911 and Ireland in 1913. Joined the Volunteers in 1913. Fought alongside his wife in the General Post Office during the 1916 Rising. Elected Sinn Féin TD for Dublin in 1918. Launched *Irish Bulletin* in 1919. Supported the Treaty. Served as Minister for Publicity in 1922, Minister for External Affairs from 1922 to 1927, and Minister for Defence, 1927–32. Remained in the Dáil until he lost his seat in 1937. Elected to the Senate in 1938, but defeated in 1943. Retired from politics in 1944. Father of Garret FitzGerald.

Michael Fogarty (1859–1955) – Born in Kilcolman, Co. Tipperary. Educated at St. Flannan's, Ennis and St. Patrick's, Maynooth. Ordained in 1885. Vice-president of St. Patrick's, Maynooth in 1903. Appointed Bishop of Killaloe in 1904. One of eighteen Catholic bishops and three Protestant bishops who signed May 1917 manifesto opposing partition. Outspoken nationalist and harsh critic of British rule in Ireland. One of the first bishops to support Sinn Féin. Trustee of the first Dáil Loan in 1919. Narrowly escaped murder by Black and Tans in December 1920. Supported Treaty and never forgave de Valera for leading opposition into Civil War. A friend and supporter of Cosgrave.

Frank Gallagher [Proinnsias Ó Gallchobhair] (1893–1962) – Born in Cork. Educated locally. Editor of *Cork Free Press* during First World War. Joined Sinn Féin in 1917. Worked with Erskine Childers on publicity staff of first Dáil in 1918. Interned in Mountjoy jail in 1920. One of the leaders of the April 1920 hunger strike. Opposed the Treaty. Assistant editor of *Poblacht na h-Eireann*. Imprisoned by Free State forces in 1922. Became editor of *The Irish Press* in 1931. Headed the Information Bureau during World War II. Deputy Director of Radio Éireann. Became member of the Board of the National Library in 1954.

Pietro Cardinal Gasparri (1852–1934) – Born in Capovallazza di Ussita, Italy to shepherds. Educated at the Minor Seminary of Nepi, Pontifical Roman Seminary and Pontifical Roman Athenaeum. Received doctorates in theology, philosophy and canon/civil law. Ordained in 1877. Professor of Ecclesiastical History and Theology at Pontifical Roman Seminary. Professor of Canon Law at Pontifical Roman Athenaeum. Faculty member of *Institut Catholique*, Paris until 1898. Elevated to Bishop in 1898. Served as Apostolic delegate to Peru from 1898 to 1901. Appointed Secretary of the Roman Curia 1901. Elevated to Cardinal in 1907. Served as Secretary of State for the Vatican from 1914 until 1930. Chamberlain of the Holy Roman Church from 1916. Co-wrote the Lateran Treaty.

Francis Neil Cardinal Gasquet (1846–1929) – Born in north London to a physician. Educated at Downside School, the College of St. Gregory, Downside and Belmont Priory. Ordained in 1874. Took the name Aidan as part of religious orders. Prior of Downside Abbey, 1878–1885.

Did research work at the British Museum and Record Office, 1885–1900. Elected abbot president of English Benedictine Confederation in 1900 and 1904. Named president of the Vulgate Commission by Pope Pius X, 1907. Elevated to Cardinal in 1914. Served as Prefect of the Vatican Secret Archives from 1917. Appointed Librarian of the Holy Roman Church in 1919. Served as Archivist of the Holy Roman Church from 1920. A respected historian of English monasticism during his life, but widely discredited afterward. He was known for his particular delight in jokes about the Irish.

<u>Thomas Patrick Gilmartin</u> (1861–1939) – Born in Rhinsinna, Castlebar, Co. Mayo. Educated at St. Jarlath's, Tuam and St. Patrick's, Maynooth. Ordained in 1883. Professor of Mathematics at St. Jarlath's, 1883–91. Appointed Dean of St. Patrick's, Maymooth in 1891, Vice President in 1904. Appointed Bishop of Clonfert in 1909. Elevated to Archbishop of Tuam in 1918. Called for a 'Truce of God' between the Irish and British. Though a strong supporter of the GAA and Gaelic League, he tended to be politically aloof and wrote little.

<u>Bernard Hackett</u> (1863–1932) – Born in Dungarvan, Co Waterford. Educated at Mt Melleray, St. John's, Waterford, and Maynooth. Ordained, 1888. Professor of Classics and Philosophy, St. John's, Waterford, 1890–1904. Joined Redemptorist Order, 1904. Became rector of Marianella, Rathgar and Mt St Alphonsus, Limerick. Appointed Bishop of Waterford and Lismore, 1916. Signed May 1917 manifesto opposing partition.

<u>John Hagan</u> (1873–1930) – Born near Rathnew, Co. Wicklow. Educated at Holy Cross, Clonliffe and the Irish College, Rome. Ordained in 1899. Obtained curacy in Dublin diocese and appointed to Maynooth, transferred to Ballytore after brief ministry and then North Anne St. Wrote for the *Irish Ecclesiastical Record* and became noticed by the Hierarchy, who recommended him for vice-rectorship of the Irish College, Rome. Appointed vice-rector, 1904. Became rector in 1920. Author of 'Notes from Rome' in the *Catholic Bulletin*, 1911–20. He was an outspoken nationalist who fought perceived English influence in Rome and over Dublin.

<u>Denis Hallinan</u> (1849–1923) – Born in Graigue, Co. Limerick. Educated at Irish College, Rome. Ordained in 1874. Author of a series of articles in the *Catholic Bulletin* critical of Britain's motives during World War I. Appointed Bishop of Limerick in 1918. Criticised for refusing to allow a Requiem Mass for John Redmond in 1918, arguing that to do so would introduce politics into the services of the Church. Vocal supporter of Sinn Féin prior to the Treaty.

<u>John Mary Harty</u> (1867–1946) – Born in Knocknagurteeny, Murroe, Co. Limerick. Educated at Crescent College, in Limerick, St. Patrick's, Thurles, St. Patrick's, Maynooth and the Pontifical Gregorian University in Rome. Ordained in 1894. Appointed to Chair of Dogmatic Theology at Maynooth in 1895, Professor of Moral Theology in 1904, and Professor of Canon Law in 1909. Co-founder and editor of the *Irish Theological Quarterly*. Appointed Archbishop of Cashel and Emly in 1913. President of the Catholic Truth Society of Ireland from 1914, and patron of the GAA from 1928. One of four Catholic bishops who attended the Irish Convention of 1917–18. One of the few bishops to actively engage in attempting to bring about peace during the Civil War. Destroyed most of his papers shortly before death, especially those discussing politics.

<u>Joseph Hoare</u> (1842–1927) – Born in Ballymahon, Co. Longford. Educated at Mt. Melleray, St. Mel's, Longford and St. Patrick's, Maynooth. Ordained in 1867. Appointed President of St. Mel's in 1875. Parish priest of Streete from 1881. Appointed Vicar-General for Ardagh and Clonmacnois in 1887. Appointed Bishop of Ardagh and Clonmacnois in 1895. Denounced the 1916 Rising as 'a mad and sinful adventure.' Did not support Sinn Féin but also strongly criticised British methods.

<u>Patrick T. Keohane</u> (1870–1939) – Born in Co. Sligo. Vice-president of the Irish National Aid and Volunteers' Dependents' Fund, 1916. Company secretary of M.H. Gill and Son publishing. Influential in publication of *Catholic Bulletin* from its inception and editor from October 1922. Senator from 1938. Strongly republican. Close friend of Hagan and regularly corresponded with him on political issues.

<u>Charles Joseph Kickham</u> (1828–1882) – Born near Cashel, Co. Tipperary to a shopkeeper. Educated at local pay school. Suffered impaired hearing and vision from a gunpowder accident at thirteen. Became interested in national politics through 1840s repeal campaign. Disillusioned with parliamentary politics as a result of Sadleir and Keogh's 1852 takeover of the tenant campaign. Joined editorial team of Fenian *Irish People* in 1863. Arrested for treason felony and imprisoned, 1865–69. Released due to ill health. Wrote *Knocknagow*, 1873. President of the Supreme Council of the IRB from 1873. Regarded by John O'Leary as the intellectual drive behind the Fenian movement.

<u>Michael Cardinal Logue</u> (1840–1924) – Born in Carrigart, Co. Donegal to a blacksmith. Educated at St. Patrick's, Maynooth. Appointed Professor of Dogmatic Theology and *Belles Lettres* at the Irish College, Paris in 1866. Ordained in 1866. Appointed Dean and Professor of Irish at Maynooth in 1876, Professor of Dogmatic and Moral Theology in 1878. Appointed Bishop of Raphoe in 1879. Elevated to Archbishop of Armagh in 1887. Elevated to Cardinal in 1893. He was a cautious and conservative nationalist who focused on the impact of political activities and decisions on the Catholic Church in Ireland.

<u>Salvatore Luzio</u> (1870–1959) – Born in Sicily. Educated at the Seminary of Girgenti, and University of St. Apollinare in Rome. Awarded doctorates in Theology, Philosophy and Canon and Civil Law. Ordained in 1893. Professor of Canon Law at Maynooth, 1897–1910. Professor of Canon Law at the Seminary of the Diocese of Rome. Received the honorary title of Secret Chamberlain to Pope Benedict XV in 1906. Served as Regent of the Apostolic Penitentiary, 1922–59.

<u>Charles McHugh</u> (1856–1926) – Born in Dreenan, Co. Tyrone. Educated at St. Columb's, Derry and St. Patrick's, Maynooth. Ordained in 1881. President of St. Columb's, Derry, 1890–1905. Appointed Bishop of Derry in 1907. Clashed with Volunteers in attempts to maintain peace in 1914. Established Anti-Partition League and Irish Nation League. Responsible for May 1917 manifesto opposing partition. Refused nomination as episcopal representative to 1917 Irish Race Convention over issue of partition. Took leading part in denunciation of Government of Ireland Act (1920). Believed that religion and politics were mixed in

Ireland and did not hesitate to air thoughts and feelings regarding partition.

Patrick McKenna (1868–1942) – Born in Moy, Co. Monaghan to farmers. Educated at Killybrone National School, St. Macarten's, Monaghan and St. Patrick's, Maynooth. Ordained in 1894. Lecturer in English at Dunboyne Institute, 1894–1896. Lecturer in Theology at St. Kiernan's, Kilkenny, 1896–1900. Appointed Chair of Theology at Maynooth in 1904. Editor and contributor to *Irish Theological Quarterly*. Appointed Bishop of Clogher in 1909.

Joseph Cardinal MacRory (1861–1945) – Born in Ballygawley, Co. Tyrone to a small farmer. Educated at St. Patrick's, Armagh and St. Patrick's, Maynooth. Ordained in 1885. Appointed Professor of Sacred Scripture and Oriental Languages at Maynooth in 1889. Chair of Hermeneutics and New Testament Exegesis. Co-founded *Irish Theological Quarterly*, 1906. Appointed vice-president of St. Patrick's, Maynooth in 1912. Appointed Bishop of Down and Connor in 1915. Appointed Archbishop of Armagh in 1928. Elevated to Cardinal in 1929. One of four Catholic bishops who attended the Irish Convention of 1917–18. He was a Sinn Féin sympathiser and vocal opponent of partition. Signed May 1917 manifesto opposing partition. He highlighted the unfair treatment of Northern Irish Catholics. In 1931 he caused outrage by stating that the Church of Ireland was not part of the church of Christ. He was also a patron of the GAA.

Valentine Emmanuel Patrick MacSwiney (1871–1945) – Hereditary Papal Marquis. Arrested after 1916 Rising, but released a day later. Unofficial Irish representative to the Vatican from 1922 to 1923. Irish delegate to the League of Nations in 1923 and 1924. Chancellor of the Order of Malta in Ireland, 1934–1939. Organizer of contributions of Irish books to the Vatican library. Known to speak eleven European languages. First cousin of Sir Vernon Kell, founder and first director general of MI5.

Mary Margaret MacSwiney [Máire Nic Suibhne] (1872–1942) – Born in London to schoolteachers. Family moved to Cork city. Failed business sent family into bankruptcy. Educated at Ursuline convent school in

Cork. Took up teaching post in private school in England in 1892. Acquired teaching diploma from University of Cambridge. Began one year noviciate with Oblates of St. Benedict while teaching at a convent school in Farnborough, but did not proceed at end of period. Returned to Cork in 1904 and taught at St. Angela's. Involved in suffrage movement, but opposed militant tactics. Left Munster Women's Franchise League in 1914 and started Cork chapter of Cumann na mBan. Fired from teaching job in 1917 due to political opinions. Elected to the Dáil for Cork city in 1920. Opposed Treaty. Re-elected in 1922 and 1923, but lost 1927 election. Vice-president of Sinn Féin and Cumann na mBan. Resigned from both in 1933 and 1934, respectively. An outspoken republican whose unwavering, militant views and strong personality caused consternation even among sympathisers and colleagues.

Terence James MacSwiney [Tordhealbhach Mac Suibhne] (1879–1920) – Born in Cork city. Educated at North Monastery Christian Brothers School and Queen's College, Cork. Part-time lecturer in business studies at Cork Municipal School of Commerce. Full-time post of commercial instructor for the Joint Technical Instruction Committee for County Cork from the end of 1911. Founder member of Cork branch of Young Ireland Society, 1899, and Cork Celtic Literary Society, 1901. Strong proponent of Irish language. Activities became overtly political from 1911. Founder and second-in-command of Cork Brigade of Irish Volunteers, 1913. Felt uneasy about part in 1916 Rising, having called for Volunteers to surrender arms to civil authorities. Arrested and detained until June 1917. Arrested and sentenced to six months, November 1917 but released after four days due to hunger strike. Arrested and detained, March 1918 – March 1919. Sinn Féin TD for Mid-Cork, 1918. Succeeded Tomás MacCurtain as Lord Mayor of Cork and commandant of Cork brigade of IRA, 1920. Arrested and sentenced to two years detention, August 1920. Began hunger strike immediately. Died seventy-four days later. Became iconic figure of Irish republicanism.

Daniel Patrick Mannix (1864–1963) – Born in Charleville, Co. Cork. Educated at Christian Brothers' schools and St. Patrick's, Maynooth. Ordained in 1890. Appointed Chair of Moral Theology at Maynooth in 1895. Served as President of Maynooth, 1903–12. Served as Coadjutor

Archbishop of Melbourne, 1912–7. Served as Archbishop of Melbourne from 1917. Refused entry to Ireland by Great Britain in 1920. Opposed Treaty, and strongly opposed partition. Once he relocated to Australia, be became known for his strong nationalist beliefs and willingness to express them in public, though while in Ireland he had been much more conservative.

Rafael María José Pedro Francisco Borja Domingo Gerardo de la Santísma Trinidad Cardinal Merry del Val y Zulueta (1865–1930) – Born in London to the secretary of the Spanish legation in London. Educated at Bayliss House, Slough, Notre Dame de Namur and St Michel, Brussels. Began clerical training in Scots College, Rome, but moved to Accademia dei Nobili Ecclesiastici at the insistence of Pope Leo XIII. Ordained in 1888. Appointed *cameriere segreto partecipante*, 1891; master of the robes and privy chamberlain to the pope, 1893. Vatican adviser on English affairs, 1895-6; drafted *Apostolicae curae*, 1896 papal encyclical that declared Anglican orders null and void. Appointed titular Archbishop of Nicaea in 1900. Elevated to Cardinal in 1903. Served as Cardinal Secretary of State, 1903–14, and Secretary of the Sacred Congregation of the Holy Office from 1914. His influence decreased substantially after the death of Pius X because of later popes' moves away from anti-modernism, of which Merry del Val had been one of the prime forces.

Patrick Morrisroe (1869–1946) – Born in Charlestown, Co. Mayo. Educated at National School, St. Nathy's, Ballaghaderreen and St. Patrick's, Maynooth. Ordained in 1893. Dean of St. Patrick's, Maynooth, 1896–1911. Appointed Bishop of Achonry in 1911. Signed May 1917 manifesto against partition. Strong supporter of Irish language revival movement.

Edward Mulhern (1863–1943) – Born in Ederney, Co. Fermanagh. Educated at St. Macarten's, Monaghan and St. Patrick's, Maynooth. Ordained in 1888. President of St. Macarten's in 1892. Awarded degree of Doctor of Divinity by Pope Leo XIII in 1895 for services in education. Appointed parish priest of Innismacsaint in 1903. Appointed Bishop of Dromore in 1916. One of the eighteen Catholic bishops and three Protestant bishops who signed the May 1917 manifesto protesting partition.

Cornelius J. 'Conn' Murphy (1869–1947) – Born in Dublin to a hardware merchant. Received BA from Royal University in 1895. First recipient of DPh from Royal University in 1906. Founding member of Gaelic League. Became active in politics during war for independence. Opposed the Treaty. Secretary of appeal delegation to Vatican in January 1923. Interned by Free State in March 1923 during which he went on hunger strike. Unsuccessfully stood for Dáil in 1923 and 1927. Known as a devout Catholic and friend of Monsignor Hagan.

Arthur O'Connor (1888–1950) – Born in Celbridge, Co. Kildare. Educated at Blackrock College and Trinity College, Dublin. Elected TD for Kildare South, 1918. Substitute Director of Agriculture, 1920; Minister of Agriculture, 1921–2. Opposed Treaty. Lost in general elections, 1923 and 1927. Remained in Sinn Féin after de Valera left, 1926. Elected titular President of the Republic at the Sinn Féin Ard Fheis. Resigned from presidency and party, 1928. Returned to Trinity College and studied law. Called to the bar. Appointed Senior Counsel, then Circuit court judge, Cork city.

Thomas O'Dea (1858–1923) – Born Carron, Kilfenora, Co. Clare. Educated at St. Flannan's, Ennis and St. Patrick's, Maynooth. Ordained, 1882. Appointed Chair of Theology at Maynooth; Vice-president of Maynooth in 1894. Bishop of Clonfert, 1903. Bishop of Galway and Kilmachuagh and Apostolic Administrator of Kilfenorain from 1909. Keen interest in University College, Galway. Began new cathedral and diocesan college. Strong temperance advocate. Fluent Irish speaker. Advocate of Gaelic League. Never took active part in politics, though a supporter of self-determination for Ireland. Received death threat from Black and Tans in 1920.

Thomas O'Doherty (1877–1936) – Born in Lissacull, Co. Roscommon. Educated at Summerhill, Sligo and St. Patrick's, Maynooth. Ordained in 1902. Professor at Summerhill from 1902 to 1910. Dean of St. Patrick's, Maynooth from 1910 to 1919. Appointed Bishop of Clonfert in 1919. Appointed Bishop of Galway and Kilmachuagh and Apostolic Administrator of Kilfenorain in 1923. Subscriber to dependents of 1916 Rising fund. House raided twice by Black and Tans. Enthusiastic supporter of the Gaelic League.

<u>Patrick Joseph Cardinal O'Donnell</u> (1856–1927) – Born in Kilraine, Co. Donegal to small farmers. Educated at local national school and St. Patrick's, Maynooth. Ordained and received Chair in Theology at Maynooth in 1880. Prefect of Dunboyne Institute, 1885. Appointed Bishop of Raphoe in 1888. Appointed Coadjutor Archbishop of Armagh in 1922, and elevated to Archbishop of Armagh in 1924. Elevated to Cardinal in 1925. Member of Congested Districts Board, 1892–1923. Very active in nationalist politics including the Irish Parliamentary Party and the United Irish League. Trustee of the IPP's parliamentary fund. Chief episcopal protector of the Ancient Order of Hibernians and secured removal of Hierarchy's ban on AOH in 1904. Chaired the Irish Race Convention in Dublin in 1896. He was one of four episcopal representatives to the Irish Race Convention of 1917–18. He remained distant from Sinn Féin during 1919–1921 and always espoused strict constitutional methods. Close, personal friend of Joseph Devlin. A fluent Irish speaker who often wrote his pastoral letters in Irish. Infamous for having appalling handwriting.

<u>Michael O'Flanagan</u> (1876–1942) – Born near Castlerea, Co. Roscommon to small farmers. Educated at local National school, Summerhill College, Sligo and St. Patrick's, Maynooth. Ordained in 1900. Professor of Irish at Summerhill College from 1900 to 1914. Delivered City Hall address during O'Donovan Rossa's funeral in 1915. Elected vice-president of Sinn Féin in 1917. Largely responsible for Count Plunkett's North Roscommon parliamentary victory in 1917. Served as vice-president of the Gaelic League, 1919–20. Opposed Treaty. Elected president of Sinn Féin in 1933, but was expelled from the party in 1936 for participating in Radio Éireann broadcast. Suspended by bishop on multiple occasions for violating orders against political activities, and was only granted permission to publicly celebrate Mass in 1938 through permission of papal nuncio. Believed that priests had a right and duty to participate in political life.

<u>John Joseph O'Kelly [Scéilg]</u> (1872–1957) – Born on Valentia Island, Co. Kerry to a successful farmer. Educated at local National Schools. Founding member of the Keating Branch of the Gaelic League, 1901; Sinn Féin at inaugural meeting, 1905. Became member of the executive of the Gaelic League, 1914. Joined Irish Volunteers, 1914. Editor of

Catholic Bulletin, 1911–22. Joined Irish National League, 1916. Treasurer of the Irish National Aid and Volunteers' Dependents' Fund, 1916. Arrested and deported to England, 1917. Elected Sinn Féin TD for Louth in 1918. Elected Leas Ceann Comhairle of the Dáil, 1919–21. Minister of Irish; Minister for Education, 1921–22. Opposed the Treaty. President of the Gaelic League, 1919–23. Republican envoy to the USA and Australia, 1922–4. President of Sinn Féin, 1926–31. Devout and conservative Catholic.

Seán Thomas O'Kelly [Seán Tomás Ua Ceallaigh] (1882–1966) – Born in Dublin. Educated by the Christian Brothers. Joined the Gaelic League in 1898, Sinn Féin in 1905. Elected general secretary of the Gaelic League, 1915. Appointed Pearse's staff captain prior to Easter Rising. Elected Sinn Féin TD for College Green in 1918. Served as Ceann Comhairle of the First Dáil. Represented Irish Republic as an envoy at post-WWI treaty negotiations in Paris. Republican ambassador to Paris during war for independence. Also served as republican envoy to USA and Italy. Opposed Treaty. Jailed for duration of the Civil War. Founding member of Fianna Fail. Served as Minister for Local Government, 1932–39; Minister for Finance, 1939–45. Vice-President of Executive Council, 1932–37 and Tánaiste, 1937–45. Elected President of Ireland in 1945 and 1952. Retired in 1959.

Kevin Roantree O'Shiel [Caoimhín Ó Siadhail] (1891–1970) – Born in Omagh, Co. Tyrone to a solicitor. Educated by Christian Brothers, convent preparatory schools in Oxford and Bath, St. George's, Surrey and Mount St. Mary's Jesuit school, Derby. Studied law at Trinity College, Dublin but did not complete course due to father's illness. Attended King's Inns. Called to bar in 1913. Joined Irish Volunteers in 1914; Sinn Féin in 1917. Member of the Anti-Partition League and the Irish Nation League. Represented Omagh at 1917 Mansion House Convention. Unsuccessfully stood for South Antrim and Fermanagh North seats in 1918. Acted as judge in republican courts from 1919 to 1921. Appointed special judicial commissioner of Dáil Éireann for agrarian disputes in May 1920, and judicial commissioner of Land Commission in September 1920. Supported Treaty. Legal secretary to Provisional Government. Member of the constitution committee. Assistant legal adviser to Executive Council. Adviser to Michael Collins on Northern Ireland in 1922. Director of the North-Eastern Boundary Bureau, 1922–25. Substitute delegate for Fourth Assembly of the League of Nations, 1923. Land commissioner, 1923–63.

Charles O'Sullivan (1858–1927) – Born in Ballyfinane, Firies, Co Kerry. Educated at St. Brendan's, Killarney, and Maynooth. Ordained, 1884. Served as curate, 1884–1900; parish priest, 1902–1917. Appointed Bishop of Kerry, 1917. One of three Irish bishops to visit Terence MacSwiney while on hunger strike. Never identified himself with party politics but was known to hold strong, independent nationalist views. One of the harshest ecclesiastical critics of anti-Treaty republicans.

Pope Pius XI (1857–1939) – Born Ambrogio Damiano Achille Ratti in Desio, Italy. Ordained in 1879. Received doctorates in Philosophy, Canon Law and Theology from the Pontifical Gregorian University, Rome. Worked in Ambrosian Library, 1888–1911. Appointed Chief Librarian, 1907. Appointed Vice-Prefect of Vatican Library, 1911; Prefect, 1914. Appointed Apostolic visitor to Poland, 1918. Appointed Archbishop of Milan, 1921. Elevated to Cardinal at the same time. Elected pope in 1922. He pushed for greater incorporation of religious values into economic and political activities and was less dismissive of democracy than previous popes.

George Noble Plunkett (1851–1948) – Born in Dublin. Educated in Nice, Clongowes Wood and Trinity College, Dublin. Awarded Papal Countship in 1884 for donations to the Little Company of Mary. Clericalist until Parnell divorce scandal. Ran for Parliament as IPP candidate in 1892 (Parnellite), 1895 and 1898. President of the Society for the Preservation of the Irish Language. Director of the National Museum, 1907–16. Vice-president of the Royal Irish Academy, 1908–09, 1911–14. President of the Royal Society of Antiquaries of Ireland. Father of Joseph Mary Plunkett, who swore him into IRB in 1916. Successfully sought papal blessing for Rising volunteers. Ejected by Royal Dublin Society after 1916 Rising. Elected Sinn Féin MP/TD for North Roscommon, 1917–27. Republican Foreign Minister from April 1919 to November 1921, Minister for Fine Arts from August 1921. Opposed Treaty. Helped write appeal to the Vatican against October pastoral. Split with de Valera in 1926 and remained republican until his death.

<u>Michael Sheehan</u> (1870–1945) – Born in Waterford. Educated at Augustian School, Dungarvan, St. John's, Waterford, St. Patrick's, Maynooth, University of Griefswald, University of Oxford and University of 'Bonn, where he received his PhD Ordained in 1895. Appointed to Chair of Ancient Classics at Maynooth. Awarded honorary DD by Vatican. Chief examiner in Latin and Greek under the Intermediate Board. Elected Commissioner of Intermediate Education. Vice-president of Maynooth in 1919. Appointed Coadjutor Archbishop of Sydney in 1922. Resigned in 1937, and returned permanently to Ireland. Made a Papal Count in 1938. Fluent Irish speaker.

<u>Hanna Sheehy-Skeffington</u> (1877–1946) – Born in Kanturk, Co. Cork to David Sheehy, IRB member and future MP. Family moved to Dublin in 1887. Educated at the Dominican Convent in Eccles Street and St. Mary's University College. Received her BA from the Royal University, 1899, MA in 1902, both in languages. Deeply involved in suffragette movement and, along with husband Francis, founded the Irish Women's Franchise League in 1908. Founding member of the Irish Women's Workers' Union in 1911. Messenger to GPO during 1916 Rising. Appointed to Sinn Féin executive in 1917. Judge in republican courts in 1920. Opposed Treaty. Appointed to Fianna Fail executive in 1926 but resigned as protest against de Valera's taking of the oath. Editor of *Republican File* in 1931; assistant editor of *An Phoblacht* shortly thereafter. Objected to place of women in 1937 constitution. Founder of the Women's Social and Progressive League. Stood as independent candidate in 1943 elections, demanding equality for women.

<u>Peter Christopher Yorke</u> (1864–1925) – Born in Galway into shipowning family. Educated at St. Joseph's, St. Jarlath's, Tuam and St. Patrick's, Maynooth. Transferred to St. Mary's Seminary, Baltimore in 1886 at the request of his mother. Ordained in 1887. Sent by bishop for postgraduate studies in theology at Catholic University of America in 1889. Moved to San Francisco in 1891. Appointed editor of archdiocese's organ, Monitor until 1898. Appointed head of Catholic Truth Society. Co-founder of San Francisco *Leader* in 1902. Awarded *Laurea Nomine Sanctae Sedis* by Pius X in 1906 for work on Catholic education. Forced to sever official ties with the *Leader* in 1909 due to dissatisfaction of Apostolic delegate. Early supporter of physical force nationalism

and Easter Rising. Cousin of John MacBride. Elected California state president of the Friends of Irish Freedom in 1917, national vice-president in 1919. Appointed state organiser of AARIR by de Valera in 1920, and elected state president in 1921. Initially quiet on the Treaty, but became outspoken against it by spring, 1922. Strong proponent of the Gaelic League and the Irish-Ireland movement.

Appendix B:
Monsignor Salvatore Luzio's
Report to Cardinal Gasparri

THE IRISH QUESTION

A desire for independence has existed in Ireland for centuries. The Irish have always wished to make Ireland a nation separate from England, which has subjugated and persecuted its people for more than seven hundred years. The celebrated 'Home Rule' or 'autonomy' long promised to the Irish by England was never granted. Because of this, 10 or 15 years ago, the Irish formed the secret society 'Soein Fein' [sic] and have procured munitions, funds and provisions to start a revolution and acquire independence. The war offered them this opportunity, as the English troops were occupied elsewhere, while the Irish had defied English conscription laws.

In fact, the week following Easter Sunday 1916, they proclaimed the Republic under the command of the famous agitator and organiser de Valera

The English then resolved to take vigorous measures against Ireland and began a harsh and bloody battle with the army of the Irish Republic. This action, however, consolidated the existence of the organisation which it was intended to destroy. In 1918, the first republican general election was held and in January 1919 the first Parliament of the Republic was formed. In 1920, another election took place, and republican courts, public offices, ministries, etc., began to function. England, unable to suppress through bloodshed this tremendous desire for freedom, proposed an armistice in order to conclude a treaty with Ireland and to grant her a certain amount of liberty.

The Irish delegates left for London to conclude this treaty, with orders not to be satisfied with anything less than a Republic, i.e. full freedom and independence for Ireland. It happened, however, that under the threat of the continuation of the war, the delegates signed a treaty which fell short of creating an Irish Republic, and instead put the country on the same footing as other dominions of the British Empire, i.e. Canada, Australia, South Africa, etc. The treaty was signed on 6 December 1921. It divided Ireland into two legislative zones (parliaments): one for the 5 [*sic*] counties in the north, the other for the remaining 26 counties.

The treaty needed to be accepted by the people and general elections were scheduled for June 1922. At that time, Collins, who was the leader of those who accepted the treaty, and de Valera, leader of the opposition, in order to avoid further complications, made a pact in May 1922, to have all the deputies sitting in the republican parliament re-elected, irrespective of their stance on the treaty; they also agreed to have 4 ministers anti and 5 pro in the new cabinet. This was done, perhaps with the intention of creating a provisional government and then re-examining and modifying the treaty with England as well as the constitution. England opposed this pact, claiming that it violated the treaty. Collins broke the pact on the eve of the elections, publishing a manifesto on the very day of the elections. As can be imagined, the elections were chaotic, nevermind to say that many, such as the Farmers, the Workers, and the Independents, for example, unaware of the breaking of the Collins–de Valera pact, elected their own candidates. It was from this point that the great question arose. The pro-treaty side declared that they had the majority. The anti-treaty side denied this, since not all of the voters knew of the breaking of the electoral pact and therefore voted for candidates for whom they would not otherwise have voted. Furthermore, each party, in order to gain a majority, appropriated 30 deputies from the other parties who had declared that they had been elected for peace – peace with England, as the pro-treaty side interpreted it, or peace between the parties, as the republicans understood. Unable to resolve the question peacefully, they split into two camps to dispute the government of the nation. Collins set up a government of the 'Free State', echoing the treaty with England. De Valera continued to call himself President of the Republic. The Free State, aided by England in terms of munitions and finances, after some time, gained the upper hand.

Of these two parties, or more accurately, these two governments, the

Republican government is much more religious, preferring the ancient and genuine Catholic faith of the Irish people. The ministers of the Free State are almost all young men, aged 25 – 30, fanatical, proud, raised aloft by England in this turbulent time. They have given up on the oath that one had to take before sitting in Parliament, the oath that is taken in the Protestant Parliament of England and in that of the 6 counties of Northern Ireland. Out of 30 Senators, President Cosgrave has chosen 18 freemasons. In the constitution, Art. 8, it is stated that all religions are equal in the eyes of the Free State. Something which seems incredible in Catholic Ireland! And to think that this is the government supported by the ecclesiastical hierarchy (Document 1).

APPEALS TO THE HOLY SEE

While this struggle raged, appeals from Ireland reached the Holy See that it might use its good judgment to intervene. However, as I managed to establish, these appeals were not made so that the Holy See might decide this most difficult political question of its own accord, one in which, in any case, the Irish insisted that the Holy See should not intervene. Rather, the appeals centred on a moral and religious problem of great significance, which had caused much damage. The appeals made by Miss Mo. Sweney [*sic*], by Count Plunket [*sic*], by the Committee for the appeal to the Holy See signed by Doctor Murphy and by Prof. Clery etc., can be seen, and this was confirmed to me by countless republicans and by a declaration by the same Prof. Cleary (Document 2).

This question arose due to the following less than prudent act by the Bishops. While the two parties had engaged in a bloody struggle disputing the government of the nation, the Bishops, in October of 1922, published a pastoral, signed by all of them, in which they decided an apparently very dubious political fact – that of the legitimacy of the Irish Government, declaring the Free State to be legitimate and that, as such, the republicans were all rebels. But an even greater evil, however, was that of having wished to mix the Sacraments with an extremely debatable political fact which they had neither authority to decide, nor certain data which would enable them to do so justly; a decision to which both the faithful and non-believers felt bound to adhere. They stated that the republicans were rebels and that in opposing the legitimate Free State through force, they were committing a grave crime and could not, if they continued to do so, be absolved and receive the sacraments. Moreover, they inflicted suspension 'ipso facto incurrenda' upon the priests who absolved such republicans. What happened next is easy to predict. The republicans, not accepting the decision of the Bishops regarding the legitimacy of the Free State naturally rejected the implications of that decision, that is that they were assassins, rebels and unworthy of receiving the sacraments. This scandalous fact meant, and still means that some priests with republican ideals give confession and sacraments to republicans, while others who accept the decision of the Bishops do not. The faithful therefore know to whom they must turn to receive the sacraments and they marvel at how the religion is not equal in the eyes of all priests and begin to believe that each one shapes it according to his own wishes (Document 3).

The evil was further aggravated by the fact that the priests who favoured the decision of the Bishops, in order to show themselves as zealous, took things to the extreme, not only refusing confession to those republicans who had fought and facilitated the use of violence, but also to those who had never been involved in politics but who had only republican ideals, i.e. they desired, as the Irish have always done, the complete freedom of their native land. And there are imprudent priests that, before confession, inquire as to the nature of the penitent's political beliefs, and if he says that he has republican ideals, he will be thrown out and the priests will refuse to hear his confession.

But the most unhappy position is that of the 14 or 15,000 who cannot chose [sic] their Confessor, but are restricted to the chaplain of the prison, who, having been sent by the Bishop with precise instructions, denies absolution to all, and there are many thousands of Catholics, most of whom take communion very frequently, who can no longer avail of the sacraments and could not even fulfil until now the Easter precept. All the appeals I heard every day in Ireland centred on this and were made with such insistence that they truly provoked great sadness. The Bishops, in my opinion, rely too much on the profound piety of the Irish people. If it had not been for this profound piety I believe that Ireland would have witnessed the defection of thousands from the Catholic Church. In my opinion, it is necessary to rectify this abnormal situation immediately, especially now that hostilities have ceased and thus the reason given up to now of the opposition being guilty of opposing with force a legitimate (according to the Bishops) government no longer applies. And it is also necessary to prohibit the Bishops entirely from taking part in politics, as this has always brought disastrous consequences for the ecclesiastical authorities and for the religion. The Irish people love their priests and respect them because it is from them that they receive the sacraments; but they respect the Bishops very little because they see them very little and only hear their voices when they speak about politics, which do not always conform to the aspirations of the people and are often contradictory. For example, when Ireland rose up against England, the Bishops, with few exceptions, joined forces with the republicans; indeed, one of the Bishops, Mons. Fogarty, was a member of the Committee which collected funds in order to sustain the republican armed forces. All the Bishops then opposed the military conscription laws which England had the right to impose on Ireland as a part of the United Kingdom. Therefore, the right-thinking Irish people could not understand how the same Bishops who encouraged them to fight for the republic, now denied them the sacraments for continuing to do so. The same war was in question, first against England and now against a treaty drawn up by England, which had set up, in its place, a government known as the Free State (Document 4). Such a provision preventing the Bishops from getting involved with politics would be received with general approval by all the Irish, even by those who are in favour of the Free State. Several different people told me this, among them, and this was no surprise to me, the very President of the Free State, Cosgrave.

MY MISSION

I was summoned by the Secretary of State in early March and informed that the Holy Father wished to send me to Ireland to gather information on the strange conditions in which that nation found itself and to see whether it would be suitable to publish a letter from the Holy Father and to help in any way I could with the pacification of their souls. In fact, I was given a pontifical letter by the Secretary of State as well as another letter signed by Card. Gasparri addressed to Card. Logue, which said that I had been sent to Ireland to gather the above information and to facilitate peace, and it asked Card. Logue to give me access to and contact with eminent personages and anyone else with whom I could have an exchange of ideas regarding the above ends.

This mission was kept secret. The Bishops of Ireland and the

Government of the Free State did not officially participate in it before my departure from Rome. This silence was later said to have been interpreted by the ecclesiastical hierarchy and by the government as a lack of respect and served, particularly in the case of the Bishops, to create a hostile atmosphere for me in Ireland, before my arrival in the region. The first news they had heard was from the 'Daily Mail' in London and they told me that this information was communicated to the press by Father Langton [sic], Card. Gasquet's secretary, but I cannot confirm the authenticity of this statement; however I do know that the said Father has propagated erroneous information regarding my mission. Thus, while here in Italy few or none knew about this mission, in Ireland it had been talked about and written about for about ten days, giving rise to conjecture of all sorts, often erroneous and always exaggerated. The Bishops, through Card. Logue, declared that they knew nothing of my visit and that they did not know why I should be sent; while on the other hand everyone maintained that it was certain that my mission related to the abnormal conditions in Ireland and more pertinently to the religious situation created by the Bishops with the publication of their pastoral.

Under such conditions, it is easy to imagine the coolness and diffidence with which the Bishops received me. Even my closest friends wanted to get rid of me.

In Dublin I stayed in the Shelbourne Hotel and took Canon Conry with me to help. The usual news agencies try to criticise him, saying that he is a very unbalanced priest. Nothing of the sort. Certainly, he was not very intelligent, but he was useful to me particularly in the area of material work. He was respected by all, and was able to help me because he knew people and things in Ireland, and having been in Rome for many years and only recently returned to Ireland, he was free from any suspicion of partisanship. He undertook all work conscientiously and for free.

ON THE PUBLICATION OF THE PONTIFICAL DOCUMENT

First and foremost I went to Armagh, as was my duty, to see Card. Logue and to give him the letter from Card. Gasparri. He received me kindly, but immediately told me that I was expected to bring approval from Rome of the actions of the Bishops in relation to the publication of the Pastoral, and therefore to reject the appeals which the Republicans had made to Rome against that action. I answered that that was not my mission, but that I did not believe that the Holy See would ratify the Bishops' decision on the legitimacy of the government of the Free State, since in doing so it would enter into a political question in which it did not wish to be involved. I said that I had come to consult him about the suitability of publishing a pontifical letter and the probability of successfully saying a few words for the sake of peace. With regard to the publication of the letter, the Cardinal expressed some difficulties, but told me to consult the other Bishops too. I then asked him to write me an introductory letter to persons of influence with whom I had to speak, especially to President Cosgrave. He responded that he did not feel he had such authorisation. I was surprised by this refusal and understood that I did not find myself in a very favourable environment.

I went to the Archbishop of Dublin who showed himself to be completely opposed to the publication of a pontifical letter owing to the damage that it might do; then, speaking of peace, he said (in a polite manner, but what he wanted to say was this) that the Holy See should not concern itself with these matters, because for politics in Ireland there was the Free State Government, and for religion, there were the Bishops, neither of which needed unwanted mediation. I had lost. I spoke to other Archbishops and Bishops and all were of the same opinion regarding the unsuitability of the publication of the pontifical letter.

Thus, I too was persuaded that the publication of the pontifical letter in its present form could give rise to false interpretations and could worsen the situation. The letter actually said that, from the reports made to Rome on the Irish situation, the Holy Father could not form an exact opinion. This would have been to the detriment of the government of the Free State which wholly maintained that it was the only legitimate government and would have embarrassed the Bishops because they had already decided the question by declaring the Free State to be legitimate and had prohibited the republicans who fought against it from receiving the sacraments. The republicans on the other hand, who were still strong, would have certainly taken the chance to fight even more and not lay down their arms. It is also stated in the letter that the Holy See had received requests from both opposing parties to intervene and to make peace. But the supporters of the Free State deny doing this, since they say that their legitimate government does not lower itself to pacts with rebels through the means of mediation; while the appeals to the Holy See, as I have said, were made primarily by the republicans for the resolution of the religious problem created by the publication of the Bishops' pastoral. Furthermore, the majority of Irish people were convinced that the reasonable way to achieve peace was that which was indicated in the pontifical letter, i.e. the cessation of hostilities and the recourse to free elections; however, the opposing parties disagreed on the particulars and especially on the methods of securing the freedom of such elections. And after the proposals of peace made by de Valera, the pontifical letter would not have had much effect.

THE PEACE MISSION

After this, I tried, if it was possible, to say a few words privately to the opposing parties in order to facilitate their reaching an agreement. First and foremost, I pressed de Valera to cease his armed opposition and to return to the legal methods of election, thus establishing the will of the majority of people regarding the form of government to adopt in Ireland. And he had the comfort of being able to succeed, as I added quickly.

After several days of my stay in Ireland, I understood the political situation very well (and everyone said so), and that was that the Free State army, aided as it was by England, had already virtually subjugated and defeated that of the Republic, and that it was only a question of months before it would end in a complete rout. But at the same time I also understood the fact that, given the stubbornness of the republicans until their army was totally defeated, they could still, through various means, bring about carnage and immense destruction. It was precisely this that I was trying to avoid, as were all those who for love of their country wanted peace through negotiation and not as an effect of the complete destruction of the republican army. This is expressed well in an article in the 'Irish Times' which I will cite later.

I went to pay a courtesy visit to the president of the Free State, Cosgrave. Also present at the meeting was the Minister for Foreign Affairs, FitzGerald. Both received me kindly. I told Cosgrave that I had given letters from the Secretary of State to Cardinal Logue and that the contents referred to him, and I also said that I was saddened that the said Cardinal had not written me a letter of introduction, even though the letter had asked him to facilitate my contact with eminent personages with whom I wished to speak. I wanted to see if he would remonstrate or be difficult. He did nothing of the sort; on the contrary, when I said that while in Ireland I wished to say a few good words, if possible, in order to help the cause of peace, he showed me great deference and we spoke for three hours about the details of the negotiations that could have developed, and he finished by saying that he did not wish to talk directly to the republicans as this would not be decorous for the government, but that he could understand what I had said to him after having seen the leaders of the other party. Cosgrave, unlike some other ministers was disposed to peace by negotiation, understanding perfectly that in this way a lasting peace could be made, while peace after the devastation of the enemy would be momentary and ephemeral since the republicans would disturb it again as soon as they had the means.

I then went to meet de Valera, leader of the republicans, who made me use highly irregular methods, since the said de Valera is still a fugitive. He also received me kindly, and I saw immediately that he had a good and devout soul, however he seemed at first indomitable with regard to the cessation of hostilities and to making peace with the Free State. I reasoned with him for two hours and after having argued with him from the side of Christian morality and religion, making him recognise that it was a crime to persist in an armed reprisal when there was a legal means to resolve the problem (i.e the elections), and that now this was much more evident, given <u>the inferiority of his army and the vain hope of resolving on his part the question with arms</u>, I thought that he would capitulate, but for now he said nothing. All this I did secretly because I thought that if the negotiations did not succeed no one would have known about the failure. The people however, desirous as they were for peace took the opportunity of my presence in Ireland to ask me to mediate in order to obtain it.

The protestant newspaper 'The Irish Times', though deferential to Catholics, wrote a wonderful article entitled 'An Opportunity' (Document 5), saying that while I, a foreign and impartial person, was in Ireland, there was a good opportunity to conduct peace talks. After the publication of this article, I received hundreds and hundreds of telegrams, letters and agendas approved by City and County Councils, as well as other bodies, all endorsing the article published by the aforementioned newspaper, and proposing that I play an intermediary role in re-establishing peace in Ireland. This general desire for peace shocked those who were opposed to peace talks, and wished instead to put an end to the question through the annihilation of the enemy on the battlefield. Among these was one of the Ministers, O'Higgins, a young man of about 30, arrogant and fanatical, who despises the Republicans because they killed his father. I am of the opinion that it is for reasons such as this, that O'Higgins and England, which has supported the Free State and aided it with monies and munitions, look upon my visit to Ireland less than favourably; and lastly (though it seems impossible), so do the Bishops of Ireland. This was made clear to me by the Archbishop of Dublin. All of them, and particularly the aforementioned minister in an article in the *Freeman's Journal* inspired by them, told me that the public's voice regarding peace was not to be heard because it did not exist, and that they would have made little of mediation as they are capable of defining the question by themselves, and that furthermore I did not have the documents which would authorise me to act in such a capacity. This last reason was merely an excuse because I had already told Cosgrave that I had shown some documents to Cardinal Logue, documents which they in fact had published. The truth of the matter is this: that the Free State government wanted the Vatican to address the letters directly to them, thinking that in doing so, the Holy See would be seen to support the decision of the Bishops, recognising it as the legitimate government, and that afterwards, the Republicans would cease their campaign. The Vatican could certainly not have done so, and not only because the Free State had the intention of using such letters for this end, and then not even to take them into consideration for the peace talks. In fact, it is said that if they had had such letters from the Vatican, they would have put them before Parliament, discussed them, and then decided on whether to admit a mediator from the Papal envoy for the peace talks. Furthermore, the Free State government was displeased, as I have said, about the [fact] that my visit to Ireland was not communicated to them beforehand; and lastly, they were especially offended by the fact that a telegram had arrived in Dublin from the Vatican with an apostolic benediction for Dr. Murphy, who had come to Rome for the appeal against the Bishops, was arrested on his return to Ireland, and then found dead after protesting by hunger strike.[1] The telegram was interpreted as a sign of protest on the part of the Vatican over the imprisonment of the said Dr. Murphy (Document 6).

So I then responded that I had not made any step towards peace talk public, but that I did not intend to involve myself in such a dispute when my mediation was neither necessary nor welcome. Thus, the incident was at an end.

Meanwhile, the Bishops who were still opposed to me, and like the English who are always underhanded in their actions, whilst supporting the Free State and giving it's government reason to make clear that it had been offended by the Vatican, and aided by the English here resident and by Minister FitzGerald, who had come specially from Ireland, returned[2] to Rome to say that it was not the case that I was remaining in Ireland in order to cooperate with the peace process.

In the meantime, de Valera had become convinced of the futility of the resistance movement had sent me the peace proposals so that I might present them to Cosgrave. But since I was no longer able to intervene in such matters, de Valera published the proposals, saying that he had been swept up in the general movement towards peace brought about by my presence and that this demonstrated his willingness to make peace and to end hostilities; thus placing all responsibility for the delay and refusal to make peace with the Free State, which in terms of public opinion is finished if it submits, and at present the last matters regarding a peace settlement are being finalised.

That was how I left things when I returned from Ireland, and I believe that I have assumed my duty perfectly regarding cooperation leading to peace, a duty which consisted primarily of inducing de Valera to end hostilities and table peace proposals. On this, I have an important document, namely a signed letter from de Valera in which he recognises that the arguments put forward by me were what induced him to end hostilities and make a proposal for peace, and that it will be in no small part due to me if this peace is concluded[3] (Document 7).

Since de Valera himself says so, I would like to believe that my arguments were truly the crucial factor in his decision; but one may also suppose that these arguments, or indeed my presence in Ireland, had been merely a simple pretext allowing him to capitulate; however, it is still true that my presence in Ireland, rather than prolonging the war, as my enemies claimed, in fact shortened it, and accelerated the declaration of peace.

This truth, which ran contrary to all that was claimed by suspect Agencies, particularly English ones, led to acts being carried out by interested parties aimed at discrediting my mission, and in part also the Holy See's intervention in the Irish Question.

In Ireland they kept watch over me around the clock, wherever I went, seeking to catch me at foul play, and I knew that to that end a person sent from England had booked himself into the hotel in which I was staying; however, they will have nothing to say about my conduct, since I always beat a gentle path. Only once did I accept an invitation to take part in a very private meeting of the Italian society, honouring a famous Italian musician upon whom had been conferred an honourific title. It seemed to me acceptable to do so, this event having nothing to do with Ireland, the English, or the parties; however, I now know that it has been said that I had assisted at a meeting honouring a Protestant. A laughable notion!! The musician is Signore Esposito, from Naples, a devout Catholic who has studied at numerous religious institutions and who was a close personal friend of the late Bishop Walsh.

I could write little or nothing of these things to the Secretary of State, since the means of correspondence was not safe. I asked the secretary for permission to use the codex and received no response; I then wrote a few letters and in particular I sent one rather long one through a priest of the Irish College, asking for directions on any further course of action, but received no response in this instance either; perhaps because, as I have said, the means of correspondence was not safe.

Consequently, I humbly propose:

1st – that the Bishops be told to lift the ban on Republicans receiving the Sacraments, especially since they have laid down their arms and returned to legal means in order to further their political ideals.

2nd – that the lay and regular clergy be completely prohibited from taking part in political affairs, since this has always led to disorder and been damaging to the Faith.

3rd – that a permanent apostolic delegation be installed in Ireland, something which is vital for that region, even if the Bishops do not wish it, as they say that they do not wish that their work be overseen.

NOTES

1. [in margin] This telegram was never sent by the [indecipherable] of the State. Signed F. Borgognini.
2. [in margin] ???
3. [in margin] Nevertheless, in the Daily Mail on 10 May 1923: 'President Cosgrave announced yesterday in the Parliament of the Free State of Ireland that the [indecipherable] of peace [indec.] de Valera were interrupted because of De Valera's [indec.] to [indec.] the conditions [indec.] by the government of [indec.] namely the controls regarding arms.' signed F. Borgognini.

Bibliography

ARCHIVAL MATERIAL

Archdiocesan Archives, Armagh
    Michael Logue papers
    Patrick O'Donnell papers
Archdiocesan Archives, Cashel
    John Harty papers
Archdiocesan Archives, Dublin
    Edward Byrne papers
    Michael Curran papers
    William Walsh papers
Archdiocesan Archives, Tuam
    Thomas Gilmartin papers
Congregazione degli Affari Ecclesiastici Straordinari Archives, Vatican
    City Inghilterra files
Cork City and County Archives
    Fr Dominic's Letter (U149)
Liam de Róiste papers (U271)
    Sinn Féin tracts (U105)
Cumbria Record Office
    Lord Howard of Penrith papers (D HW)
Diocesan Archives, Clonfert
    John Dignan papers
Diocesan Archives, Cork
    Daniel Cohalan papers
Diocesan Archives, Galway
    Thomas O'Dea papers
    Thomas O'Doherty papers
Diocesan Papers, Killaloe
    Michael Fogarty papers

Irish College, Rome Archives
  Michael Curran papers
  John Hagan papers
Jesuit Archives, Dublin
  Edward Cahill papers
  Timothy Corcoran papers
  Lambert McKenna papers
National Archives, Dublin
  Department of An Taoiseach
National Library, Dublin
  Piaras Béaslaí papers (Collection no. 44)
  Michael Curran memoir (Collection no. 9)
  Seán T. O'Ceallaigh papers (Collection no. 9)
  Geraldine Plunkett Dillon papers (Collection no. 43)
  Sheehy-Skeffington papers (Collection no. 47)
National University, Maynooth Archives
  John Hogan papers (21)
  James MacCaffrey papers (26)
Public Record Office of Northern Ireland
  Home Affairs of Northern Ireland (HA)
The Royal Archives, Windsor Castle (PS/PSO/GV)
Trinity College Dublin Archives
  John Dillon papers
University College Dublin Archives
  Frank Aiken papers (P104)C.S. Andrews papers (P91)
  Ernest Blythe papers (P24)
  Éamon de Valera papers (P150)
  Desmond FitzGerald papers (P80)
  George Gavan Duffy papers (P152)
  Mary MacSwiney papers (P48a)
  Richard Mulcahy papers (P7)
  Conn Murphy papers (P141)
  Ernie O'Malley papers (P17)
  George Noble Plunkett papers (P79)

CONTEMPORARY NEWSPAPERS/JOURNALS

Belfast Newsletter
Catholic Bulletin
Connachtman
Cork Examiner
The Derry Journal
The Derry People
Derry Weekly News and Tyrone Herald
Donegal Vindicator
Eire
The Fenian
Freeman's Journal
The Free State
The Gael
Galway Observer
Irish Catholic
Irish Catholic Herald
Irish Ecclesiastical Record
Irish Independent
Irish News and Belfast Morning News
Irish Press
Irish Statesman
Irish Theological Quarterly
Irish Times
Kerryman
The Leader (San Francisco)
Limerick Leader
An Long
Manchester Guardian
Meath Chronicle
The Moderator
The Monitor (New Jersey)
Munster News
The Nationalist and Leinster Leader
Northern Whig
An tÓglách
An Phoblacht
Plain People

Poblacht na h-Eireann
Roscommon Herald
The Separatist
Sinn Féin
Sligo Champion
Studies
The Tablet
The Times (London)
Tuam Herald
Waterford Standard
Waterford Star
Western People
Westmeath Guardian
Wicklow People
The World's News

REFERENCE MATERIAL

Canning, B.J., *Bishops of Ireland, 1870–1987* (Ballyshannon, 1987).

Catholic Encyclopedia (consulted at http://www.newadvent.org/cathen).

Dáil Debates (consulted at http://historical-debates.oireachtas.ie).

Fanning, Ronan, et al. (eds), *Documents on Irish Foreign Policy, Vols. I and II* (Dublin, 1998).

Hansard's Parliamentary Debates

Irish Catholic Directory and Almanac

Irish Jesuit Directory

Newspaper Press Directory

O'Farrell, Padraic, *Who's Who in the Irish War of Independence and Civil War, 1916–1923* (Dublin, 1997).

O'Shiel, Kevin, *Handbook of the Ulster Question* (Dublin, 1923).

Oxford Dictionary of National Biography (consulted at http://www.oxford dnb.com).

Report of the Irish Boundary Commission, 1925, introduced by Geoffrey Hand (Shannon, 1969).

The Stormont Papers (consulted at http://stormontpapers.ahds.ac.uk).

AUTOBIOGRAPHIES/CONTEMPORARY PUBLISHED WRITINGS

Andrews, C.S. 'Tod', *Dublin Made Me: An Autobiography* (Dublin, 2001 edition).

Béaslaí, P., *Michael Collins and the Making of a New Ireland* (London, 1926).

Birmingham, G. A. (James Hannay), *An Irishman Looks at his World* (London, 1919).

Brady, J. (Fr. Maurice Browne), *The Big Sycamore* (Dublin, 1958).

Browne, P., 'December the Eighth' in *Poblacht na h-Eireann*, 25 December 1922.

Clarke, K., *My Fight for Ireland's Freedom*, edited by Helen Litton (Dublin, 1997 edition).

Clery, A., *The Idea of a Nation*, edited by Patrick Maume (Dublin, 2002 edition).

Deasy, L., *Brother Against Brother* (Cork, 1998 edition).

English, R., and C. O'Malley (eds), *Prisoners: The Civil War Letters of Ernie O'Malley* (Dublin, 1991).

Gallagher, F., *Days of Fear* (London, 1928).

——, *Four Glorious Years* (Dublin, 1953).

——, *The Indivisible Island: The story of the partition of Ireland* (London, 1957).

Gogarty, O. St John, *As I Was Going Down Sackville Street* (New York, 1937).

Irish Priests, *The Will and the Way* (Dublin, 1915).

Isaacson, A. (ed.), *Irish Letters in the New York Carmelites' Archives* (Boca Raton, FL, 1988).

——, *More Irish Letters in the New York Carmelites' Archives* (Tarrytown, NY, no date).

Jones, T., *Whitehall Diary, Volume III: Ireland 1918–1925*, edited by Kenna, G.B. (Fr. John Hassan), *Facts & Figures: The Belfast Pogroms, 1920–22*, edited by Thomas Donaldson (1997 edition).

MacBride White, A., and A.N. Jeffares (eds), *The Gonne–Yeats Letters, 1893–1938: Always Your Friend* (London, 1992).

Macardle, D., *The Irish Republic: A Documented Chronicle of the Anglo-Irish Conflict and the Partitioning of Ireland, with a Detailed Account of the Period 1916–1923* (London, 1968 edition).

————, *Tragedies of Kerry, 1922–1923* (Dublin, 1998 edition).

McDonald, W., *Reminiscences of a Maynooth Professor*, edited by Denis Gwynn (Cork, 1967 edition).

————, *Some Ethical Questions of Peace and War with Special Reference to Ireland* (London, 1919).

Mangan, H. (ed.), *Poems by Alice Milligan* (Dublin, 1954).

Murphy, J.J., *The People's Primate: A Memoir of Joseph Cardinal MacRory* (Dublin, 1945).

O'Donnell, P., *The Gates Flew Open* (London, 1932).

O'Donoghue, F., *No Other Law* (Dublin, 1986 edition).

O'Flaherty, L., *A Tourist's Guide to Ireland* (London, 1930).

O'Hegarty, P.S., *The Victory of Sinn Féin* (Dublin, 1998 edition).

O'Kelly, A.A. (ed.), *The Letters of Liam O'Flaherty* (Dublin, 1996).

O'Leary, J., *Recollections of Fenians and Fenianism, in Two Volumes* (London, 1896).

O'Malley, Ernie, *On Another Man's Wound* (Dublin, 1936).

————, *The Singing Flame* (Dublin, 1978).

O'Riordan, M., *Catholicity and Progress in Ireland* (London, 1905).

Pearse, P., *Collected Works of Pádraic H. Pearse: Political Writings and Speeches* (Dublin, 1919).

Sheehan, Patrick A., *The Blindness of Dr. Gray; or, The Final Law* (London, 1909).

————, *The Graves of Kilmorna* (London, 1915).

————, *Luke Delmege* (London, 1901).

————, *My New Curate: A Story Gathered from the Stray Leaves of an Old Diary* (London, 1928).

SECONDARY SOURCES

aan de Wiel, J., *The Catholic Church in Ireland, 1914–1918: War and Politics* (Dublin, 2003).

Akenson, D., *The Irish Education Experiment: The National System of Education in the Nineteenth Century* (London, 1970).

————, *Small Differences: Irish Catholics and Irish Protestants, 1815–1922* (Dublin, 1991).

Anderson, B., *Imagined Communities: Reflections on the Origin and Spread of Nationalism* (London, 1991).

Anderson, M., and E. Bort (eds), *The Irish Border: History, Politics, Culture* (Liverpool, 1999).

Augusteijn, J., *From Public Defiance to Guerrilla Warfare: The Experience of Ordinary Volunteers in the Irish War of Independence, 1916–1921* (Dublin, 1996).

—— (ed.), *Ireland in the 1930s: New Perspectives* (Dublin, 1999).

—— (ed.), *The Irish Revolution, 1913–1923* (Basingstoke, 2002).

——, 'Political Violence and Democracy: An Analysis of the Tensions within Irish Republican Strategy', *Irish Political Studies*, 2003, 18 (1).

Baker, J., *The McMahon Family Murders* (Belfast, 2002).

Barton, B.E., *The Government of Northern Ireland, 1920–1923* (Belfast, 1980).

Bew, P., *Ideology and the Irish Question: Ulster Unionism and Irish Nationalism 1912–1916* (Oxford, 1994).

——, *Ireland: The Politics of Enmity, 1789–2006* (Oxford, 2007).

Bew, P., P. Gibbon and H. Patterson, *The State in Northern Ireland, 1921–72* (Manchester, 1979).

Biggs, M., 'The Rationality of Self-Inflicted Sufferings: Hunger Strikes by Irish Republicans, 1916–1923', Working Paper Number 2007–03, Department of Sociology, University of Oxford, February, 2007.

Blanshard, P., *The Irish and Catholic Power* (London, 1953).

Bloxham, D., 'The Armenian Genocide of 1915–1916: Cumulative Radicalization and the Development of a Destruction Policy', *Past & Present* (November 2003).

Bowman, John, *De Valera and the Ulster Question, 1917–1973* (Oxford, 1982).

Boyce, D.G. (ed.), *The Revolution in Ireland, 1879–1923* (Basingstoke, 1988).

——, *Nationalism in Ireland* (London, 1995 edition).

Boyce, D.G., and A. O'Day (eds), *The Ulster Crisis, 1885–1921* (Basingstoke, 2005).

Bromage, Mary C., *De Valera and the March of a Nation* (London, 1956).

Brown, S., and D.W. Miller (eds), *Piety and Power in Ireland: Essays in honour of Emmet Larkin* (Belfast, 2000).

Brusher, J.S., *Consecrated Thunderbolt: Father Yorke of San Francisco* (Hawthorne, NJ, 1973).

Campbell, C., *Emergency Law in Ireland, 1918–1925* (Oxford, 1994).

Campbell, F., 'The last land war? Kevin O'Shiel's memoir of the Irish revolution', *Archivium Hibernicum*, LVII (2003).

Candy, C., *Priestly Fictions: Popular Irish Novelists of the Early 20th Century* (Dublin, 1995).

Carroll, Denis, *They have fooled you again. Michael O'Flanagan (1876–1942). Priest, Republican, Social Critic* (Blackrock, 1993).

———, *Unusual Suspects: Twelve Radical Clergymen* (Blackrock, 1998).

——— (ed.), *Religion in Ireland: Past, Present and Future* (Blackrock, 1999).

Coldrey, B., *Faith and Fatherland: The Christian Brothers and the Development of Irish Nationalism, 1838–1921* (Dublin, 1988).

Coleman, M., *County Longford and the Irish Revolution, 1910–1923* (Dublin, 2006).

Collins, K., *Catholic Churchmen and the Celtic Revival in Ireland, 1848–1916* (Dublin, 2002).

Collins, P. (ed.), *Nationalism and Unionism: Conflict in Ireland, 1885–1921* (Belfast, 1994).

Comerford, R.V., *Charles J. Kickham: A Study in Irish Nationalism and Literature* (Portmarnock, 1979).

———, *The Fenians in Context: Irish Politics and Society, 1848–82* (Dublin, 1985).

Connolly, S., *Religion and Society in Nineteenth-Century Ireland* (Dundalk, 1985).

Coogan, O., *Politics and War in Meath, 1913–1923* (Dublin, 1983).

Corish, P.J. (ed.), *A History of the Irish Catholic Church, Volume 5* (Dublin, 1971).

———, *The Irish Catholic Experience: A Historical Survey* (Dublin, 1986).

———, *Maynooth College, 1795–1995* (Dublin, 1995).

Corkery, P., 'Bishop Daniel Cohalan of Cork on Republican Resistance and Hunger Strikes: A Theological Note', *Irish Theological Quarterly*, 67 (2002).

Costello, F., *Enduring the Most: The life and death of Terence Mac Swiney* (Dingle, 1995).

———, *The Irish Revolution and its Aftermath, 1916–1923: Years of Revolt* (Dublin, 2003).

Cronin, M., and J. Regan (eds), *Ireland: The Politics of Independence, 1922–49* (London, 2000).

Cruise O'Brien, C., *Ancestral Voices: Religion and Nationalism in Ireland* (Dublin, 1994).

Cruise O'Brien, M., *The Same Age as the State* (Madison, WI, 2004).

Curran, J.M., *The Birth of the Irish Free State, 1921–1923* (Alabama, 1980).

Daniel, T.K., 'Griffith on his Noble Head: The Determinants of Cumann na nGaedheal Economic Policy, 1922–32', *Irish Economic and Social History*, III (1976).

Darby, John, et al. (eds), *Political Violence: Ireland in a Comparative Perspective* (Belfast, 1990).

Davis, R., *Arthur Griffith and Non-Violent Sinn Féin* (Dublin, 1974).

Devlin, J., and R. Fanning (eds), *Religion and Rebellion* (Dublin, 1997).

Doherty, G., and D. Keogh (eds), *De Valera's Ireland* (Cork, 2003).

Donnelly, P., 'Violence and Catholic Theology', *Studies*, (Autumn 1994).

Dunphy, R., *The Making of Fianna Fáil Power in Ireland, 1923–1948* (Oxford, 1995).

Ecksteins, M., *Rites of Spring: The Great War and the Birth of the Modern Age* (New York, 1989).

Edwards, O. D., *Éamon de Valera* (Cardiff, 1987).

Edwards, O.D., and P.J. Storey, 'The Irish Press in Victorian Britain', in R. Swift and S. Gilley (eds), *The Irish in the Victorian City* (Dublin, 1985).

Edwards, R.D., *Patrick Pearse: The Triumph of Failure* (London, 1977).

Elliott, M., *The Catholics of Ulster: A History* (London, 2000).

English, R., *Radicals and the Republic: Socialist Republicanism in the Irish Free State, 1925–1937* (Oxford, 1994).

———, *Ernie O'Malley: IRA Intellectual* (Oxford, 1998).

———, *Armed Struggle: The History of the IRA, 1916–2002* (London, 2003).

———, *Irish Freedom: The History of Nationalism in Ireland* (London, 2006).

Fallon, C., 'Civil War Hungerstrikes: Women and Men', *Éire-Ireland*, 22 (1987).

Farrell, M., *Arming the Protestants: The Formation of the Ulster Special Constabulary and the Royal Ulster Constabulary, 1920–1927* (London, 1983).

Farry, M., *Sligo, 1914–1921: A Chronicle of Conflict* (Trim, 1992).

——, *The Aftermath of Revolution: Sligo, 1921–1923* (Dublin, 2000).

Ferriter, D., *The Transformation of Ireland, 1900–2000* (London, 2005).

——, *Judging Dev: A Reassessment of the Life and Legacy of Éamon de Valera* (Dublin, 2007).

Fitzpatrick, D., 'The Geography of Irish Nationalism, 1910–21', *Past and Present*, (February 1978).

—— (ed.), *Revolution?: Ireland, 1917–1923* (Dublin, 1990).

——, *Politics and Irish Life, 1913÷1921: Provincial Experience of War and Revolution* (Cork, 1998).

——, *The Two Irelands: 1912–1939* (Oxford, 1998).

——, *Harry Boland's Irish Revolution* (Cork, 2003).

Follis, B.A., *A State Under Siege: The Establishment of Northern Ireland, 1920–1925* (Oxford, 1995).

Foster, R.F., *The Irish Story: Telling Tales and Making it up in Ireland* (London, 2001).

——, *Modern Ireland, 1600–1972* (London, 1988).

Fussell, P., *The Great War and Modern Memory* (Oxford, 1975).

Garvin, T., *The Evolution of Irish Nationalist Politics* (Dublin, 1981).

——, *Nationalist Revolutionaries in Ireland, 1858–1928* (Oxford, 1987).

——, *1922: The Birth of Irish Democracy* (Dublin, 1996).

Gilchrist, M., *Wit and Wisdom: Daniel Mannix* (Melbourne, 2004).

Githens-Mazer, J., *Myths and Memories of the Easter Rising: Cultural and Political Nationalism in Ireland* (Dublin, 2006).

Goldring, M., *Faith of Our Fathers: The formation of Irish nationalist ideology, 1890–1920*, translated by Frances de Burgh-Whyte (Dublin, 1987).

Goldstrom, J.M., and L.A. Clarkson (eds), *Irish Population, Economy, and Society* (Oxford, 1981).

Green, T.R., 'Michael O'Riordan's La Recente Insurrezione in Irlanda, 1916', *Éire-Ireland*, 1993, 28 (4).

Gwynn, D., *The History of Partition, 1912–1925* (Dublin, 1950).

Harkness, D.W., *The Restless Dominion: The Irish Free State and the British Commonwealth of Nations, 1921–31* (London, 1969).

Harris, M., *The Catholic Church and the Foundation of the Northern Irish State* (Cork, 1993).

Hart, P., 'Michael Collins and the assassination of Sir Henry Wilson', *Irish Historical Studies*, xxviii (November 1992).

———, 'The Geography of Revolution in Ireland: 1917–1923', *Past and Present*, (May 1997).

———, *The IRA and its Enemies: Violence and Community in Cork* (Oxford, 1998).

———, 'The Social Structure of the Irish Republican Army, 1916–23', *Historical Journal*, 42 (1999).

———, *The IRA at War, 1916–1923* (Oxford, 2003).

Healy, James, 'The Civil War Hunger-Strike – October 1923', *Studies*, 71 (1982).

Hechter, M., *Containing Nationalism* (Oxford, 2000).

Hepburn, A.C., 'The Ancient Order of Hibernians in Irish Politics, 1905–1914', *Cithara*, 10 (1971).

Hopkinson, M., *Green Against Green: The Irish Civil War* (Dublin, 1988).

———, *The Irish War of Independence* (Montreal, 2003).

Hutchinson, J., *The Dynamics of Cultural Nationalism: The Gaelic Revival and the Creation of the Irish Nation State* (London, 1987).

Hutton, S., and P. Stewart (eds), *Ireland's Histories: Aspects of State, Society and Ideology* (London, 1991).

Inglis, T., *Moral Monopoly: The Rise and Fall of the Catholic Church in Modern Ireland* (Dublin, 1987).

Inoue, K., 'Propaganda of Dail Eireann: From Truce to Treaty', *Éire-Ireland*, 32 (1997).

Isaacson, A., *Always Faithful: The New York Carmelites, the Irish People and Their Freedom Movement* (Middletown, NY, 2004).

———, *Carmel in New York: The Province of St. Elias, 1906–1926* (Maspeth, NY, no date).

Kelly, M.J., *The Fenian Ideal and Irish Nationalism, 1882–1916* (Woodbridge, 2006).

Keogh, D., *The Vatican, the Bishops and Irish Politics: 1919–39* (Cambridge, 1986).

————, *Ireland and the Vatican: The Politics and Diplomacy of Church-State Relations, 1922–1960* (Cork, 1995).

Kiernan, C., *Daniel Mannix and Ireland* (Morwell, Victoria, 1984).

Kissane, B., 'Voluntaristic Democratic Theory and the Origins of the Irish Civil War', *Civil Wars*, 2 (1999).

————, 'Explaining the Intractability of the Irish Civil War', *Civil Wars*, 3 (2000).

————, *The Politics of the Irish Civil War* (Oxford, 2005).

Kleinrichert, D., *Republican Internment and the Prison Ship Argenta, 1922* (Dublin, 2001).

Kostick, C., *Revolution in Ireland: Popular Militancy, 1917–1923* (London, 1996).

Laffan, M., *The Partition of Ireland, 1911–1925* (Dundalk, 1983).

————, *The Resurrection of Ireland: The Sinn Féin Party, 1916–1923* (Cambridge, 1999).

Larkin, E., 'Church, State, and Nation in Modern Ireland', *The American Historical Review*, 80 (Dec. 1975).

————, *The Historical Dimensions of Irish Catholicism* (Washington, D.C., 1997).

Lee, J.J., *Ireland, 1912–1985: Politics and Society* (Cambridge, 1989).

Legg, M.-L., *Newspapers and Nationalism: The Irish Provincial Press, 1850–1892* (Dublin, 1999).

Leslie, S., *Cardinal Gasquet* (London, 1953).

Long, P., 'Organisation and Development of the Pro-Treaty Forces, 1922–1924', *Irish Sword*, 20 (1997).

Longford, Earl of, and T.P. O'Neill, *Eamon de Valera* (London, 1970).

Lynch, R., *The Northern IRA and the Early Years of Partition, 1920–1922* (Dublin, 2006).

Lyons, F.S.L., *Ireland since the Famine* (London, 1971).

————, *Culture and Anarchy in Ireland, 1890–1939* (Oxford, 1979).

Macaulay, A., *The Holy See, British Policy and the Plan of Campaign in Ireland, 1885–93* (Dublin, 2002).

MacDonagh, O., 'Ambiguity in Nationalism: The Case of Ireland', *Historical Studies*, 19 (1981).

————, *States of Mind: A Study of Anglo-Irish Conflict, 1780–1980* (London, 1983).

MacDonagh, O., et al. (eds), *Irish Culture and Nationalism, 1750–1950* (London, 1983).

Martin, F.X. and F.J. Byrne, *The Scholar Revolutionary: Eoin MacNeill, 1867–1945, and the Making of the New Ireland* (Shannon, 1973).

Martin, G., 'The Origins of Partition', in M. Anderson and E. Bort (eds), *The Irish Border: History, Politics, Culture* (Liverpool, 1999).

Maume, P., 'Nationalism and partition: the political thought of Arthur Clery', *Irish Historical Studies*, xxxi (November 1998).

———, *The Long Gestation: Irish Nationalist Life, 1891–1918* (Dublin, 1999).

McConville, Seán, *Irish Political Prisoners, 1848–1922: Theatres of War* (London, 2003).

McDermott, J., *Northern Divisions: The Old IRA and the Belfast Pogroms, 1920–22* (Dublin, 2001).

McGee, O., *The IRB: The Irish Republican Brotherhood from the Land League to Sinn Féin* (Dublin, 2005).

McHugh, R., 'The Catholic Church and the Rising', in O. Dudley Edwards and F. Pyle (eds), *1916: The Easter Rising* (London, 1968).

McRedmond, L., *To the Greater Glory: A History of the Irish Jesuits* (Dublin, 1991).

Miller, D.W., *Church, State and Nation in Ireland, 1898–1921* (Dublin, 1973).

Moran, G. (ed.), *Radical Irish Priests, 1660–1970* (Dublin, 1998).

Moran, S.F., *Patrick Pearse and the Politics of Redemption: The Mind of the Easter Rising, 1916* (Washington, D.C., 1994).

Morrissey, T.J., *Edward J. Byrne, 1872–1941: The Forgotten Archbishop of Dublin* (Blackrock, 2010).

———, *William J. Walsh, Archbishop of Dublin, 1841–1921: No Uncertain Voice* (Dublin, 2000).

Murphy, J.H., *Catholic Fiction and Social Reality in Ireland, 1873–1922* (London, 1997).

Murray, P., *Oracles of God: The Roman Catholic Church and Irish Politics, 1922–37* (Dublin, 2000).

———, 'Obsessive Historian: Eamon de Valera and the Policing of his Reputation', *Proceedings of the Royal Irish Academy*, 101C (2001).

Newsinger, John, '"I Bring Not Peace But A Sword": The Religious Motif in the Irish War of Independence', *Journal of Contemporary History*, 13 (1978).

———, 'Revolution and Catholicism in Ireland, 1848–1923', *European Studies Review*, 9 (1979).

———, 'Canon and Martial Law: William O'Brien, Catholicism and Irish Nationalism', *Éire-Ireland*, 19 (1981).

Ni Dhonnchadha, M., and T. Dorgan (eds), *Revising the Rising* (Derry, 1991).

Novick, B., *Conceiving Revolution: Irish Nationalist Propaganda during the First World War* (Dublin, 2001).

O'Callaghan, M., 'Old Parchment and Water: The Boundary Commission of 1925 and the Copperfastening of the Irish Border', *Bullán*, 4 (1999/2000).

O'Carroll, J.P., and J.A. Murphy (eds), *De Valera and His Times* (Cork, 1986).

O'Connor, U., *Oliver St. John Gogarty: A Poet and his Times* (London, 1964).

Ó Corráin, Daithí, 'Ireland in his heart north and south': the contribution of Ernest Blythe to the partition question', *Irish Historical Studies*, xxxv (May 2006).

O'Farrell, P., *Ireland's English Question: Anglo-Irish Relations, 1534–1970* (London, 1971).

Ó Fiaich, T., 'The Catholic Clergy and the Independence Movement', *Capuchin Annual*, 1970.

O'Halloran, C., *Partition and the Limits of Irish Nationalism* (Dublin, 1987).

O'Halpin, E., *Defending Ireland: The Irish State and Its Enemies Since 1922* (Oxford, 1999).

O'Shea, J., *Priests, Politics and Society in Post Famine Ireland: A Study of County Tipperary, 1850–1891* (Dublin, 1983).

Parkinson, A.F., *Belfast's Unholy War* (Dublin, 2004).

Paseta, S., *Before the Revolution: Nationalism, Social Change and Ireland's Catholic Elite, 1879–1922* (Cork, 1999).

Phoenix, E., *Northern Nationalism: Nationalist Politics, Partition and the Catholic Minority in Northern Ireland, 1890–1940* (Belfast, 1994).

Prager, J., *Building Democracy in Ireland: Political Order and Cultural Integration in a Newly Independent Nation* (Cambridge, 1986).

Privilege, J., *Michael Logue and the Catholic Church in Ireland, 1879–1925* (Manchester, 2009).

Rafferty, O.P., 'The Catholic Bishops and Revolutionary Violence in Ireland: Some Nineteenth and Twentieth Century Comparisons', *Studies*, 83 (1994).

———, *Catholicism in Ulster: An Interpretative History* (London, 1994).

———, *The Church, the State and the Fenian Threat, 1861–75* (London, 1999).

Rees, R., and A.C. Hepburn, *Ireland, 1905–1925* (Newtownards, 1998).

Regan, J.M., *The Irish Counter-Revolution, 1921–1936: Treatyite Politics and Settlement in Independent Ireland* (Dublin, 1999).

Ring, J., *Erskine Childers* (London, 1996).

Rumpf, E., and A.C. Hepburn, *Nationalism and Socialism in Twentieth Century Ireland* (Liverpool, 1977).

Santamaria, B.A., *Daniel Mannix: The Quality of Leadership* (Carlton, 1983).

Sweeney, G., 'Irish Hunger Strikes and the Cult of Self-Sacrifice', *The Journal of Contemporary History*, 28 (1993).

Tierney, M., *Eoin MacNeill: Scholar and Man of Action, 1867–1945*, edited by F.X. Martin,(Oxford, 1980).

Titley, E.B., *Church, State and the Controlling of Schooling in Ireland, 1900–1944* (Kingston, 1983).

Townshend, C., *The British Campaign in Ireland, 1919–1921: The Development of Political and Military Policies* (Oxford, 1975).

———, *Political Violence in Ireland: Government and Resistance since 1848* (Oxford, 1984).

———, *Easter 1916: The Irish Rebellion* (London, 2005).

———, 'The Meaning of Irish Freedom: Constitutionalism in the Free State', *Transactions of the Royal Historical Society*, 8 (1998).

Walker, G., 'Propaganda and Conservative Nationalism During the Irish Civil War', *Éire-Ireland*, 22 (1987).

Ward, M., *Unimaginable Revolutionaries: Women and Irish Nationalism* (London, 1983).

———, *Maud Gonne: a life* (London, 1993).

———, *Hanna Sheehy-Skeffington: a life* (Dublin, 1997).

Whyte, J.H., '1916 – Revolution and Religion', in F.X. Martin (ed.), *Leaders and Men of the Easter Rising: Dublin 1916* (London, 1967).

———, *Church and State in Modern Ireland, 1923–1970* (Dublin, 1971).

Wilson, T.K., *Frontiers of Violence: Conflict and Identity in Ulster and Upper Silesia, 1918–1922* (Oxford, 2010).

————, '"The most terrible assassination that has yet stained the name of Belfast" the McMahon murders in context', *Irish Historical Studies*, Vol. 37, No. 145 (May 2010).

UNPUBLISHED THESES

Maguire, G.E., 'The Political and Military Causes of the Divisions in the Nationalist Movement, January 1921 to August 1923' D.Phil. Thesis, Oxford, 1985.

Murphy, Brian P., 'J.J. O'Kelly (Sceilg) and the Catholic Bulletin: Cultural Considerations – Gaelic, Religious and National, 1898–1926' Ph.D. Thesis, NUI, Dublin, 1986.

Wilson, Tim, 'Boundaries, Identity and Violence: Ulster and Upper Silesia in a Context of Partition, 1918-1922', D.Phil Thesis, Oxford, 2007.

Index